Shojo B

WANTED

Story & Art by Matsuri Hino

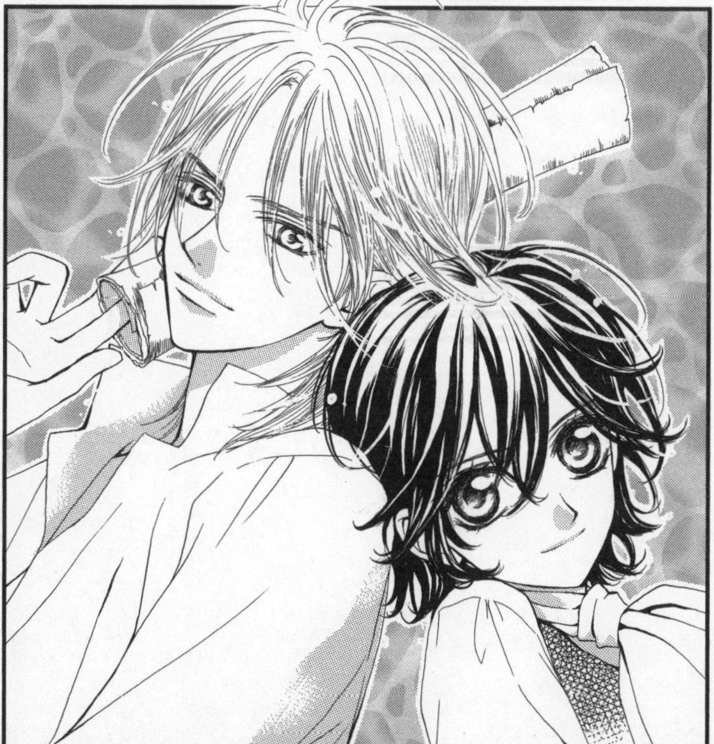

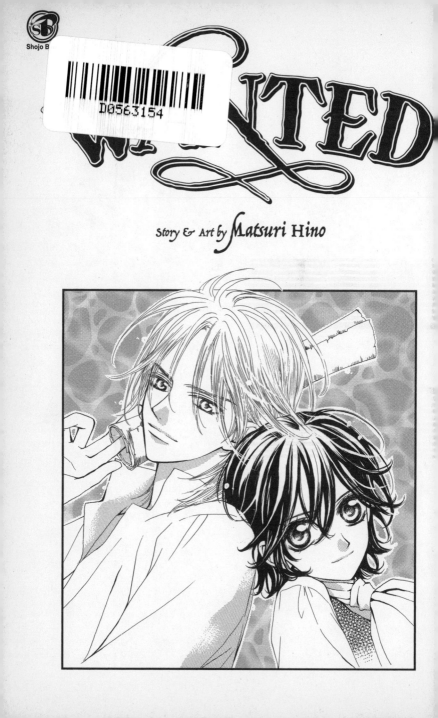

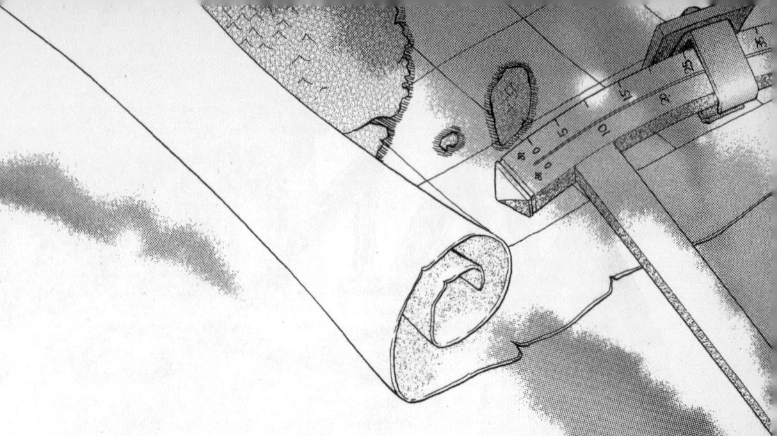

Contents

Thanks to my readers, I had my pirate manga compiled into one volume. Thank you. There may be readers of this book who are reading my manga for the first time... (I'm nervous about that... 3) This manga is different from MeruPuri (which I drew at the same time as Wanted) in that the hero is in his mid-20s and the guys around him are pretty old... It follows that the story must be a bit sordid. But it's also a story where the heroine boards a pirate ship alone; the ship's captain is handsome, he has merry comrades, and they all go on adventures, so I hope you don't analyze it too much and just enjoy.

樋野まつり
Matsuri Hino

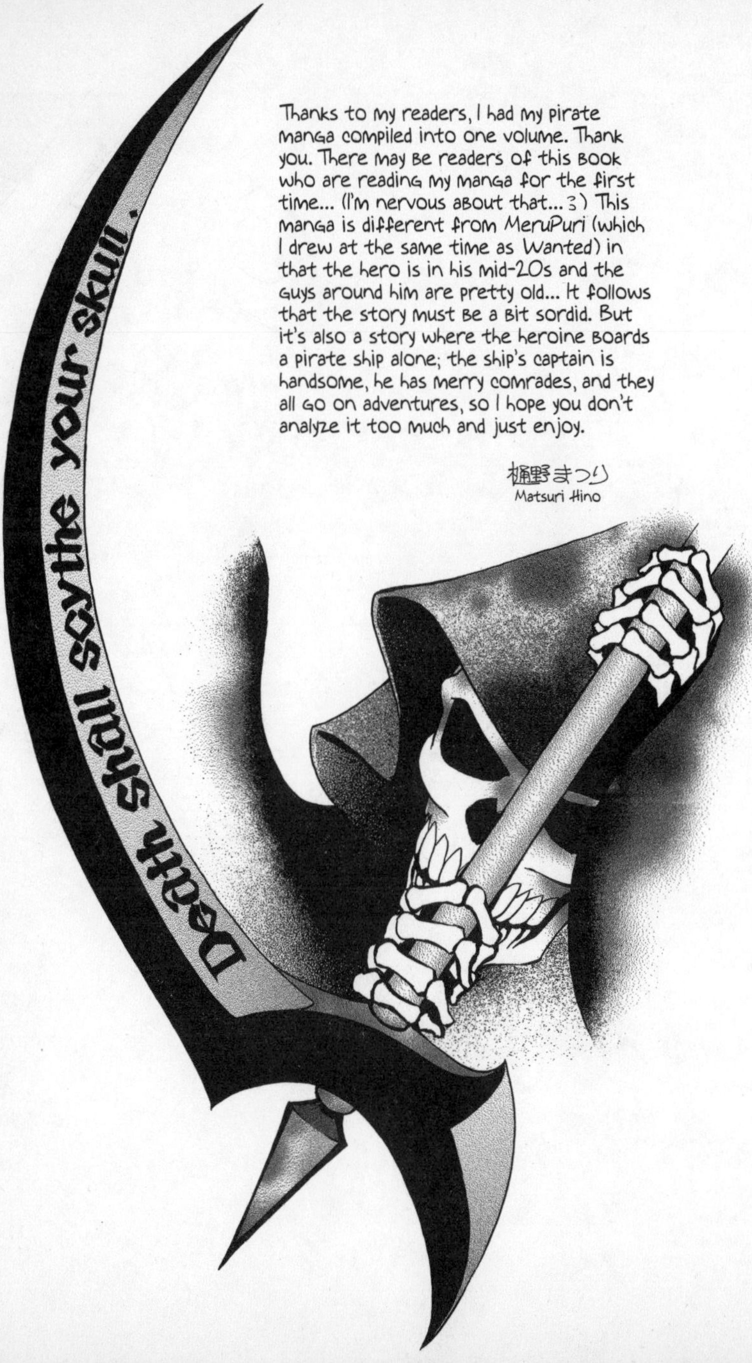
Death shall scythe your skull.

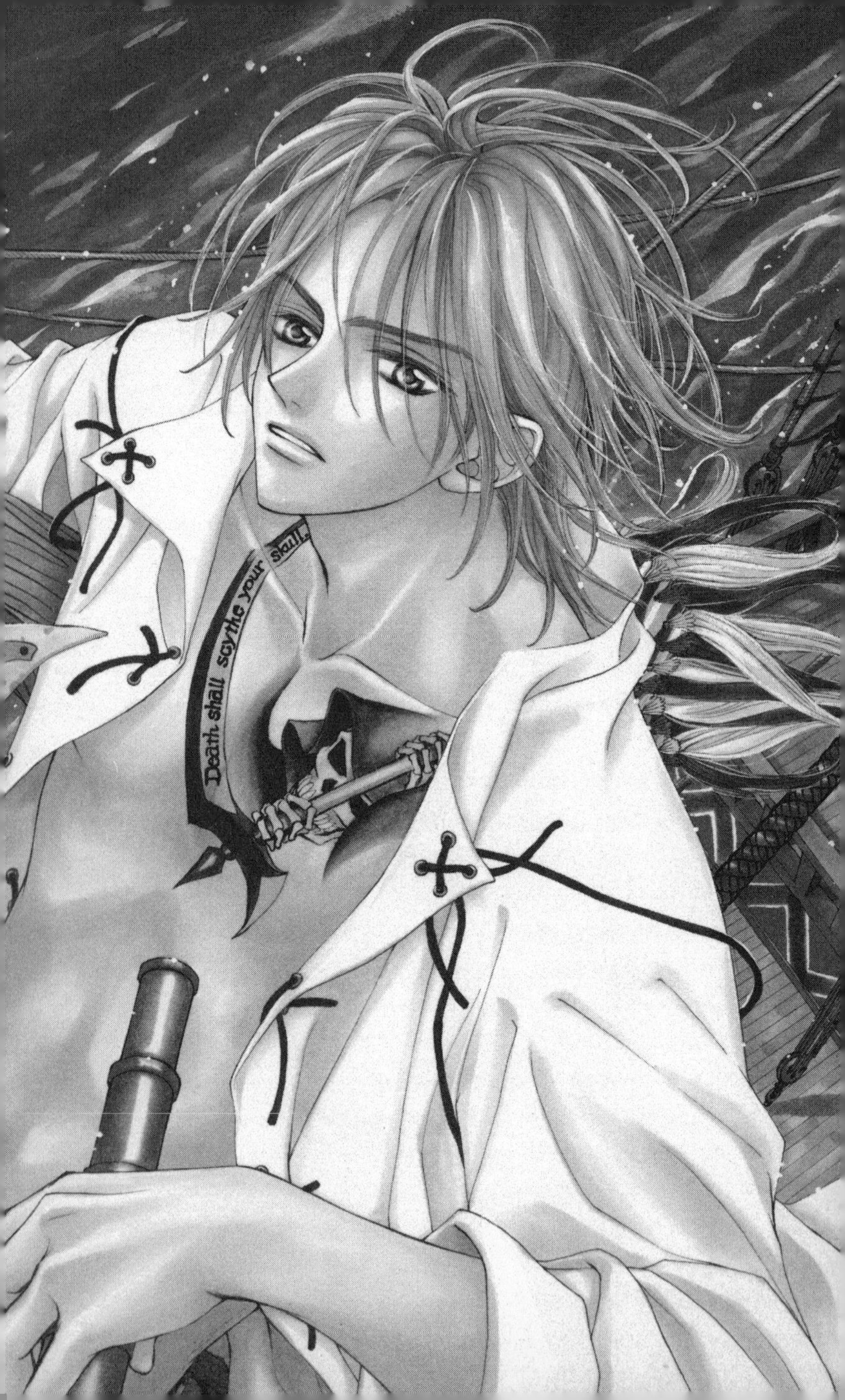
Death shall scythe your skull.

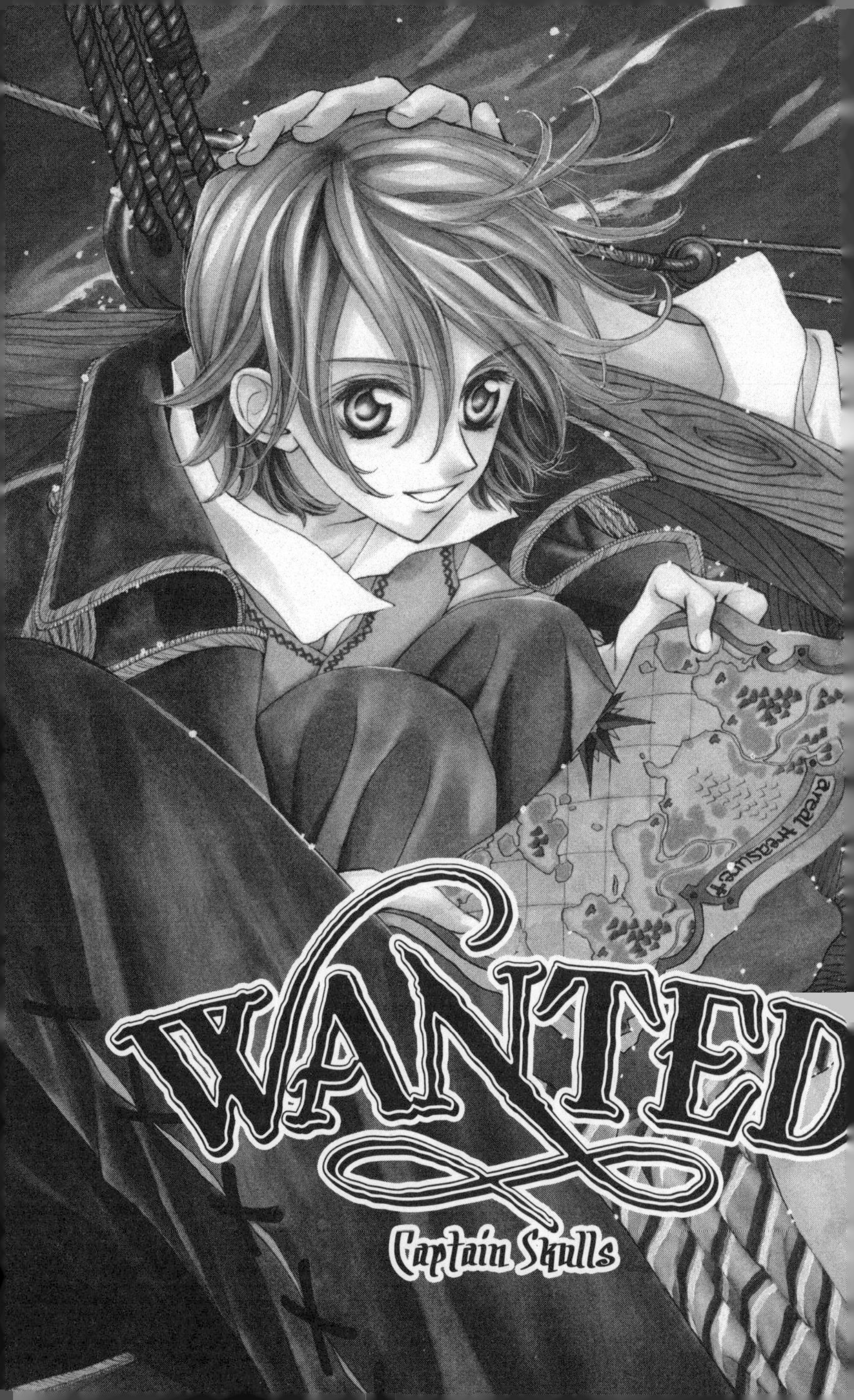
a real treasure
WANTED
Captain Skulls

WANTED

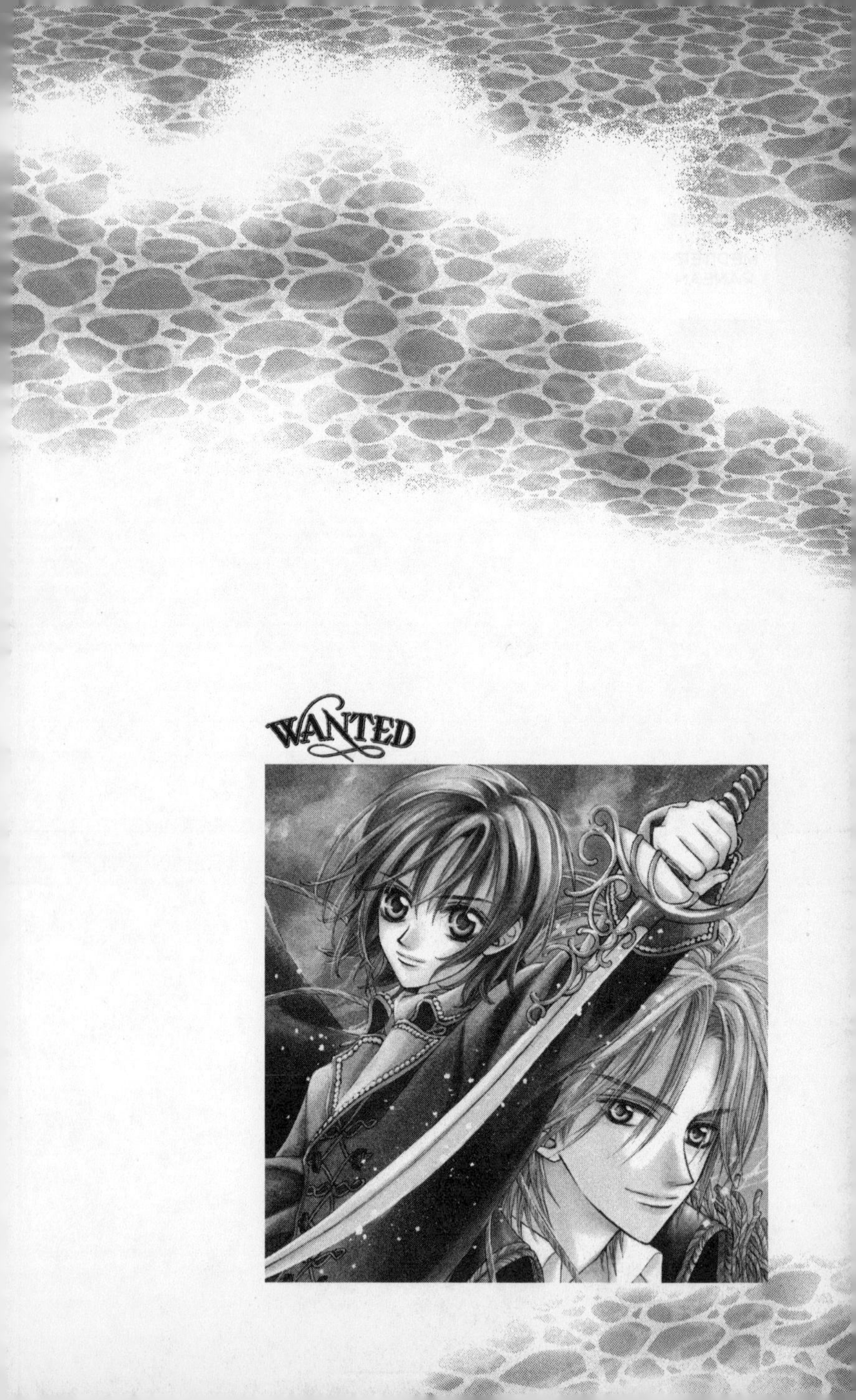

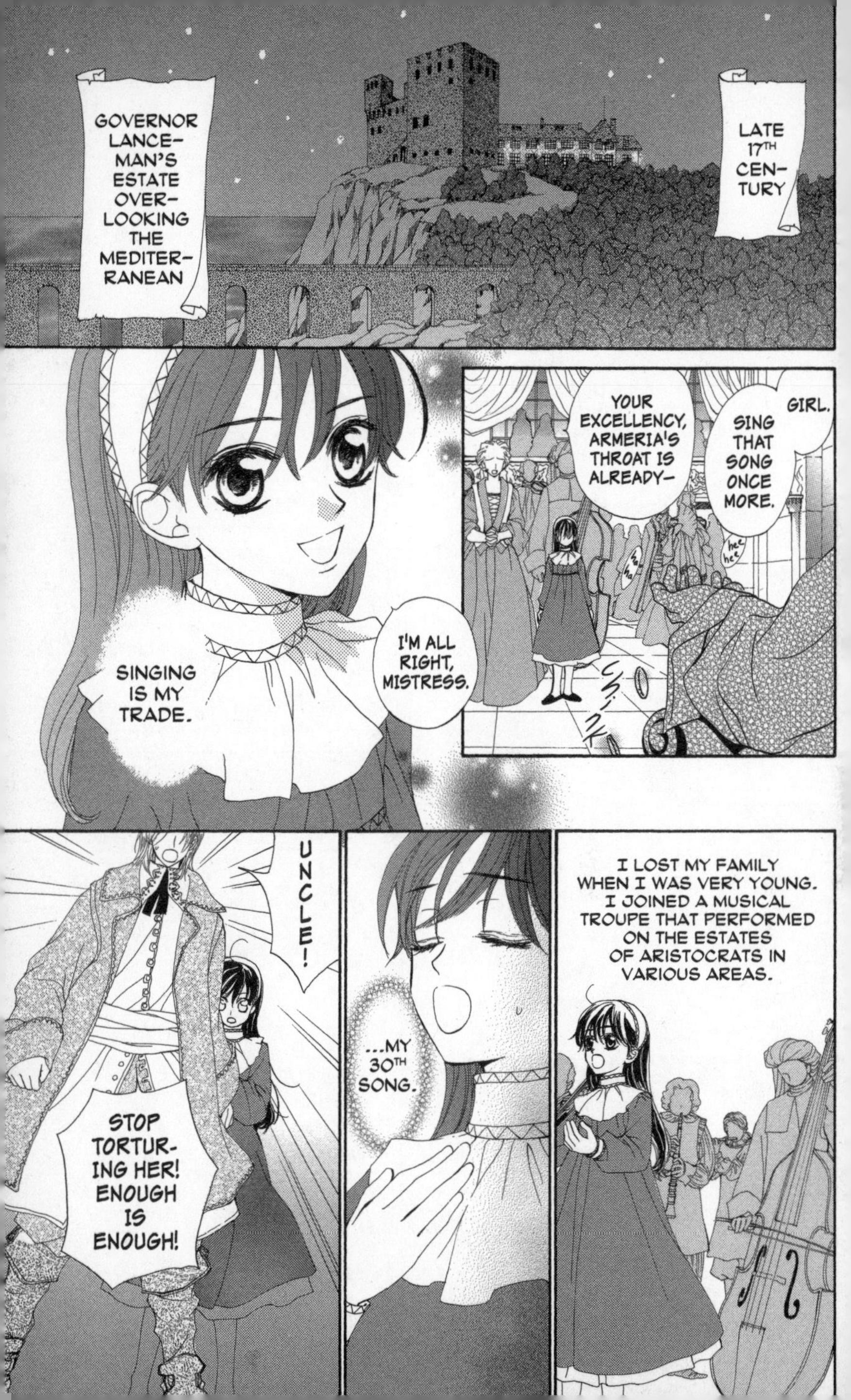
LATE 17TH CENTURY
GOVERNOR LANCEMAN'S ESTATE OVERLOOKING THE MEDITERRANEAN
GIRL.
SING THAT SONG ONCE MORE.
hee hee
ha ha
YOUR EXCELLENCY, ARMERIA'S THROAT IS ALREADY—
CHINK
I'M ALL RIGHT, MISTRESS.
SINGING IS MY TRADE.
I LOST MY FAMILY WHEN I WAS VERY YOUNG. I JOINED A MUSICAL TROUPE THAT PERFORMED ON THE ESTATES OF ARISTOCRATS IN VARIOUS AREAS.
...MY 30TH SONG.
UNCLE!
STOP TORTURING HER! ENOUGH IS ENOUGH!

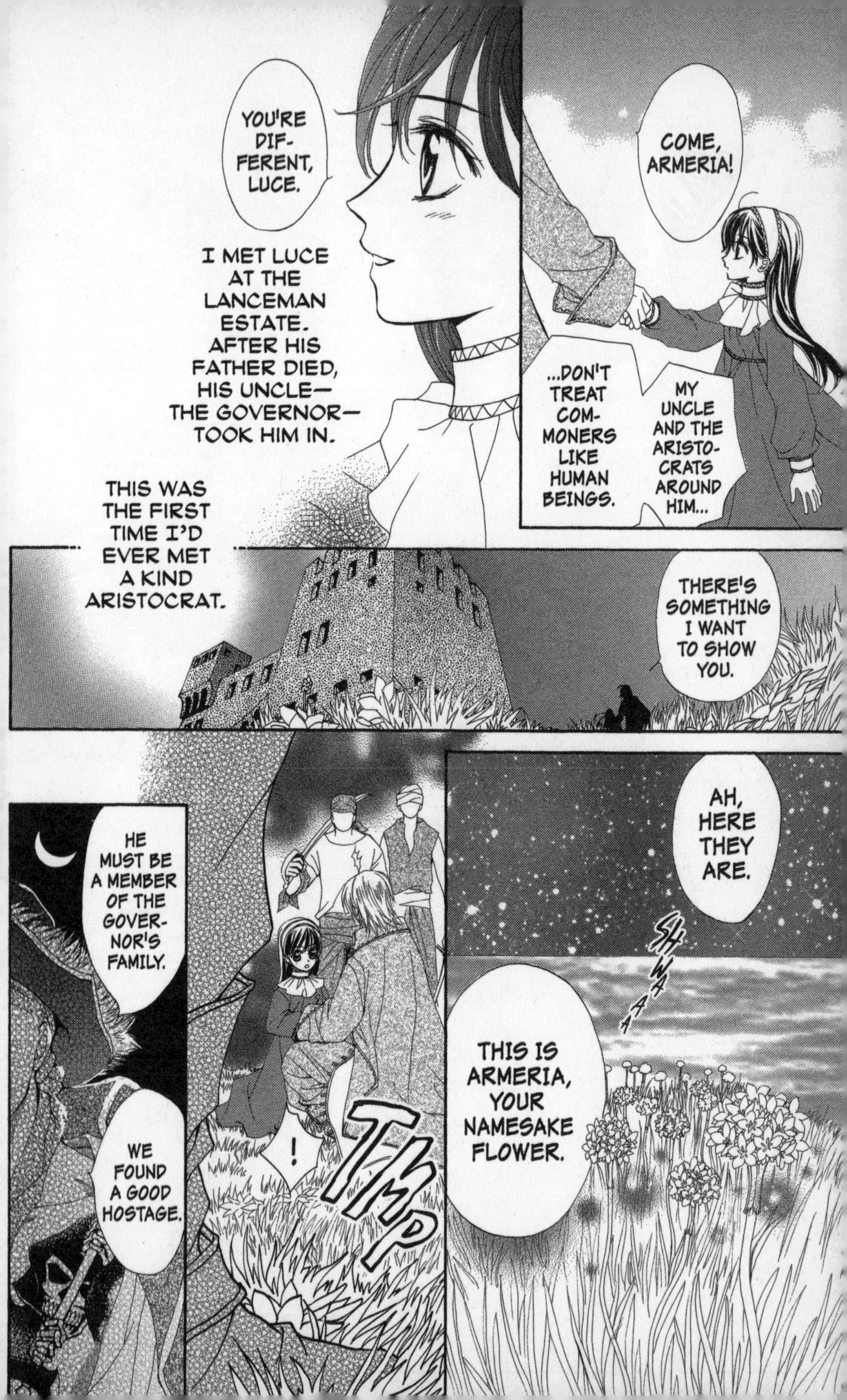
COME, ARMERIA!
MY UNCLE AND THE ARISTOCRATS AROUND HIM...
...DON'T TREAT COMMONERS LIKE HUMAN BEINGS.
YOU'RE DIFFERENT, LUCE.
I MET LUCE AT THE LANCEMAN ESTATE. AFTER HIS FATHER DIED, HIS UNCLE—THE GOVERNOR—TOOK HIM IN.
THIS WAS THE FIRST TIME I'D EVER MET A KIND ARISTOCRAT.
THERE'S SOMETHING I WANT TO SHOW YOU.
AH, HERE THEY ARE.
SHWAAA
THIS IS ARMERIA, YOUR NAMESAKE FLOWER.
TMP
!
HE MUST BE A MEMBER OF THE GOVERNOR'S FAMILY.
WE FOUND A GOOD HOSTAGE.

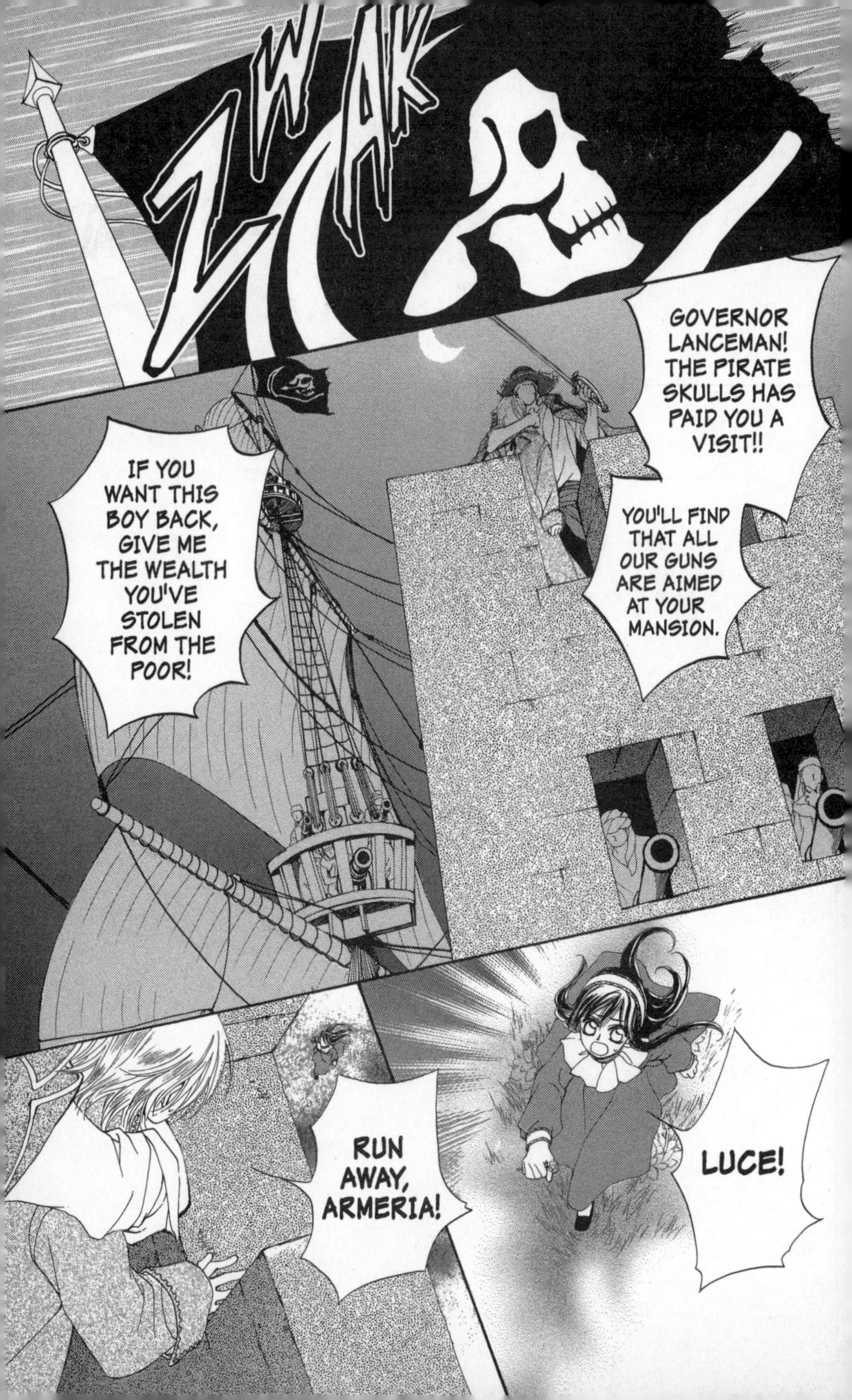
ZWAK
GOVERNOR LANCEMAN! THE PIRATE SKULLS HAS PAID YOU A VISIT!!
YOU'LL FIND THAT ALL OUR GUNS ARE AIMED AT YOUR MANSION.
IF YOU WANT THIS BOY BACK, GIVE ME THE WEALTH YOU'VE STOLEN FROM THE POOR!
LUCE!
RUN AWAY, ARMERIA!

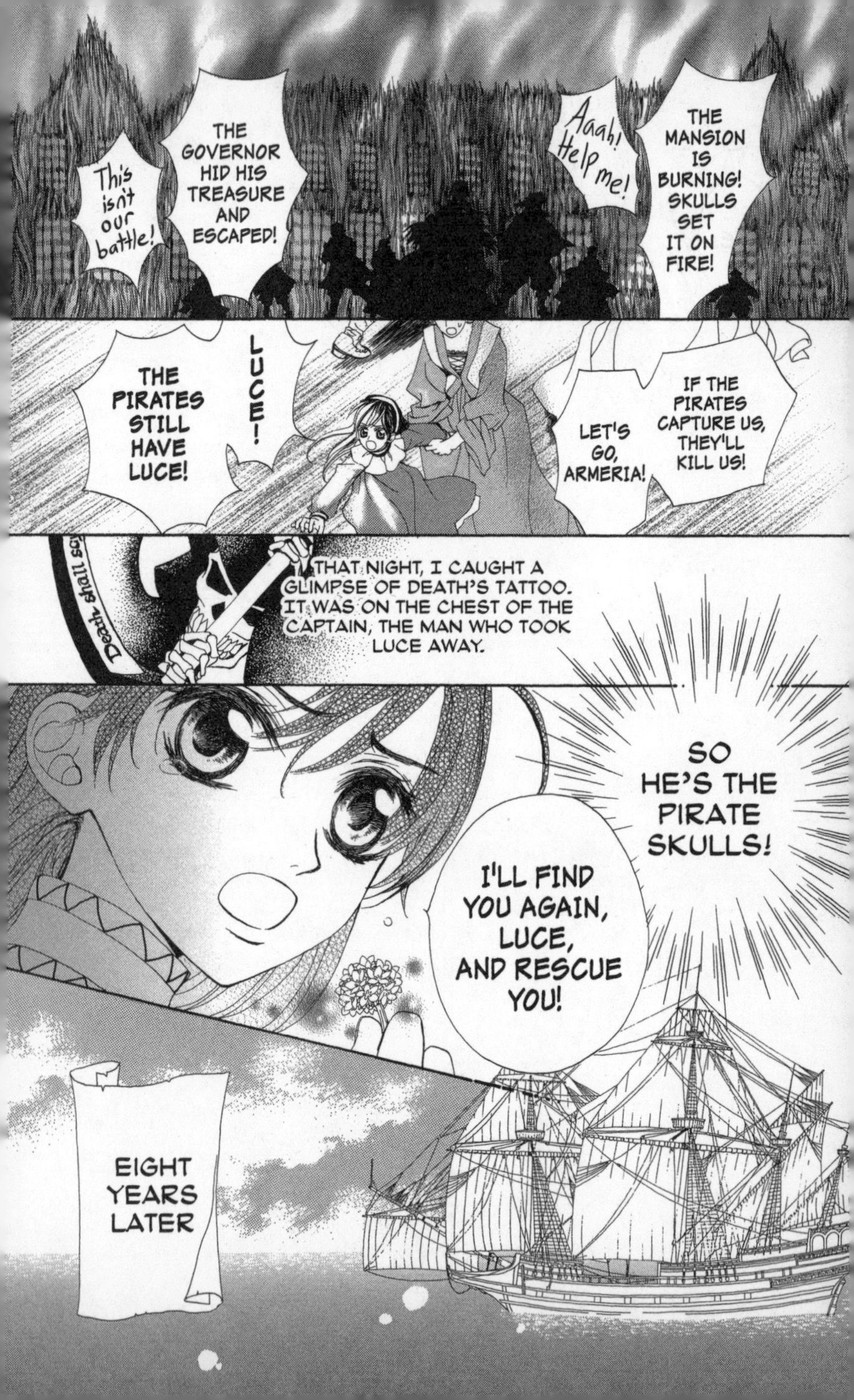
THE MANSION IS BURNING! SKULLS SET IT ON FIRE!
Aaah! Help me!
THE GOVERNOR HID HIS TREASURE AND ESCAPED!
This isn't our battle!
IF THE PIRATES CAPTURE US, THEY'LL KILL US!
LET'S GO, ARMERIA!
LUCE!
THE PIRATES STILL HAVE LUCE!
THAT NIGHT, I CAUGHT A GLIMPSE OF DEATH'S TATTOO. IT WAS ON THE CHEST OF THE CAPTAIN, THE MAN WHO TOOK LUCE AWAY.
SO HE'S THE PIRATE SKULLS!
I'LL FIND YOU AGAIN, LUCE, AND RESCUE YOU!
EIGHT YEARS LATER

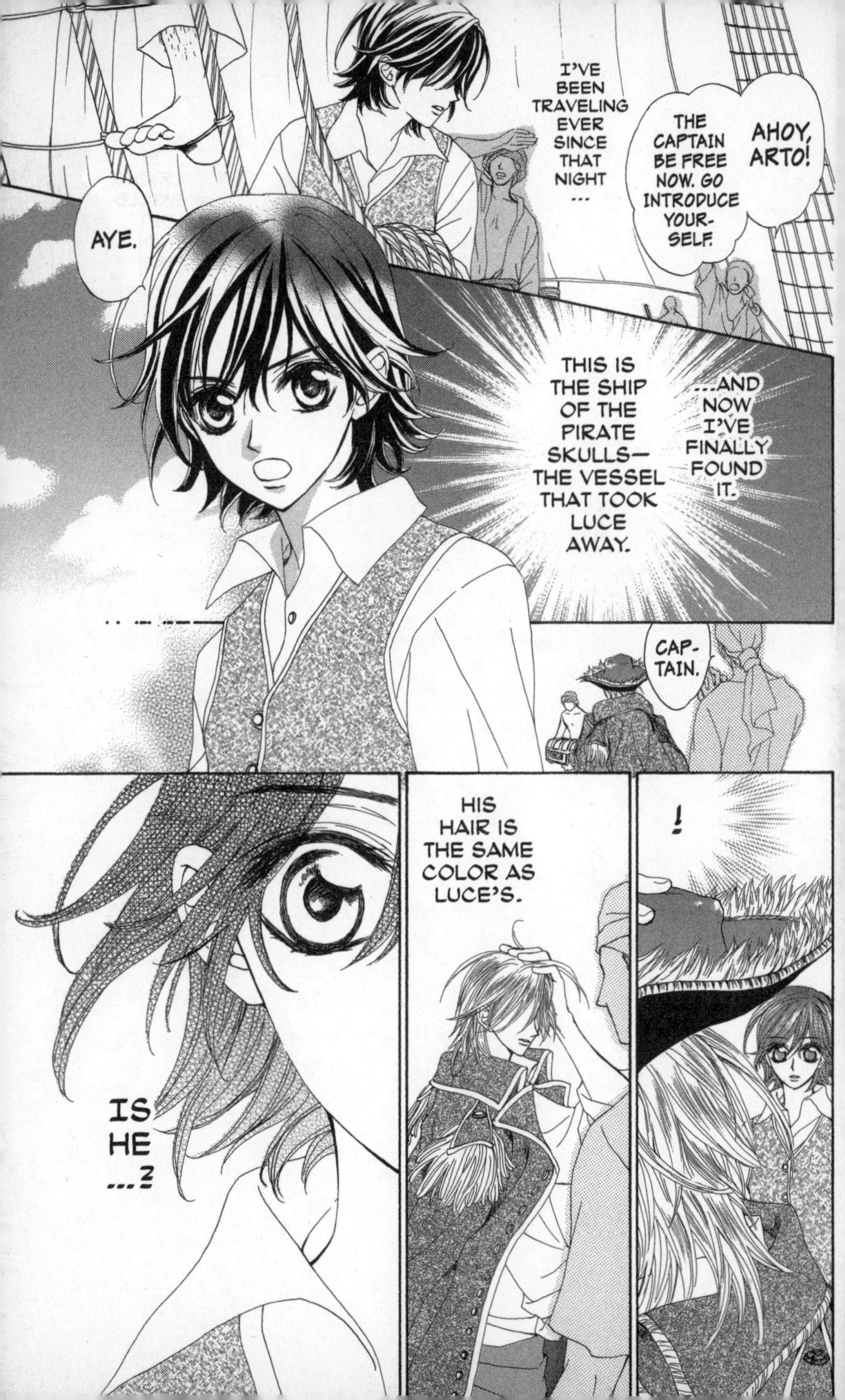
AHOY, ARTO!
THE CAPTAIN BE FREE NOW. GO INTRODUCE YOURSELF.
I'VE BEEN TRAVELING EVER SINCE THAT NIGHT ...
AYE.
...AND NOW I'VE FINALLY FOUND IT.
THIS IS THE SHIP OF THE PIRATE SKULLS—THE VESSEL THAT TOOK LUCE AWAY.
CAPTAIN.
!
HIS HAIR IS THE SAME COLOR AS LUCE'S.
IS HE ...?

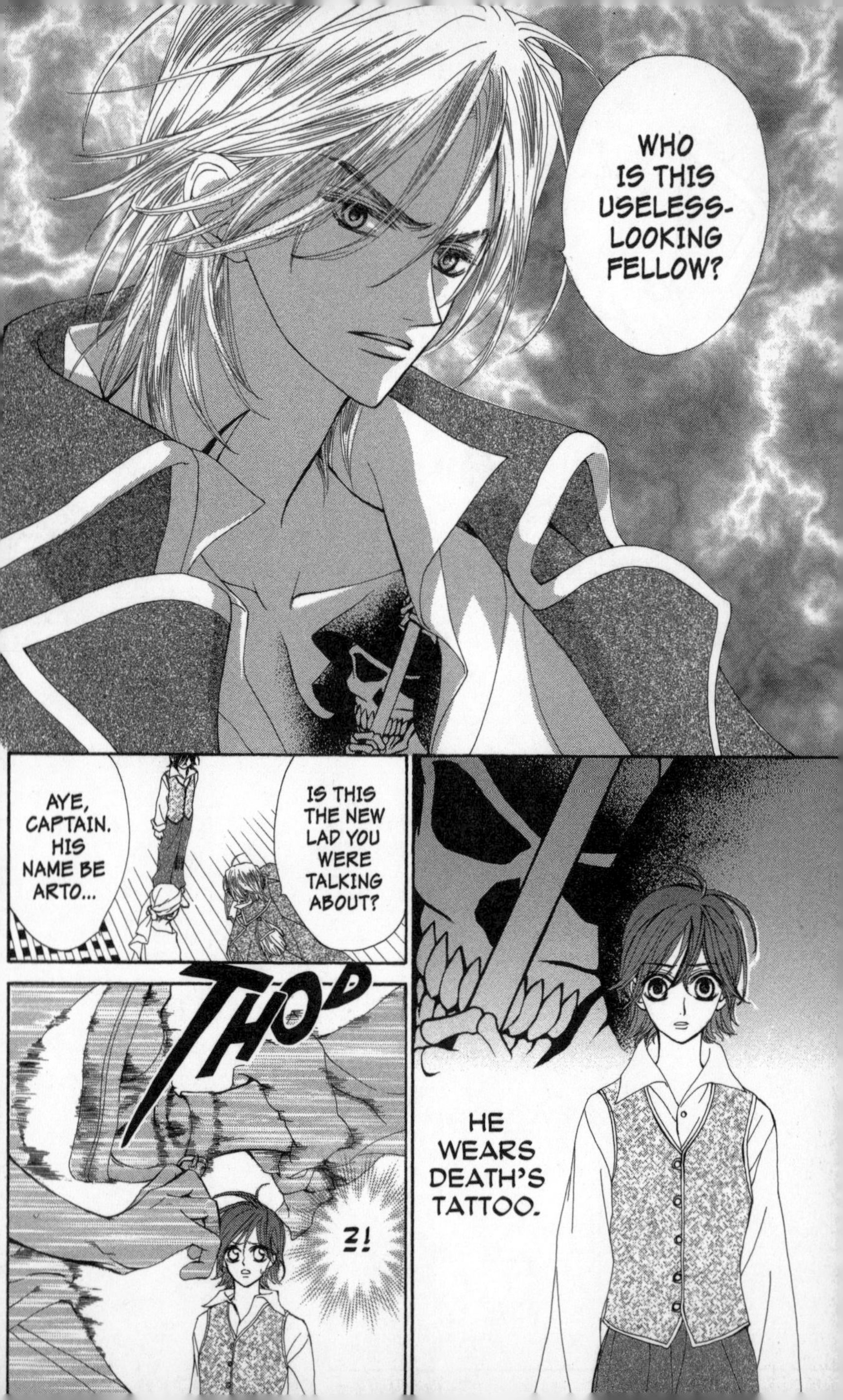
WHO IS THIS USELESS-LOOKING FELLOW?
HE WEARS DEATH'S TATTOO.
IS THIS THE NEW LAD YOU WERE TALKING ABOUT?
AYE, CAPTAIN. HIS NAME BE ARTO...
THOD
?!

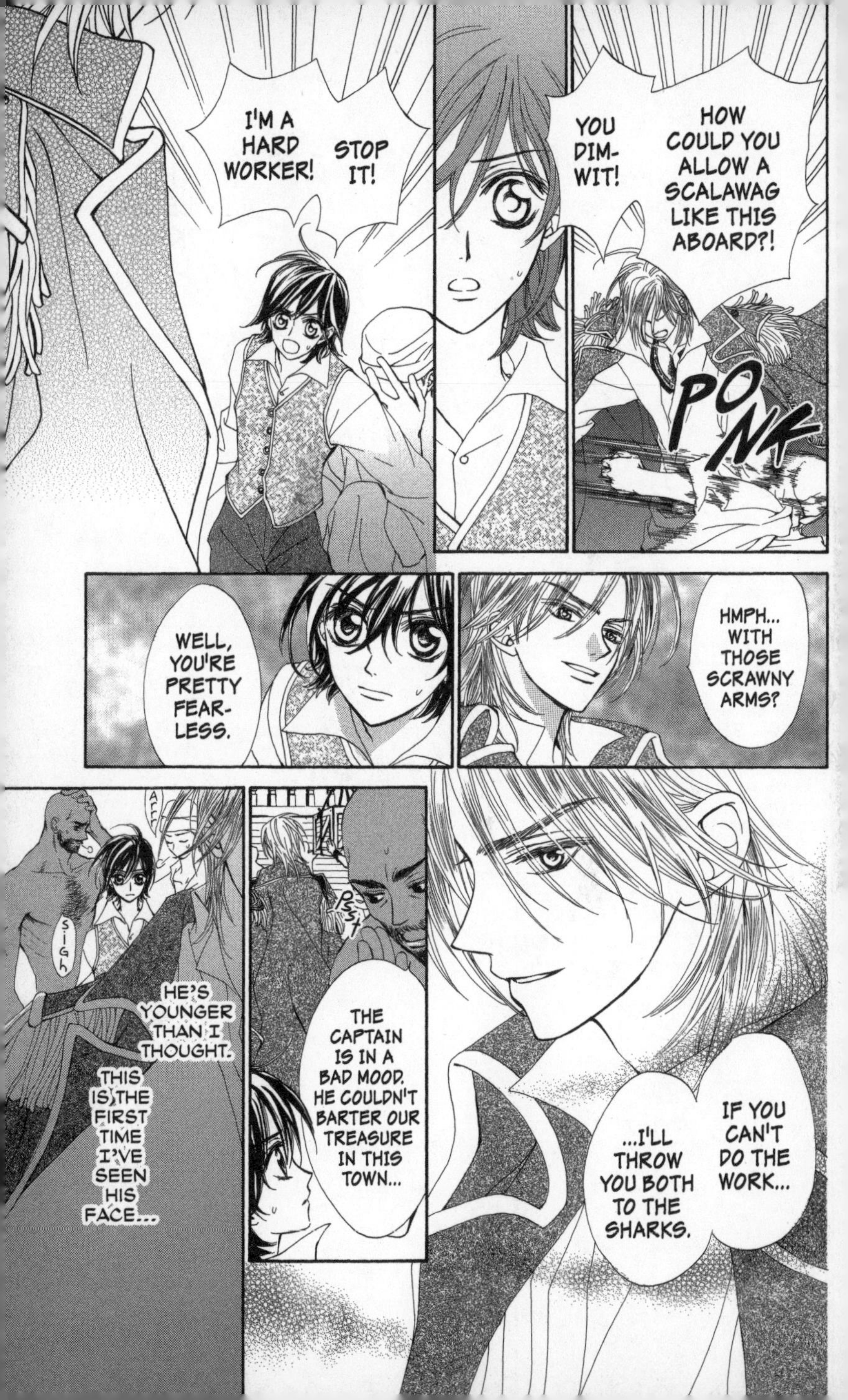
HOW COULD YOU ALLOW A SCALAWAG LIKE THIS ABOARD?!
YOU DIM-WIT!
PONK
STOP IT!
I'M A HARD WORKER!
HMPH... WITH THOSE SCRAWNY ARMS?
WELL, YOU'RE PRETTY FEARLESS.
IF YOU CAN'T DO THE WORK...
...I'LL THROW YOU BOTH TO THE SHARKS.
Pssst
THE CAPTAIN IS IN A BAD MOOD. HE COULDN'T BARTER OUR TREASURE IN THIS TOWN...
Arrr
sigh
HE'S YOUNGER THAN I THOUGHT.
THIS IS THE FIRST TIME I'VE SEEN HIS FACE...

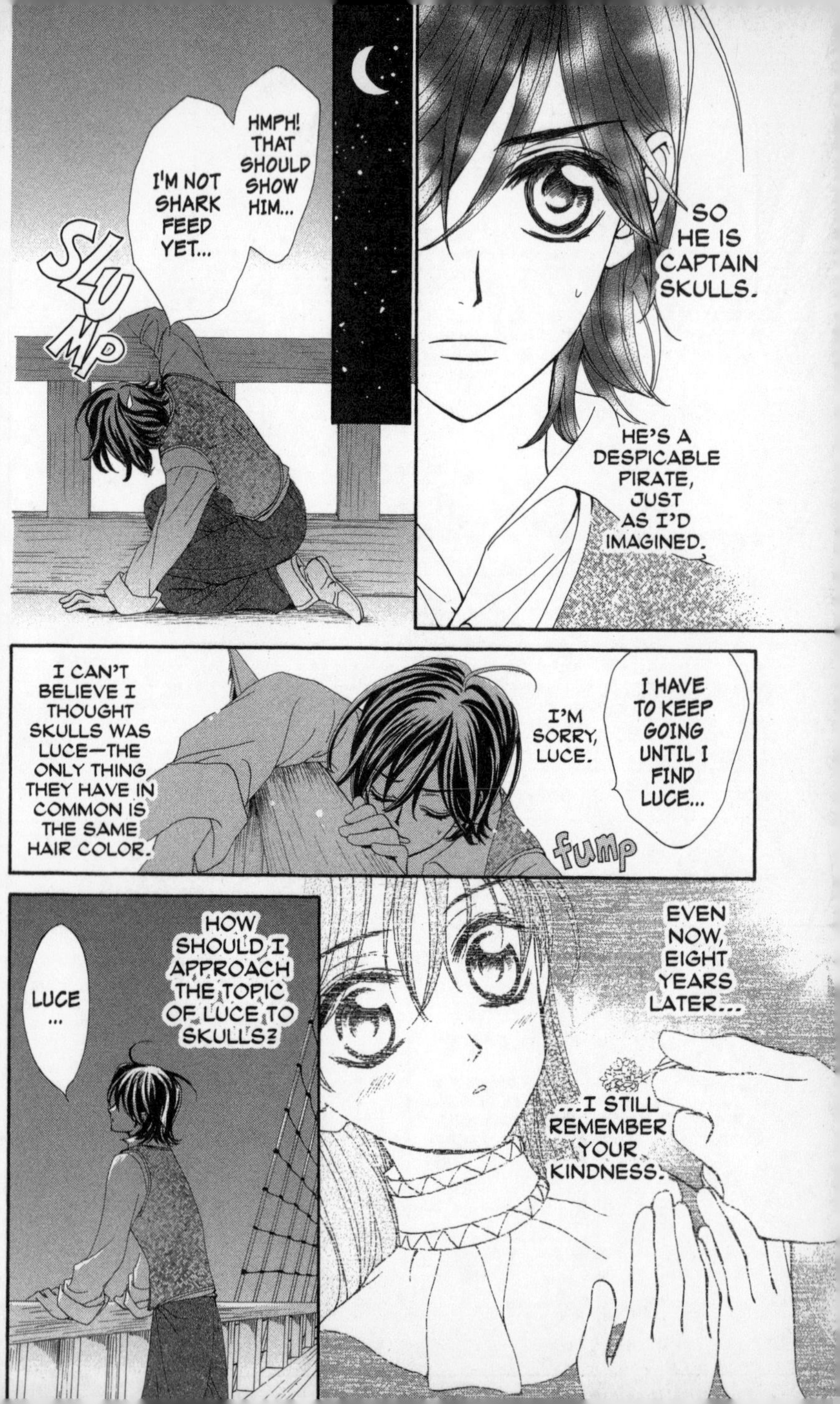
SO HE IS CAPTAIN SKULLS.
HE'S A DESPICABLE PIRATE, JUST AS I'D IMAGINED.
HMPH! THAT SHOULD SHOW HIM...
I'M NOT SHARK FEED YET...
SLUMP
I HAVE TO KEEP GOING UNTIL I FIND LUCE...
I'M SORRY, LUCE.
fump
I CAN'T BELIEVE I THOUGHT SKULLS WAS LUCE—THE ONLY THING THEY HAVE IN COMMON IS THE SAME HAIR COLOR.
EVEN NOW, EIGHT YEARS LATER...
...I STILL REMEMBER YOUR KINDNESS.
HOW SHOULD I APPROACH THE TOPIC OF LUCE TO SKULLS?
LUCE ...

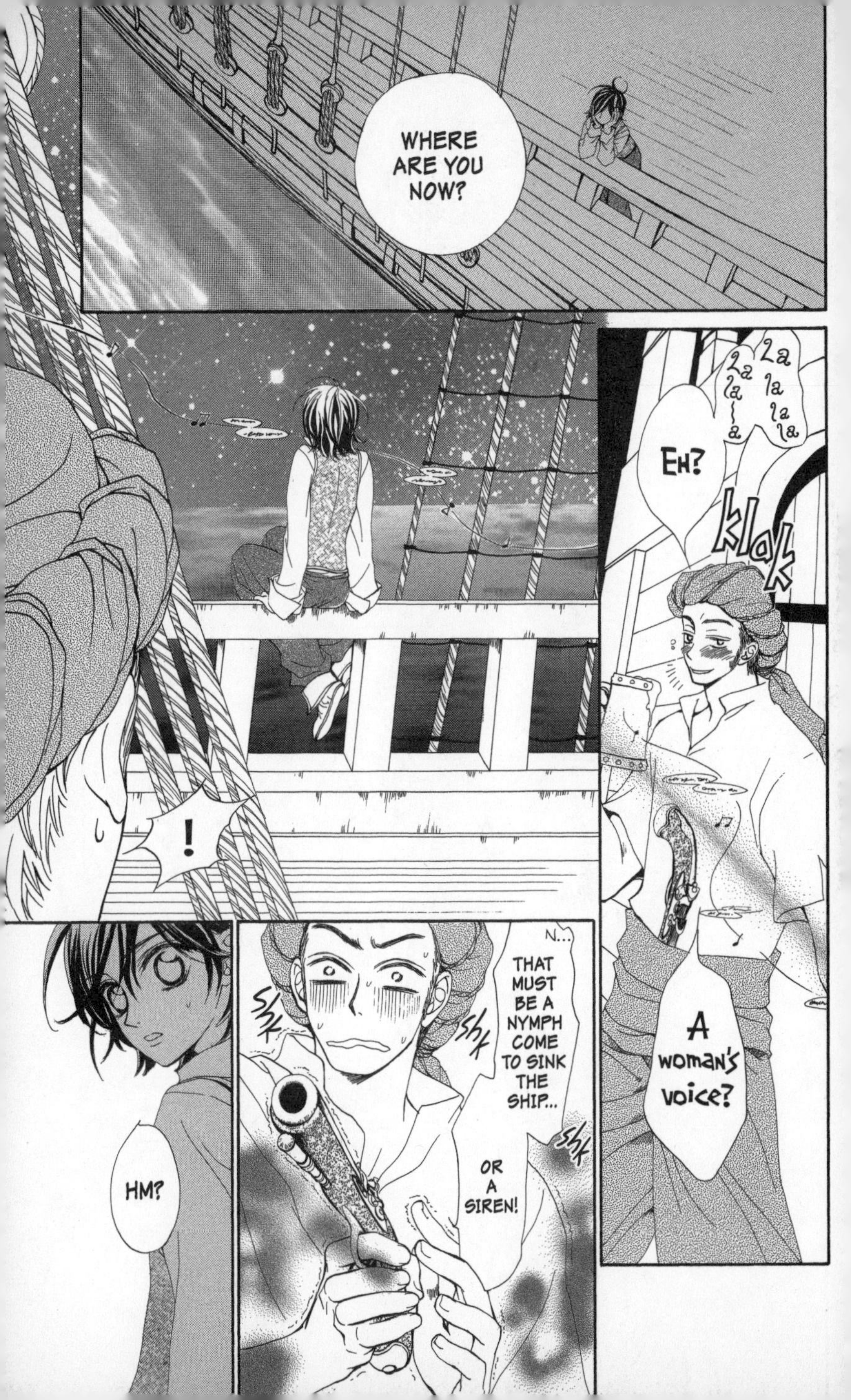
WHERE ARE YOU NOW?
La la la la
La la la~a
EH?
klak
A woman's voice?
!
N...
THAT MUST BE A NYMPH COME TO SINK THE SHIP...
shk
shk
shk
OR A SIREN!
HM?

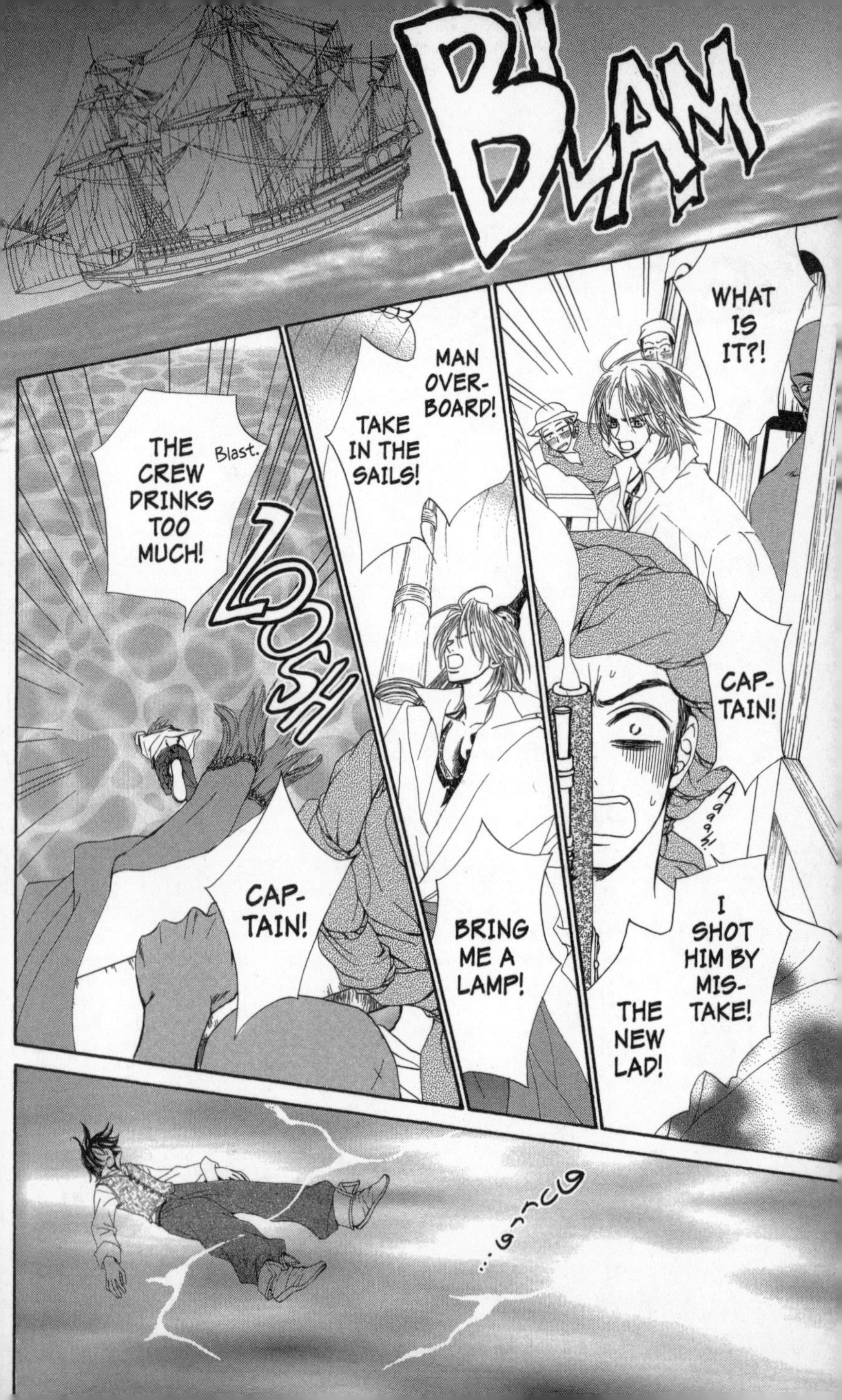

BLAM
WHAT IS IT?!
CAP-TAIN!
Aaagh!
I SHOT HIM BY MIS-TAKE!
THE NEW LAD!
MAN OVER-BOARD!
TAKE IN THE SAILS!
BRING ME A LAMP!
THE CREW DRINKS TOO MUCH!
Blast.
WOOSH
CAP-TAIN!
...gurgle

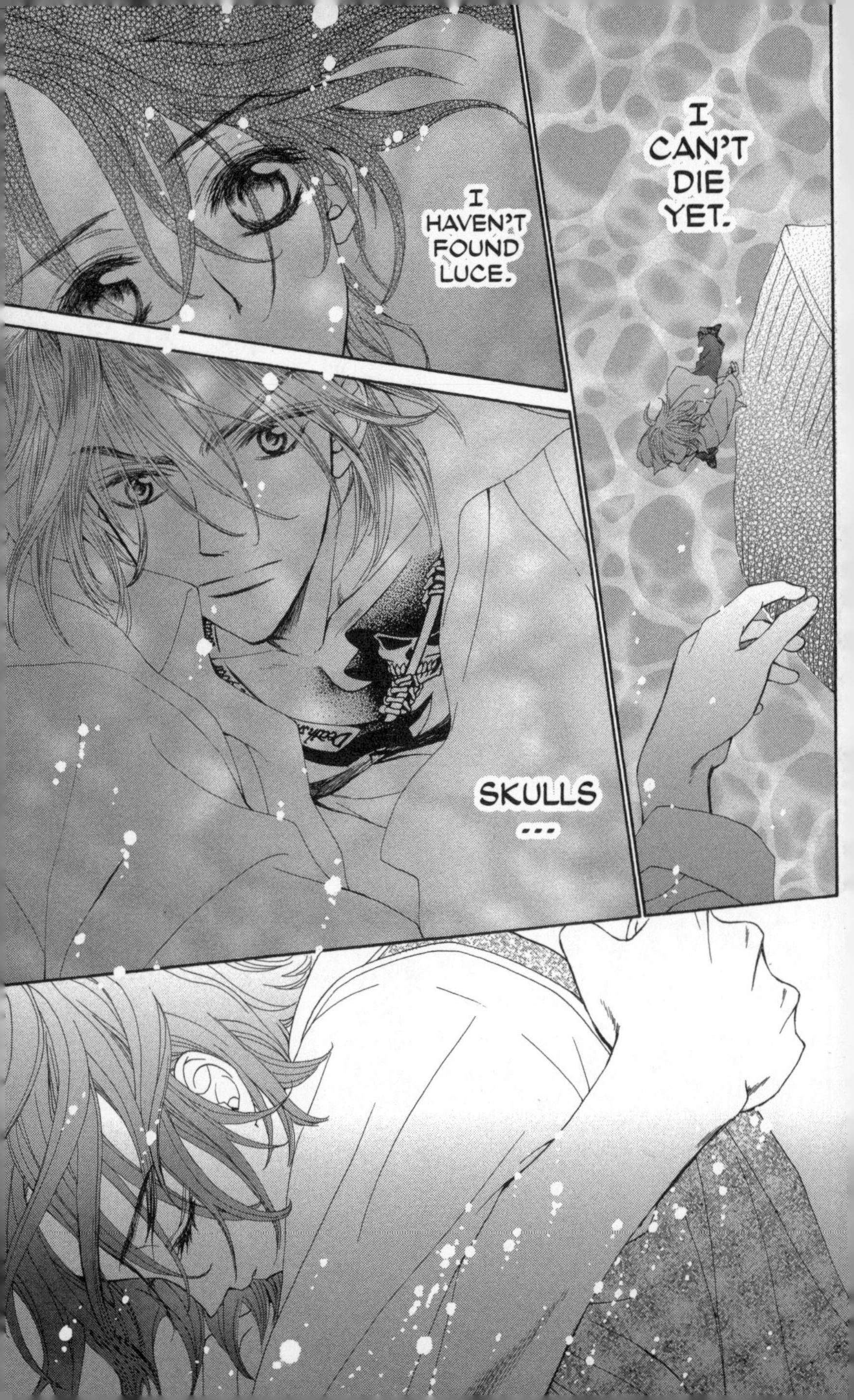
I CAN'T DIE YET.
I HAVEN'T FOUND LUCE.
SKULLS ...

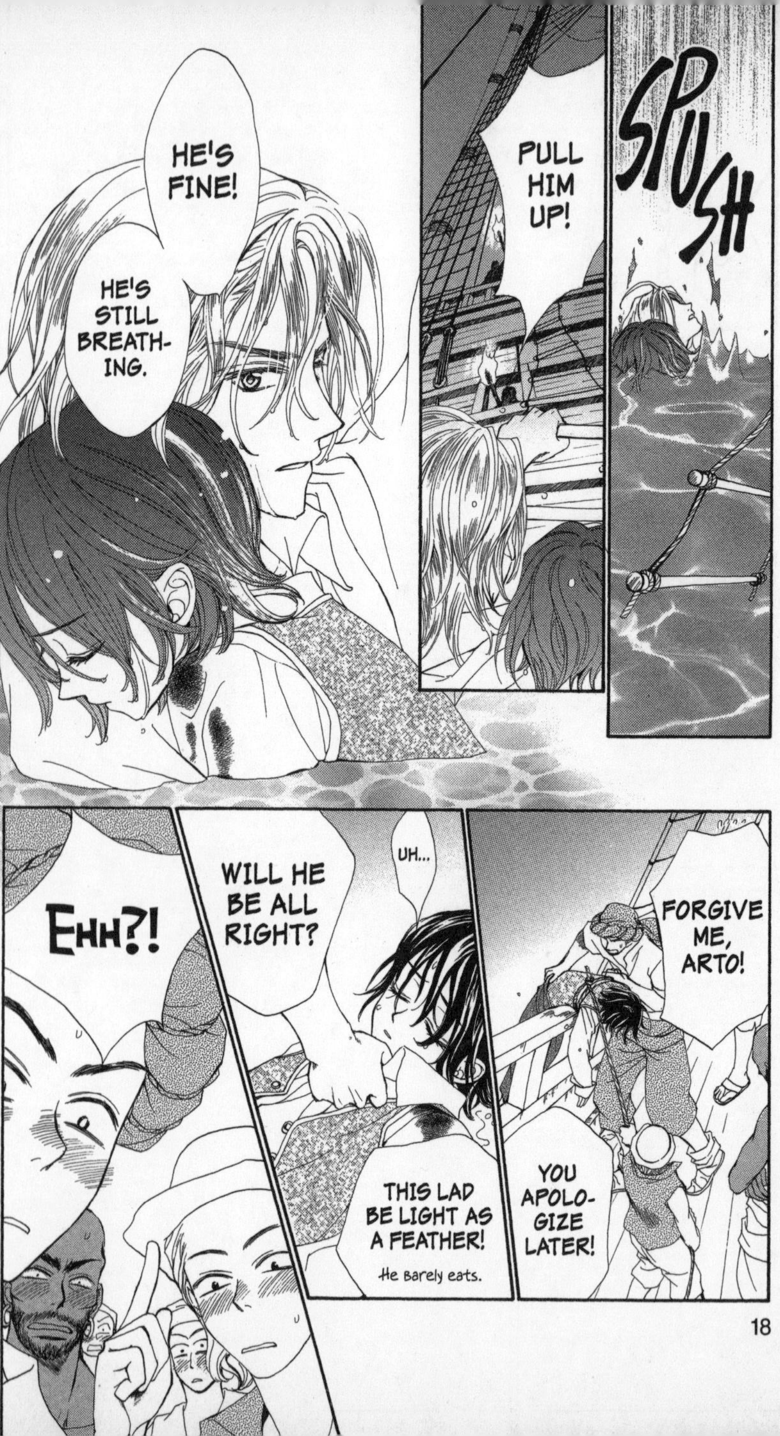
SPUSH
PULL HIM UP!
HE'S FINE!
HE'S STILL BREATHING.
FORGIVE ME, ARTO!
YOU APOLOGIZE LATER!
UH...
WILL HE BE ALL RIGHT?
THIS LAD BE LIGHT AS A FEATHER!
He barely eats.
EHH?!

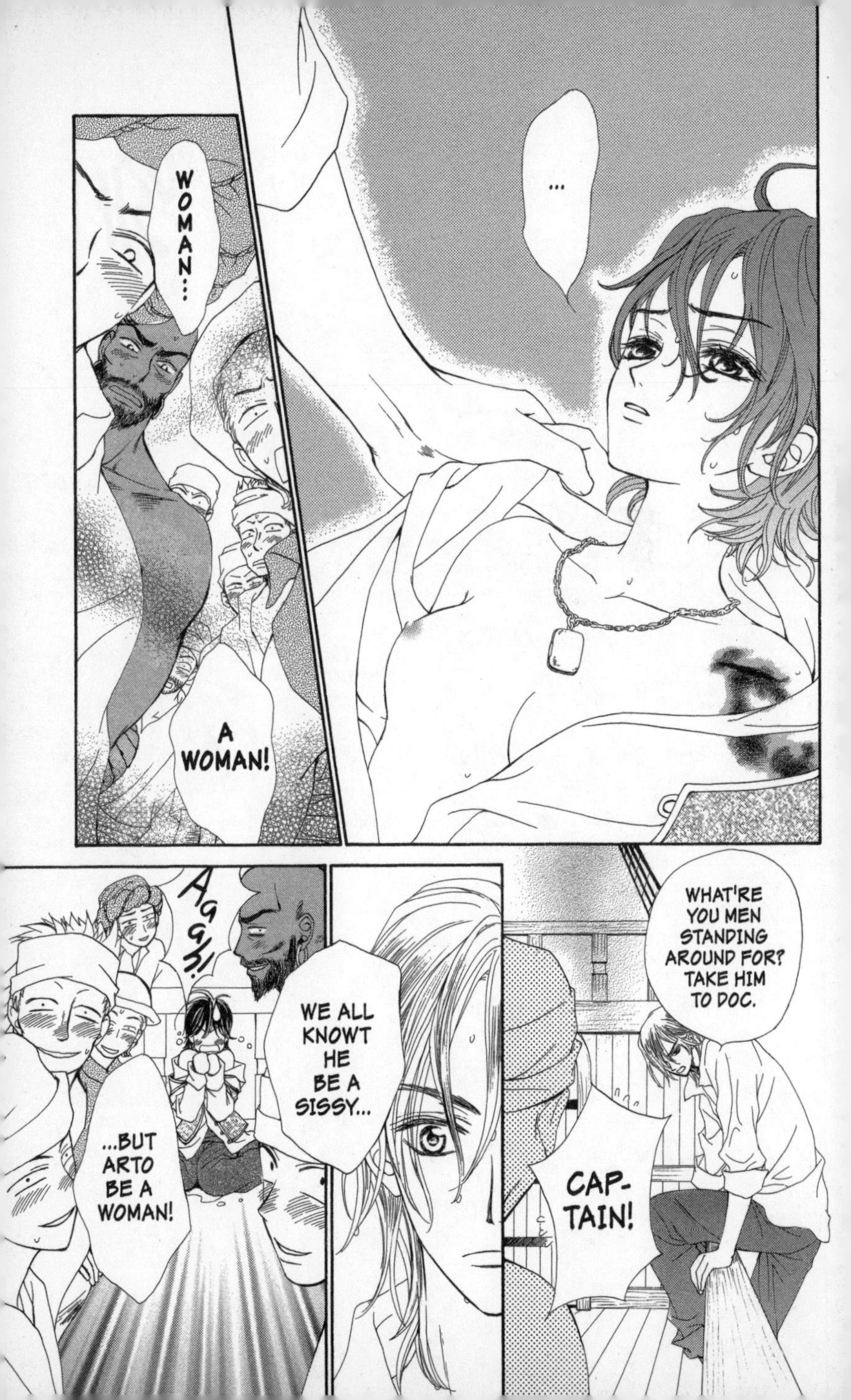
...
WOMAN...
A WOMAN!
WHAT'RE YOU MEN STANDING AROUND FOR? TAKE HIM TO DOC.
CAP-TAIN!
Aggh!
WE ALL KNOWT HE BE A SISSY...
...BUT ARTO BE A WOMAN!

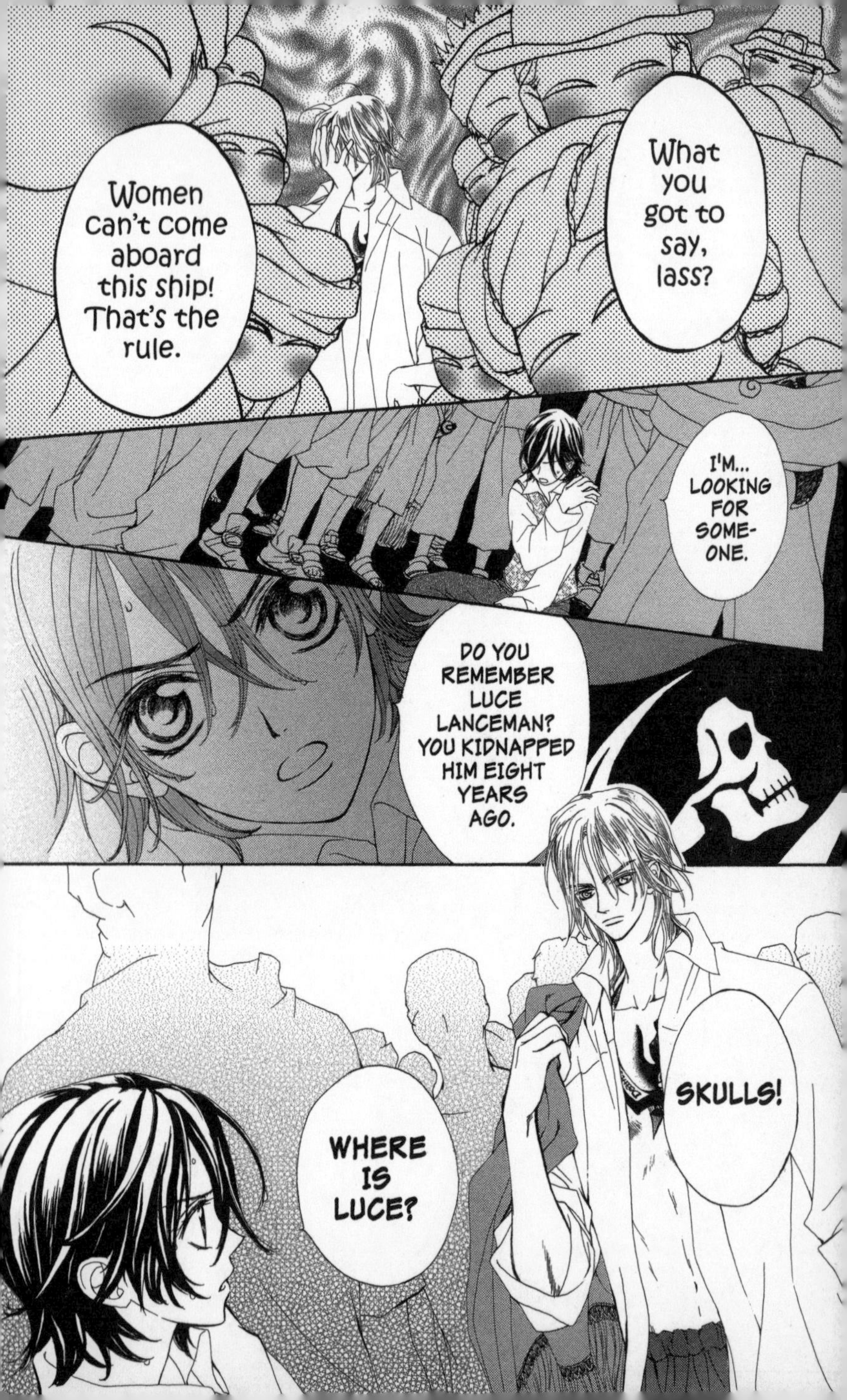
What you got to say, lass?
Women can't come aboard this ship! That's the rule.
I'M... LOOKING FOR SOME-ONE.
DO YOU REMEMBER LUCE LANCEMAN? YOU KIDNAPPED HIM EIGHT YEARS AGO.
SKULLS!
WHERE IS LUCE?

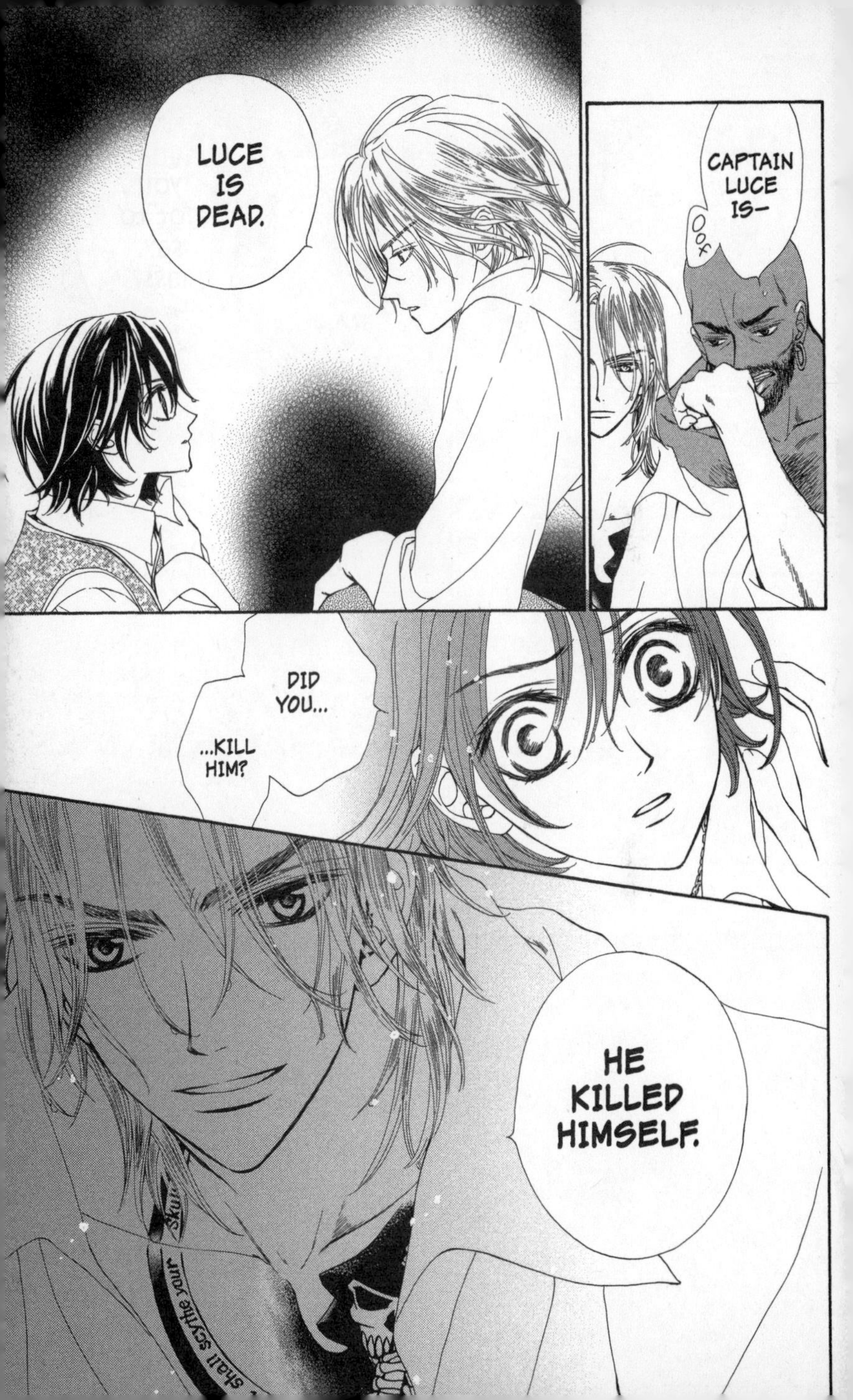
CAPTAIN LUCE IS—
Oof
LUCE IS DEAD.
DID YOU...
...KILL HIM?
HE KILLED HIMSELF.

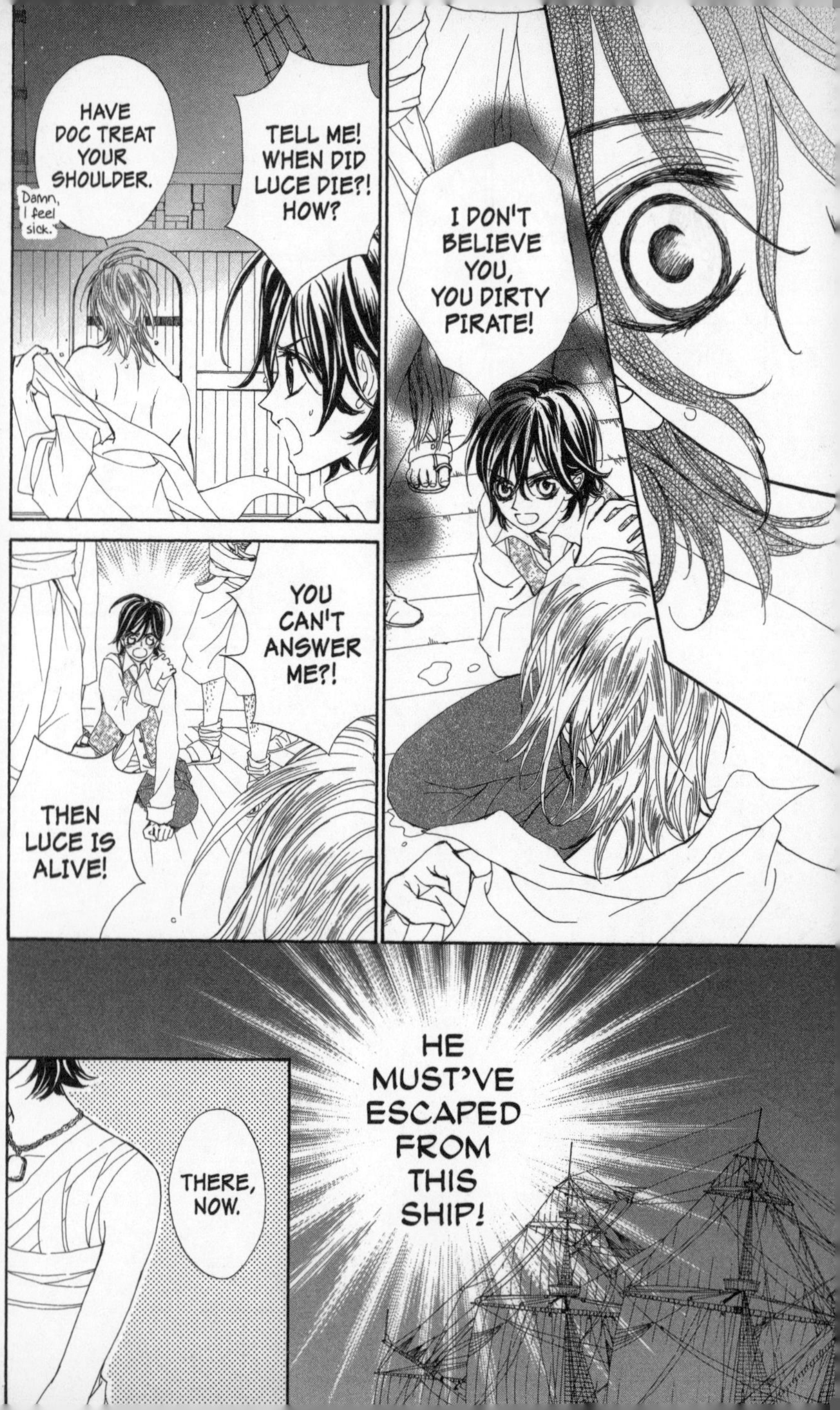
I DON'T BELIEVE YOU, YOU DIRTY PIRATE!
TELL ME! WHEN DID LUCE DIE?! HOW?
HAVE DOC TREAT YOUR SHOULDER.
Damn, I feel sick.
YOU CAN'T ANSWER ME?!
THEN LUCE IS ALIVE!
HE MUST'VE ESCAPED FROM THIS SHIP!
THERE, NOW.

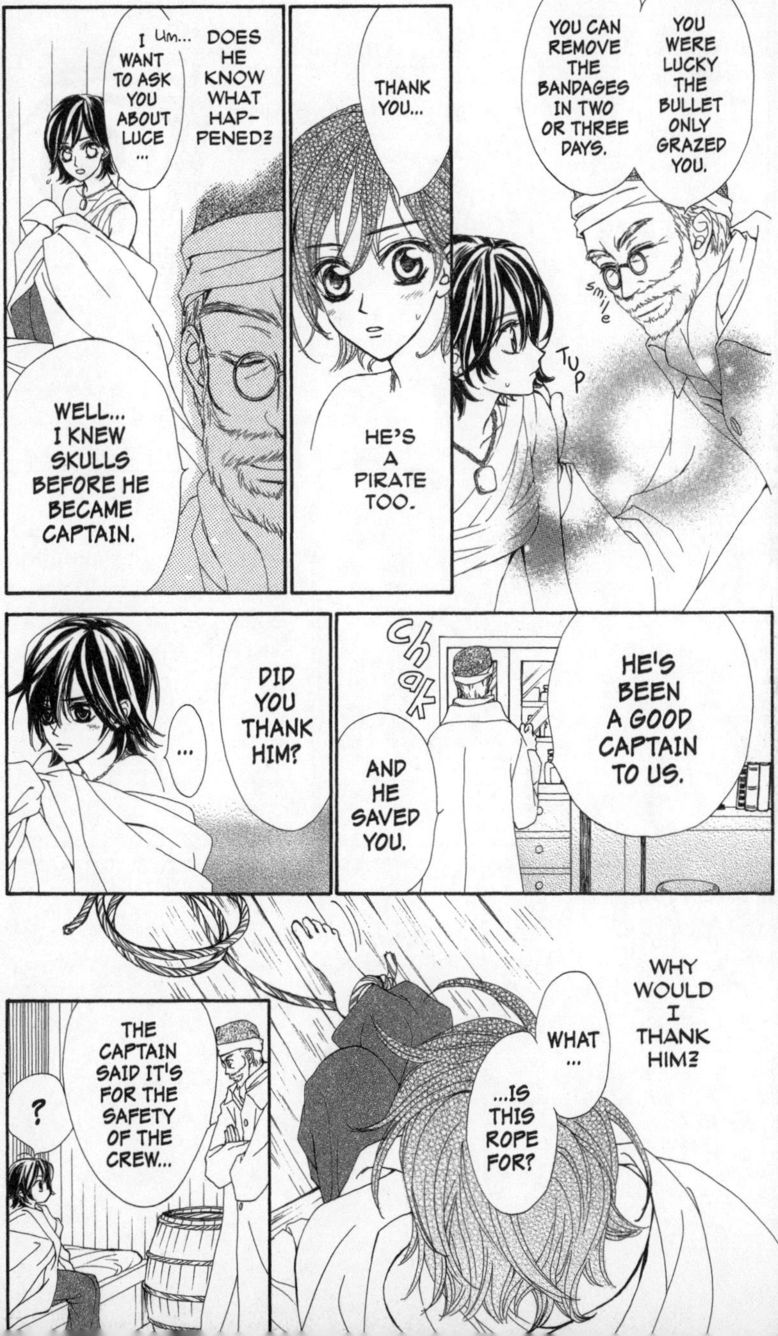
YOU WERE LUCKY THE BULLET ONLY GRAZED YOU.
YOU CAN REMOVE THE BANDAGES IN TWO OR THREE DAYS.
smile
TUP
THANK YOU...
HE'S A PIRATE TOO.
DOES HE KNOW WHAT HAP-PENED?
Um... I WANT TO ASK YOU ABOUT LUCE...
WELL... I KNEW SKULLS BEFORE HE BECAME CAPTAIN.
HE'S BEEN A GOOD CAPTAIN TO US.
Chak
AND HE SAVED YOU.
DID YOU THANK HIM?
...
WHY WOULD I THANK HIM?
WHAT...
...IS THIS ROPE FOR?
THE CAPTAIN SAID IT'S FOR THE SAFETY OF THE CREW...
?

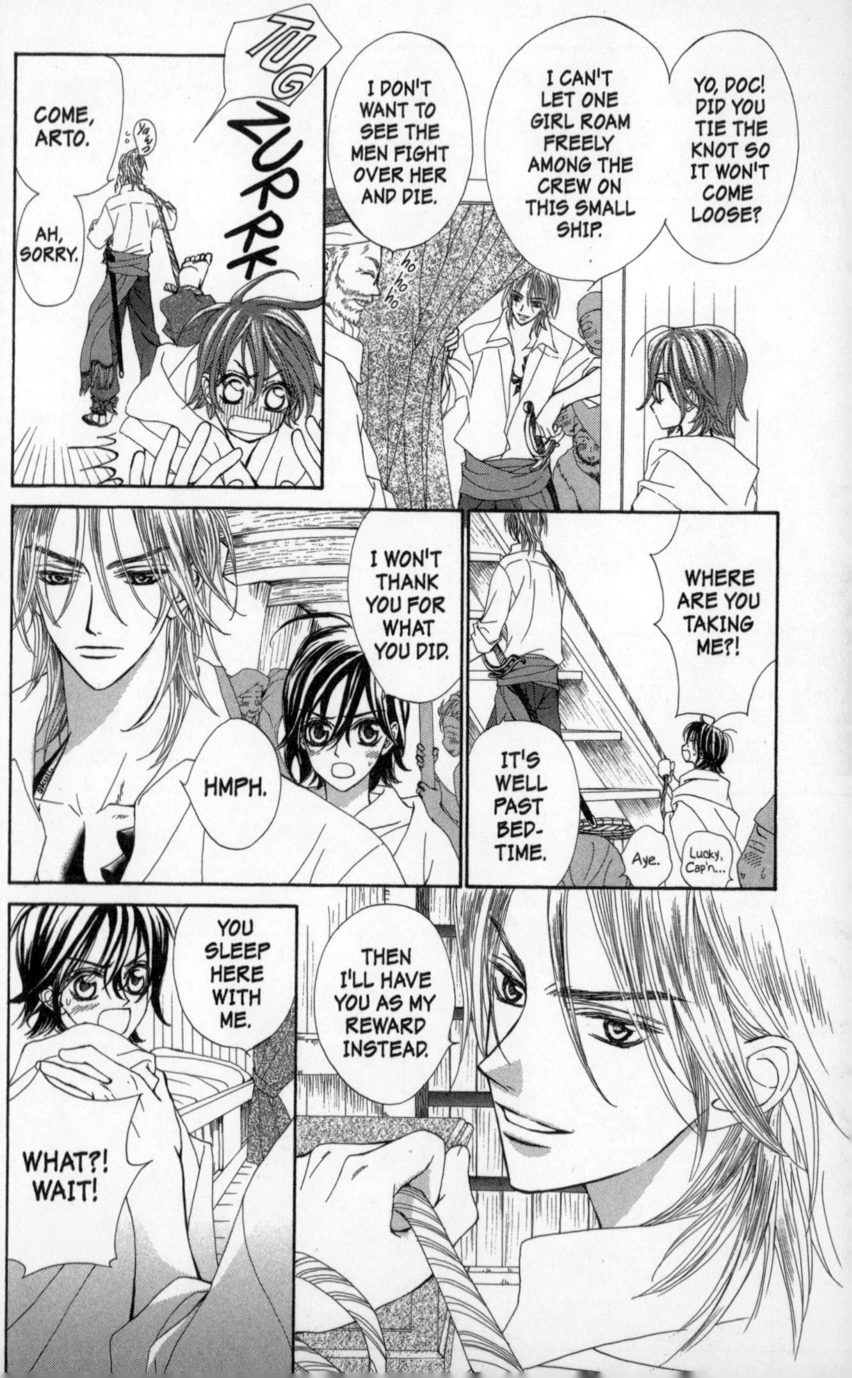
YO, DOC! DID YOU TIE THE KNOT SO IT WON'T COME LOOSE?
I CAN'T LET ONE GIRL ROAM FREELY AMONG THE CREW ON THIS SMALL SHIP.
I DON'T WANT TO SEE THE MEN FIGHT OVER HER AND DIE.
ho ho ho ho
TUG
ZURRK
COME, ARTO.
Yawn
AH, SORRY.
WHERE ARE YOU TAKING ME?!
IT'S WELL PAST BED-TIME.
Lucky, Cap'n...
Aye.
I WON'T THANK YOU FOR WHAT YOU DID.
HMPH.
THEN I'LL HAVE YOU AS MY REWARD INSTEAD.
YOU SLEEP HERE WITH ME.
WHAT?! WAIT!

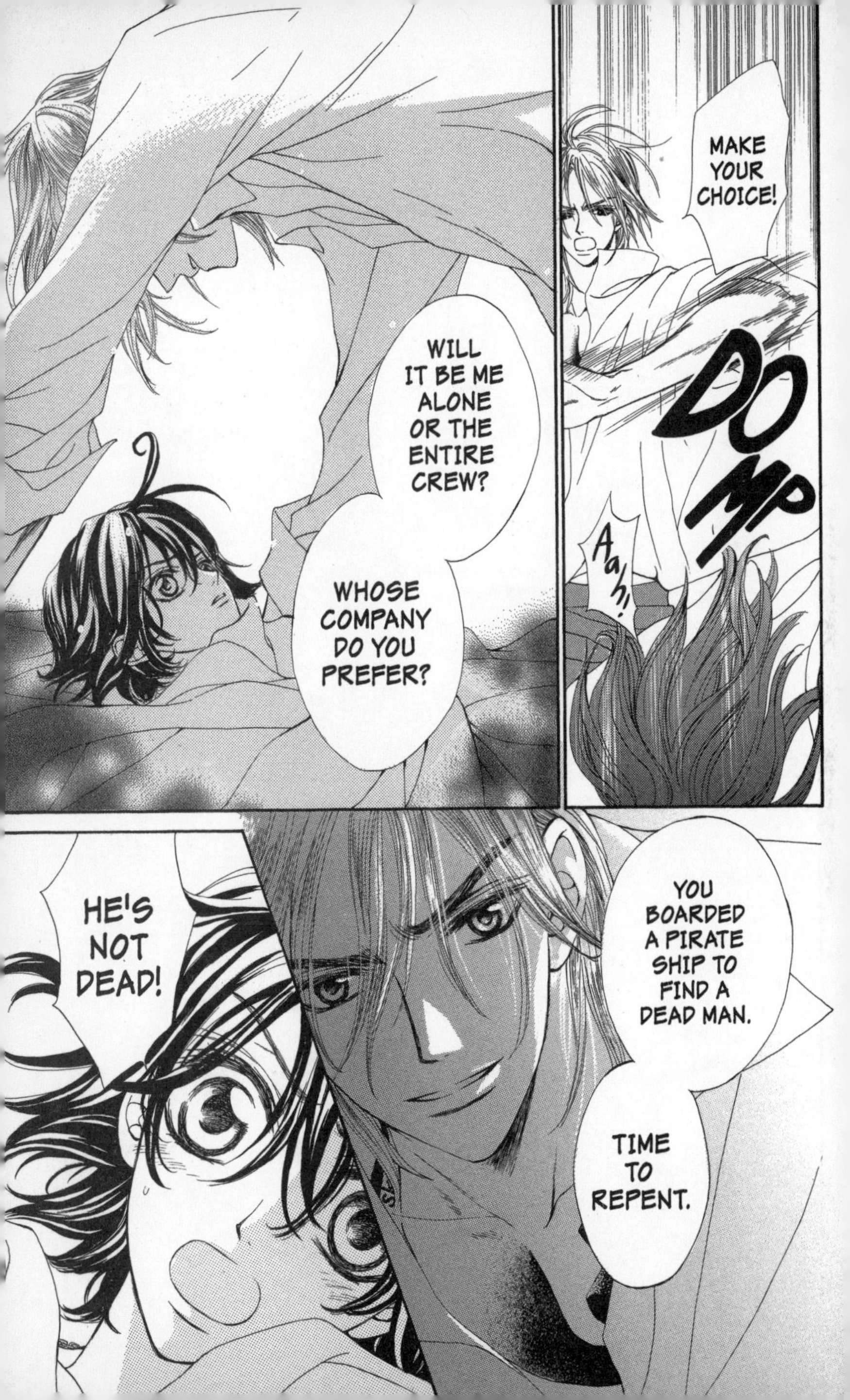
MAKE YOUR CHOICE!
DOMP
Aah!
WILL IT BE ME ALONE OR THE ENTIRE CREW?
WHOSE COMPANY DO YOU PREFER?
YOU BOARDED A PIRATE SHIP TO FIND A DEAD MAN.
TIME TO REPENT.
HE'S NOT DEAD!

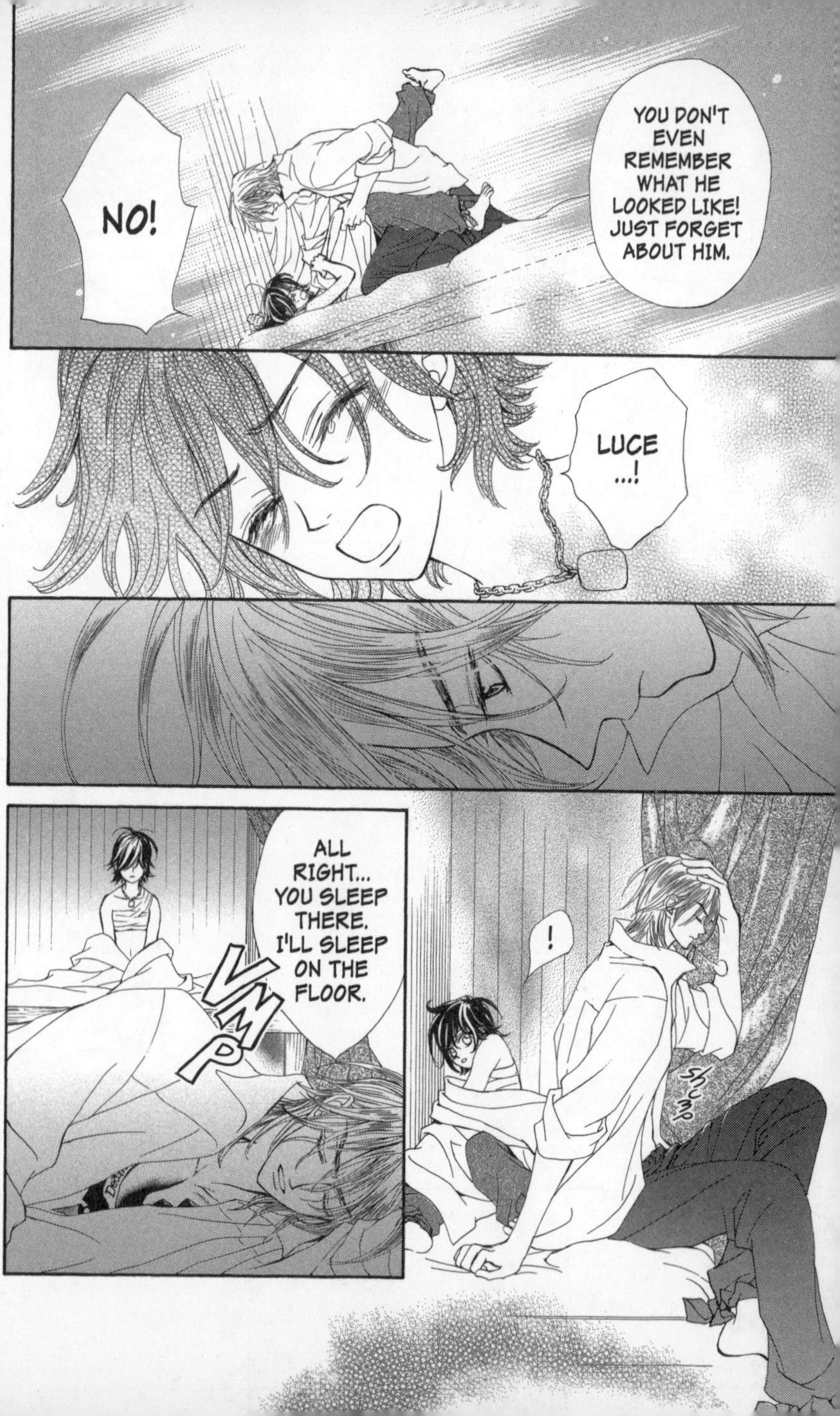
YOU DON'T EVEN REMEMBER WHAT HE LOOKED LIKE! JUST FORGET ABOUT HIM.
NO!
LUCE ...!
!
SHUMP
ALL RIGHT... YOU SLEEP THERE. I'LL SLEEP ON THE FLOOR.
VMP

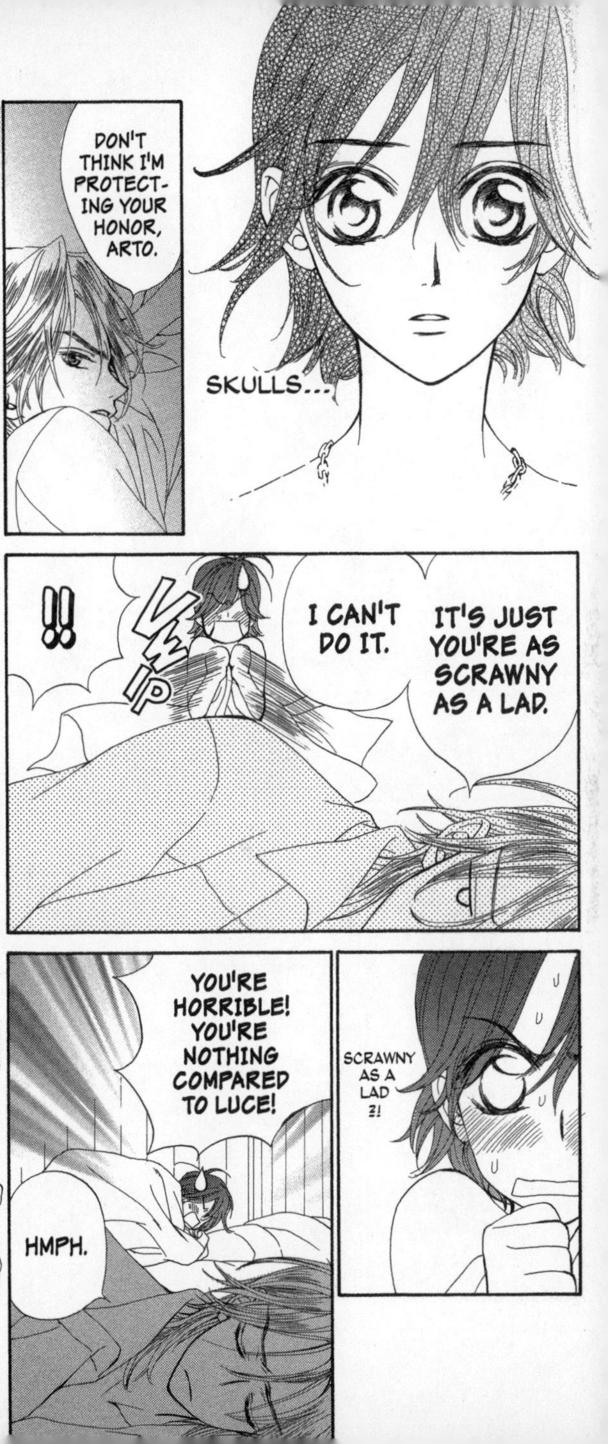
SKULLS...
DON'T THINK I'M PROTECTING YOUR HONOR, ARTO.
IT'S JUST YOU'RE AS SCRAWNY AS A LAD.
I CAN'T DO IT.
VWIP
!!
SCRAWNY AS A LAD ?!
YOU'RE HORRIBLE! YOU'RE NOTHING COMPARED TO LUCE!
HMPH.

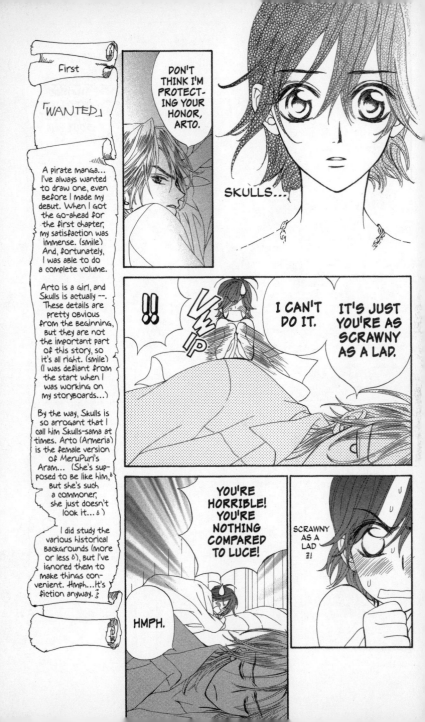

First

「WANTED」

A pirate manga... I've always wanted to draw one, even before I made my debut. When I got the go-ahead for the first chapter, my satisfaction was immense. (smile) And, fortunately, I was able to do a complete volume.

Arto is a girl, and Skulls is actually --. These details are pretty obvious from the beginning, but they are not the important part of this story, so it's all right. (smile) (I was defiant from the start when I was working on my storyboards...)

By the way, Skulls is so arrogant that I call him Skulls-sama at times. Arto (Armeria) is the female version of MeruPuri's Aram... (She's supposed to be like him, but she's such a commoner, she just doesn't look it...)

I did study the various historical backgrounds (more or less), but I've ignored them to make things convenient. Hmph...It's fiction anyway.

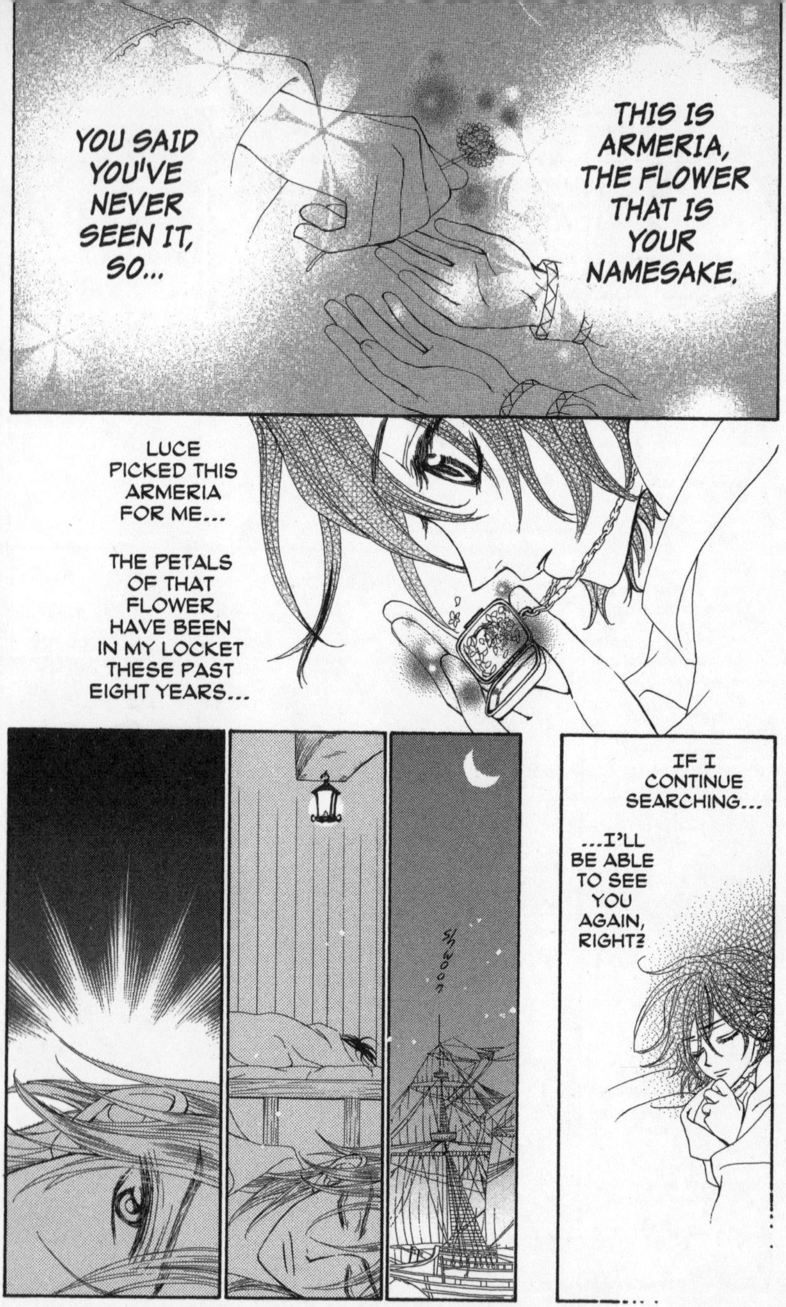
THIS IS ARMERIA, THE FLOWER THAT IS YOUR NAMESAKE.
YOU SAID YOU'VE NEVER SEEN IT, SO...
LUCE PICKED THIS ARMERIA FOR ME...
THE PETALS OF THAT FLOWER HAVE BEEN IN MY LOCKET THESE PAST EIGHT YEARS...
IF I CONTINUE SEARCHING...
...I'LL BE ABLE TO SEE YOU AGAIN, RIGHT?

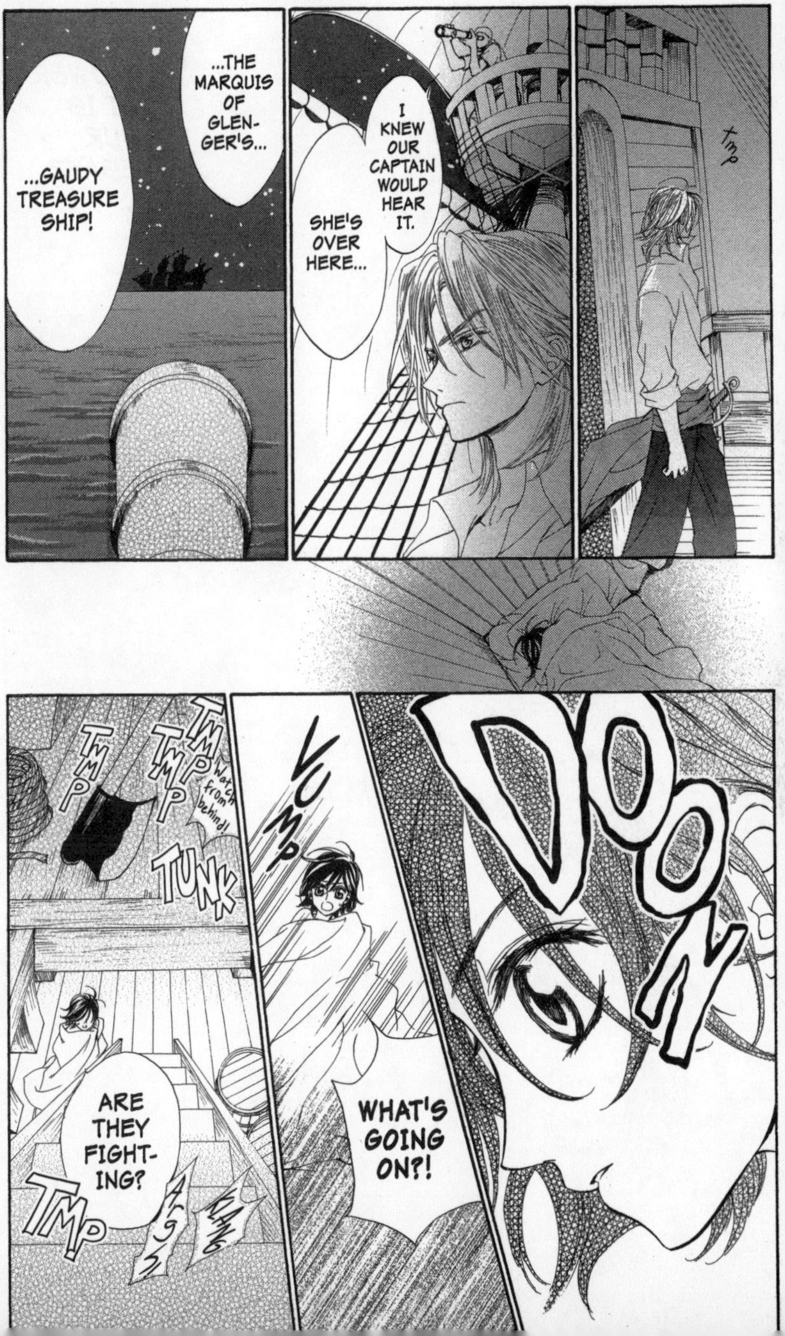
tmp
I KNEW OUR CAPTAIN WOULD HEAR IT.
SHE'S OVER HERE...
...THE MARQUIS OF GLENGER'S...
...GAUDY TREASURE SHIP!
DOOON
VUMP
WHAT'S GOING ON?!
TMP
TMP
TMP
Watch from behind!
TUNK
ARE THEY FIGHTING?
TMP
KLANG
Argh!!

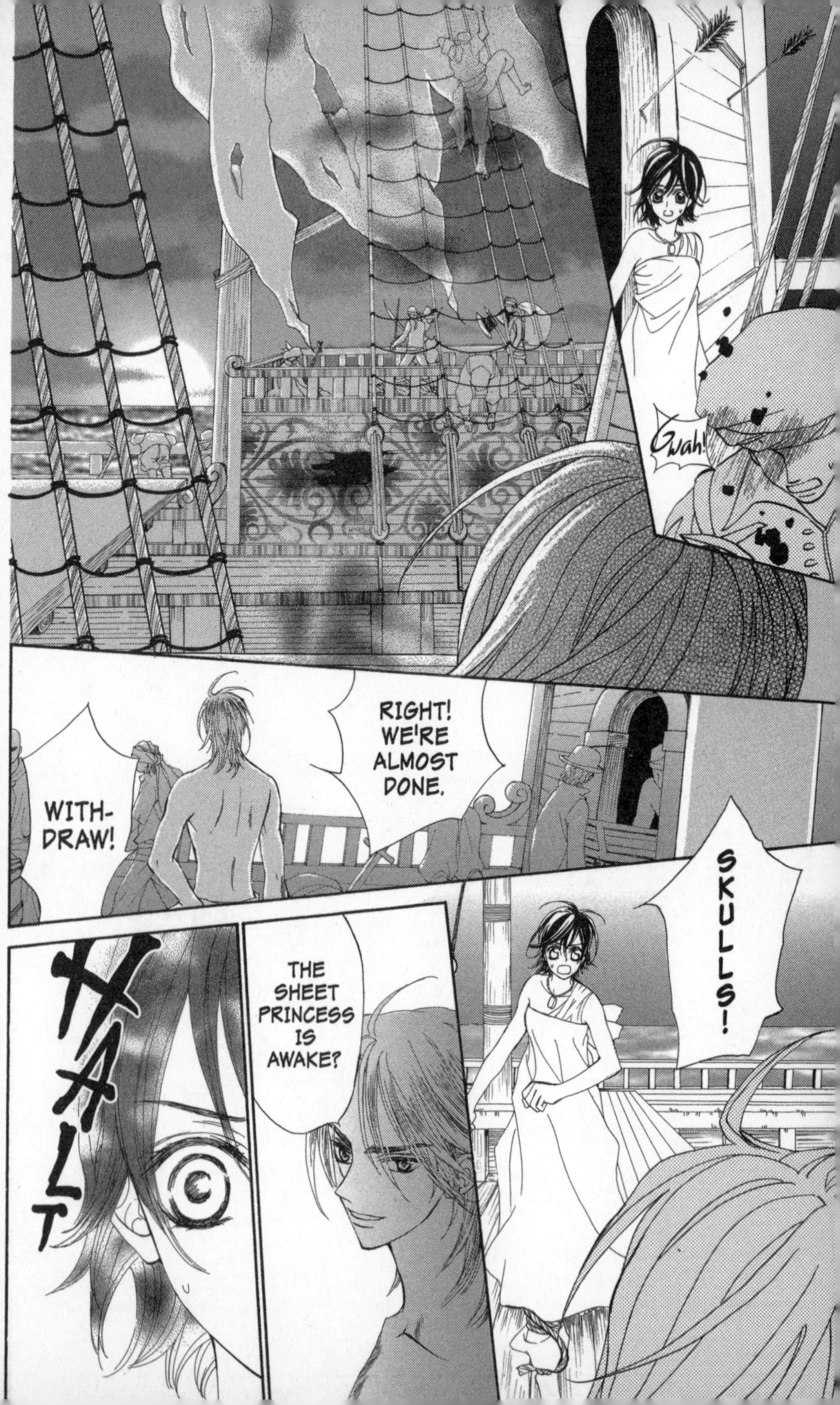
Gwah!
RIGHT! WE'RE ALMOST DONE.
WITH-DRAW!
SKULLS!
THE SHEET PRINCESS IS AWAKE?
HALT

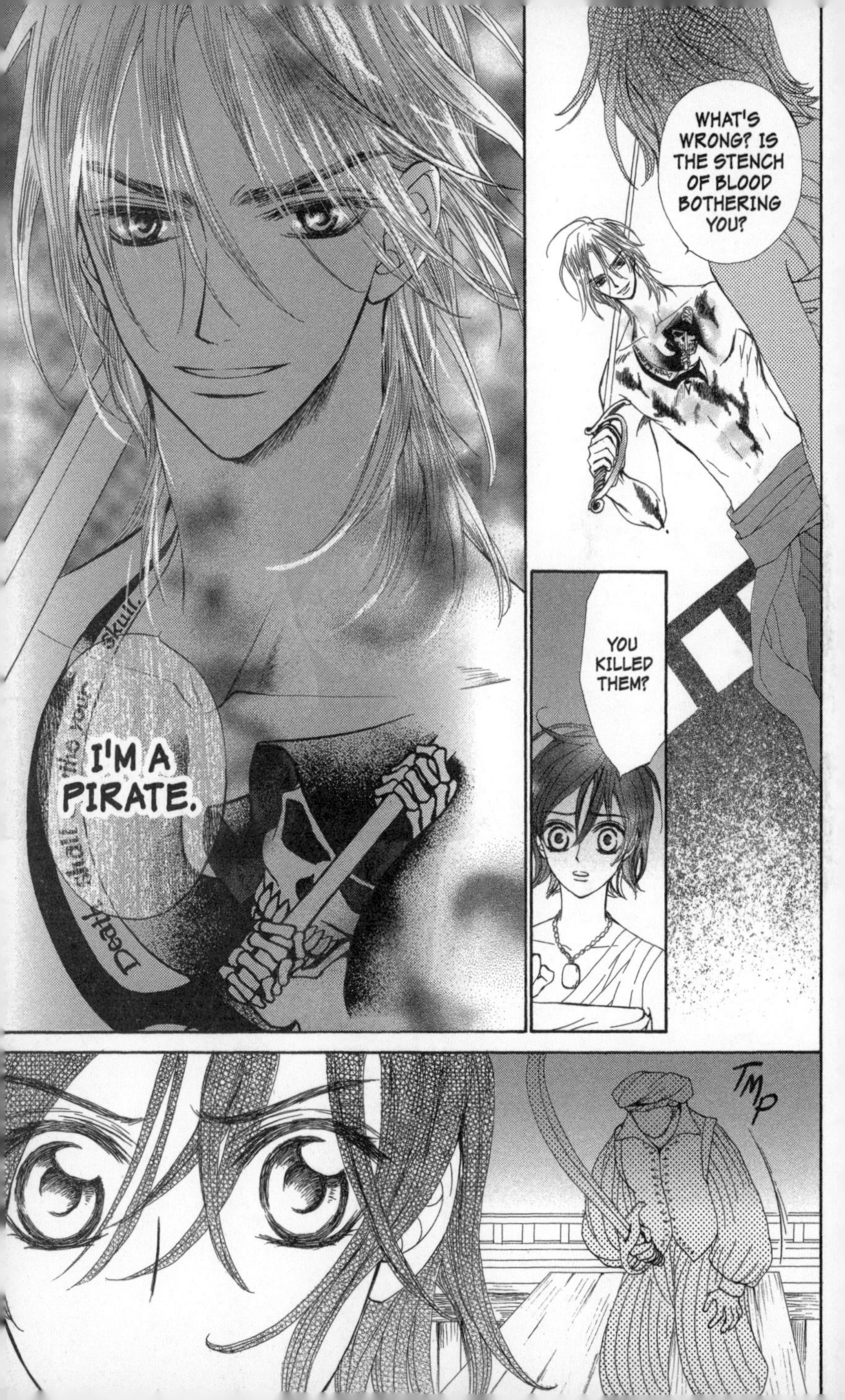
WHAT'S WRONG? IS THE STENCH OF BLOOD BOTHERING YOU?
YOU KILLED THEM?
I'M A PIRATE.
TMP

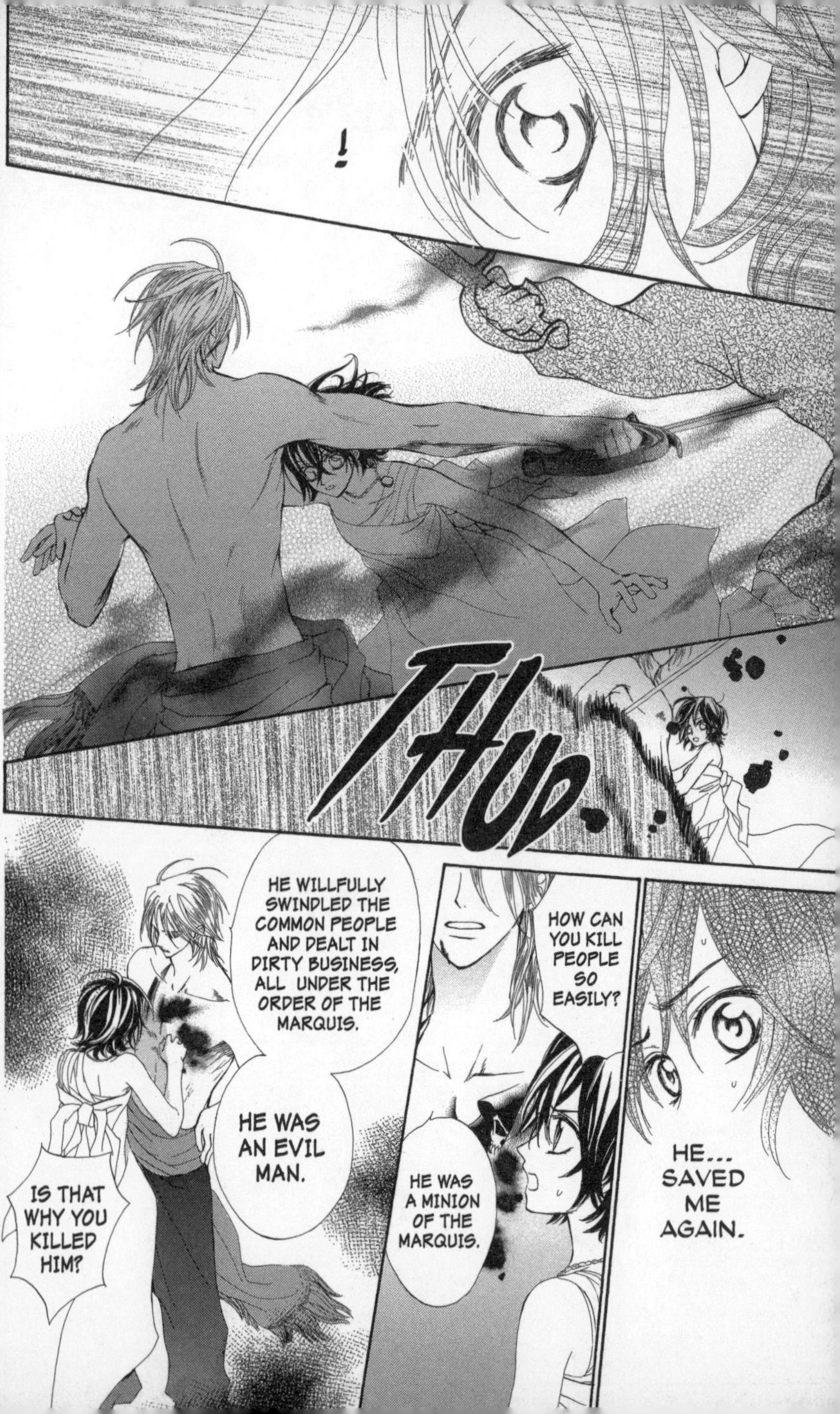
!
THUD
HE... SAVED ME AGAIN.
HOW CAN YOU KILL PEOPLE SO EASILY?
HE WAS A MINION OF THE MARQUIS.
HE WILLFULLY SWINDLED THE COMMON PEOPLE AND DEALT IN DIRTY BUSINESS, ALL UNDER THE ORDER OF THE MARQUIS.
HE WAS AN EVIL MAN.
IS THAT WHY YOU KILLED HIM?

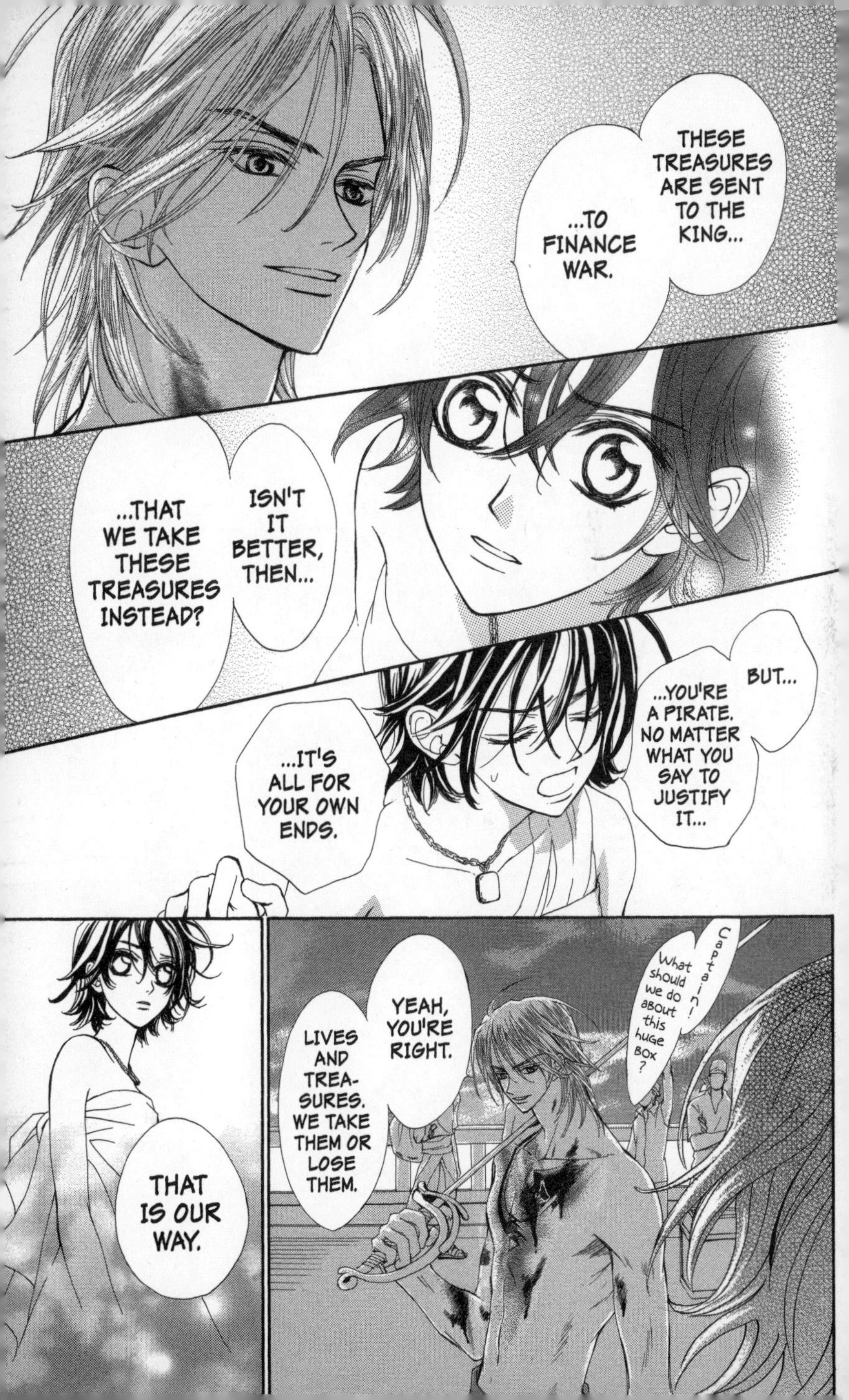
THESE TREASURES ARE SENT TO THE KING...
...TO FINANCE WAR.
ISN'T IT BETTER, THEN...
...THAT WE TAKE THESE TREASURES INSTEAD?
BUT...
...YOU'RE A PIRATE. NO MATTER WHAT YOU SAY TO JUSTIFY IT...
...IT'S ALL FOR YOUR OWN ENDS.
Captain!
What should we do about this huge box?
YEAH, YOU'RE RIGHT.
LIVES AND TREA-SURES. WE TAKE THEM OR LOSE THEM.
THAT IS OUR WAY.

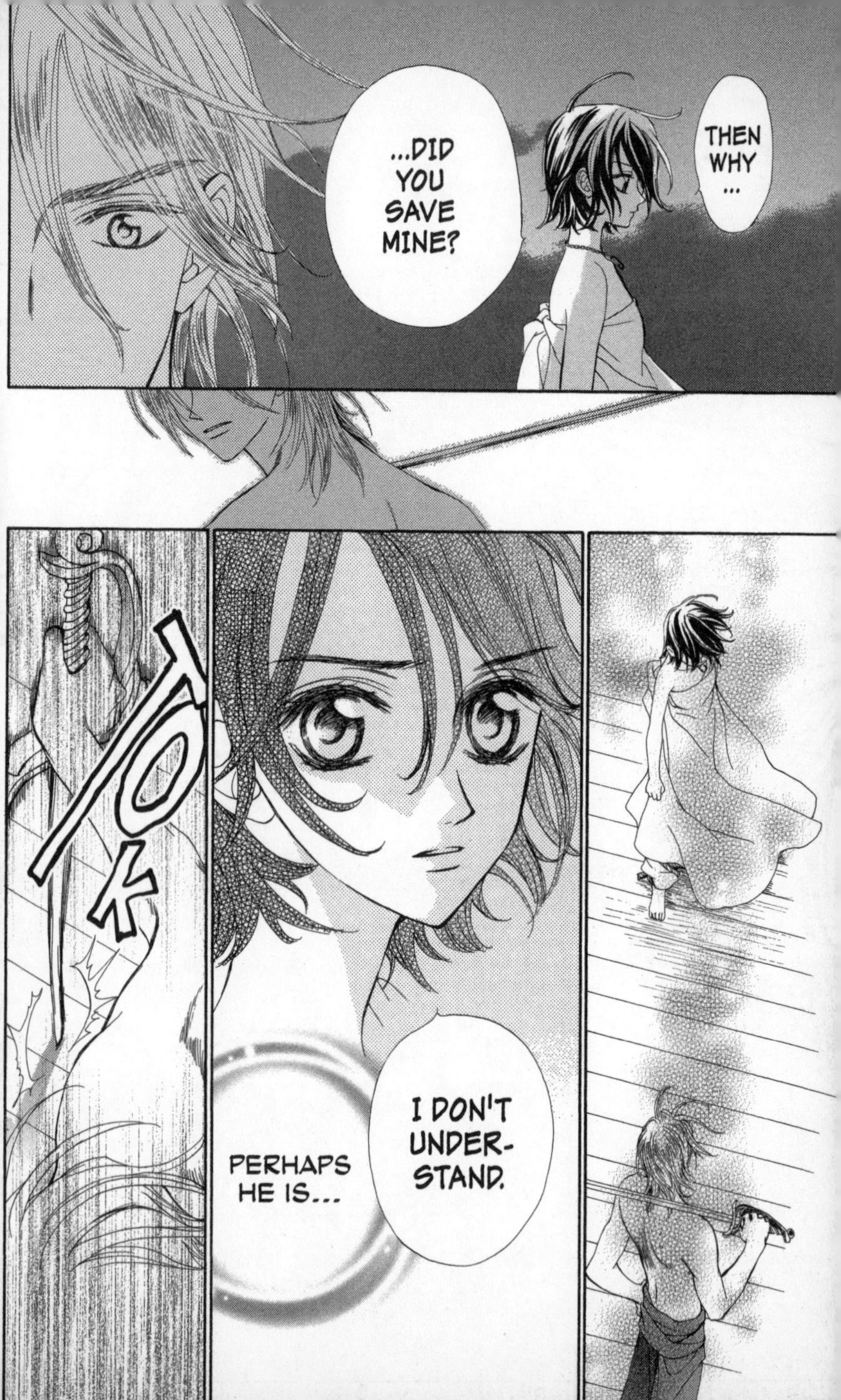
THEN WHY ...
...DID YOU SAVE MINE?
I DON'T UNDER-STAND.
PERHAPS HE IS...
TOK

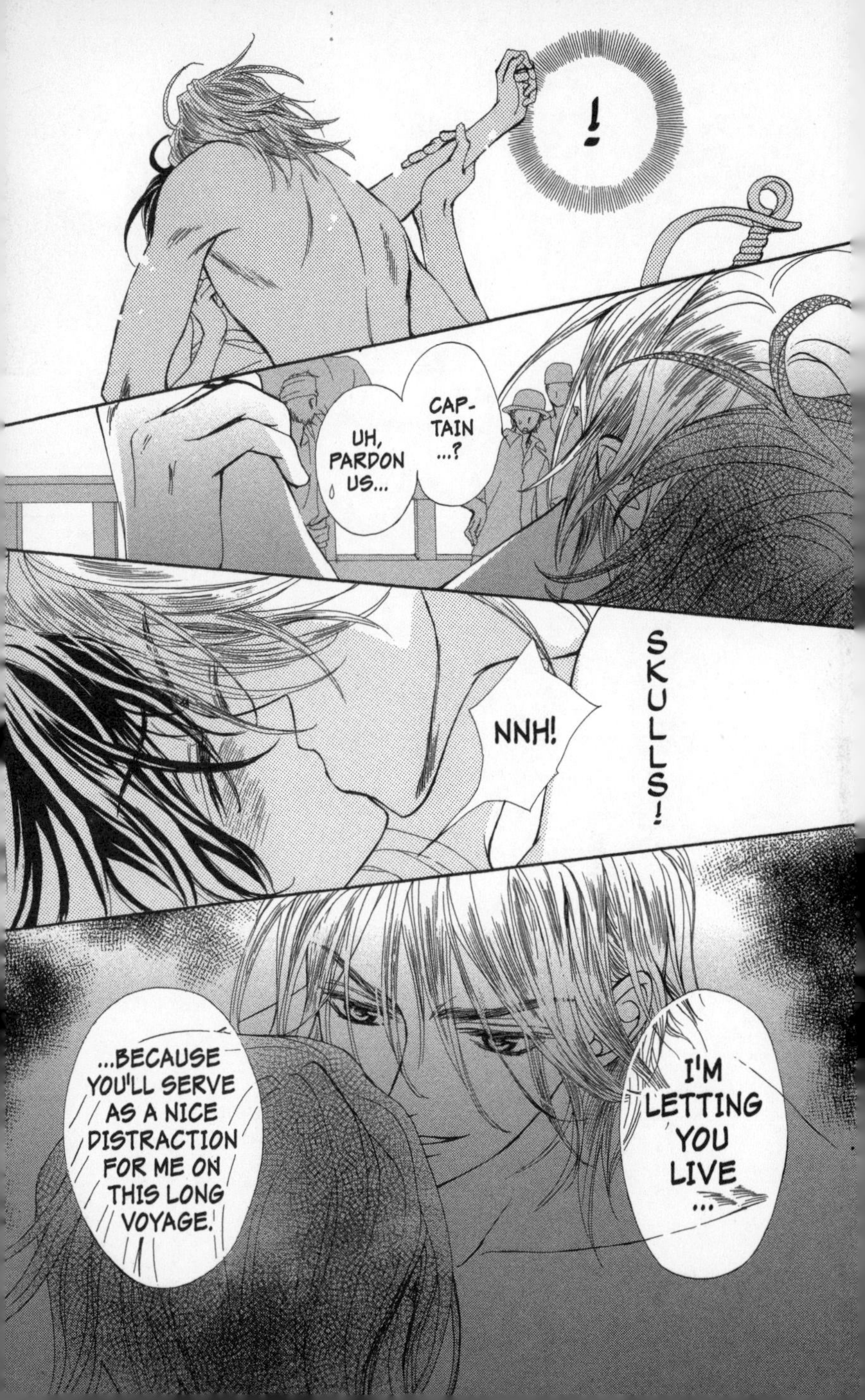
!
CAP-TAIN ...?
UH, PARDON US...
SKULLS!
NNH!
I'M LETTING YOU LIVE ...
...BECAUSE YOU'LL SERVE AS A NICE DISTRACTION FOR ME ON THIS LONG VOYAGE.

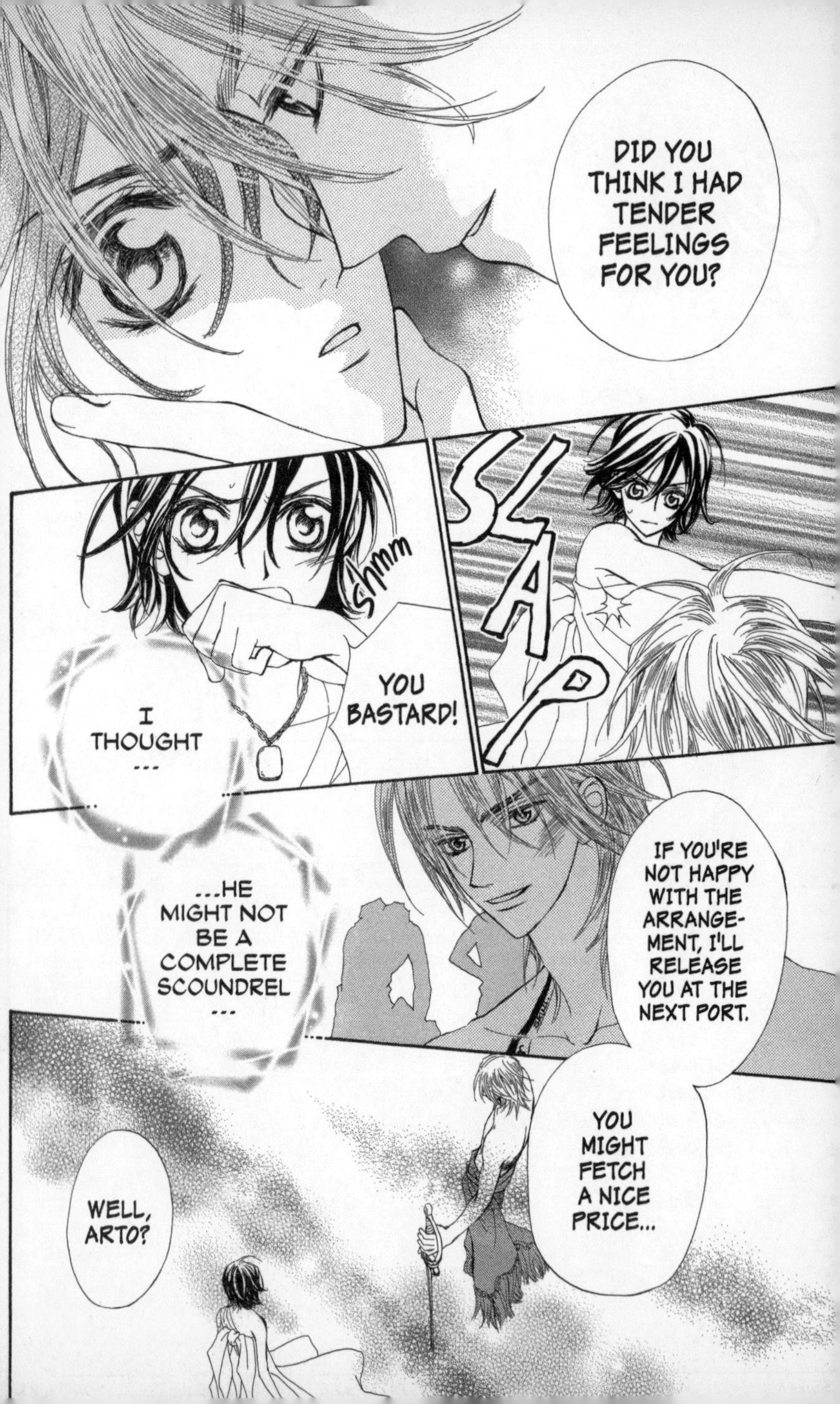
DID YOU THINK I HAD TENDER FEELINGS FOR YOU?
SLAP
shmm
YOU BASTARD!
I THOUGHT...
IF YOU'RE NOT HAPPY WITH THE ARRANGE-MENT, I'LL RELEASE YOU AT THE NEXT PORT.
...HE MIGHT NOT BE A COMPLETE SCOUNDREL...
YOU MIGHT FETCH A NICE PRICE...
WELL, ARTO?

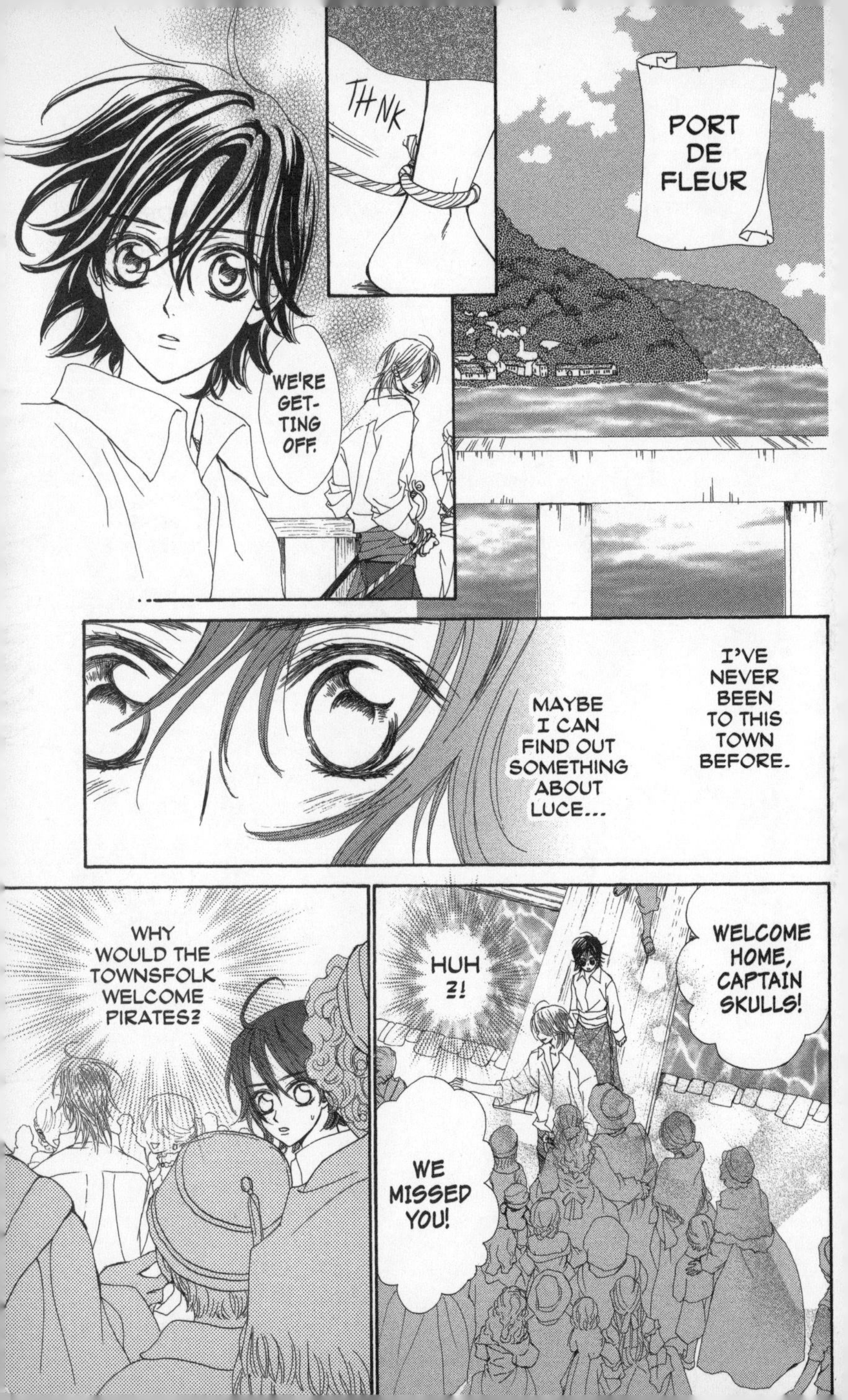
PORT DE FLEUR
THNK
WE'RE GET-TING OFF.
I'VE NEVER BEEN TO THIS TOWN BEFORE.
MAYBE I CAN FIND OUT SOMETHING ABOUT LUCE...
WELCOME HOME, CAPTAIN SKULLS!
HUH?!
WE MISSED YOU!
WHY WOULD THE TOWNSFOLK WELCOME PIRATES?

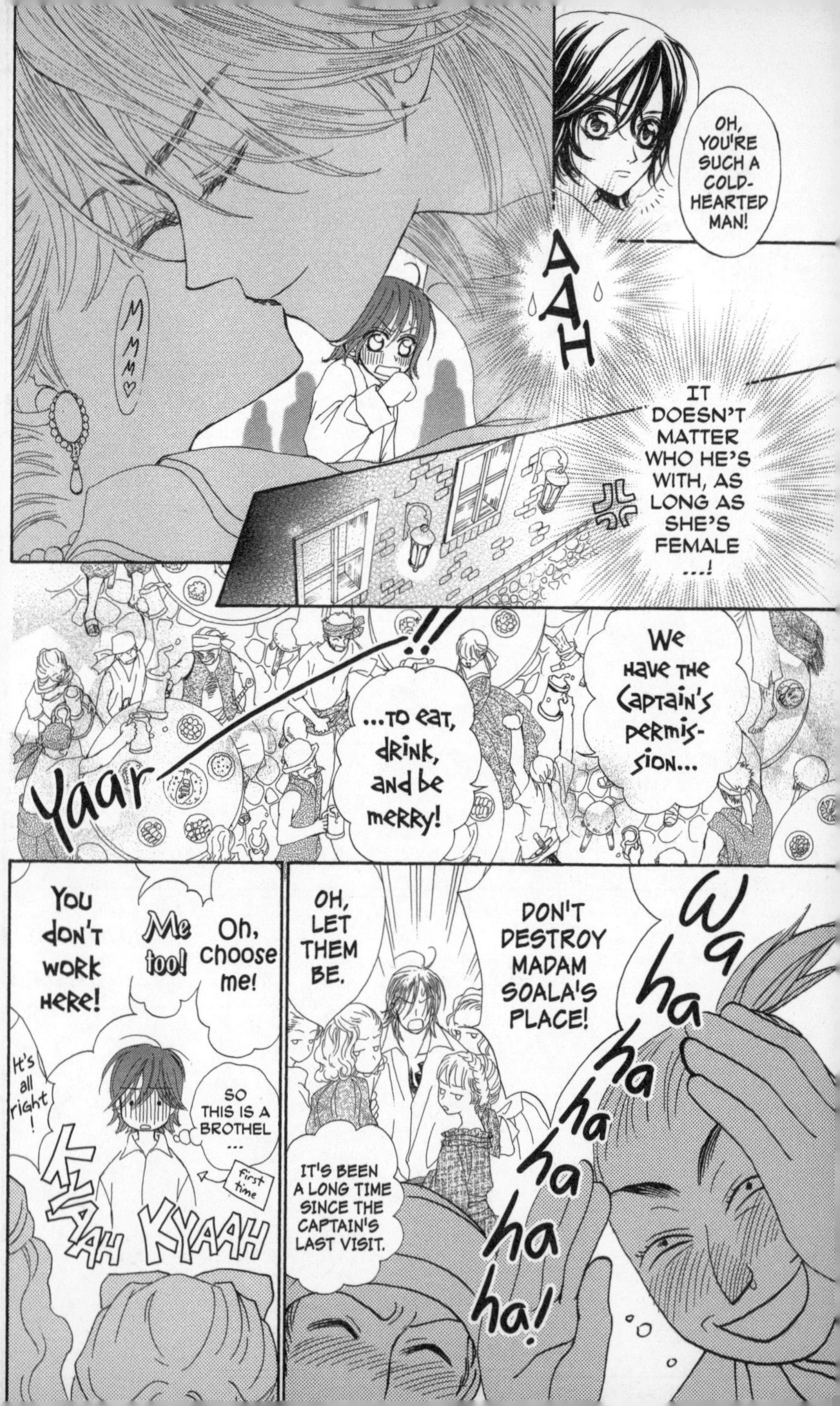
OH, YOU'RE SUCH A COLD-HEARTED MAN!
AAH
MMM♡
IT DOESN'T MATTER WHO HE'S WITH, AS LONG AS SHE'S FEMALE ...!
We have the Captain's permis-sion...
...to eat, drink, and be merry!
!!
Yaar
Wa ha ha ha ha ha ha ha ha!
DON'T DESTROY MADAM SOALA'S PLACE!
OH, LET THEM BE.
IT'S BEEN A LONG TIME SINCE THE CAPTAIN'S LAST VISIT.
Oh, choose me!
Me too!
You don't work here!
SO THIS IS A BROTHEL ...
It's all right!
First time
KYAAH KYAAH

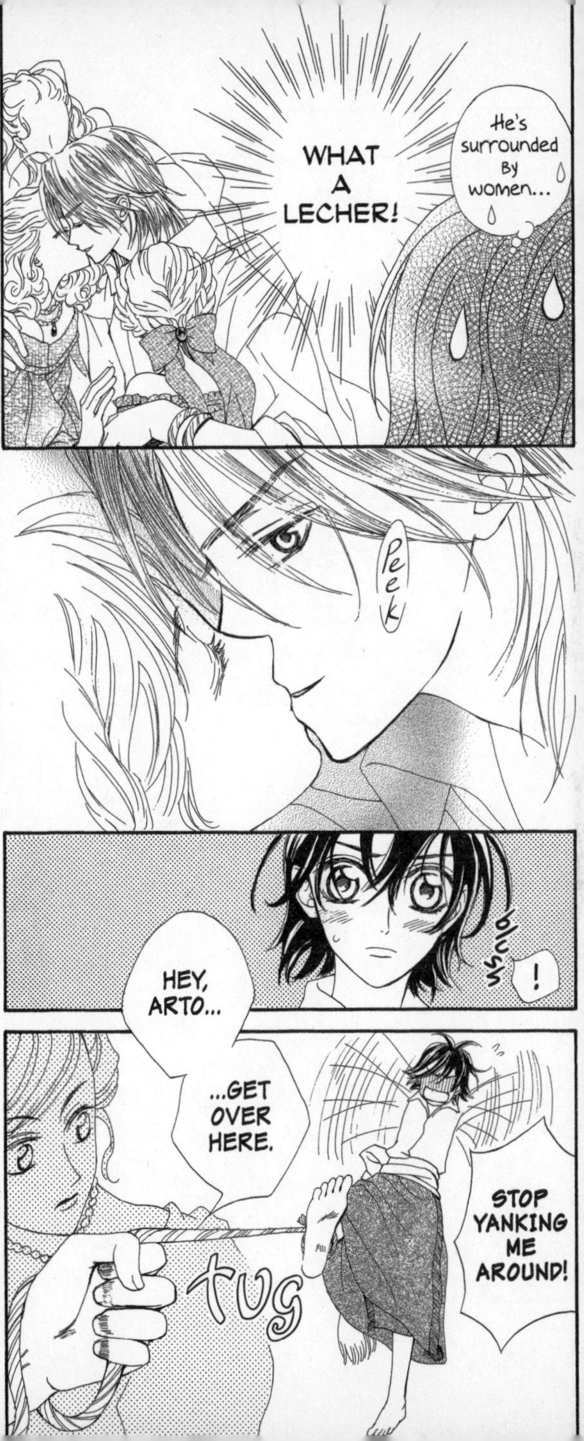
He's surrounded by women...
WHAT A LECHER!
Peek
!
blush
HEY, ARTO...
...GET OVER HERE.
tug
STOP YANKING ME AROUND!

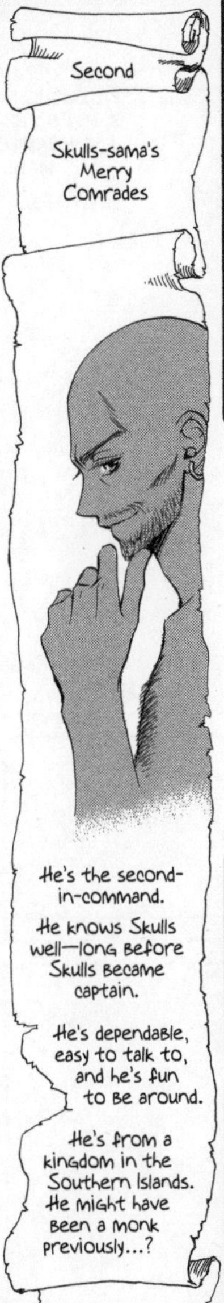
Second
Skulls-sama's Merry Comrades
He's the second-in-command.
He knows Skulls well—long before Skulls became captain.
He's dependable, easy to talk to, and he's fun to be around.
He's from a kingdom in the Southern Islands. He might have been a monk previously...?

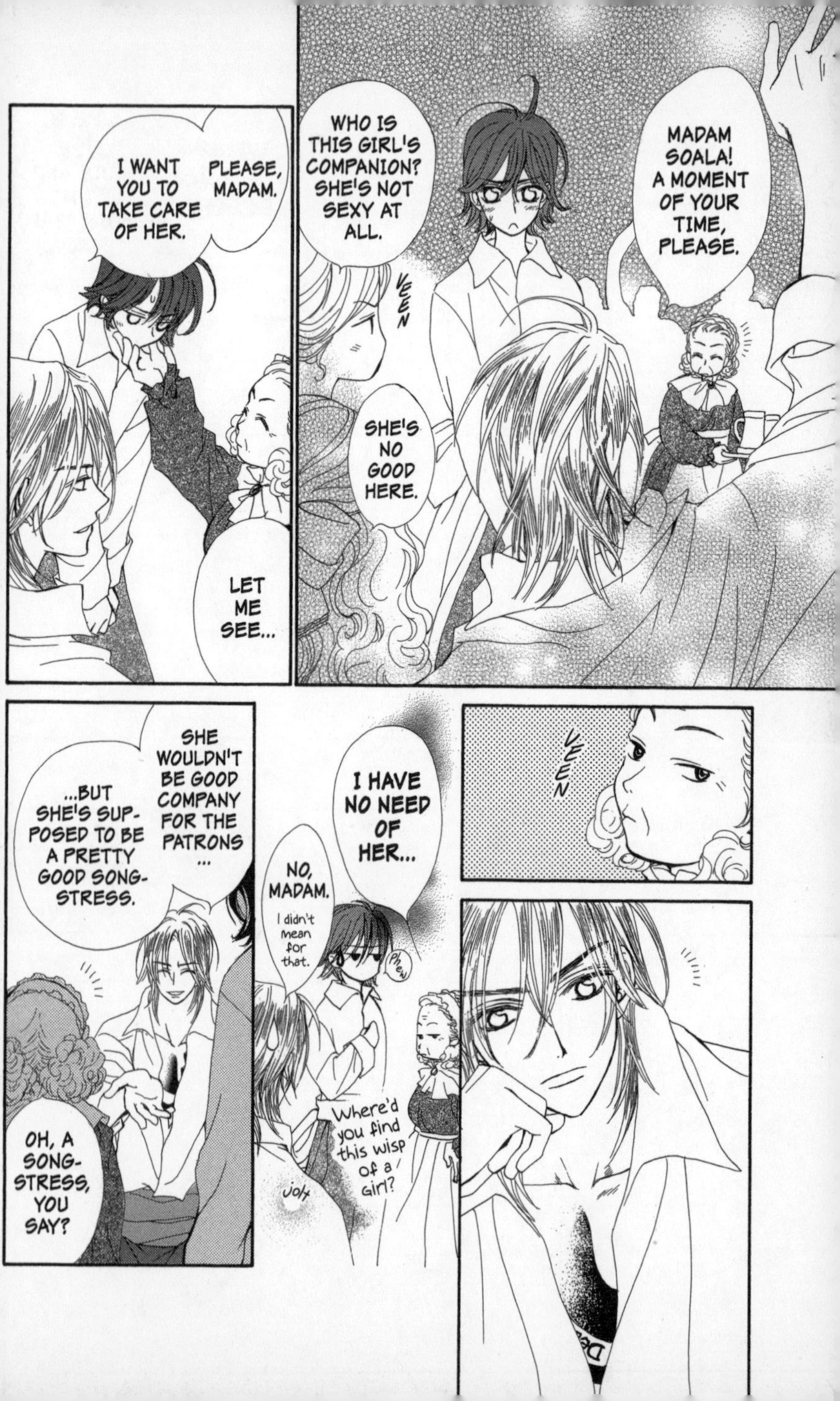
MADAM SOALA! A MOMENT OF YOUR TIME, PLEASE.
WHO IS THIS GIRL'S COMPANION? SHE'S NOT SEXY AT ALL.
VEEN
SHE'S NO GOOD HERE.
PLEASE, MADAM.
I WANT YOU TO TAKE CARE OF HER.
LET ME SEE...
VEEN
I HAVE NO NEED OF HER...
NO, MADAM.
I didn't mean for that.
Phew
Where'd you find this wisp of a girl?
Jolt
SHE WOULDN'T BE GOOD COMPANY FOR THE PATRONS ...
...BUT SHE'S SUP-POSED TO BE A PRETTY GOOD SONG-STRESS.
OH, A SONG-STRESS, YOU SAY?

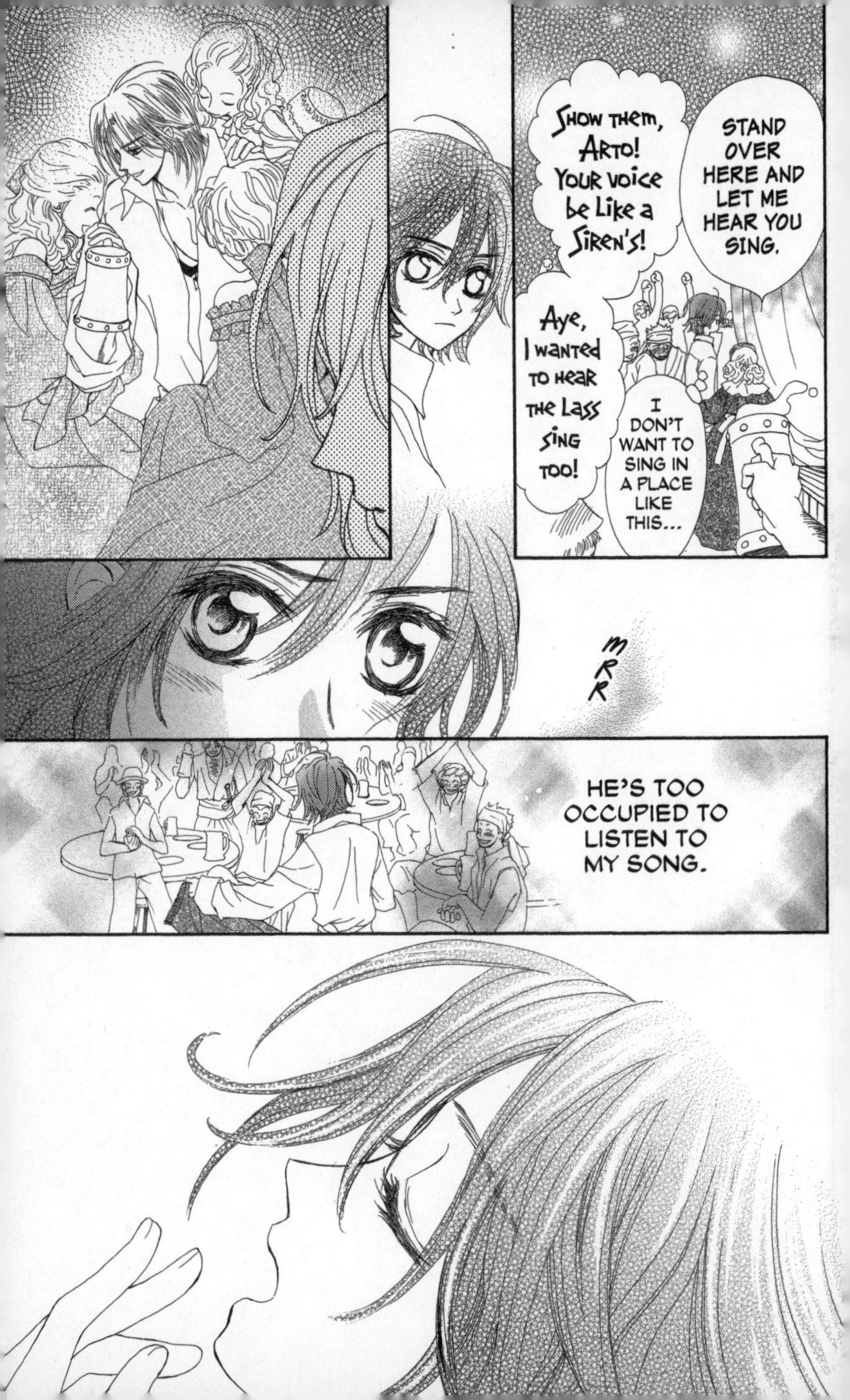
STAND OVER HERE AND LET ME HEAR YOU SING.
Show them, Arto! Your voice be like a Siren's!
I DON'T WANT TO SING IN A PLACE LIKE THIS...
Aye, I wanted to hear the lass sing too!
MRR
HE'S TOO OCCUPIED TO LISTEN TO MY SONG.

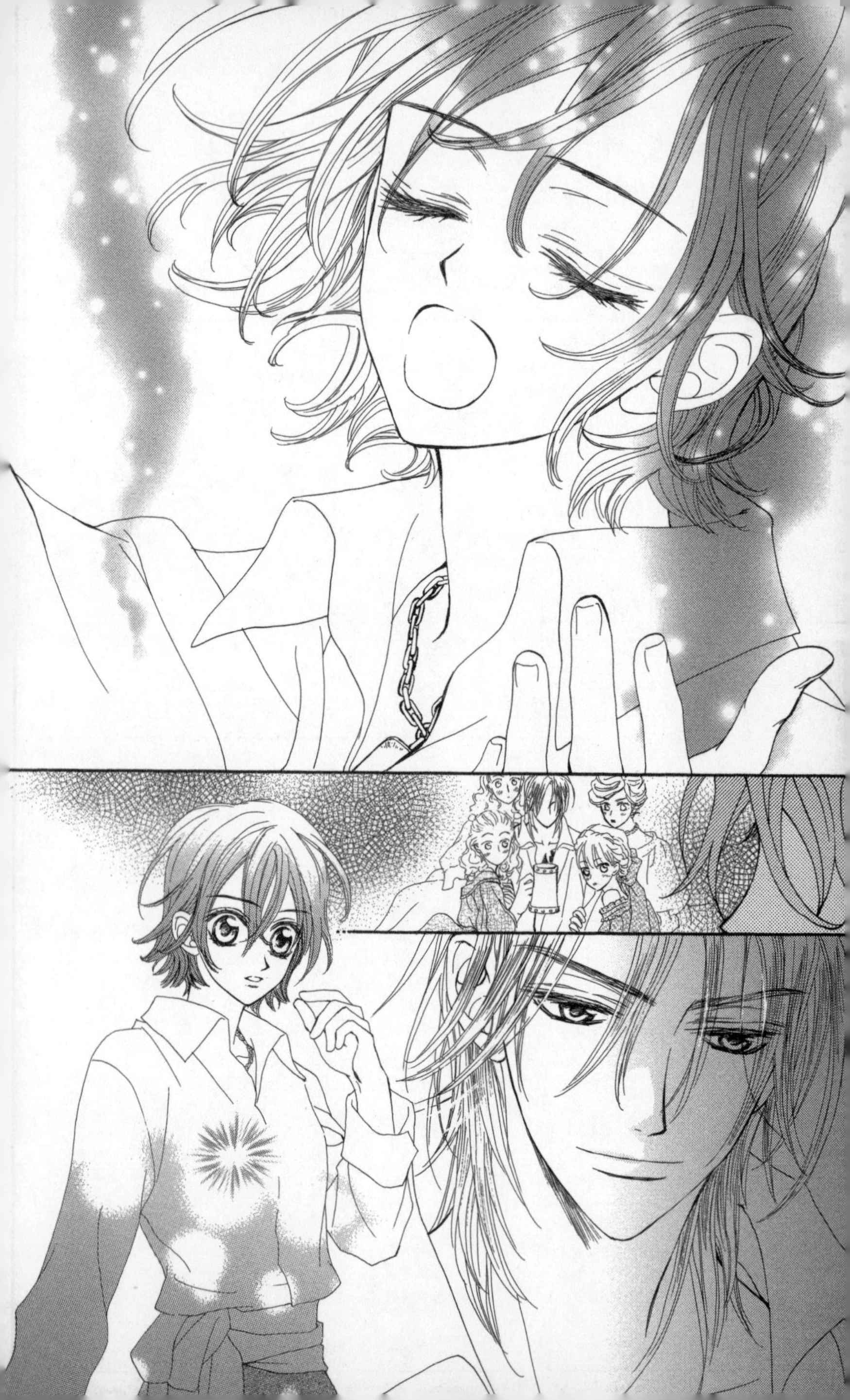

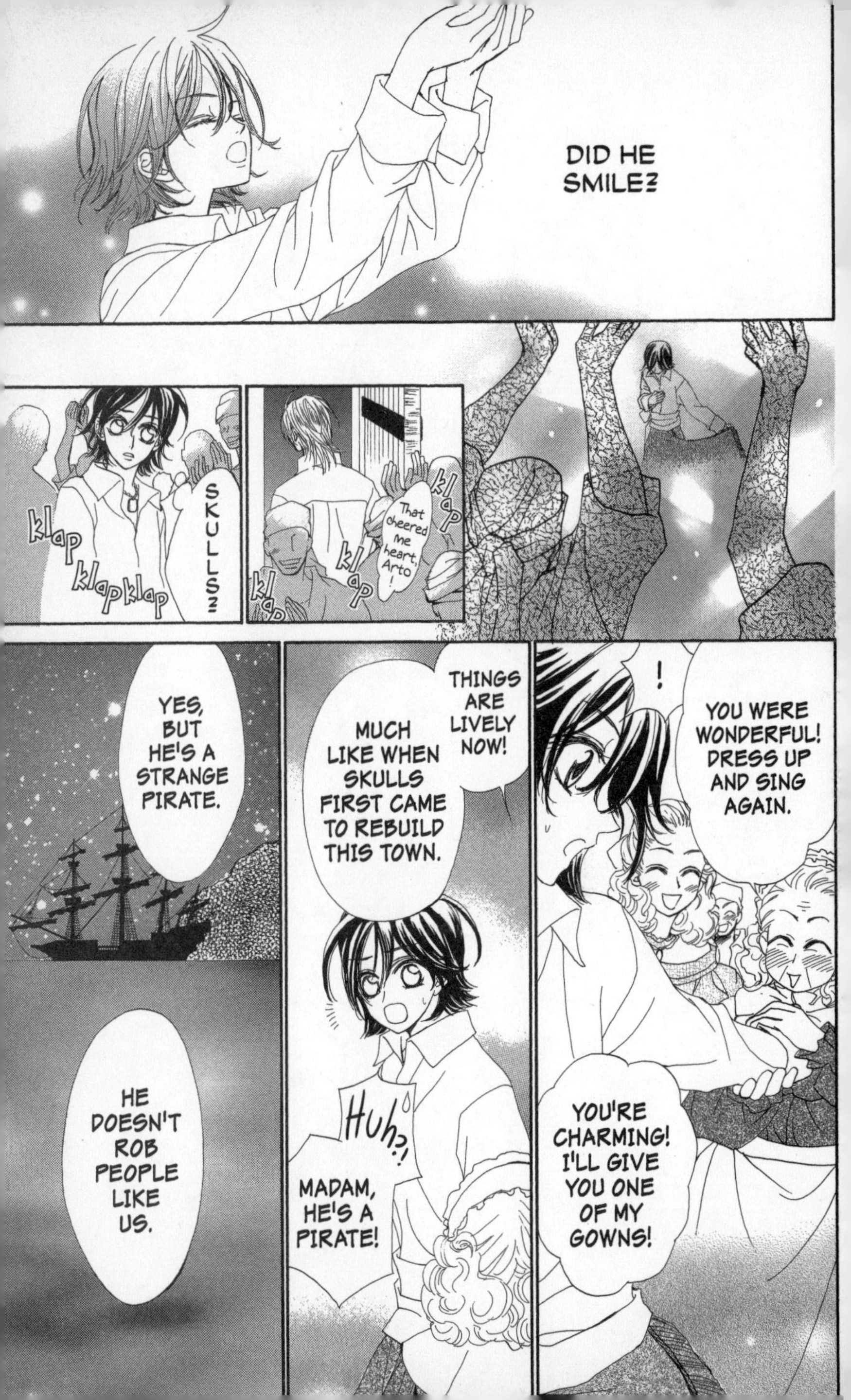
DID HE SMILE?
klap
That cheered me heart, Arto!
klap
SKULLS?
klap klapklap
!
YOU WERE WONDERFUL! DRESS UP AND SING AGAIN.
YOU'RE CHARMING! I'LL GIVE YOU ONE OF MY GOWNS!
THINGS ARE LIVELY NOW!
MUCH LIKE WHEN SKULLS FIRST CAME TO REBUILD THIS TOWN.
Huh?!
MADAM, HE'S A PIRATE!
YES, BUT HE'S A STRANGE PIRATE.
HE DOESN'T ROB PEOPLE LIKE US.

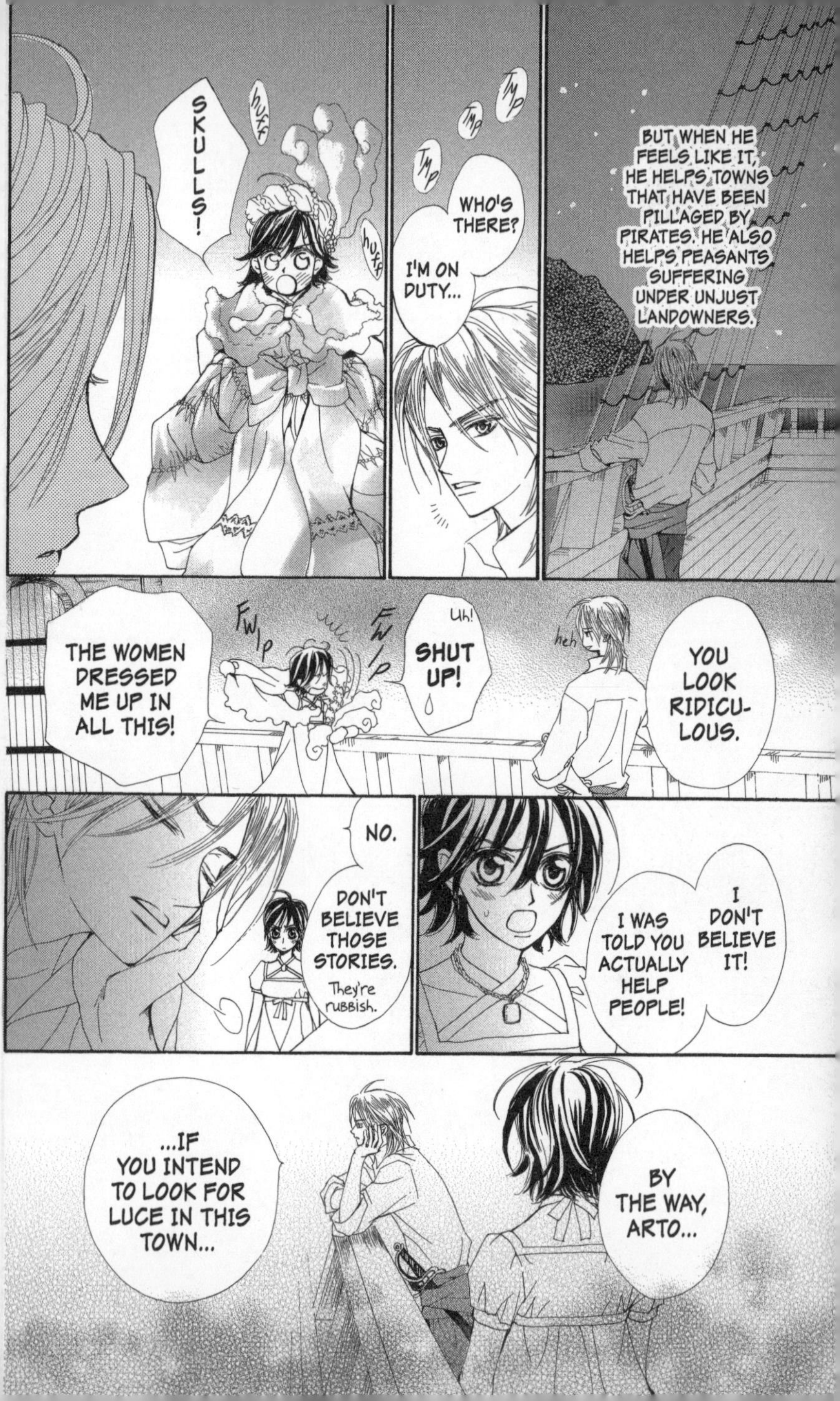
BUT WHEN HE FEELS LIKE IT, HE HELPS TOWNS THAT HAVE BEEN PILLAGED BY PIRATES. HE ALSO HELPS PEASANTS SUFFERING UNDER UNJUST LANDOWNERS.
TMP TMP TMP
WHO'S THERE?
I'M ON DUTY...
huff huff
SKULLS!
heh
YOU LOOK RIDICULOUS.
Uh!
SHUT UP!
FWIP FWIP
THE WOMEN DRESSED ME UP IN ALL THIS!
I DON'T BELIEVE IT!
I WAS TOLD YOU ACTUALLY HELP PEOPLE!
NO.
DON'T BELIEVE THOSE STORIES.
They're rubbish.
BY THE WAY, ARTO...
...IF YOU INTEND TO LOOK FOR LUCE IN THIS TOWN...

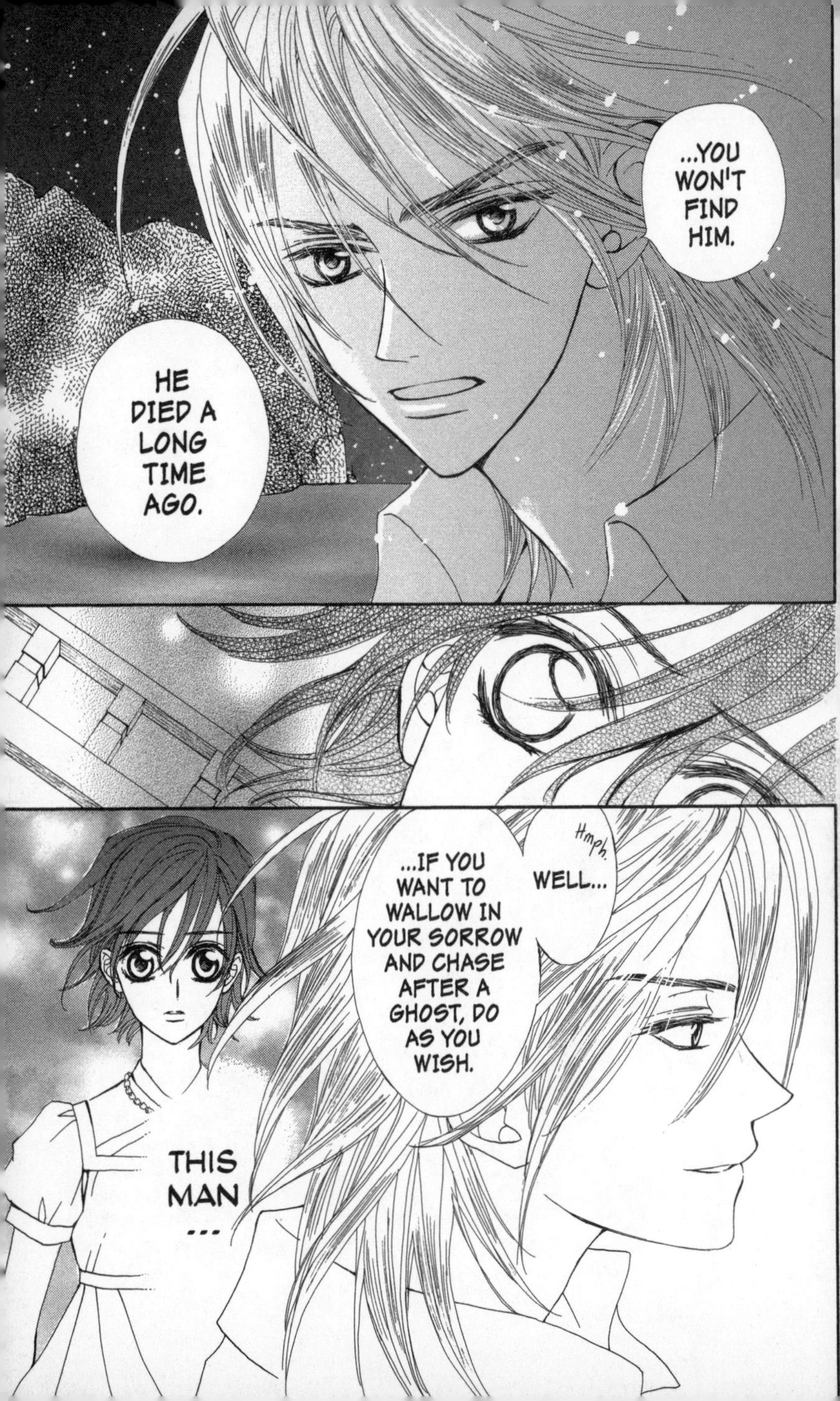
...YOU WON'T FIND HIM.
HE DIED A LONG TIME AGO.
Hmph.
WELL...
...IF YOU WANT TO WALLOW IN YOUR SORROW AND CHASE AFTER A GHOST, DO AS YOU WISH.
THIS MAN ...

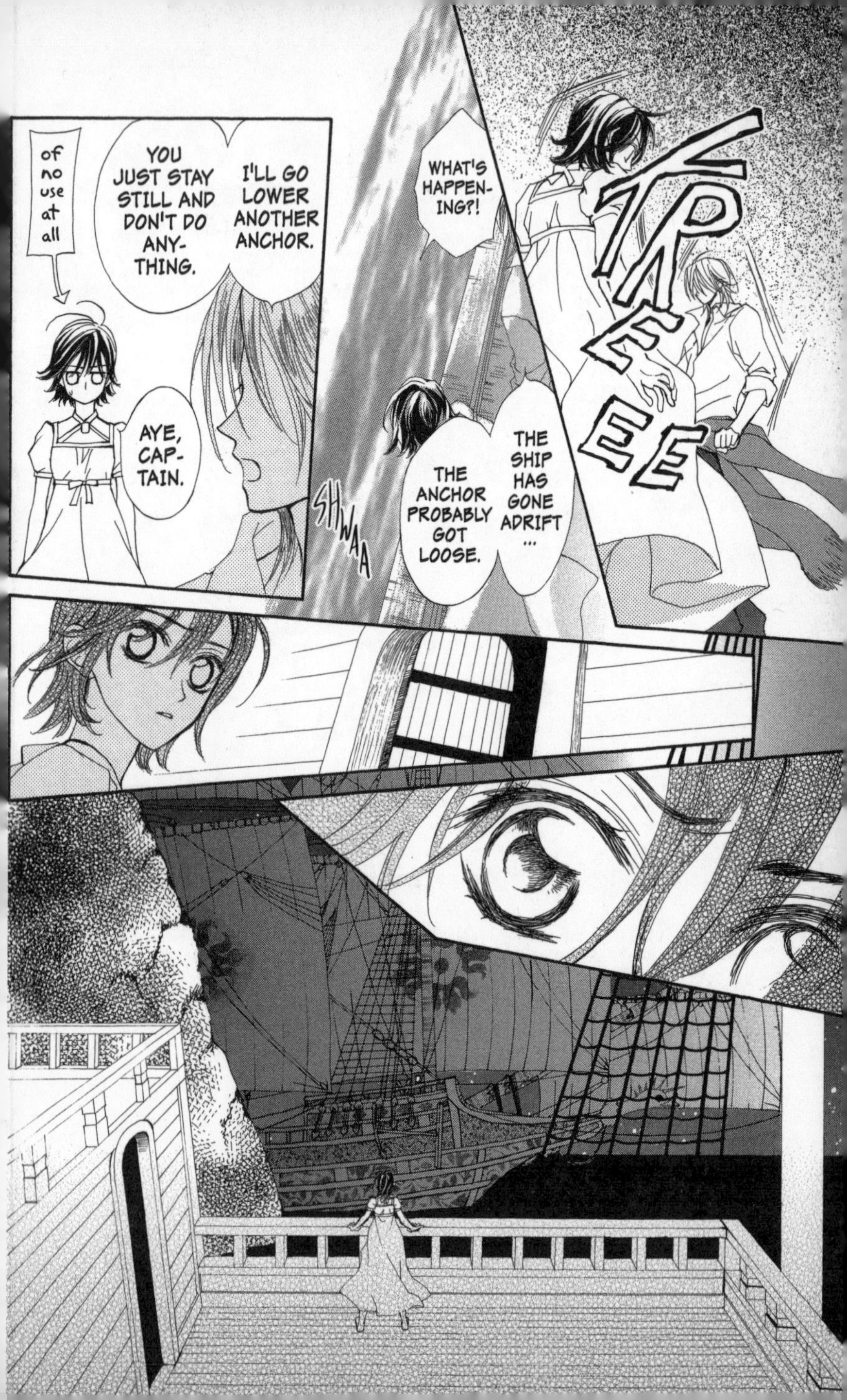
TRAEE
WHAT'S HAPPENING?!
THE SHIP HAS GONE ADRIFT...
THE ANCHOR PROBABLY GOT LOOSE.
SHWAA
I'LL GO LOWER ANOTHER ANCHOR.
YOU JUST STAY STILL AND DON'T DO ANYTHING.
of no use at all
AYE, CAPTAIN.

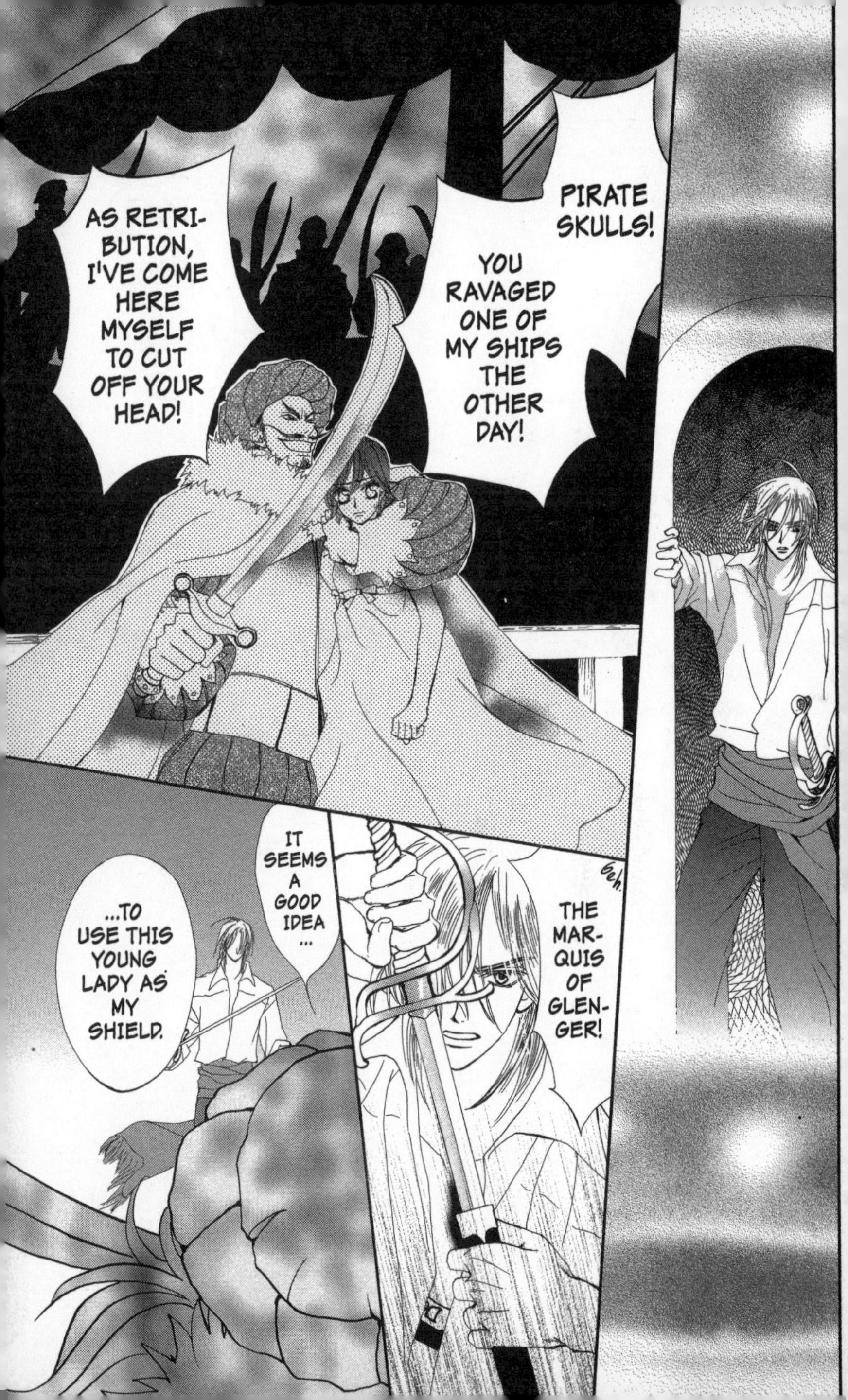
PIRATE SKULLS!
YOU RAVAGED ONE OF MY SHIPS THE OTHER DAY!
AS RETRIBUTION, I'VE COME HERE MYSELF TO CUT OFF YOUR HEAD!
THE MARQUIS OF GLENGER!
IT SEEMS A GOOD IDEA...
...TO USE THIS YOUNG LADY AS MY SHIELD.

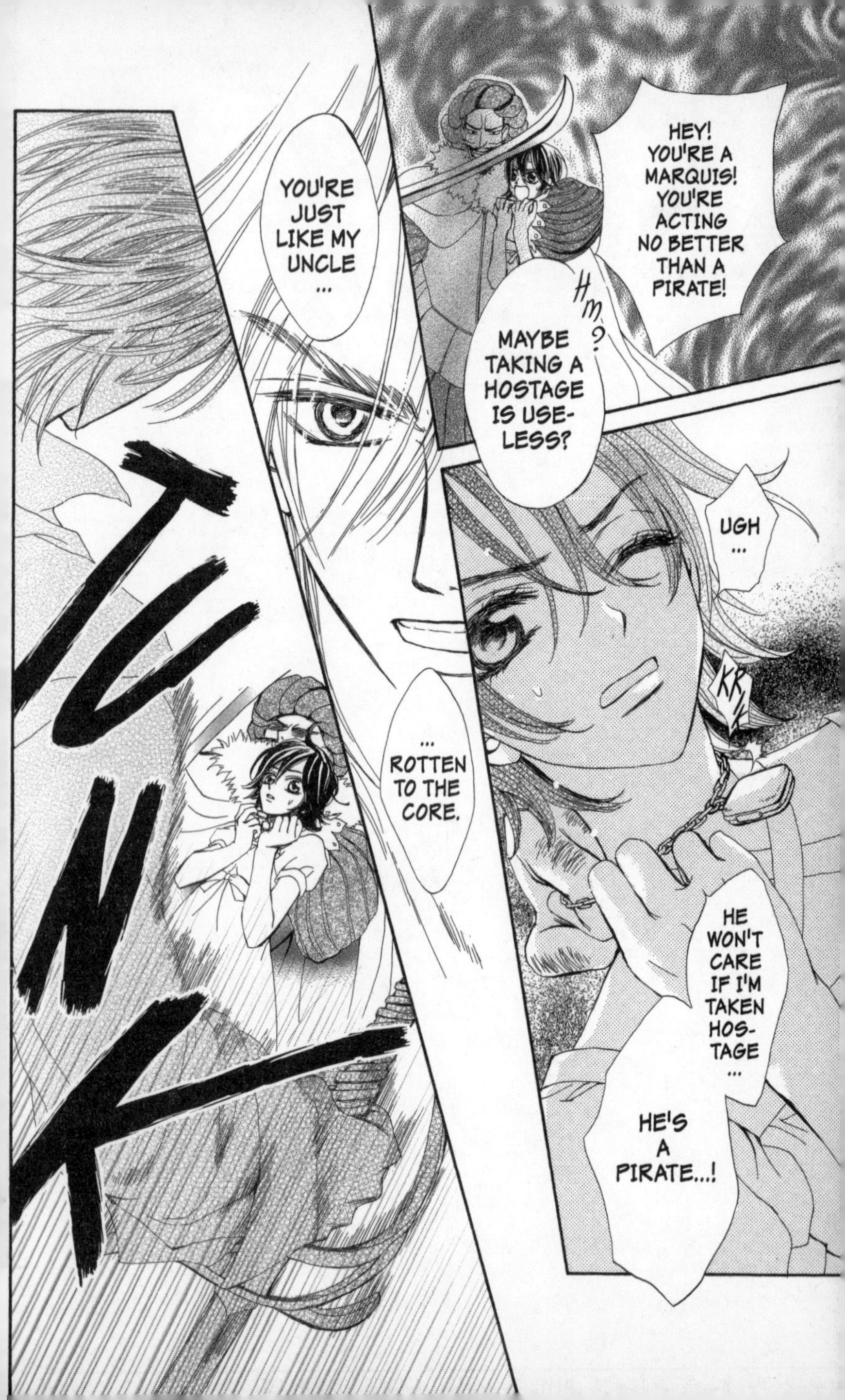
HEY! YOU'RE A MARQUIS! YOU'RE ACTING NO BETTER THAN A PIRATE!
HM?
MAYBE TAKING A HOSTAGE IS USE-LESS?
UGH ...
KRIK
HE WON'T CARE IF I'M TAKEN HOS-TAGE ...
HE'S A PIRATE...!
YOU'RE JUST LIKE MY UNCLE ...
... ROTTEN TO THE CORE.
TUNK

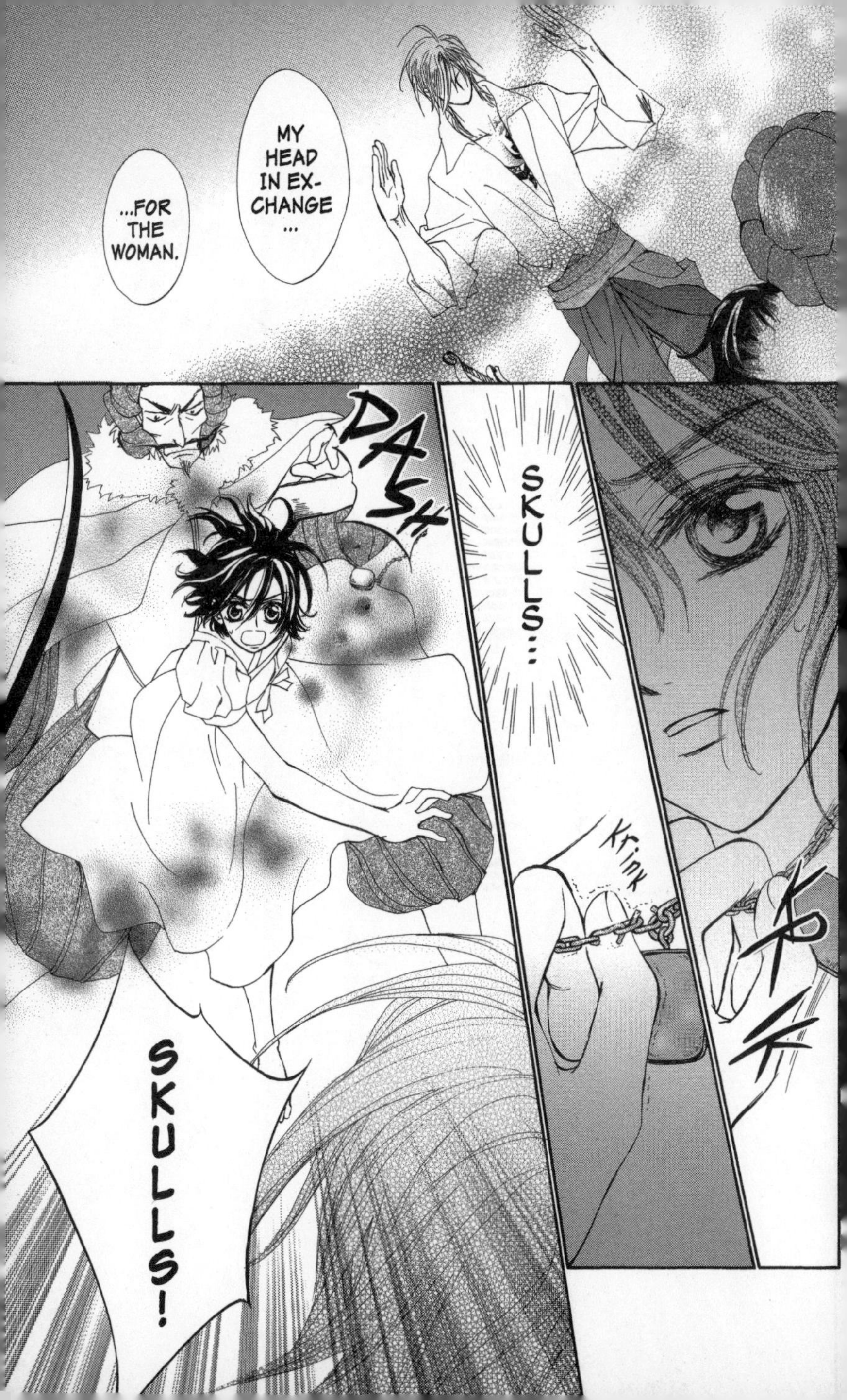

MY HEAD IN EX-CHANGE ...
...FOR THE WOMAN.
KRIK
SKULLS...
Krink
DASH
SKULLS!

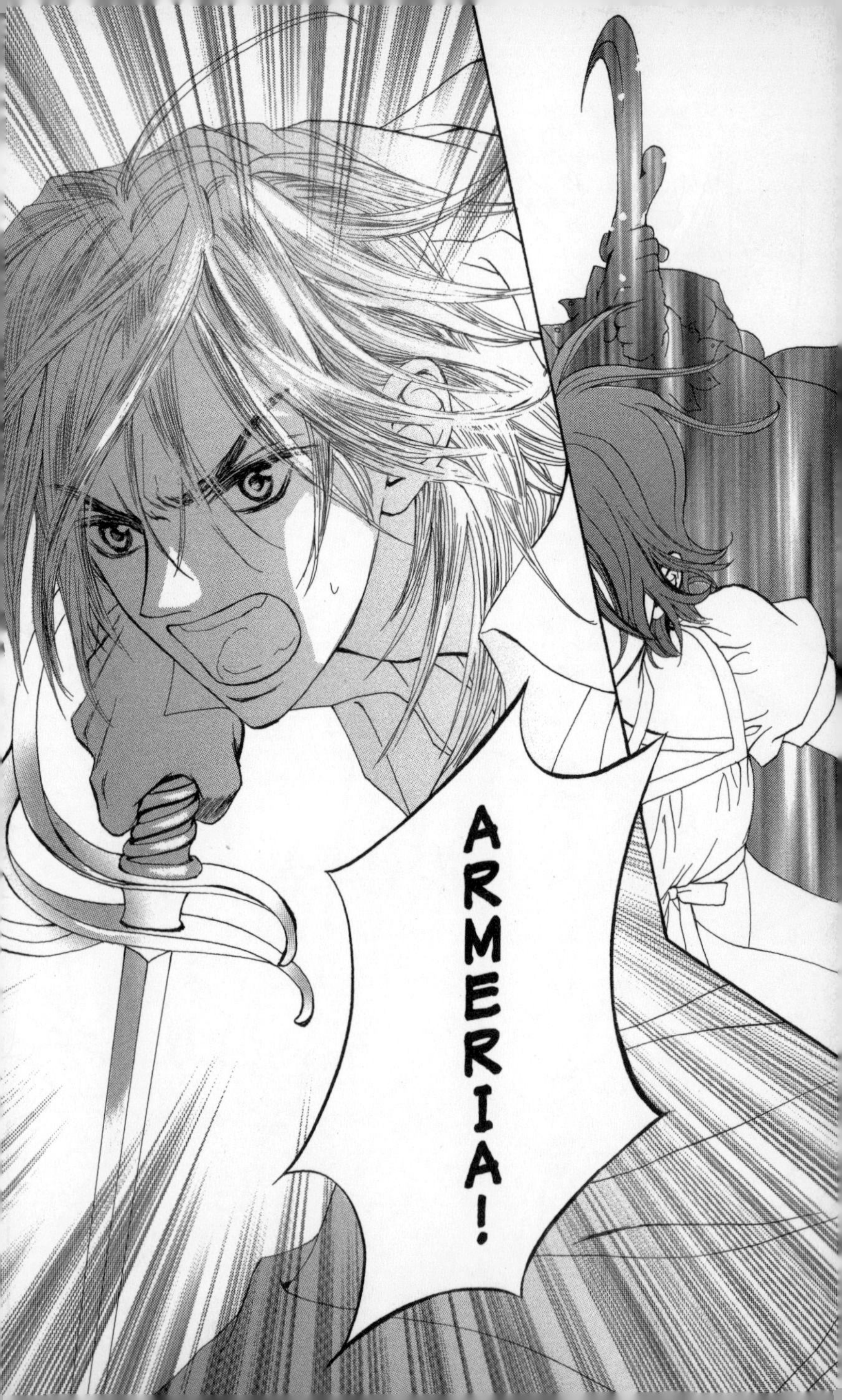
ARMERIA!

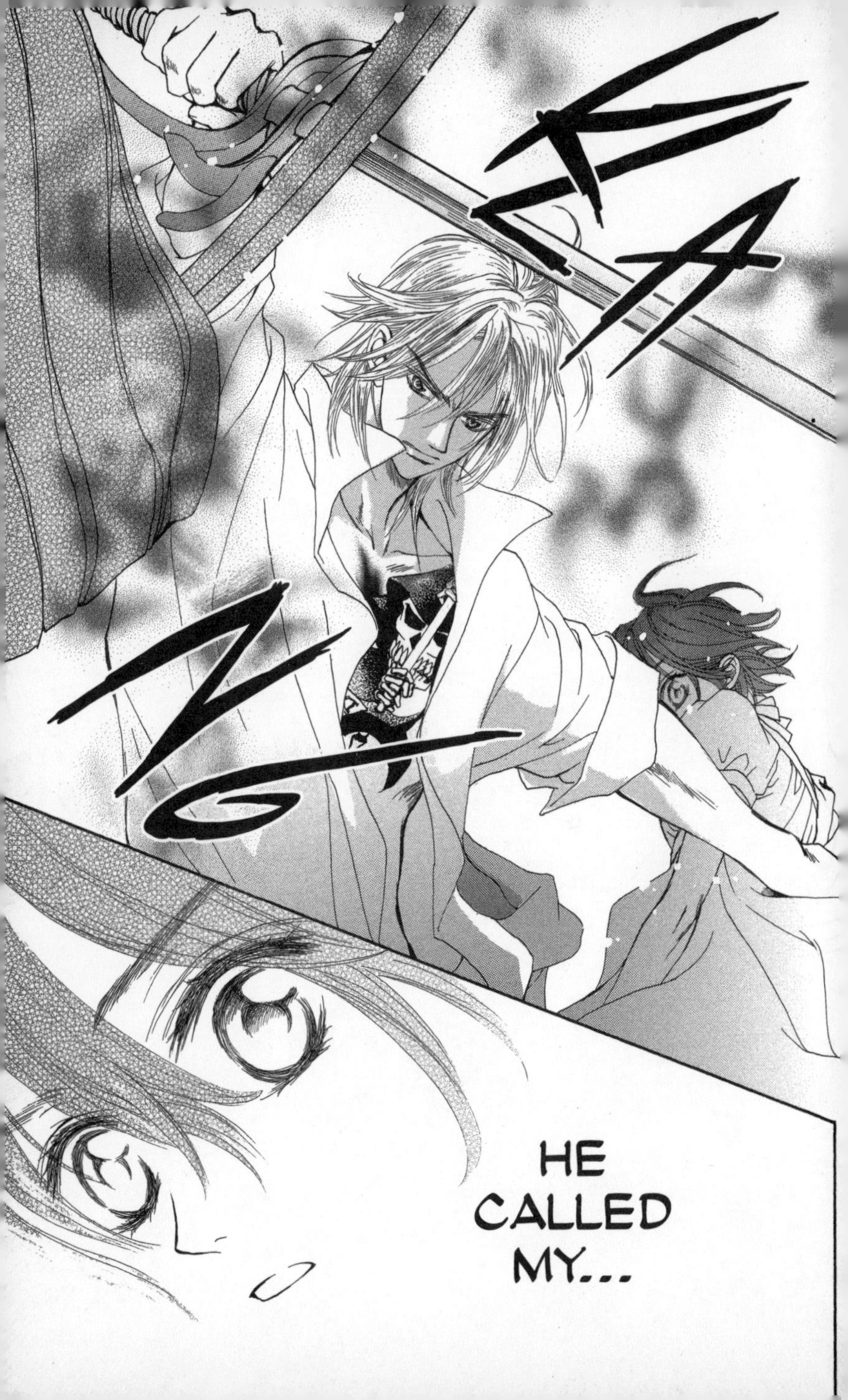
KANG
HE CALLED MY...

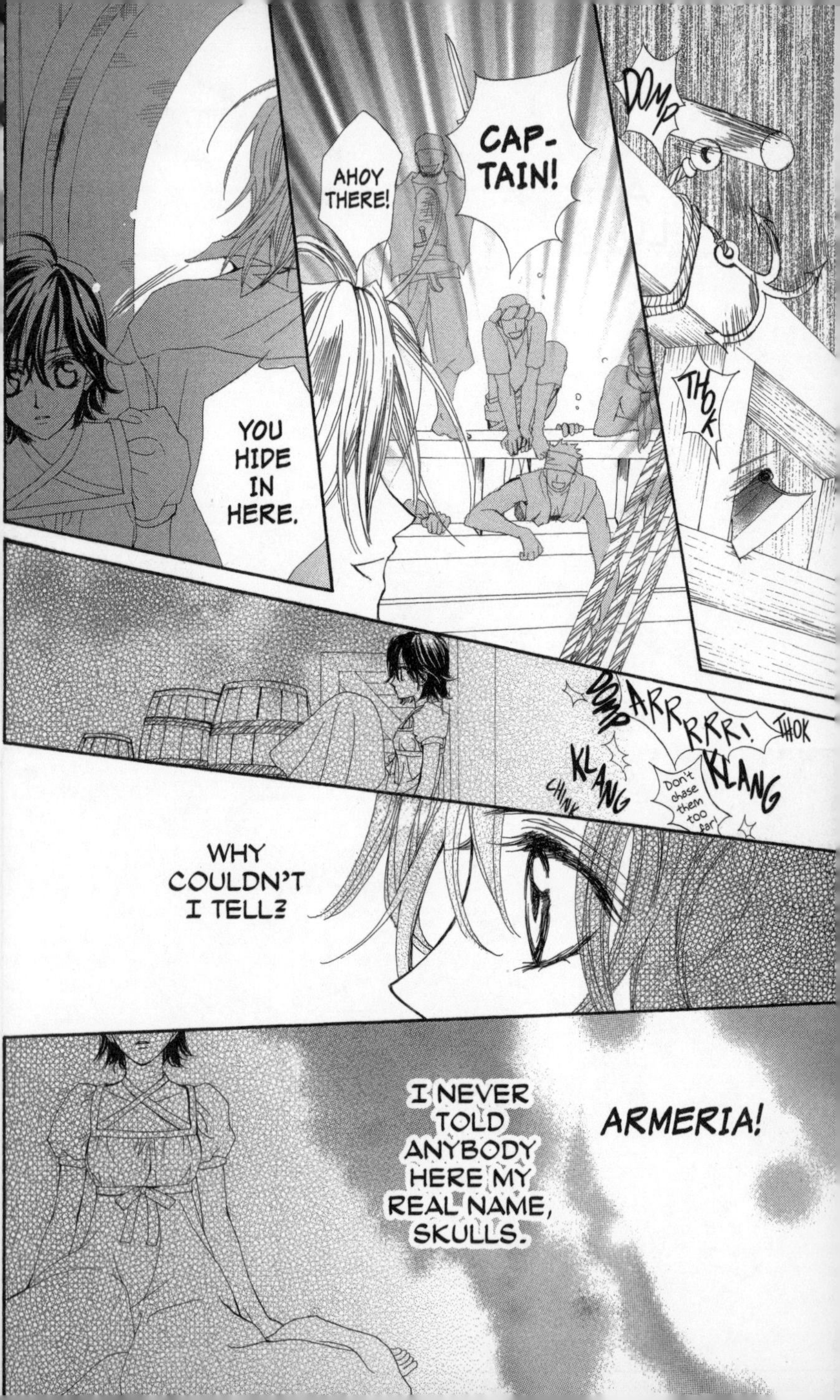
DOMP
THOK
CAP-TAIN!
AHOY THERE!
YOU HIDE IN HERE.
DOMP
ARRRRRR!
THOK
KLANG
Don't chase them too far!
KLANG
CHINK
WHY COULDN'T I TELL?
ARMERIA!
I NEVER TOLD ANYBODY HERE MY REAL NAME, SKULLS.

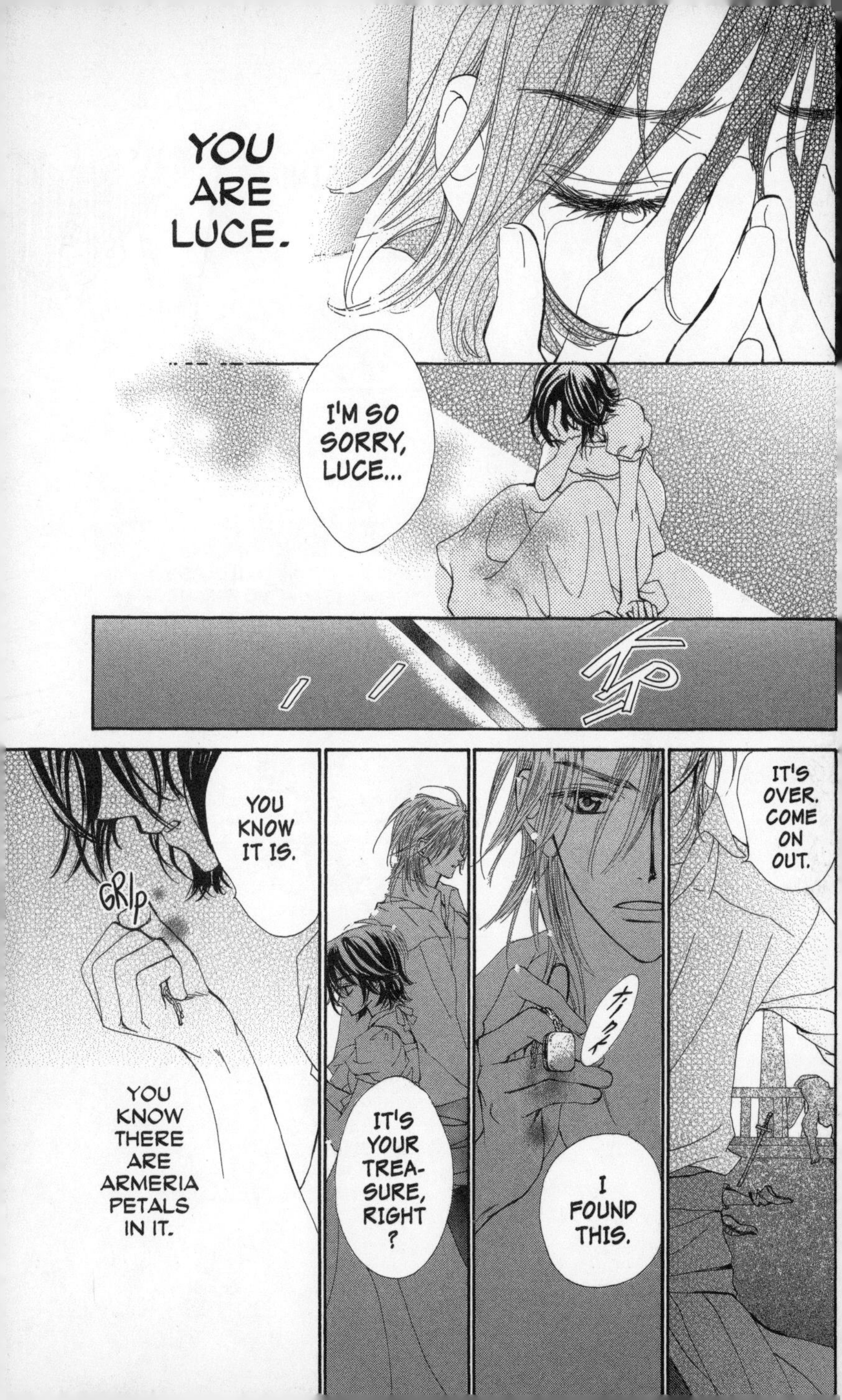
YOU ARE LUCE.
I'M SO SORRY, LUCE...
IT'S OVER. COME ON OUT.
I FOUND THIS.
IT'S YOUR TREA-SURE, RIGHT?
YOU KNOW IT IS.
GRIP
YOU KNOW THERE ARE ARMERIA PETALS IN IT.

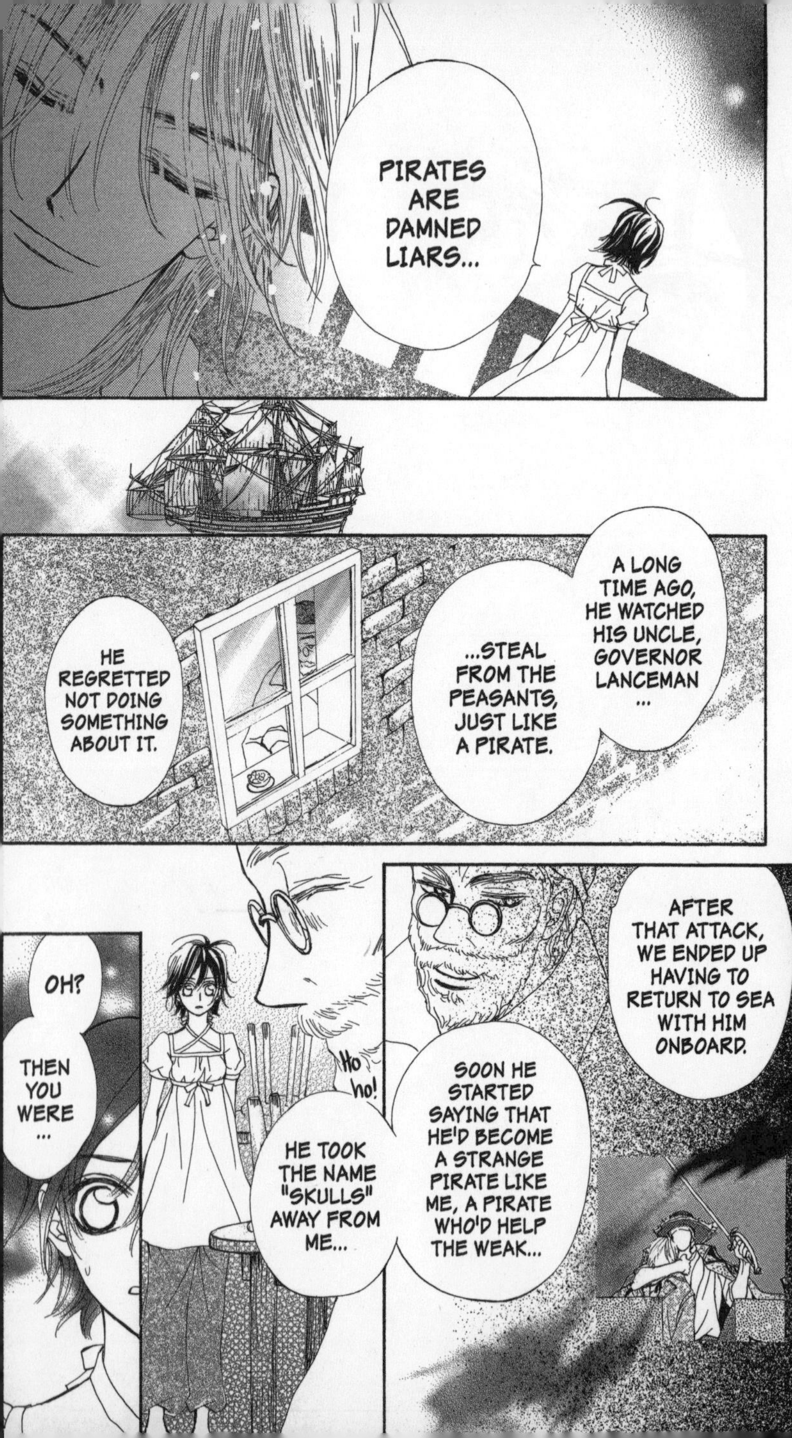
PIRATES ARE DAMNED LIARS...
A LONG TIME AGO, HE WATCHED HIS UNCLE, GOVERNOR LANCEMAN ...
...STEAL FROM THE PEASANTS, JUST LIKE A PIRATE.
HE REGRETTED NOT DOING SOMETHING ABOUT IT.
AFTER THAT ATTACK, WE ENDED UP HAVING TO RETURN TO SEA WITH HIM ONBOARD.
SOON HE STARTED SAYING THAT HE'D BECOME A STRANGE PIRATE LIKE ME, A PIRATE WHO'D HELP THE WEAK...
Ho ho!
HE TOOK THE NAME "SKULLS" AWAY FROM ME...
OH?
THEN YOU WERE ...

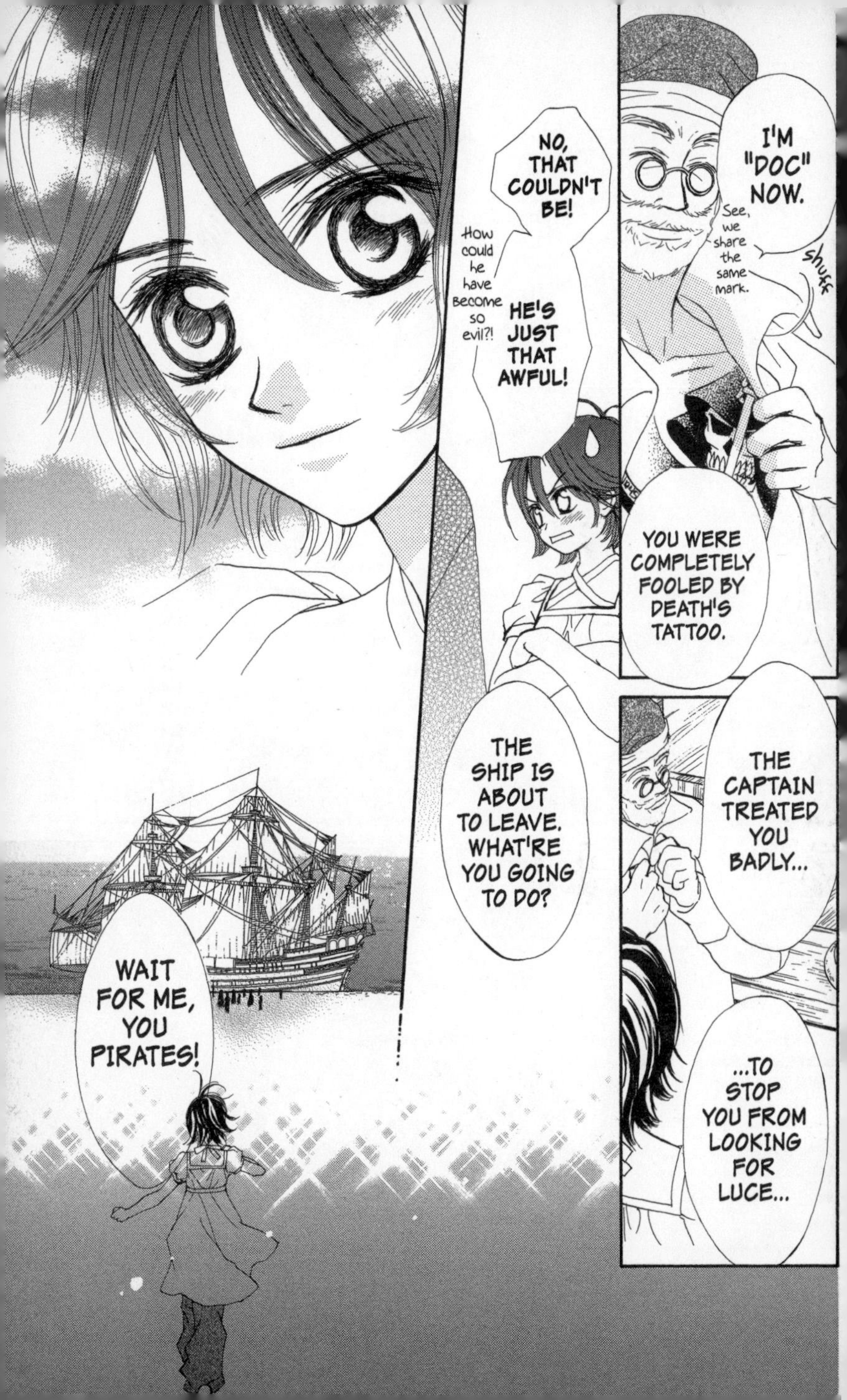
I'M "DOC" NOW.
See, we share the same mark.
shuff
YOU WERE COMPLETELY FOOLED BY DEATH'S TATTOO.
THE CAPTAIN TREATED YOU BADLY...
...TO STOP YOU FROM LOOKING FOR LUCE...
NO, THAT COULDN'T BE!
How could he have become so evil?!
HE'S JUST THAT AWFUL!
THE SHIP IS ABOUT TO LEAVE. WHAT'RE YOU GOING TO DO?
WAIT FOR ME, YOU PIRATES!

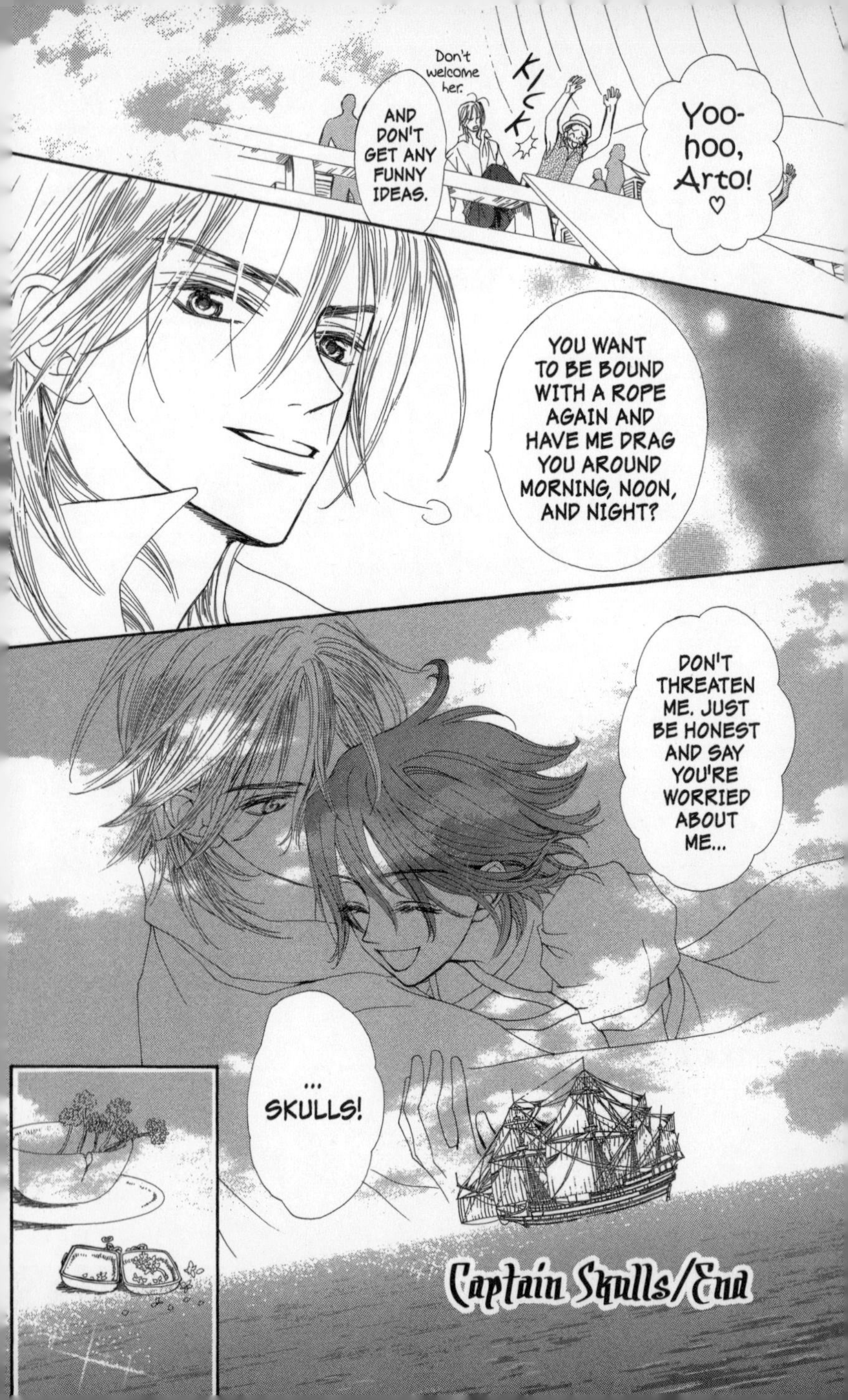
Yoo-hoo, Arto! ♡
KICK
Don't welcome her.
AND DON'T GET ANY FUNNY IDEAS.
YOU WANT TO BE BOUND WITH A ROPE AGAIN AND HAVE ME DRAG YOU AROUND MORNING, NOON, AND NIGHT?
DON'T THREATEN ME. JUST BE HONEST AND SAY YOU'RE WORRIED ABOUT ME...
... SKULLS!
Captain Skulls/End

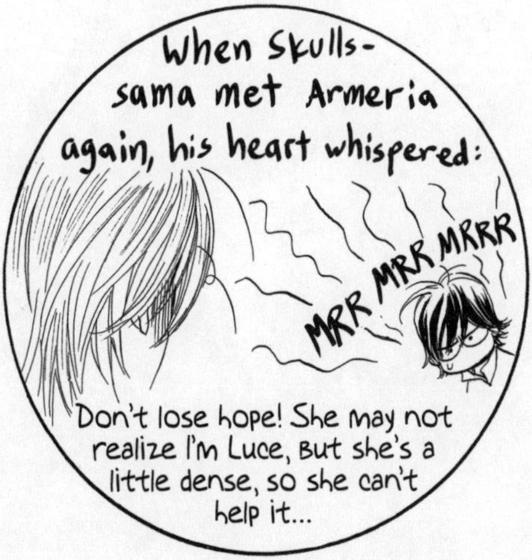
When Skulls-sama met Armeria again, his heart whispered:
MRR MRR MRRR
Don't lose hope! She may not realize I'm Luce, but she's a little dense, so she can't help it...

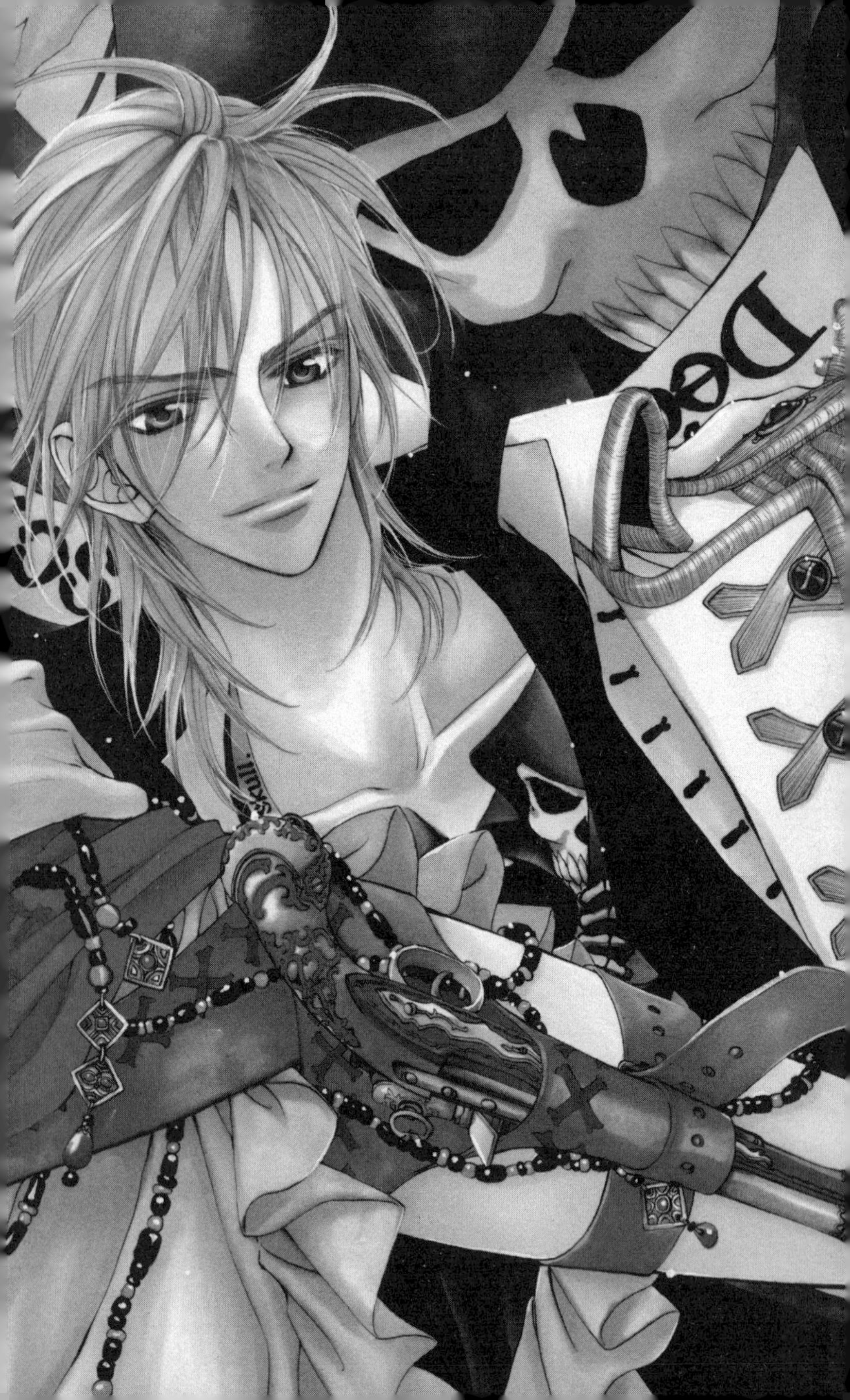

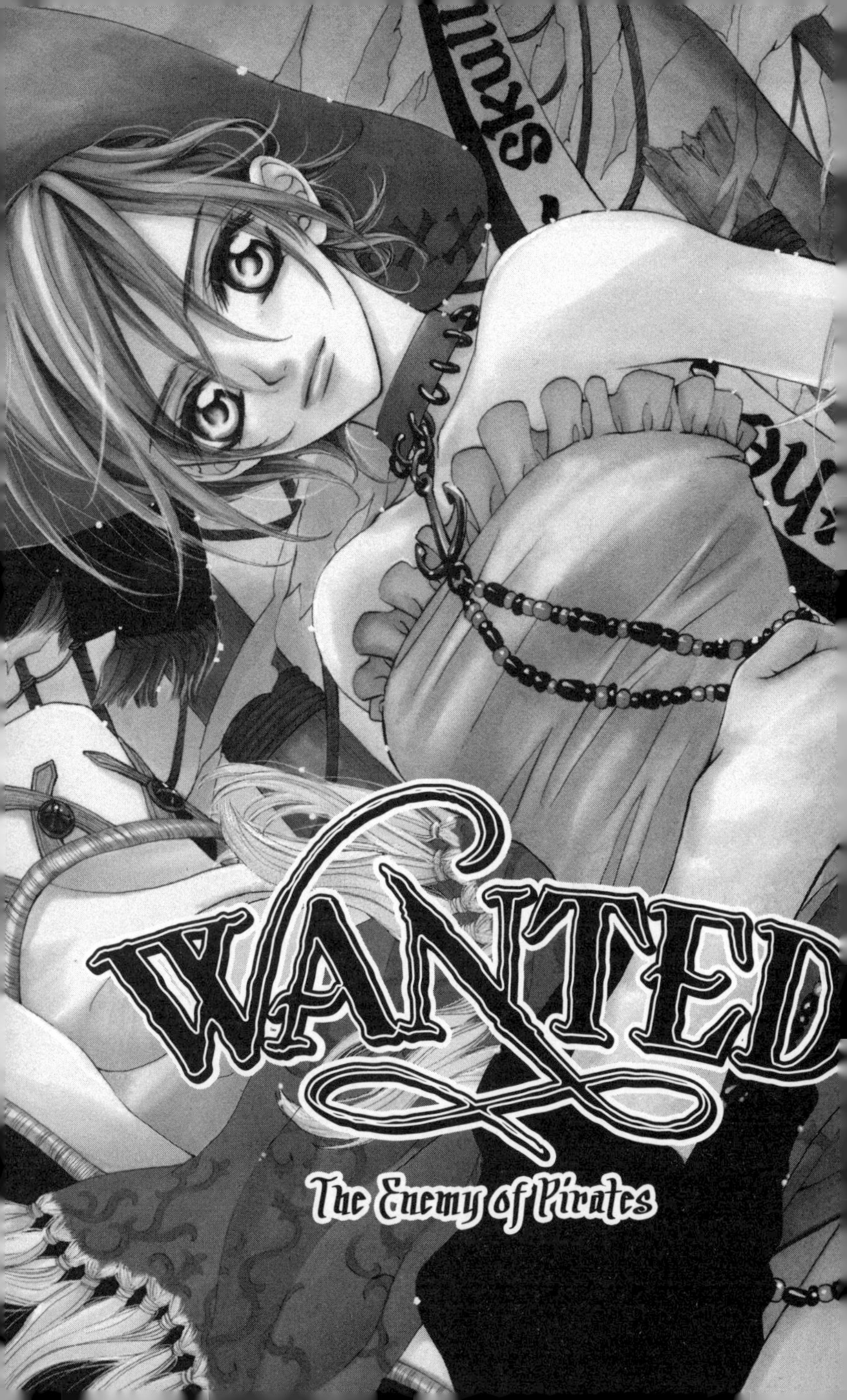
Skull
WANTED
The Enemy of Pirates

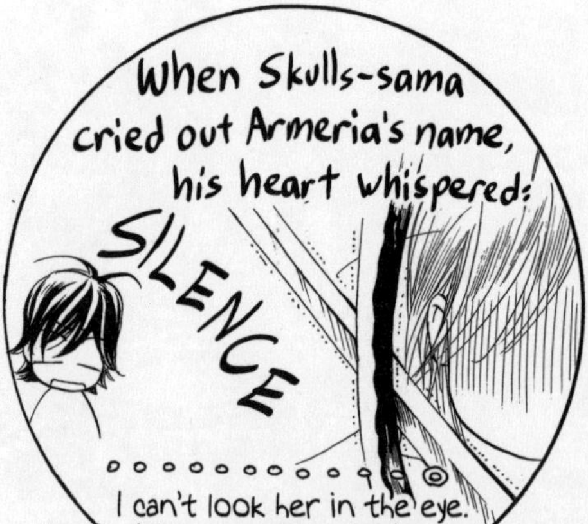
When Skulls-sama cried out Armeria's name, his heart whispered:
SILENCE
ooooooooooooo
I can't look her in the eye. I just revealed who I am. I'm an idiot!

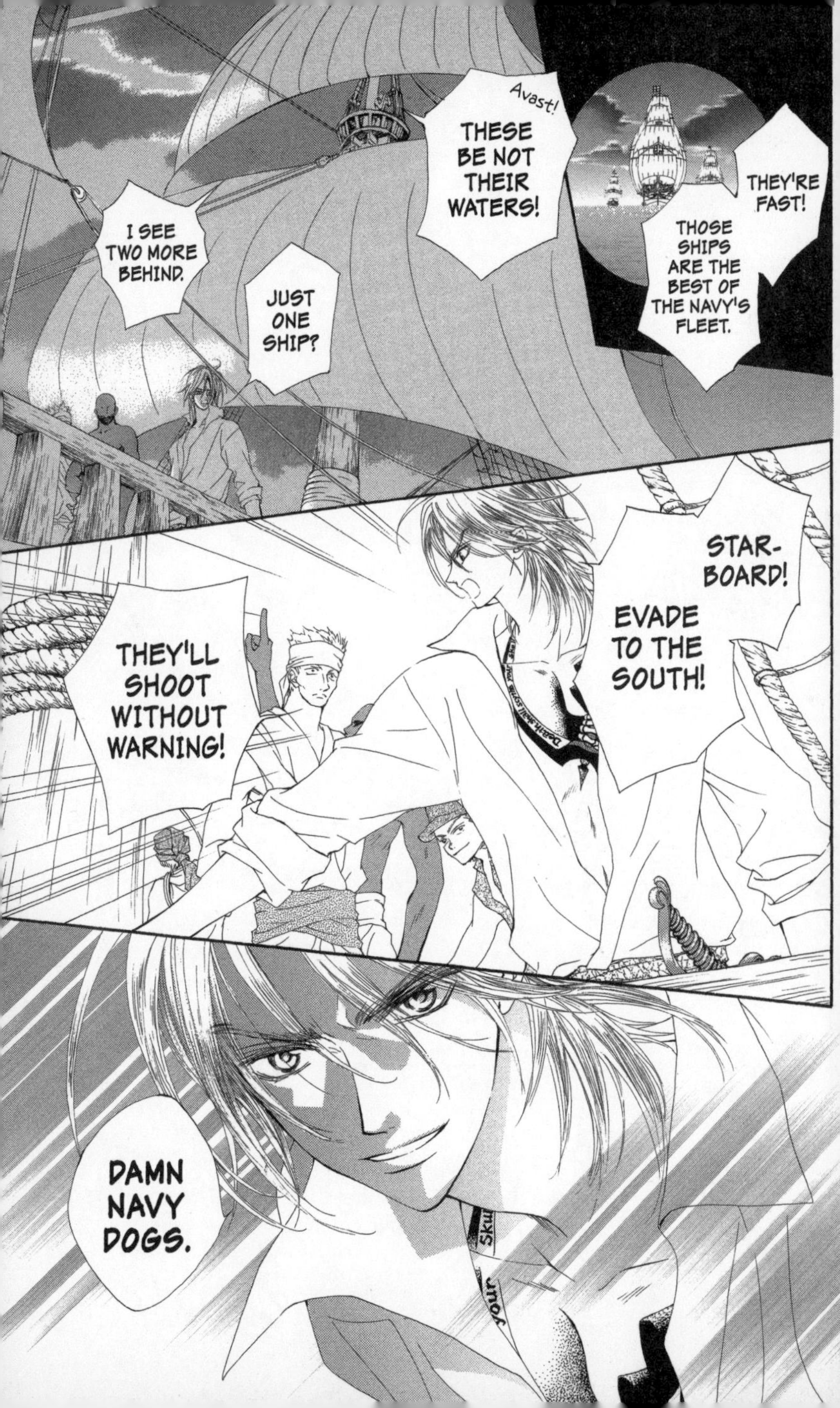
THEY'RE FAST!
THOSE SHIPS ARE THE BEST OF THE NAVY'S FLEET.
Avast!
THESE BE NOT THEIR WATERS!
JUST ONE SHIP?
I SEE TWO MORE BEHIND.
STAR-BOARD!
EVADE TO THE SOUTH!
THEY'LL SHOOT WITHOUT WARNING!
DAMN NAVY DOGS.

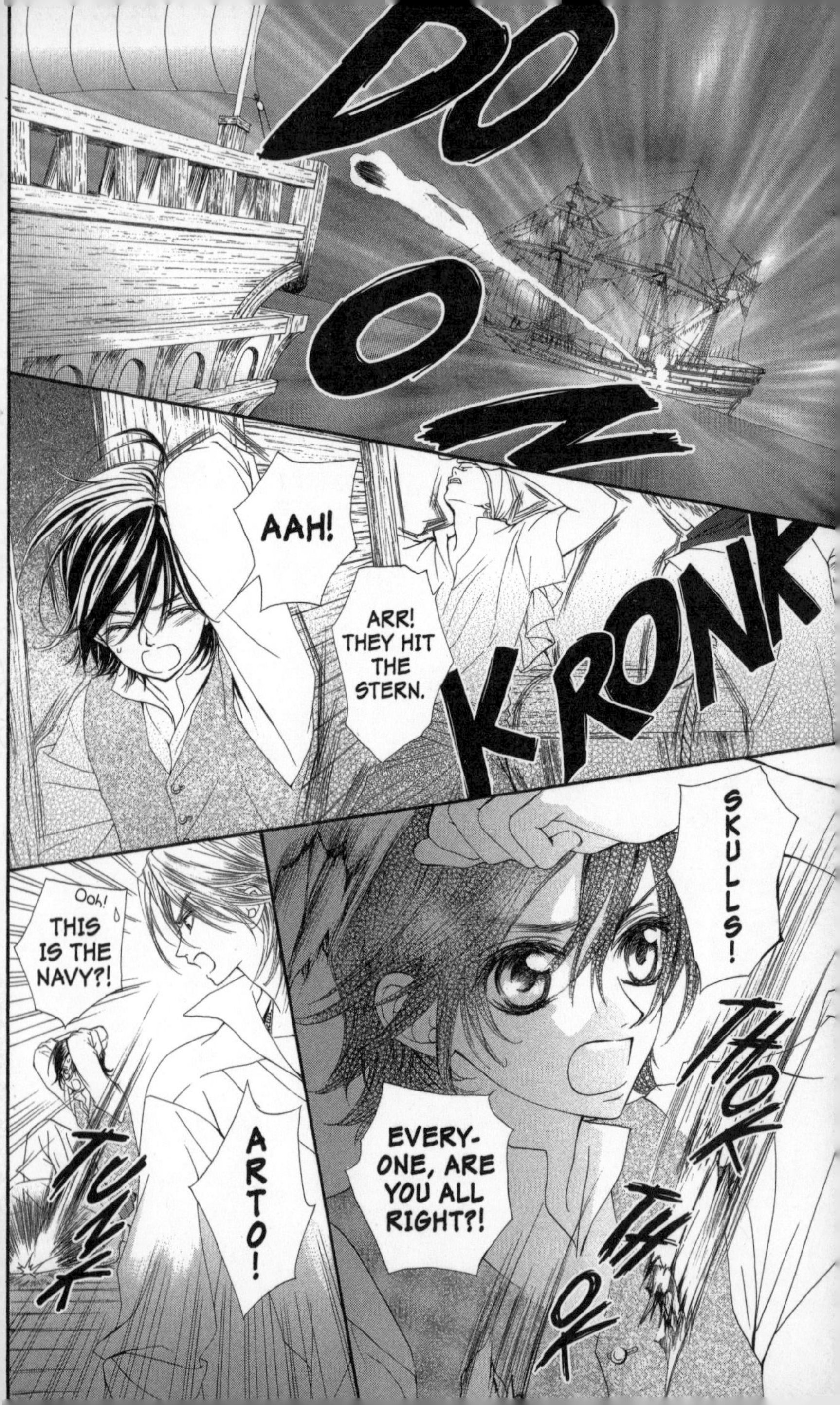
DOON
KRONK
AAH!
ARR! THEY HIT THE STERN.
SKULLS!
THOK THOK
EVERY-ONE, ARE YOU ALL RIGHT?!
Ooh! THIS IS THE NAVY?!
ARTO!
TUNK

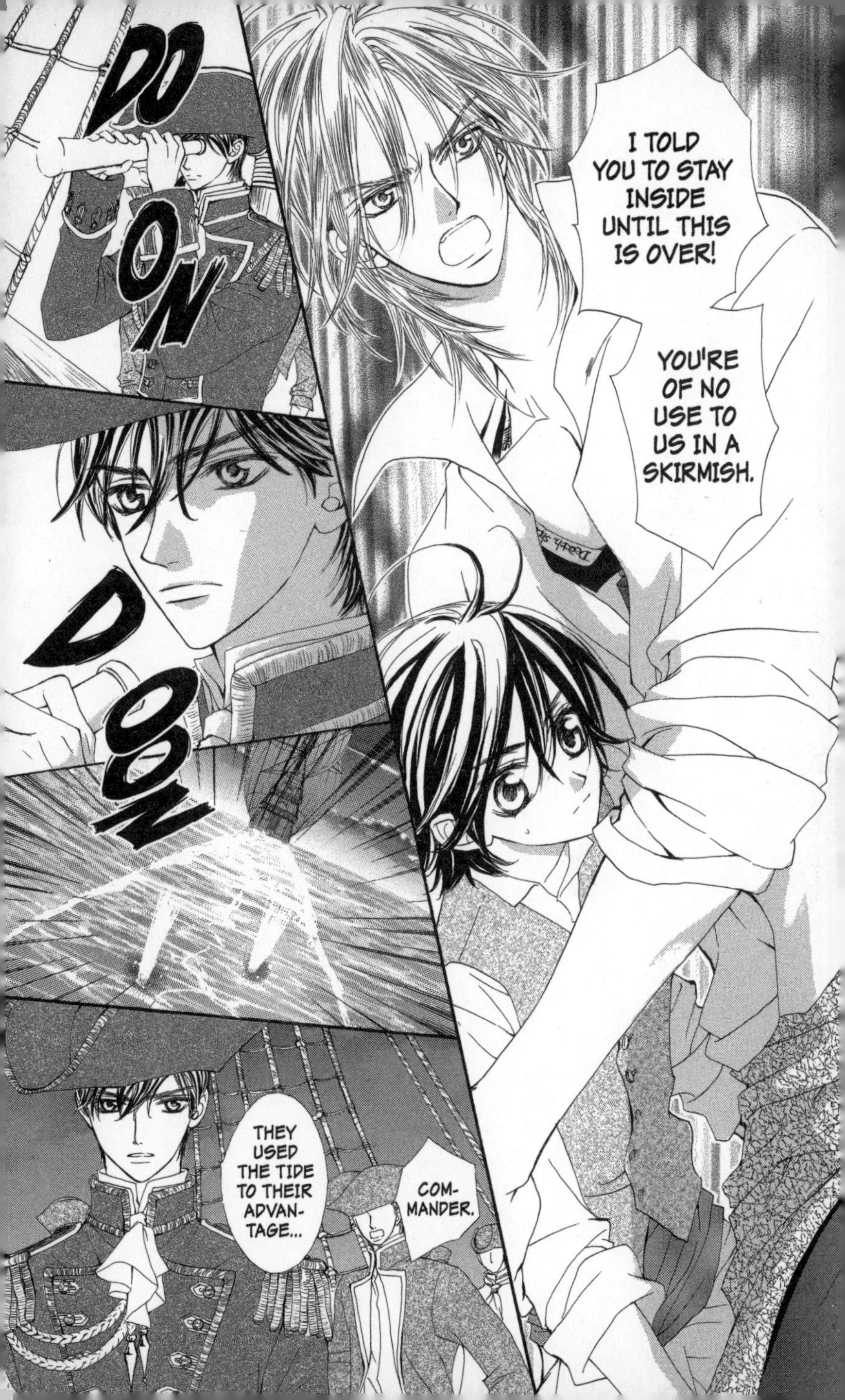
I TOLD YOU TO STAY INSIDE UNTIL THIS IS OVER!
YOU'RE OF NO USE TO US IN A SKIRMISH.
DO DON
DOOON
COM-MANDER.
THEY USED THE TIDE TO THEIR ADVAN-TAGE...

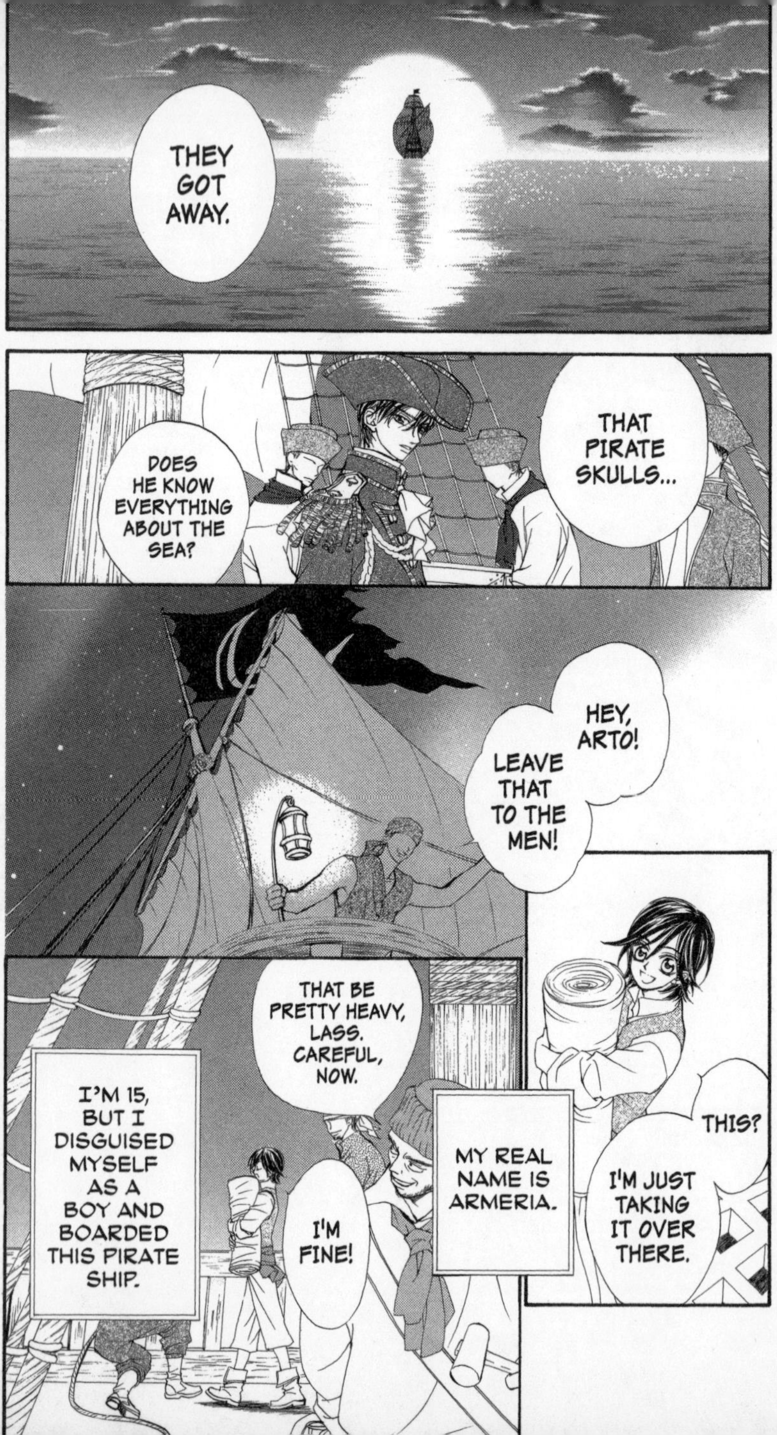
THEY GOT AWAY.
THAT PIRATE SKULLS...
DOES HE KNOW EVERYTHING ABOUT THE SEA?
HEY, ARTO!
LEAVE THAT TO THE MEN!
THIS?
I'M JUST TAKING IT OVER THERE.
MY REAL NAME IS ARMERIA.
THAT BE PRETTY HEAVY, LASS. CAREFUL, NOW.
I'M FINE!
I'M 15, BUT I DISGUISED MYSELF AS A BOY AND BOARDED THIS PIRATE SHIP.

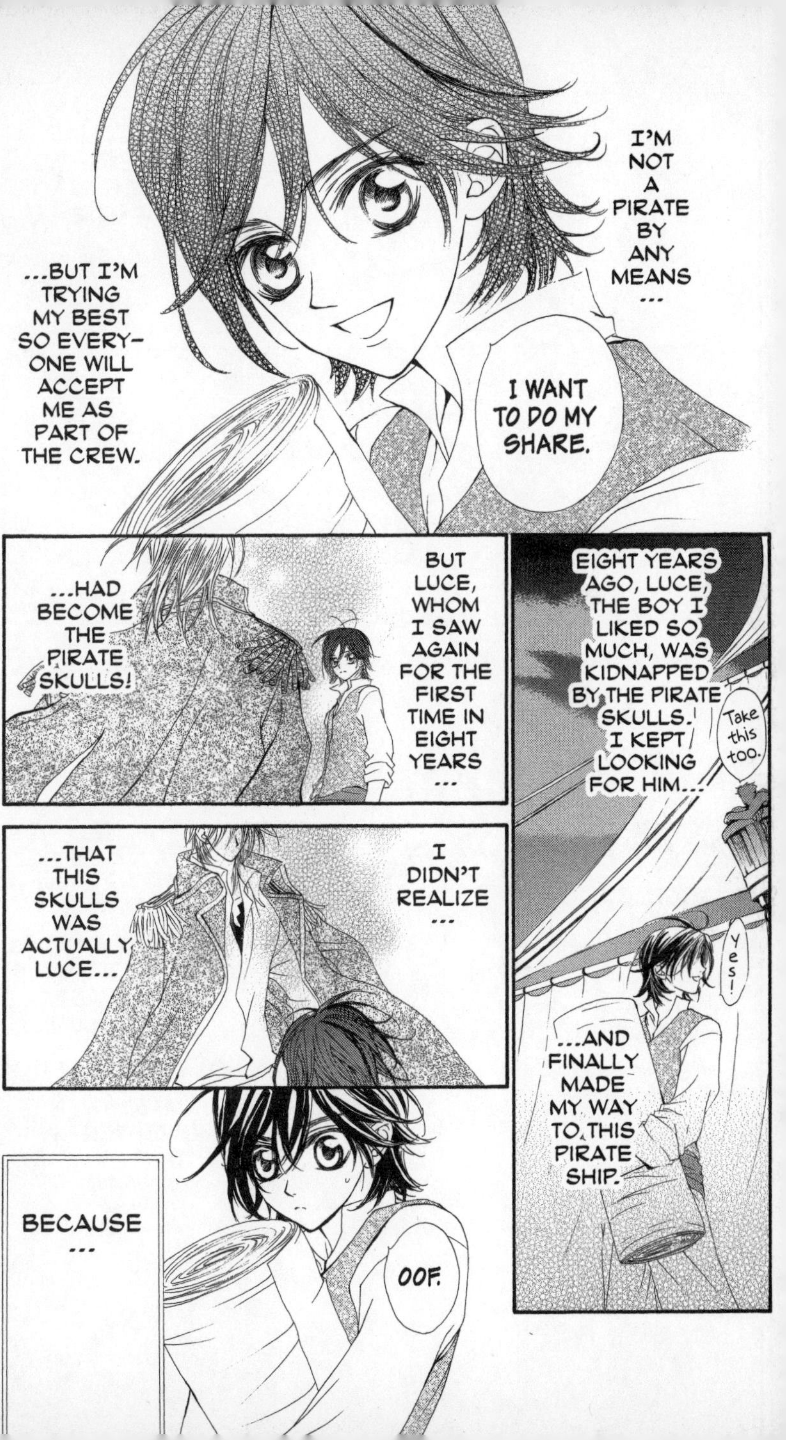
I'M NOT A PIRATE BY ANY MEANS...
I WANT TO DO MY SHARE.
...BUT I'M TRYING MY BEST SO EVERY-ONE WILL ACCEPT ME AS PART OF THE CREW.
EIGHT YEARS AGO, LUCE, THE BOY I LIKED SO MUCH, WAS KIDNAPPED BY THE PIRATE SKULLS. I KEPT LOOKING FOR HIM...
Take this too.
Yes!
...AND FINALLY MADE MY WAY TO THIS PIRATE SHIP.
BUT LUCE, WHOM I SAW AGAIN FOR THE FIRST TIME IN EIGHT YEARS...
...HAD BECOME THE PIRATE SKULLS!
I DIDN'T REALIZE...
...THAT THIS SKULLS WAS ACTUALLY LUCE...
OOF.
BECAUSE...

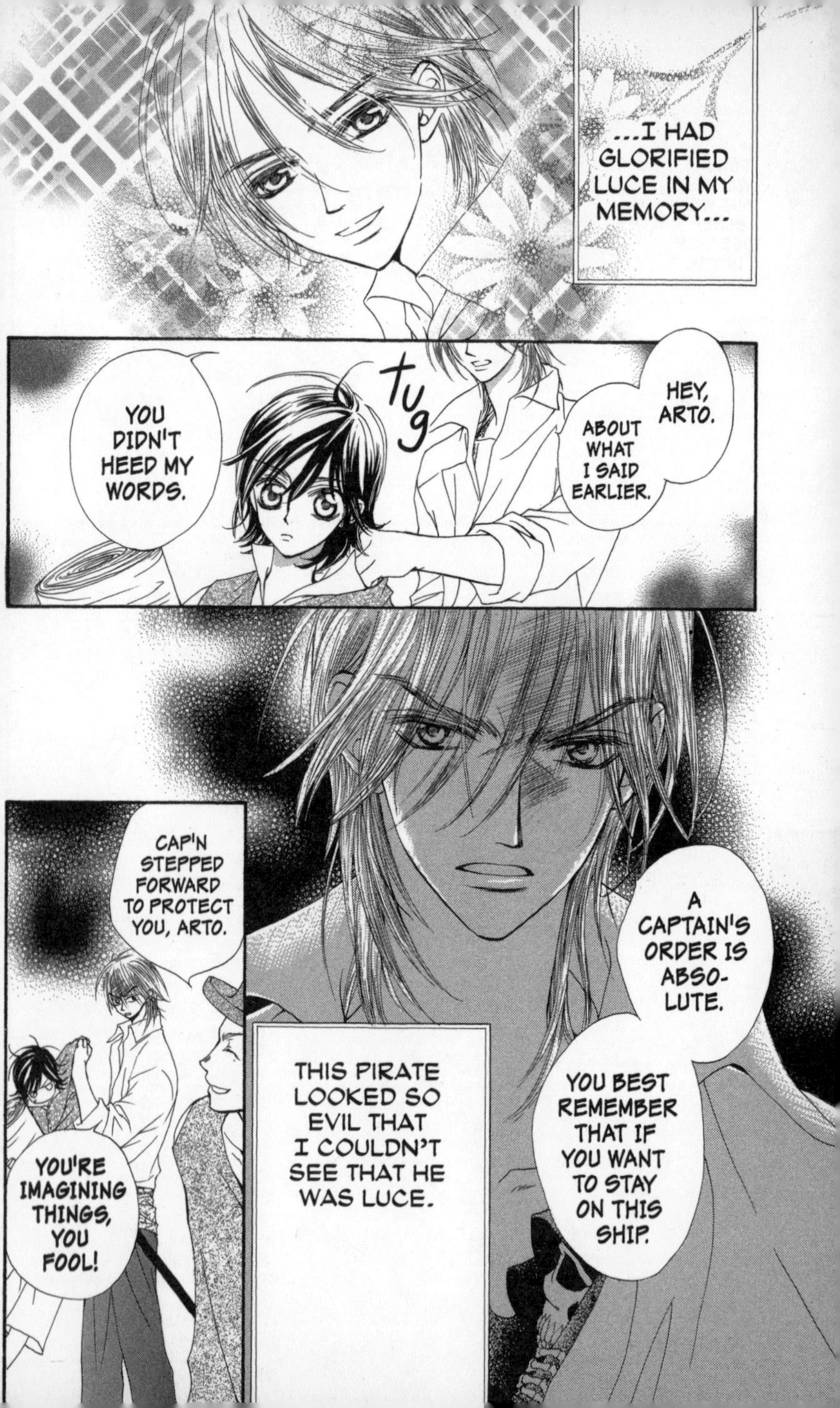
...I HAD GLORIFIED LUCE IN MY MEMORY...
HEY, ARTO.
ABOUT WHAT I SAID EARLIER.
TUG
YOU DIDN'T HEED MY WORDS.
A CAPTAIN'S ORDER IS ABSO-LUTE.
YOU BEST REMEMBER THAT IF YOU WANT TO STAY ON THIS SHIP.
THIS PIRATE LOOKED SO EVIL THAT I COULDN'T SEE THAT HE WAS LUCE.
CAP'N STEPPED FORWARD TO PROTECT YOU, ARTO.
YOU'RE IMAGINING THINGS, YOU FOOL!

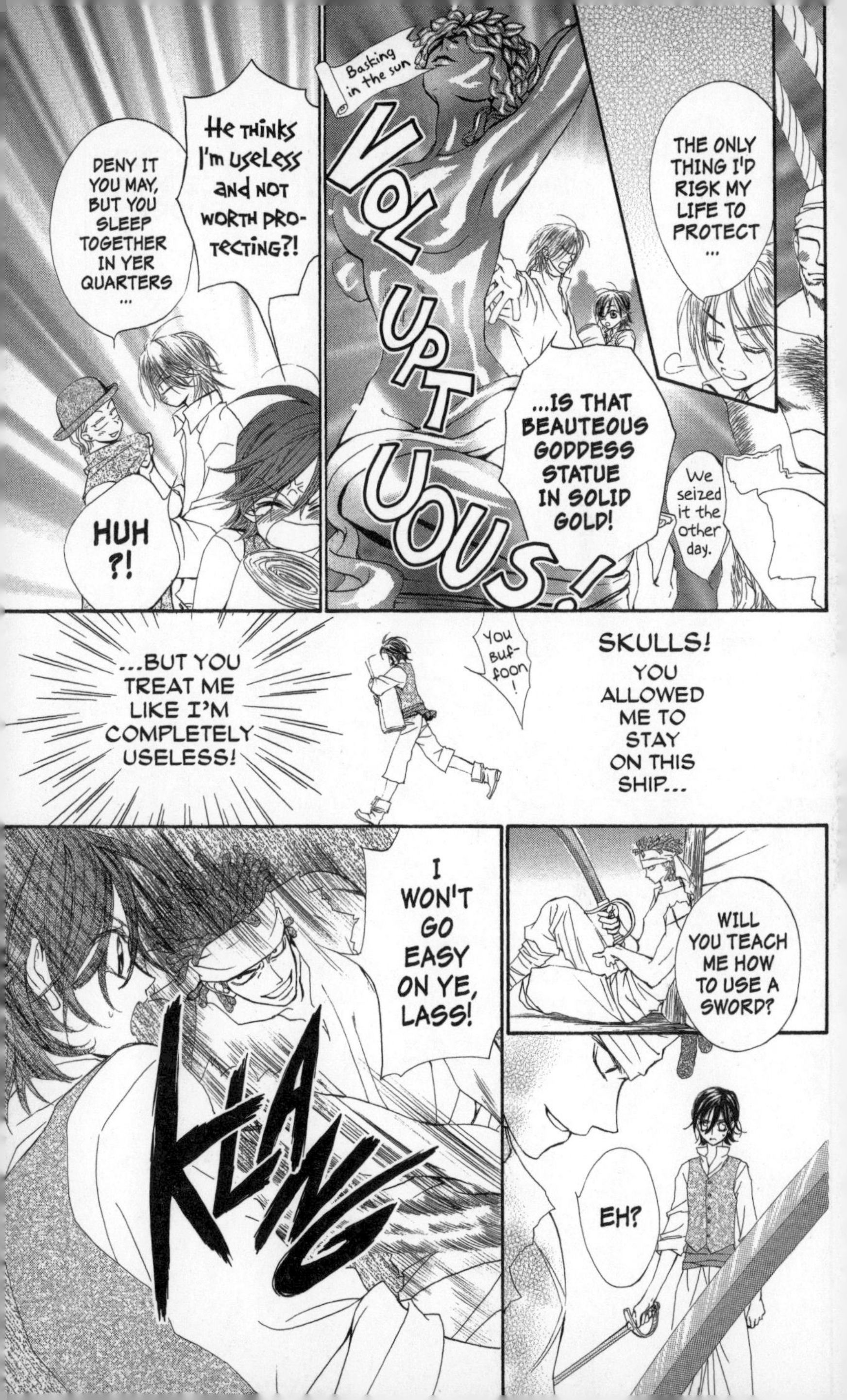
THE ONLY THING I'D RISK MY LIFE TO PROTECT ...
Basking in the sun
VOLUPTUOUS...!
...IS THAT BEAUTEOUS GODDESS STATUE IN SOLID GOLD!
We seized it the other day.
He thinks I'm useless and not worth protecting?!
DENY IT YOU MAY, BUT YOU SLEEP TOGETHER IN YER QUARTERS ...
HUH ?!
SKULLS!
YOU ALLOWED ME TO STAY ON THIS SHIP...
You buffoon!
...BUT YOU TREAT ME LIKE I'M COMPLETELY USELESS!
WILL YOU TEACH ME HOW TO USE A SWORD?
EH?
I WON'T GO EASY ON YE, LASS!
KLANG

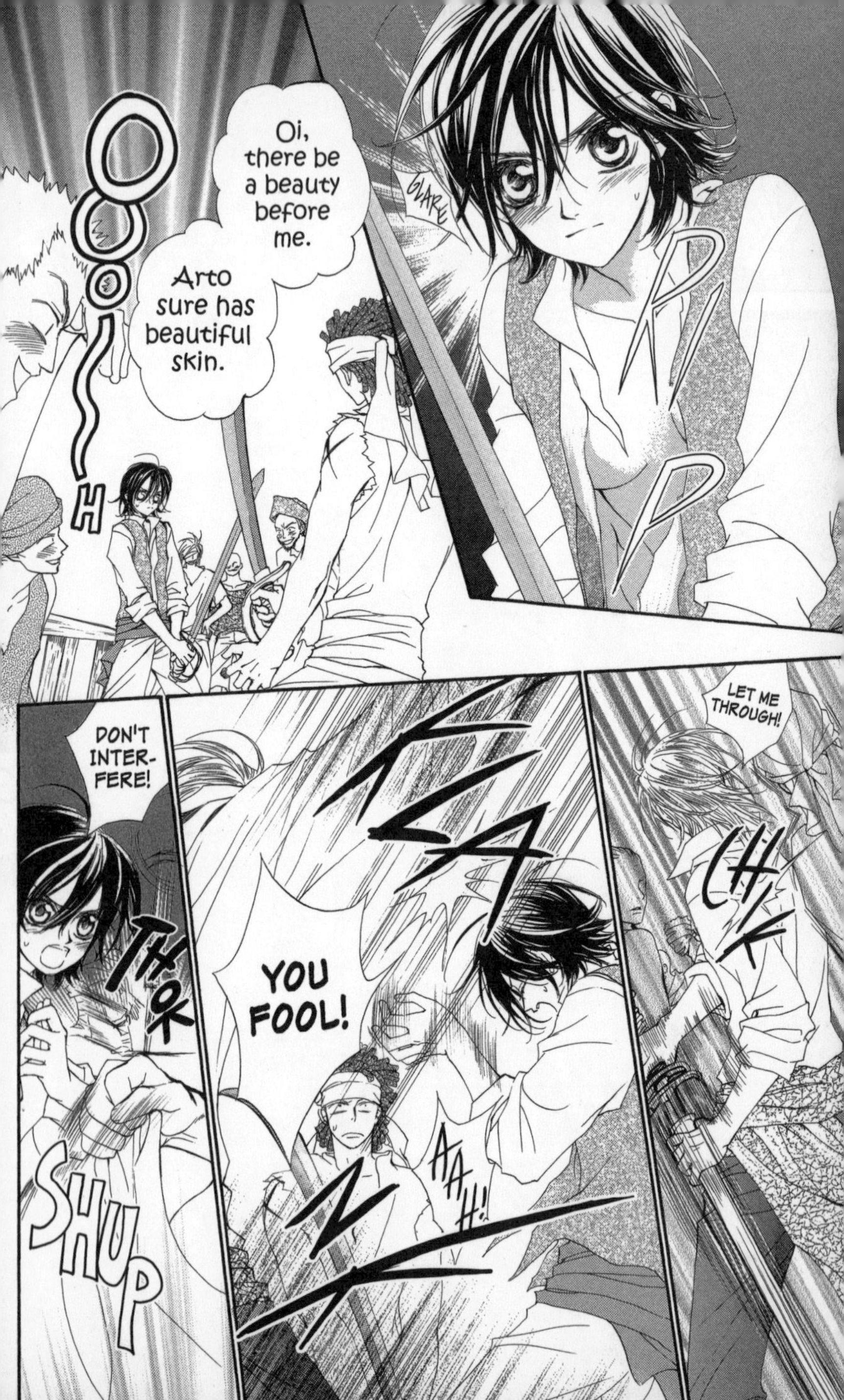
GLARE
RIP
Oi, there be a beauty before me.
Arto sure has beautiful skin.
OOOOH
LET ME THROUGH!
CHIK
KLANK
YOU FOOL!
AAH!
DON'T INTER-FERE!
THOK
SHUP

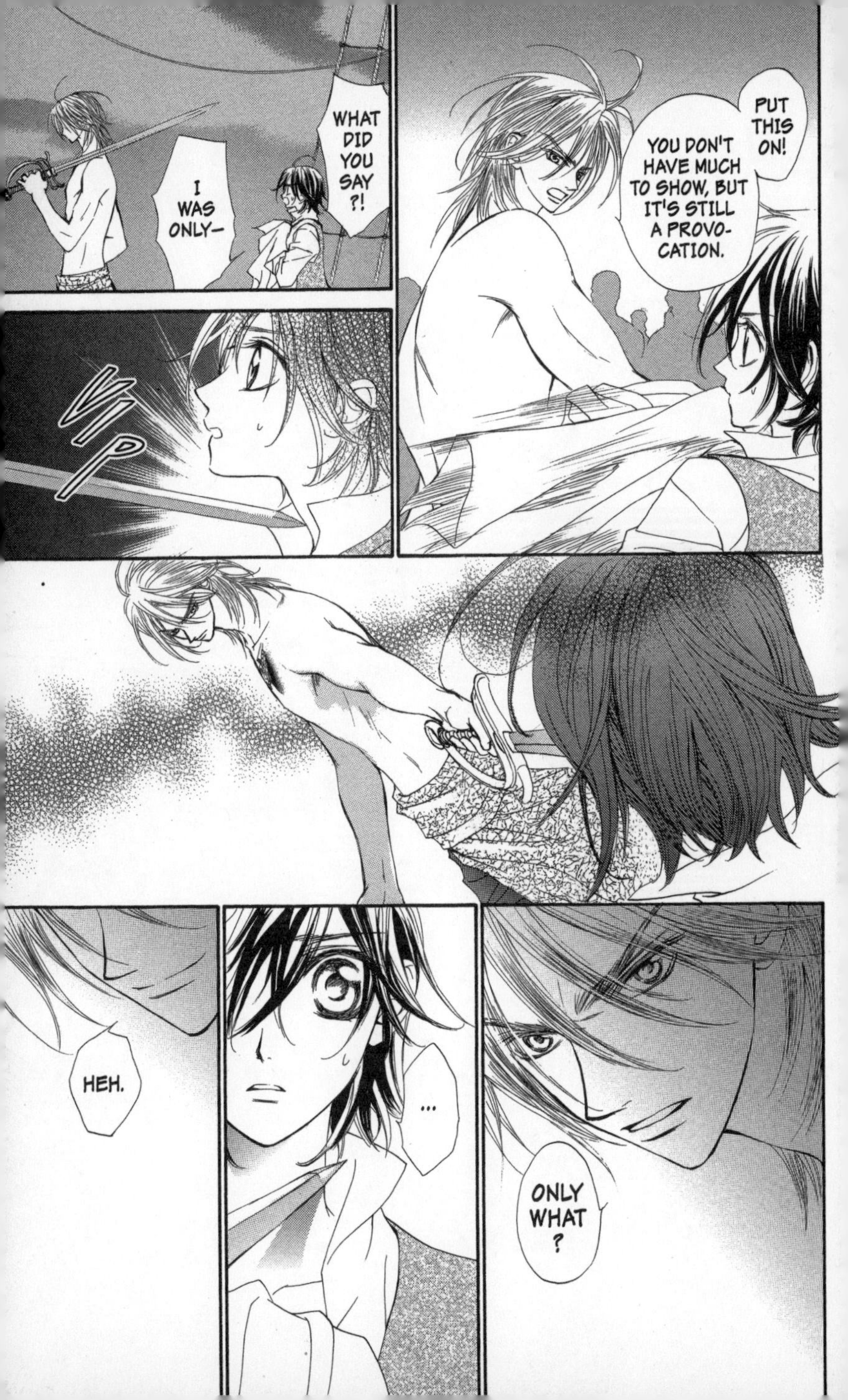
PUT THIS ON!
YOU DON'T HAVE MUCH TO SHOW, BUT IT'S STILL A PROVOCATION.
WHAT DID YOU SAY?!
I WAS ONLY—
VIP
ONLY WHAT?
...
HEH.

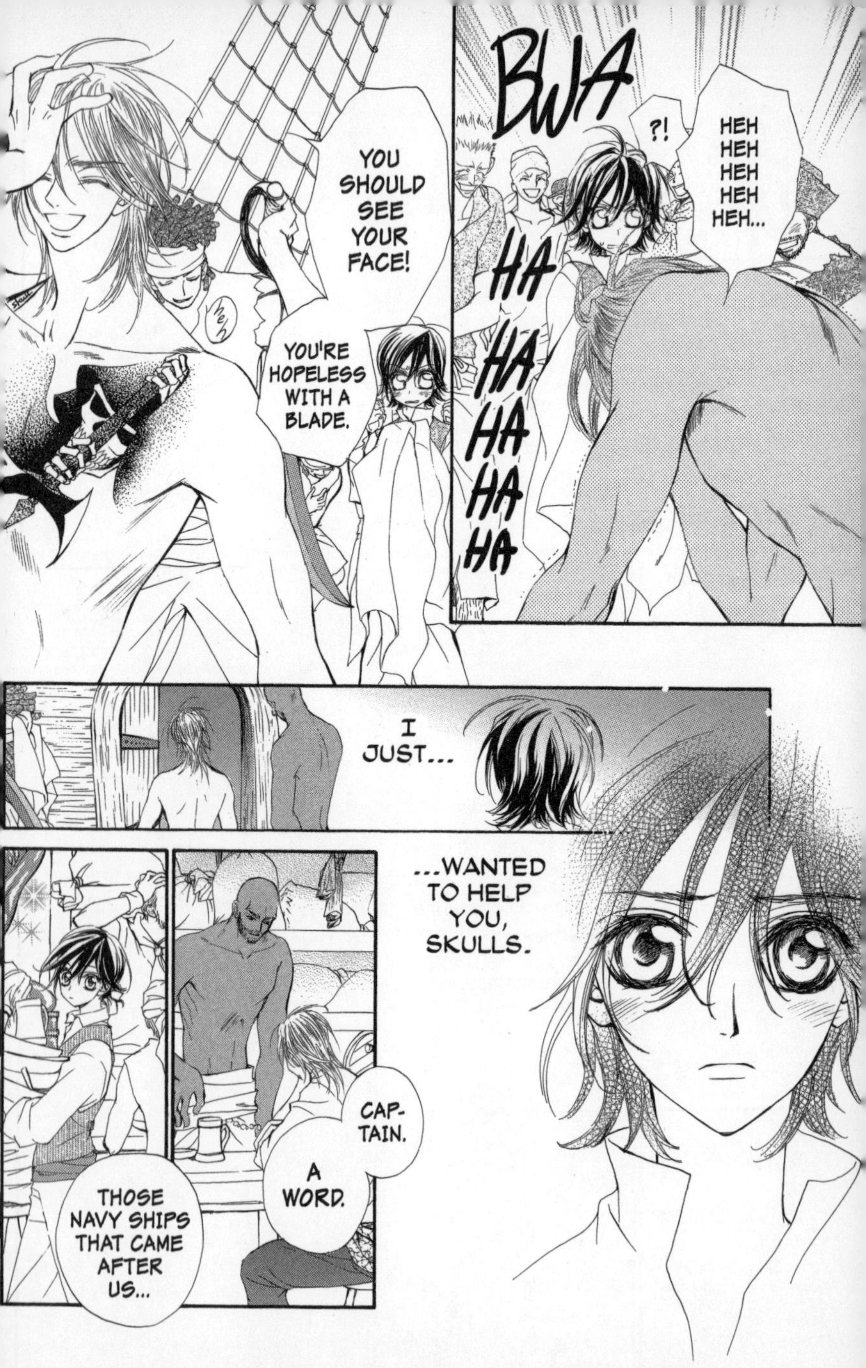
HEH HEH HEH HEH HEH...
?!
BWA
HA HA HA HA HA HA
YOU SHOULD SEE YOUR FACE!
YOU'RE HOPELESS WITH A BLADE.
I JUST...
...WANTED TO HELP YOU, SKULLS.
CAP-TAIN.
A WORD.
THOSE NAVY SHIPS THAT CAME AFTER US...

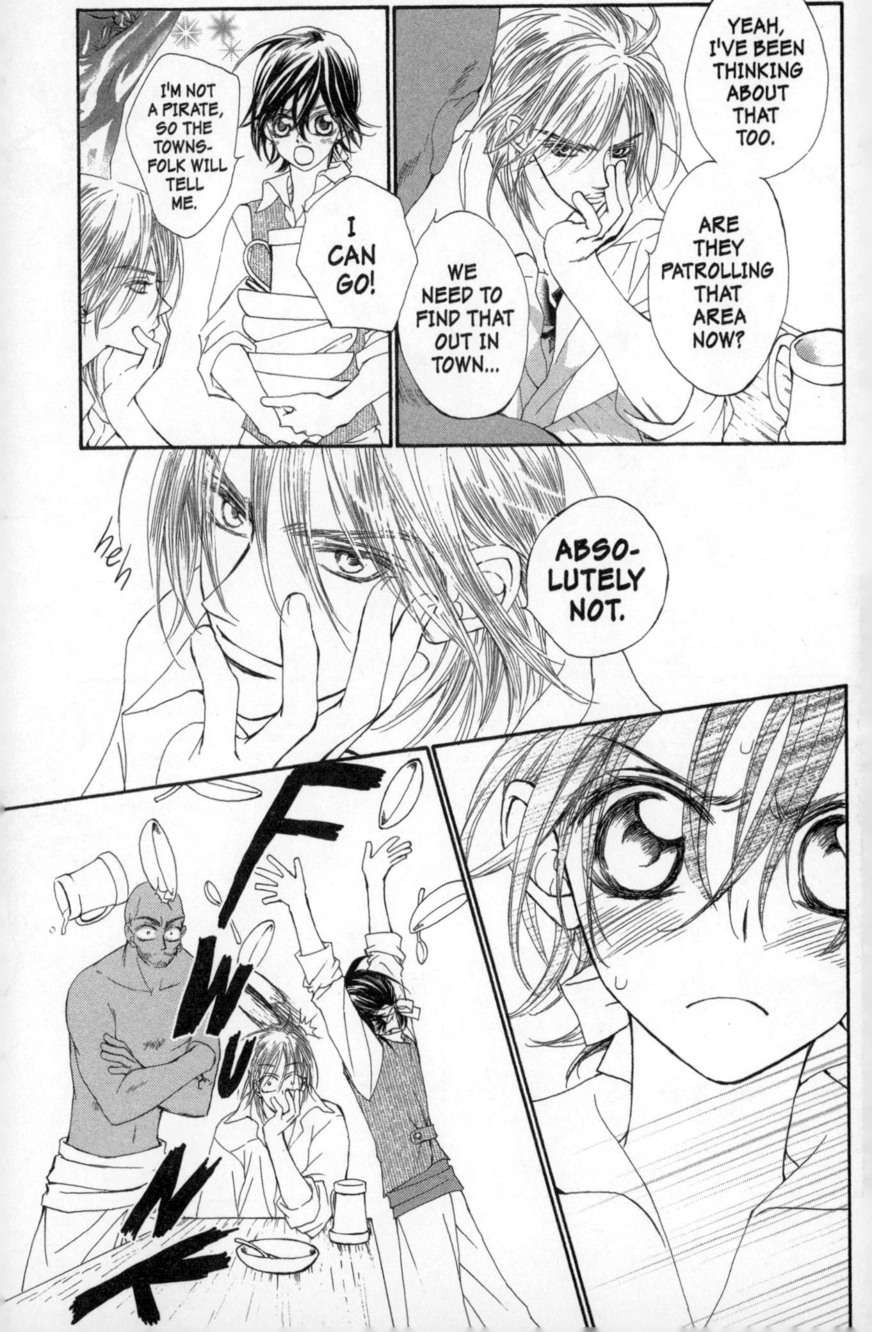
YEAH, I'VE BEEN THINKING ABOUT THAT TOO.
ARE THEY PATROLLING THAT AREA NOW?
WE NEED TO FIND THAT OUT IN TOWN...
I CAN GO!
I'M NOT A PIRATE, SO THE TOWNS-FOLK WILL TELL ME.
ABSO-LUTELY NOT.
heh
FWUNK

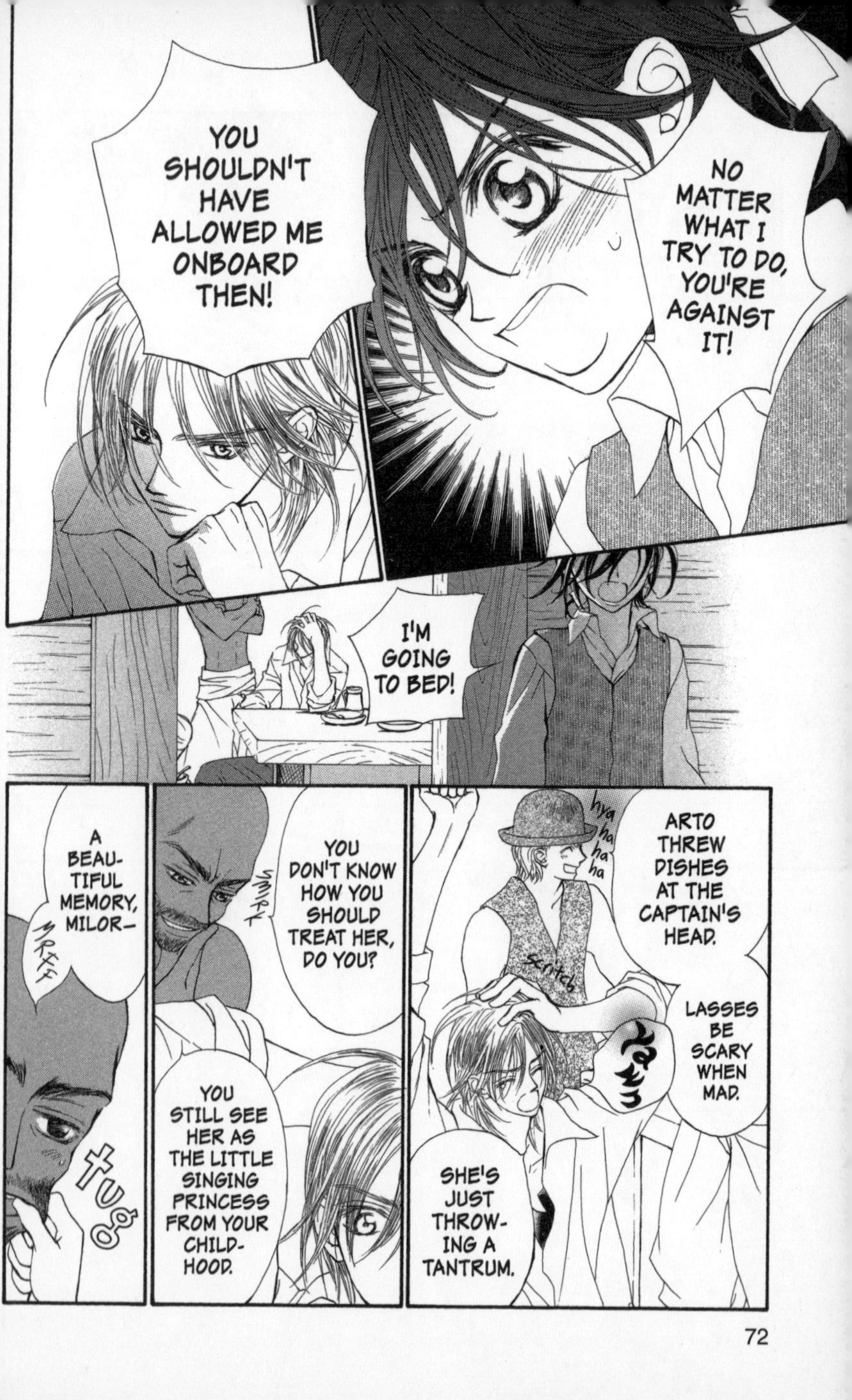

NO MATTER WHAT I TRY TO DO, YOU'RE AGAINST IT!
YOU SHOULDN'T HAVE ALLOWED ME ONBOARD THEN!
I'M GOING TO BED!
hya ha ha ha
ARTO THREW DISHES AT THE CAPTAIN'S HEAD.
scritch
LASSES BE SCARY WHEN MAD.
SHE'S JUST THROWING A TANTRUM.
YOU DON'T KNOW HOW YOU SHOULD TREAT HER, DO YOU?
SMIRK
YOU STILL SEE HER AS THE LITTLE SINGING PRINCESS FROM YOUR CHILDHOOD.
A BEAUTIFUL MEMORY, MILOR—
MRFF
tug

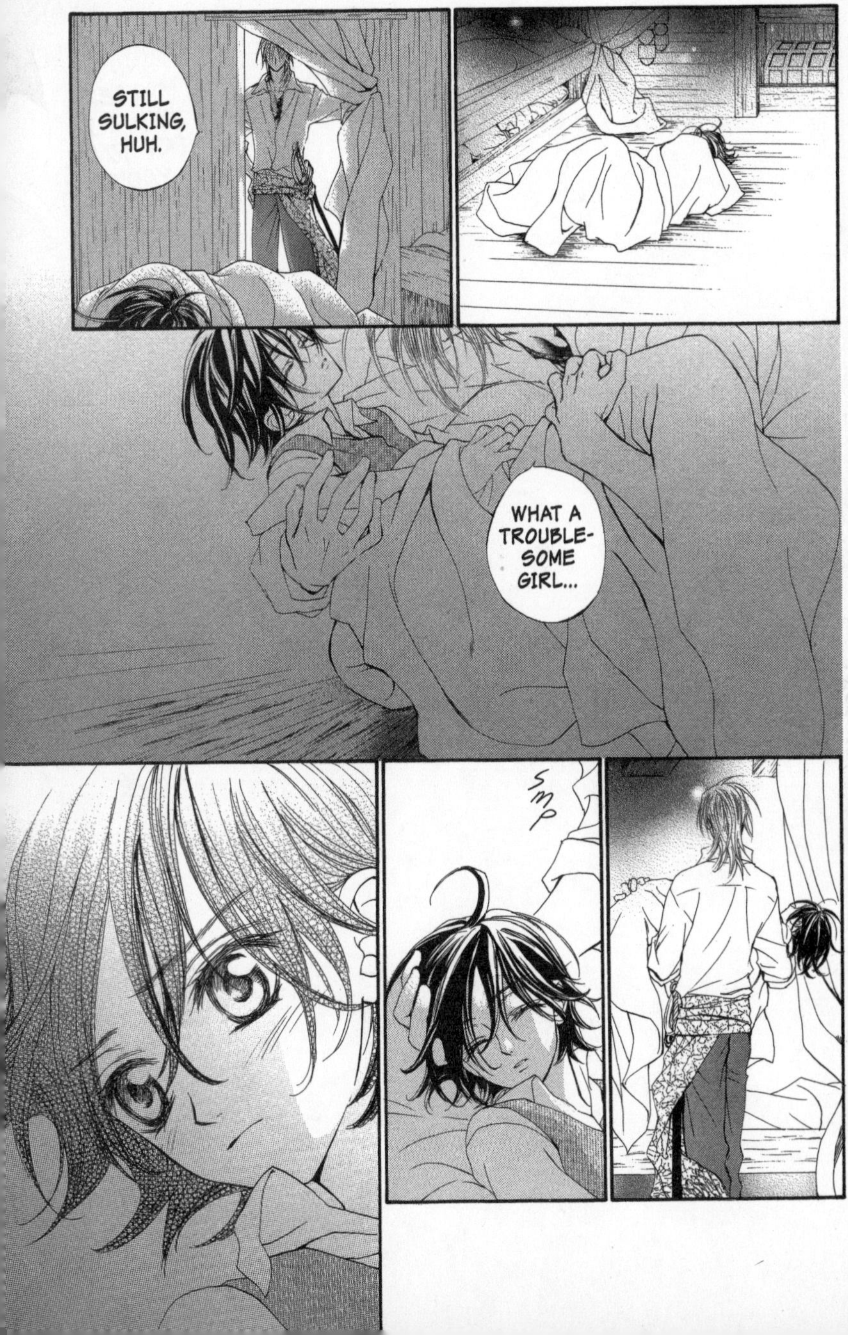
STILL SULKING, HUH.
WHAT A TROUBLE-SOME GIRL...
SMP

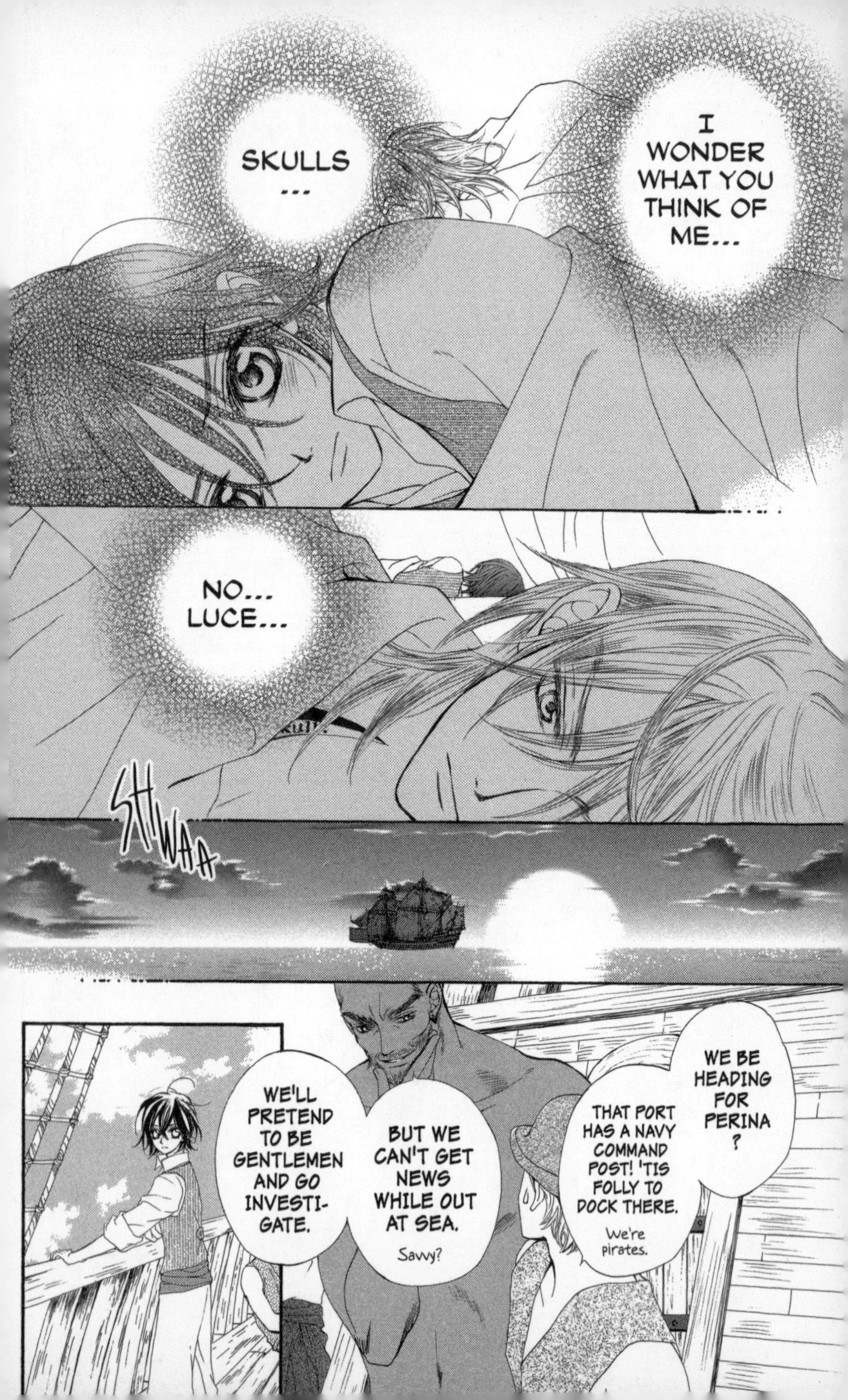
I WONDER WHAT YOU THINK OF ME...
SKULLS...
NO... LUCE...
SHWAA
WE BE HEADING FOR PERINA?
THAT PORT HAS A NAVY COMMAND POST! 'TIS FOLLY TO DOCK THERE.
We're pirates.
BUT WE CAN'T GET NEWS WHILE OUT AT SEA.
Savvy?
WE'LL PRETEND TO BE GENTLEMEN AND GO INVESTI-GATE.

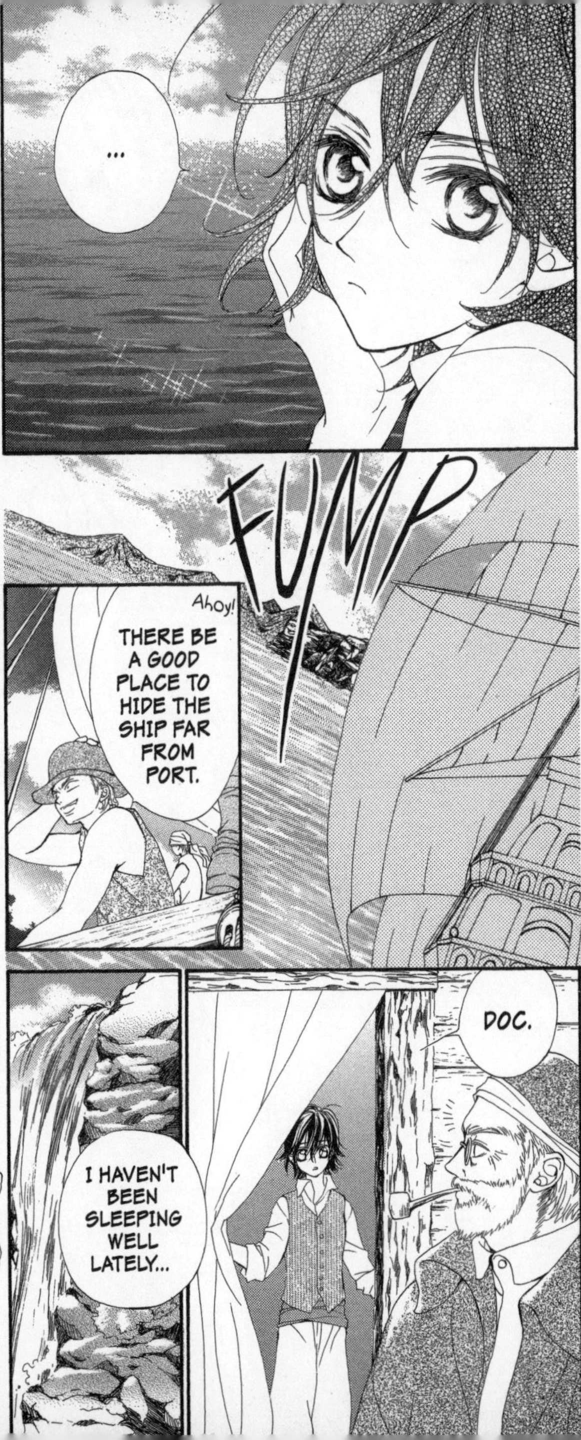
...
FUMP
Ahoy!
THERE BE A GOOD PLACE TO HIDE THE SHIP FAR FROM PORT.
DOC.
I HAVEN'T BEEN SLEEPING WELL LATELY...

Third

Skulls-sama's Merry Comrades

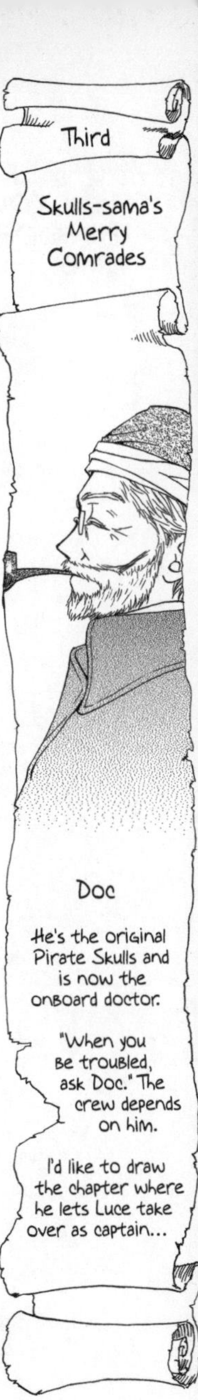

Doc

He's the original Pirate Skulls and is now the onboard doctor.

"When you be troubled, ask Doc." The crew depends on him.

I'd like to draw the chapter where he lets Luce take over as captain...

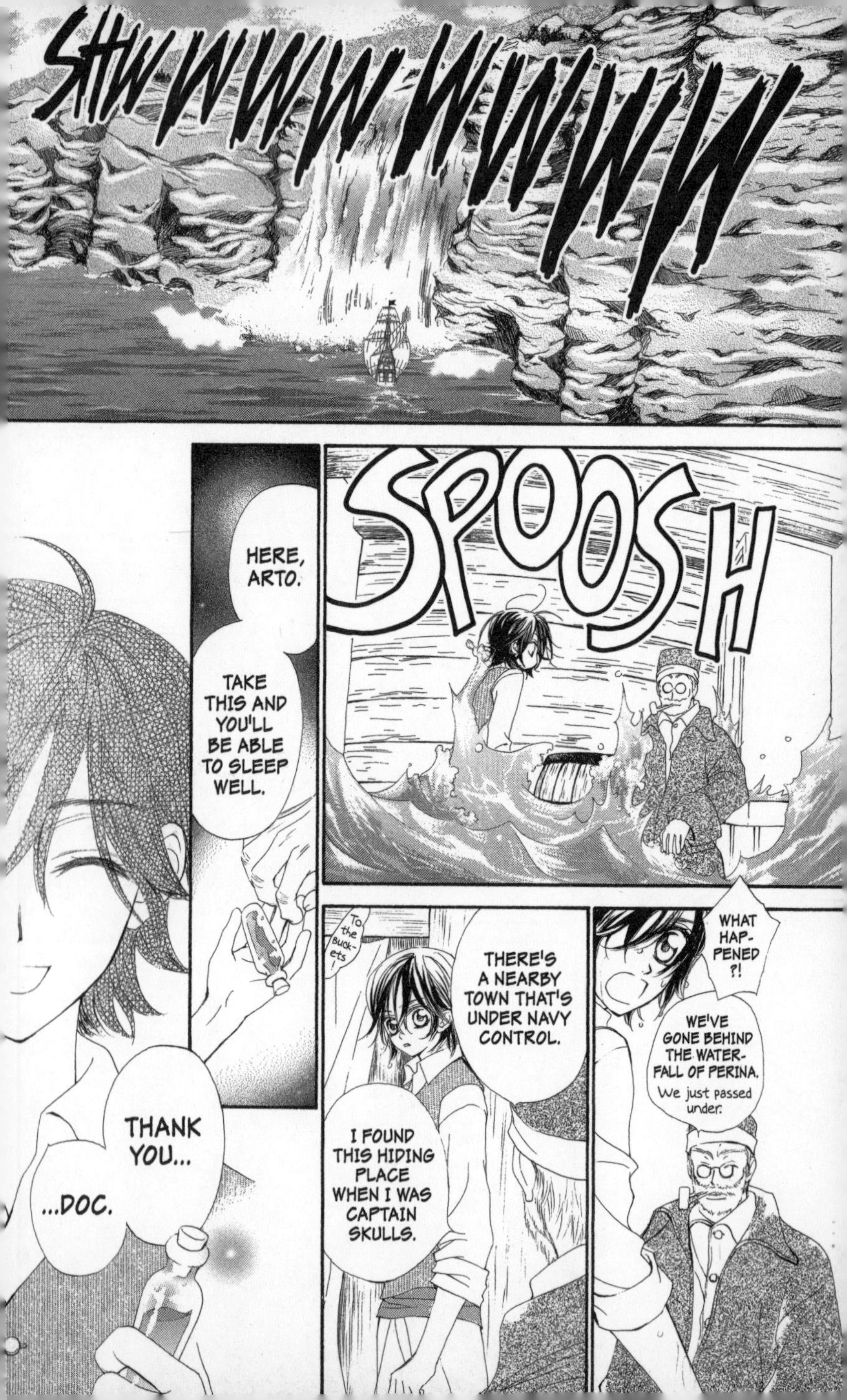
SHWWWWWWWWWWN
SPOOSH
WHAT HAP-PENED?!
WE'VE GONE BEHIND THE WATER-FALL OF PERINA.
We just passed under.
To the Buck-ets!
THERE'S A NEARBY TOWN THAT'S UNDER NAVY CONTROL.
I FOUND THIS HIDING PLACE WHEN I WAS CAPTAIN SKULLS.
HERE, ARTO.
TAKE THIS AND YOU'LL BE ABLE TO SLEEP WELL.
THANK YOU...
...DOC.

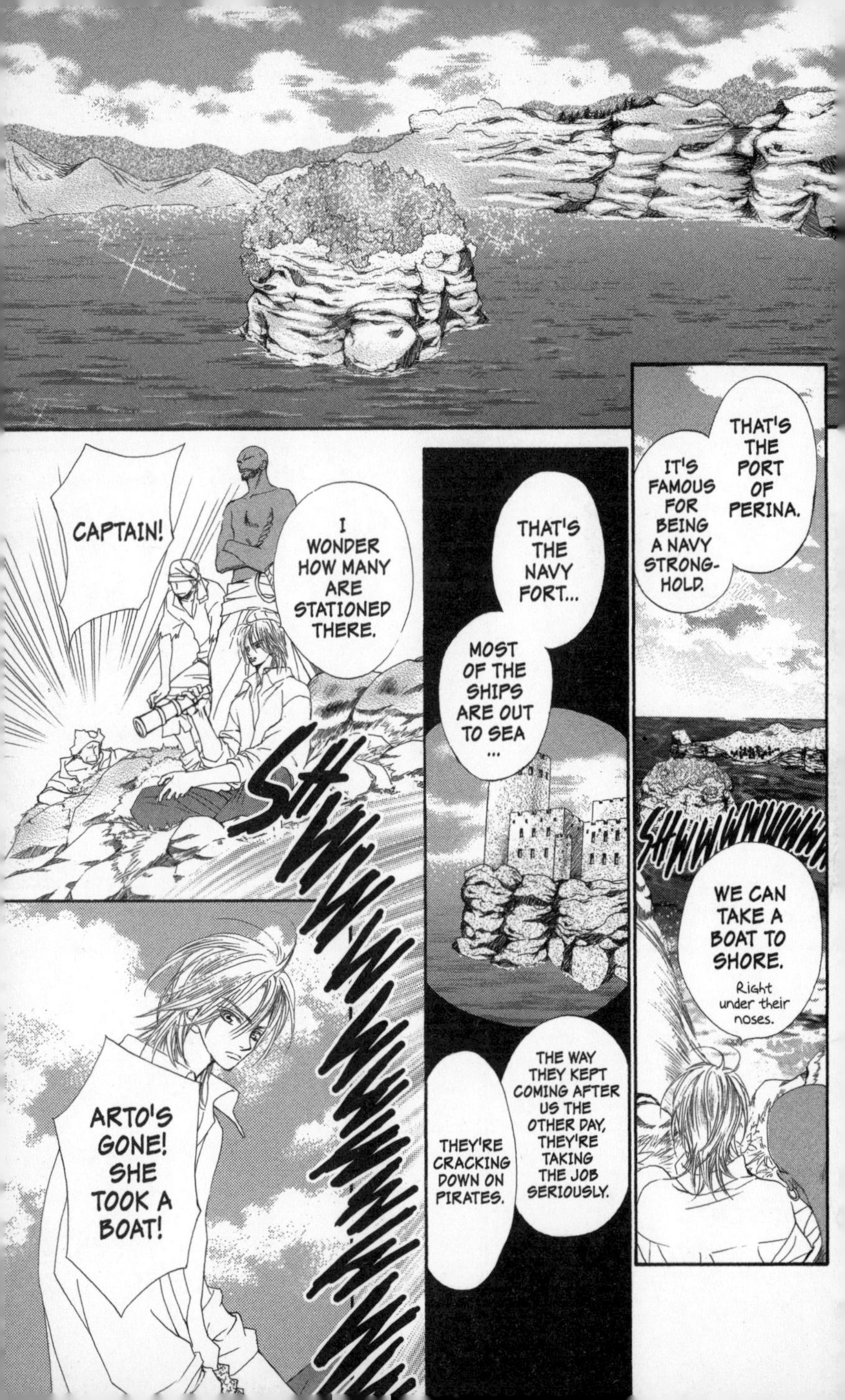
THAT'S THE PORT OF PERINA.
IT'S FAMOUS FOR BEING A NAVY STRONG-HOLD.
SHWWWWWWWWW
WE CAN TAKE A BOAT TO SHORE.
Right under their noses.
THAT'S THE NAVY FORT...
MOST OF THE SHIPS ARE OUT TO SEA ...
THE WAY THEY KEPT COMING AFTER US THE OTHER DAY, THEY'RE TAKING THE JOB SERIOUSLY.
THEY'RE CRACKING DOWN ON PIRATES.
I WONDER HOW MANY ARE STATIONED THERE.
CAPTAIN!
SHWWWWWWWWWWWW
ARTO'S GONE! SHE TOOK A BOAT!

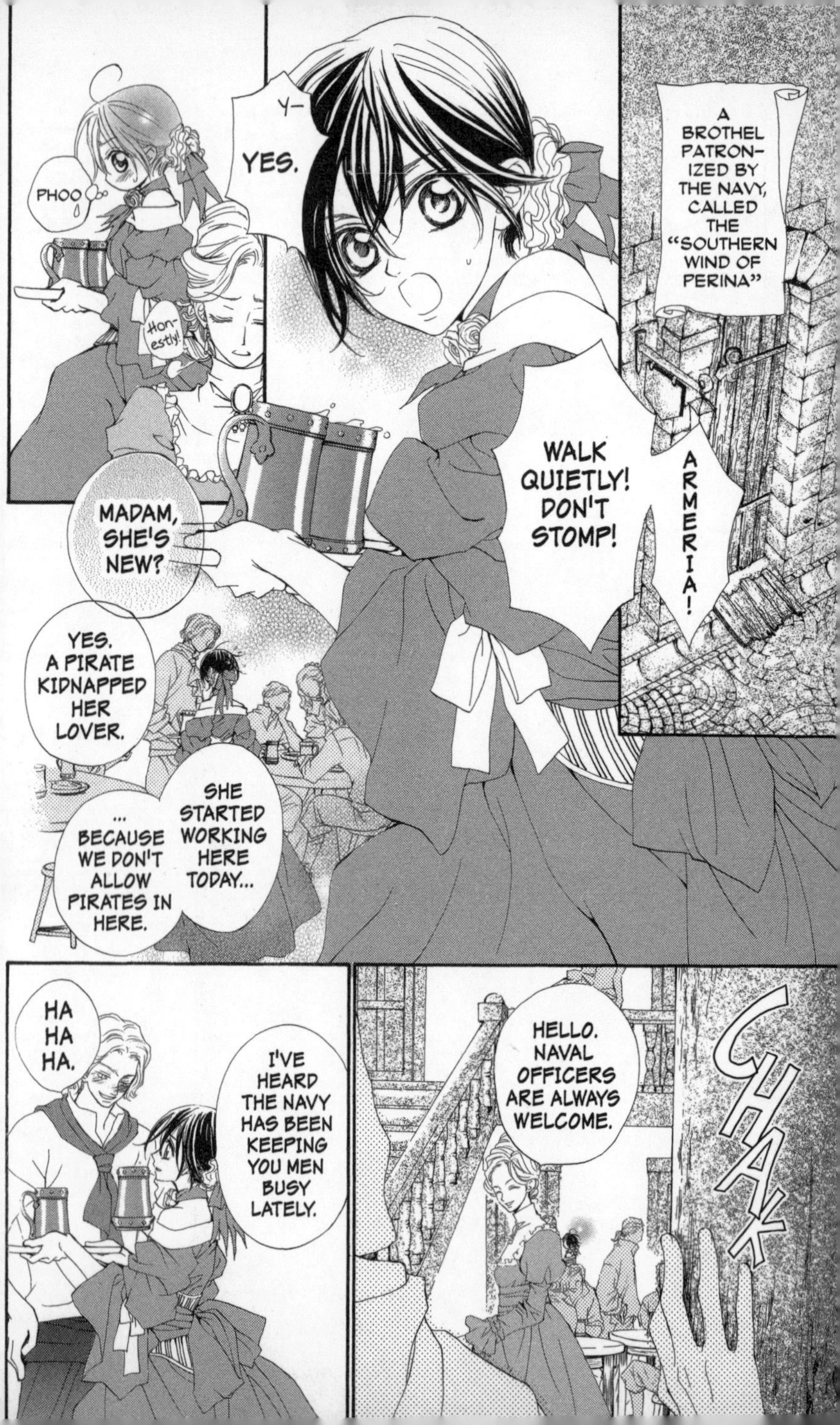
A BROTHEL PATRONIZED BY THE NAVY, CALLED THE "SOUTHERN WIND OF PERINA"
ARMERIA!
WALK QUIETLY! DON'T STOMP!
Y— YES.
PHOO
Honestly!
MADAM, SHE'S NEW?
YES. A PIRATE KIDNAPPED HER LOVER.
SHE STARTED WORKING HERE TODAY...
... BECAUSE WE DON'T ALLOW PIRATES IN HERE.
CHAK
HELLO. NAVAL OFFICERS ARE ALWAYS WELCOME.
I'VE HEARD THE NAVY HAS BEEN KEEPING YOU MEN BUSY LATELY.
HA HA HA.

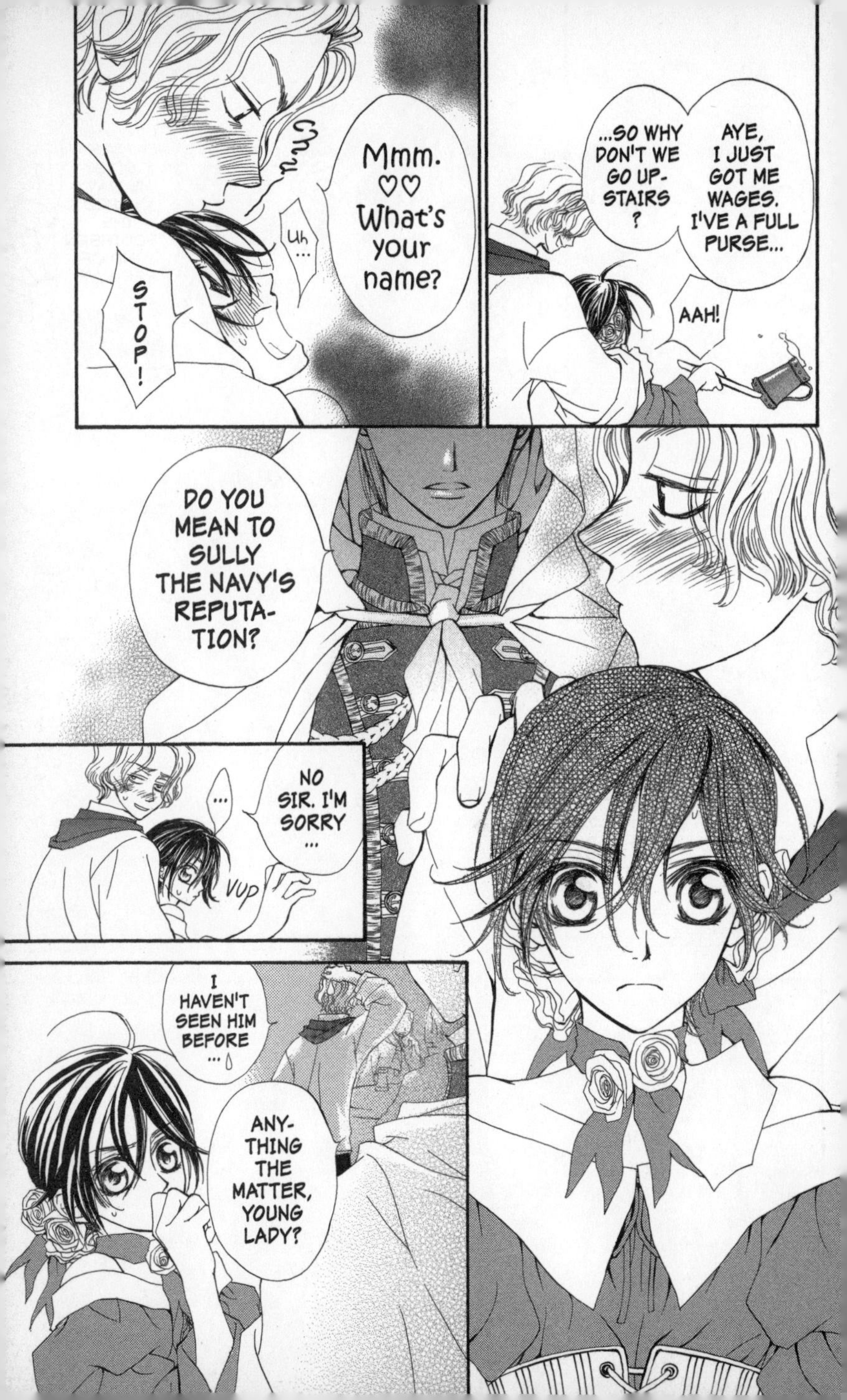
AYE, I JUST GOT ME WAGES. I'VE A FULL PURSE...
...SO WHY DON'T WE GO UP-STAIRS?
AAH!
Mmm. ♡♡ What's your name?
Chu
Uh...
STOP!
DO YOU MEAN TO SULLY THE NAVY'S REPUTA-TION?
NO SIR. I'M SORRY...
...
VUP
I HAVEN'T SEEN HIM BEFORE...
ANY-THING THE MATTER, YOUNG LADY?

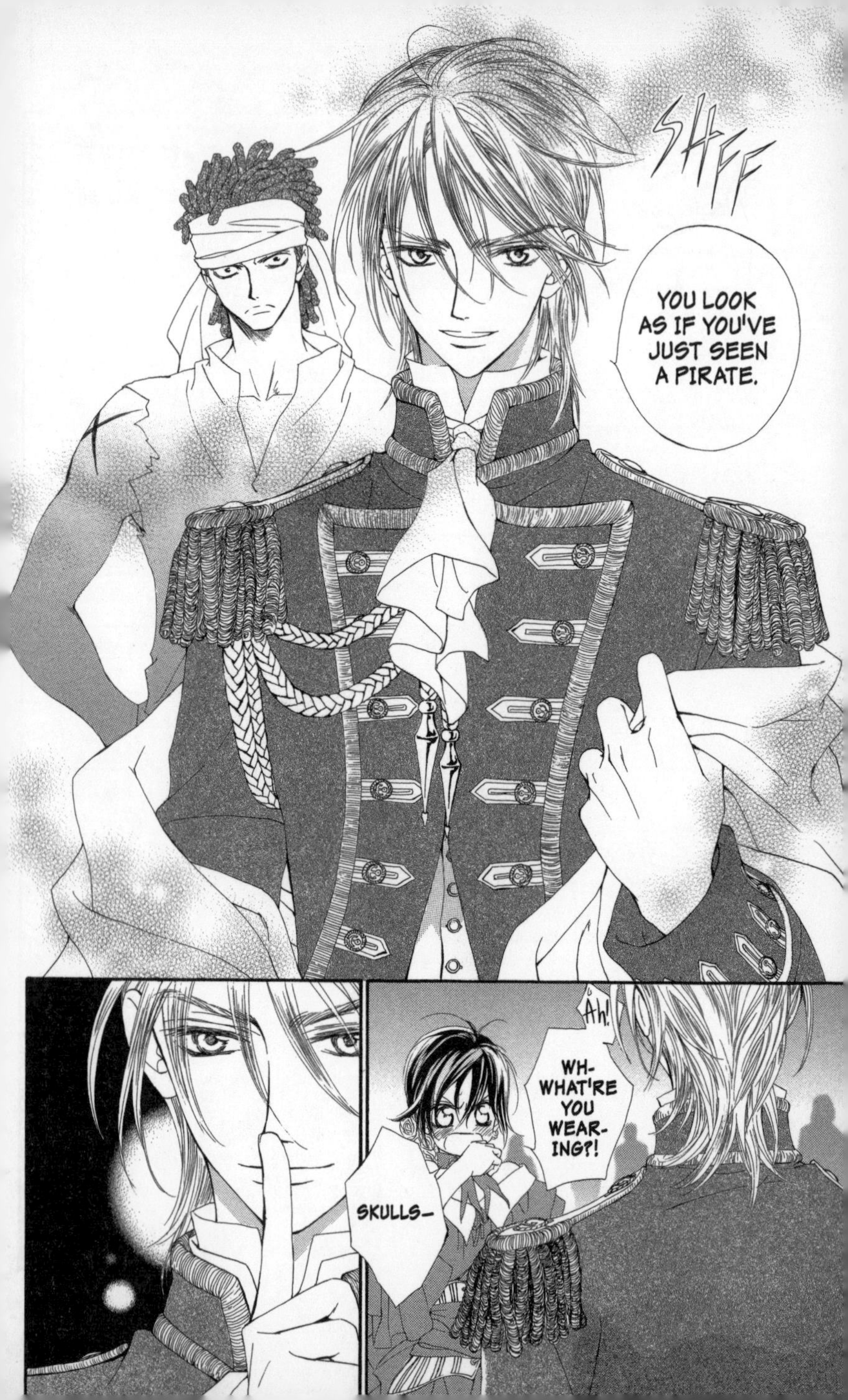
SHFF
YOU LOOK AS IF YOU'VE JUST SEEN A PIRATE.
Ah!
WH-WHAT'RE YOU WEARING?!
SKULLS–

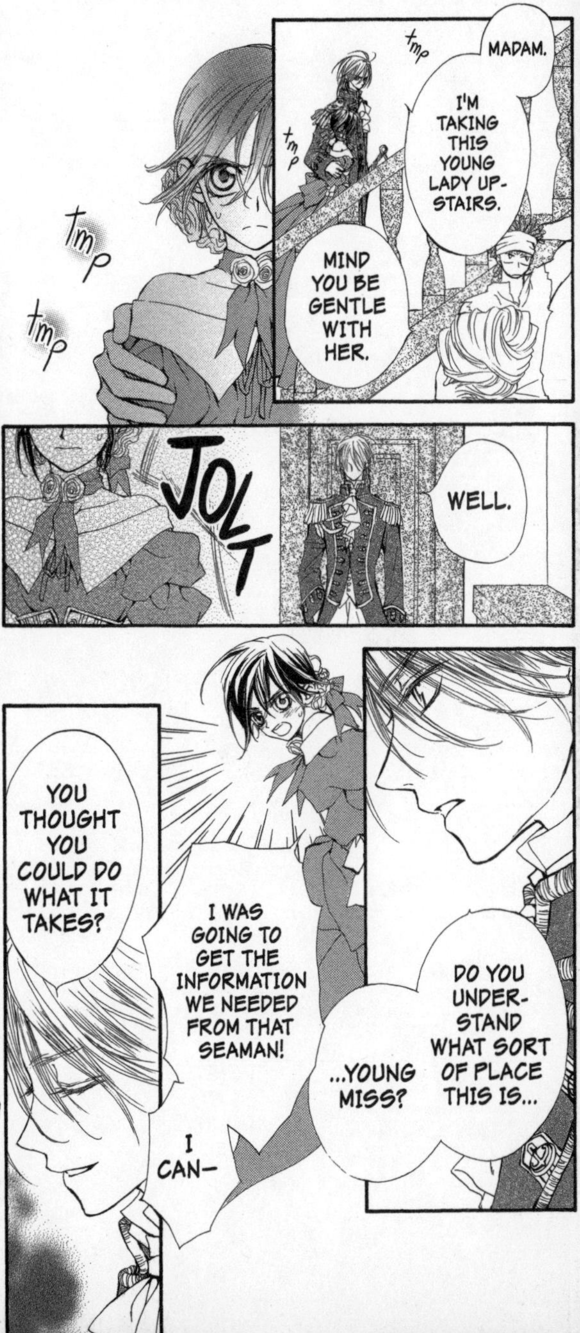
tmp
MADAM.
I'M TAKING THIS YOUNG LADY UP-STAIRS.
tmp
MIND YOU BE GENTLE WITH HER.
tmp
tmp
WELL.
JOLT
DO YOU UNDER-STAND WHAT SORT OF PLACE THIS IS...
...YOUNG MISS?
I WAS GOING TO GET THE INFORMATION WE NEEDED FROM THAT SEAMAN!
I CAN–
YOU THOUGHT YOU COULD DO WHAT IT TAKES?

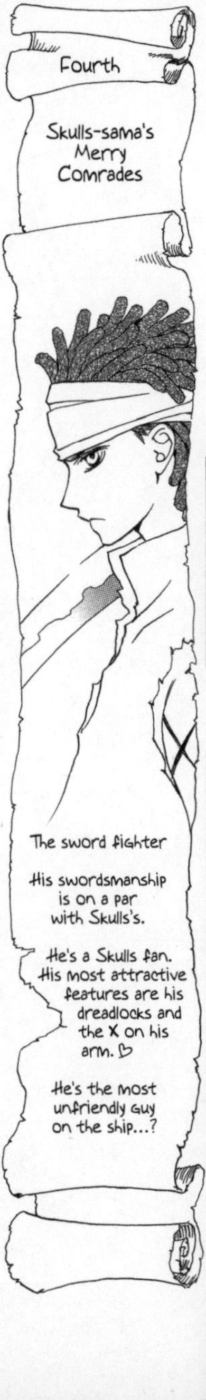
Fourth
Skulls-sama's Merry Comrades
The sword fighter
His swordsmanship is on a par with Skulls's.
He's a Skulls fan. His most attractive features are his dreadlocks and the X on his arm. ♡
He's the most unfriendly guy on the ship...?

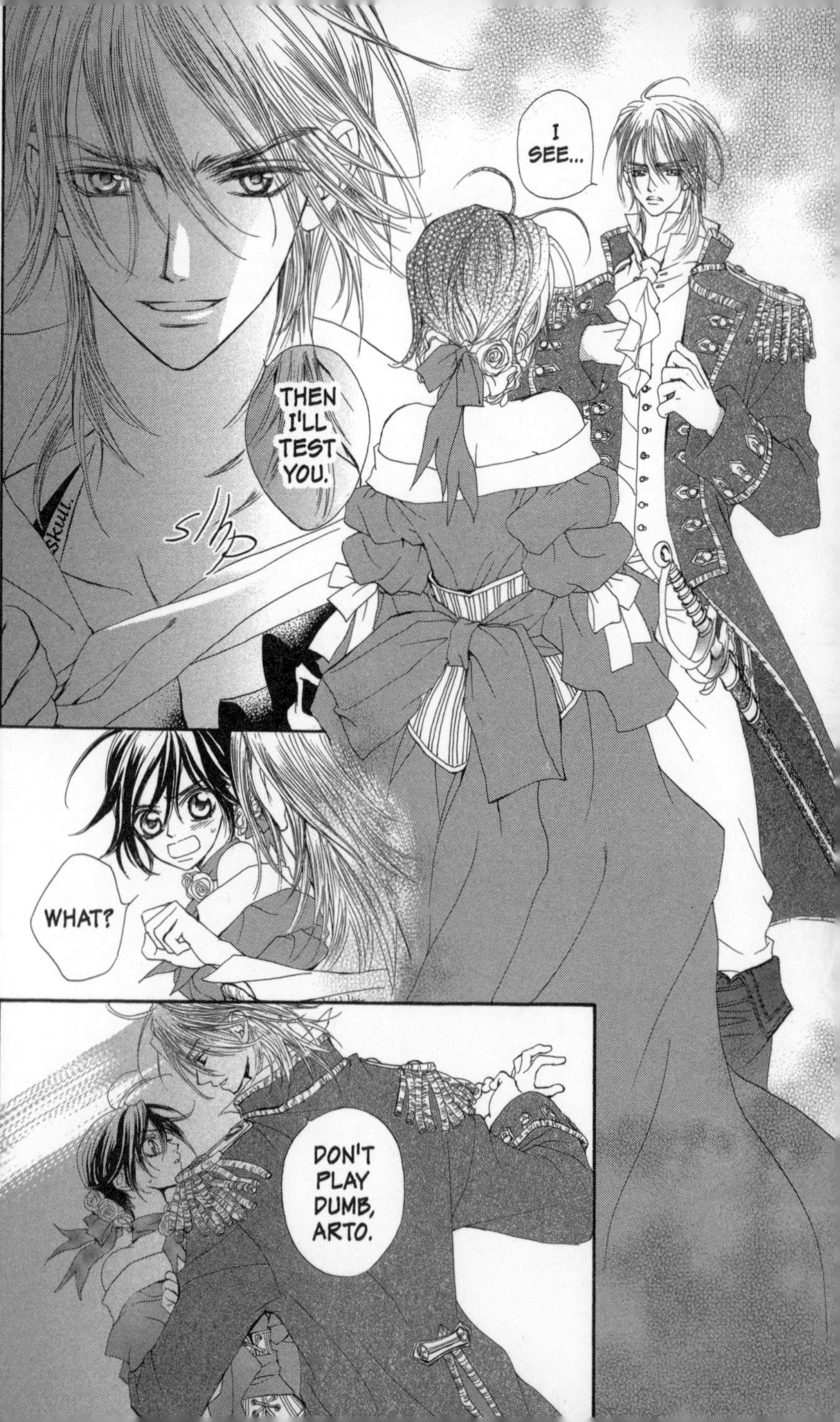
I SEE...
THEN I'LL TEST YOU.
skull.
WHAT?
DON'T PLAY DUMB, ARTO.

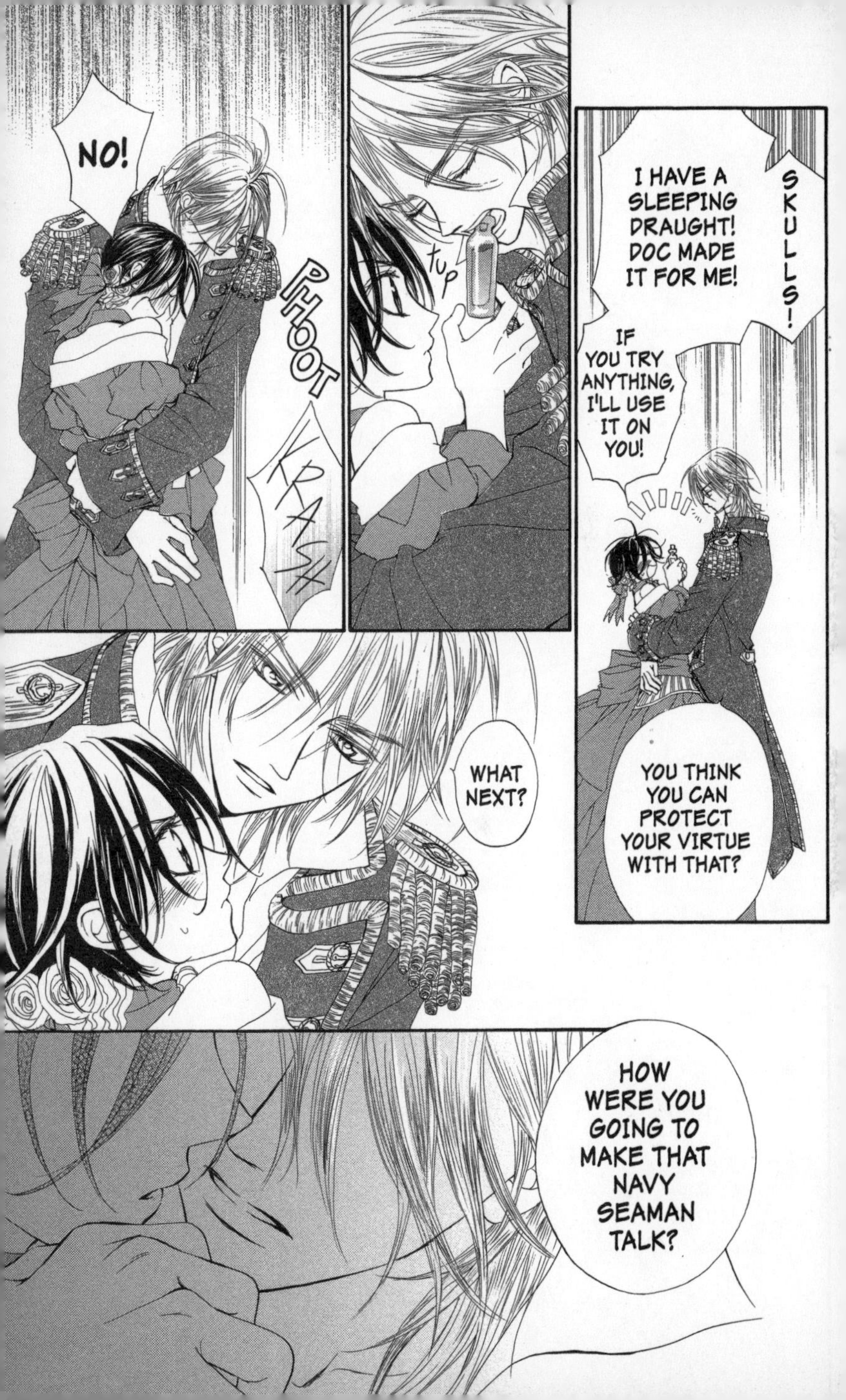
SKULLS!
I HAVE A SLEEPING DRAUGHT! DOC MADE IT FOR ME!
IF YOU TRY ANYTHING, I'LL USE IT ON YOU!
YOU THINK YOU CAN PROTECT YOUR VIRTUE WITH THAT?
TUP
NO!
PHOOT
KRASH
WHAT NEXT?
HOW WERE YOU GOING TO MAKE THAT NAVY SEAMAN TALK?

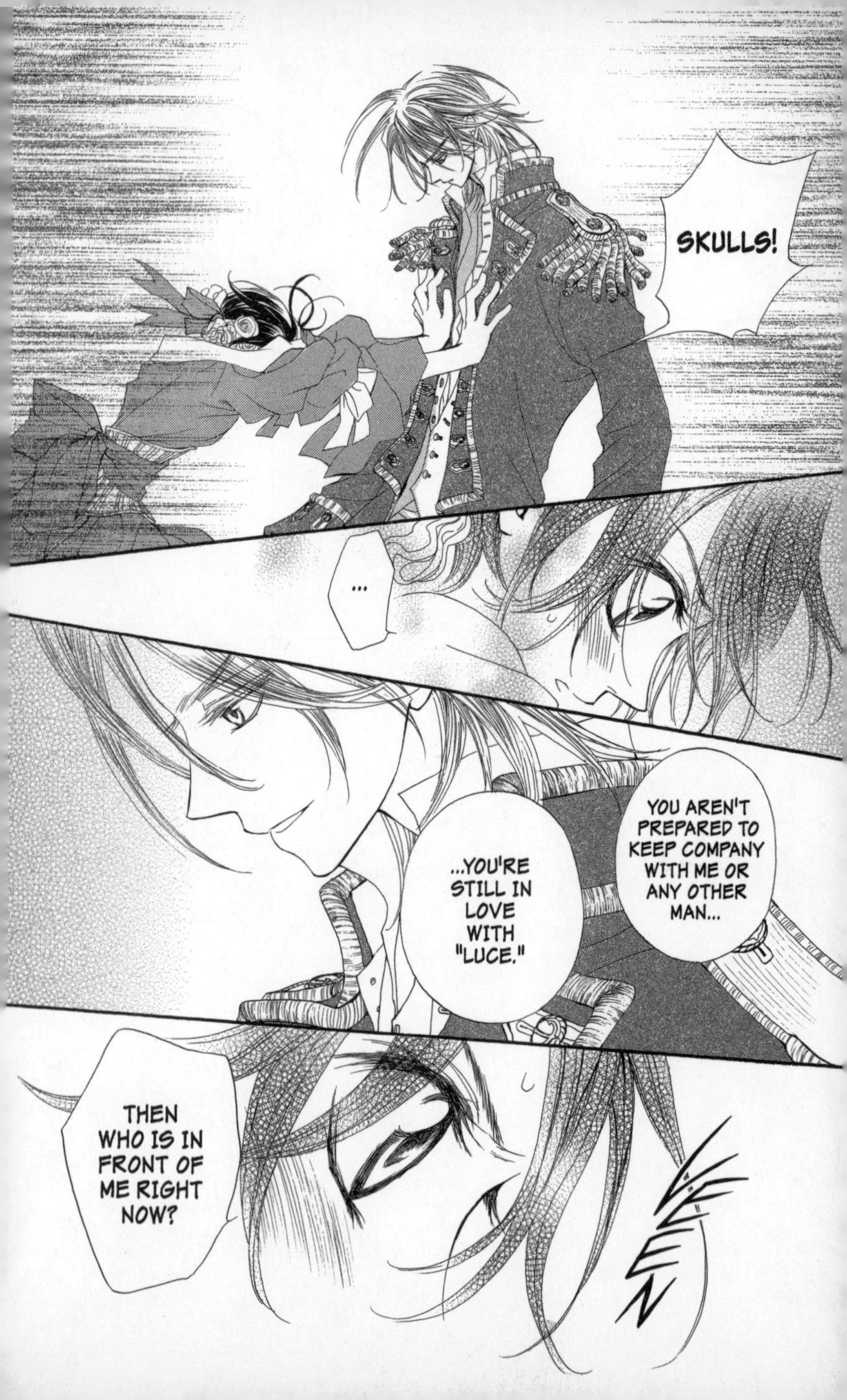
SKULLS!
...
YOU AREN'T PREPARED TO KEEP COMPANY WITH ME OR ANY OTHER MAN...
...YOU'RE STILL IN LOVE WITH "LUCE."
THEN WHO IS IN FRONT OF ME RIGHT NOW?
VEEN

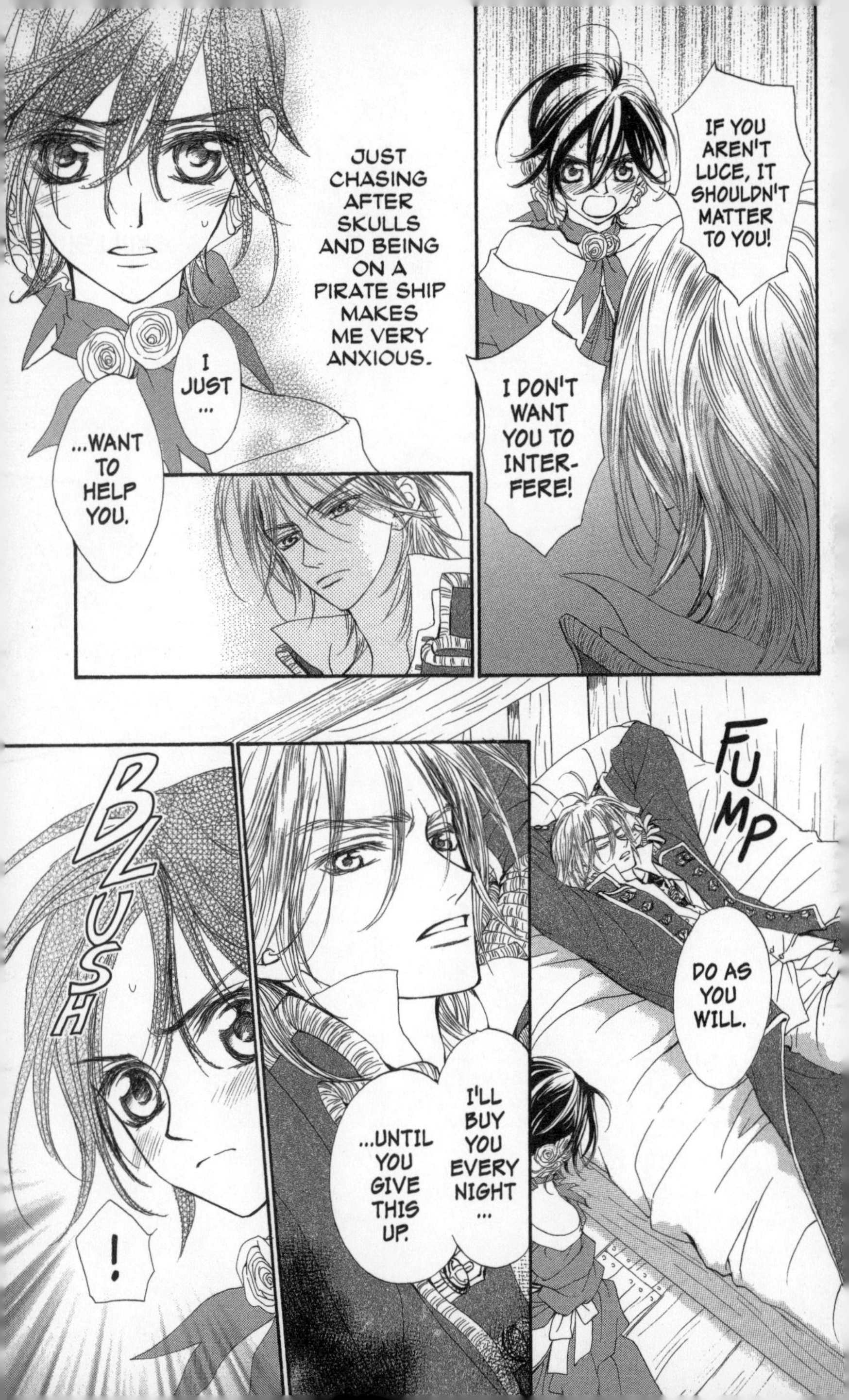
IF YOU AREN'T LUCE, IT SHOULDN'T MATTER TO YOU!
I DON'T WANT YOU TO INTERFERE!
JUST CHASING AFTER SKULLS AND BEING ON A PIRATE SHIP MAKES ME VERY ANXIOUS.
I JUST...
...WANT TO HELP YOU.
FUMP
DO AS YOU WILL.
I'LL BUY YOU EVERY NIGHT...
...UNTIL YOU GIVE THIS UP.
BLUSH
!

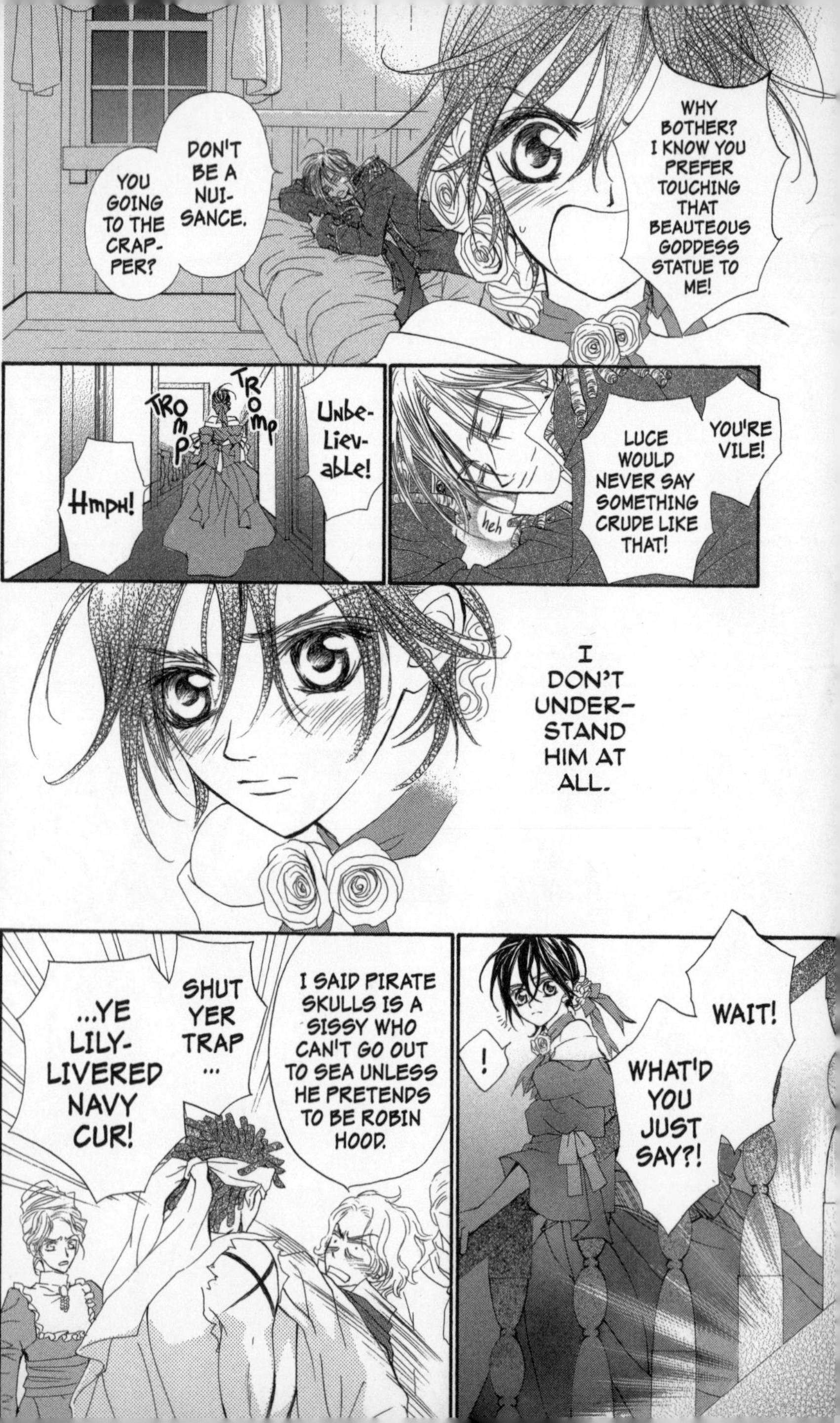
WHY BOTHER? I KNOW YOU PREFER TOUCHING THAT BEAUTEOUS GODDESS STATUE TO ME!
DON'T BE A NUISANCE.
YOU GOING TO THE CRAPPER?
YOU'RE VILE!
LUCE WOULD NEVER SAY SOMETHING CRUDE LIKE THAT!
heh
Unbelievable!
TROMP TROMP
Hmph!
I DON'T UNDERSTAND HIM AT ALL.
WAIT!
WHAT'D YOU JUST SAY?!
!
I SAID PIRATE SKULLS IS A SISSY WHO CAN'T GO OUT TO SEA UNLESS HE PRETENDS TO BE ROBIN HOOD.
SHUT YER TRAP...
...YE LILY-LIVERED NAVY CUR!

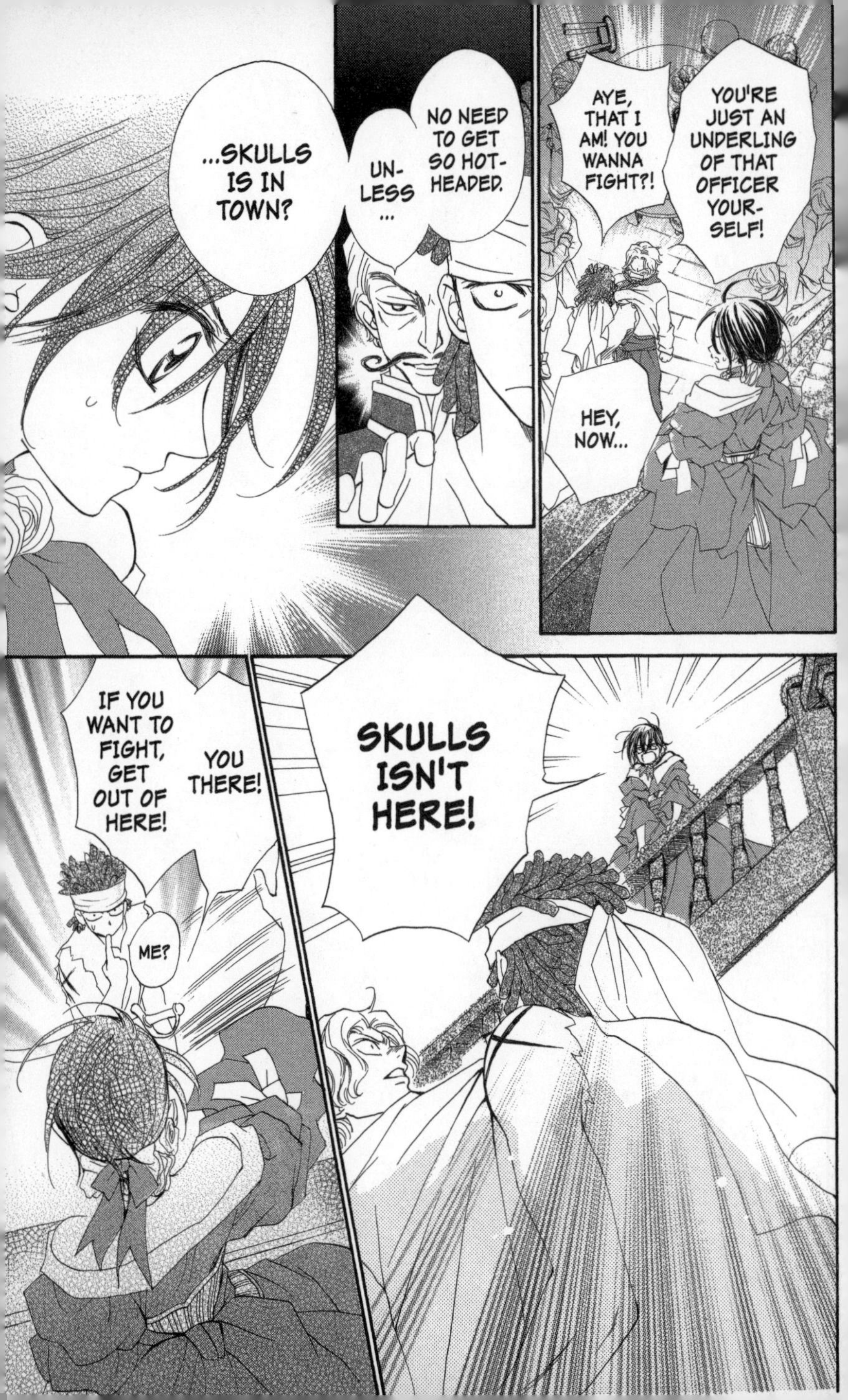
YOU'RE JUST AN UNDERLING OF THAT OFFICER YOURSELF!
AYE, THAT I AM! YOU WANNA FIGHT?!
HEY, NOW...
NO NEED TO GET SO HOT-HEADED.
UNLESS...
...SKULLS IS IN TOWN?
SKULLS ISN'T HERE!
YOU THERE!
IF YOU WANT TO FIGHT, GET OUT OF HERE!
ME?

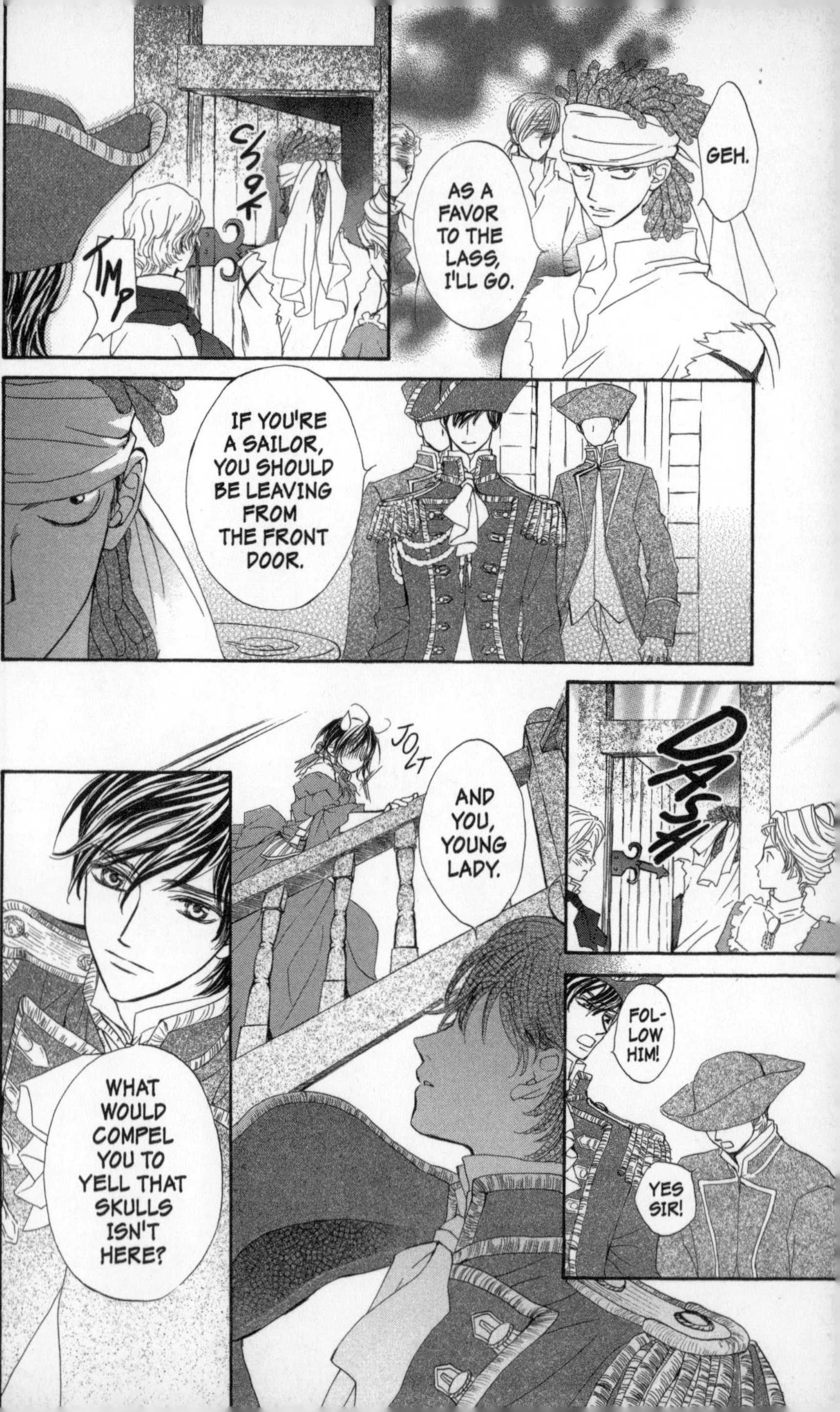
GEH.
AS A FAVOR TO THE LASS, I'LL GO.
CLACK
TMP
IF YOU'RE A SAILOR, YOU SHOULD BE LEAVING FROM THE FRONT DOOR.
DASH
FOL-LOW HIM!
YES SIR!
JOLT
AND YOU, YOUNG LADY.
WHAT WOULD COMPEL YOU TO YELL THAT SKULLS ISN'T HERE?

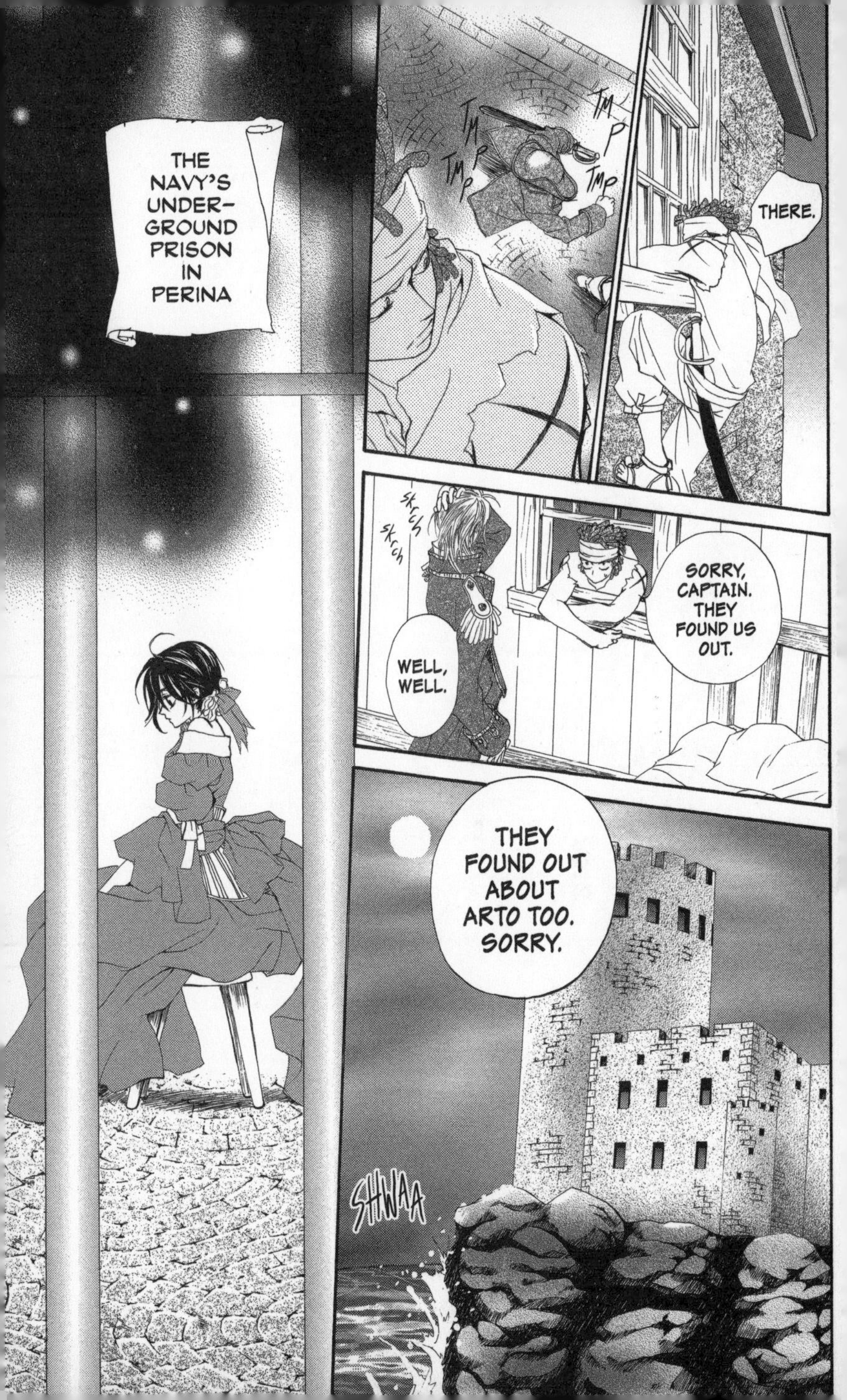
TMP TMP
TMP TMP
THERE.
SKRCH SKRCH
SORRY, CAPTAIN. THEY FOUND US OUT.
WELL, WELL.
THEY FOUND OUT ABOUT ARTO TOO. SORRY.
SHWAA
THE NAVY'S UNDER-GROUND PRISON IN PERINA

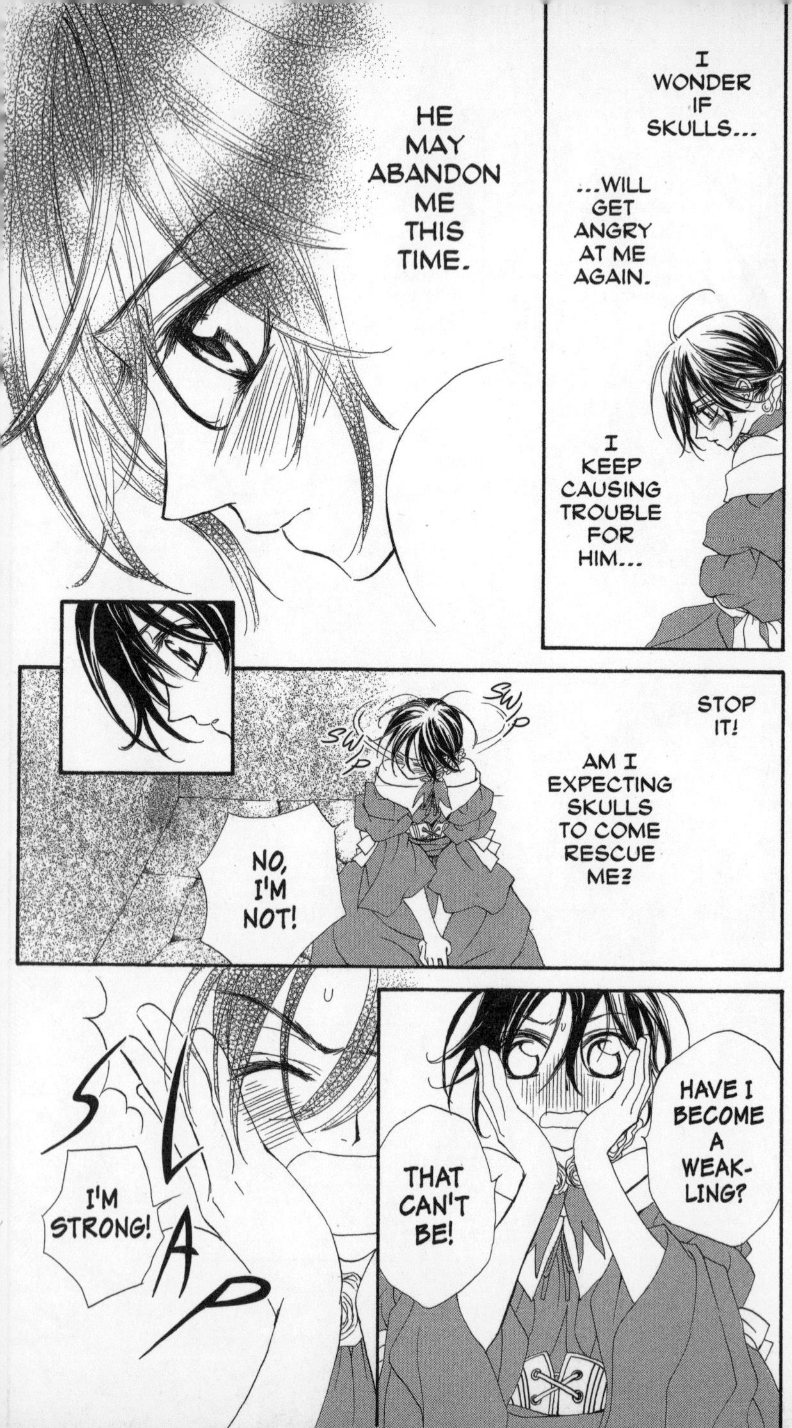
I WONDER IF SKULLS...
...WILL GET ANGRY AT ME AGAIN.
I KEEP CAUSING TROUBLE FOR HIM...
HE MAY ABANDON ME THIS TIME.
STOP IT!
AM I EXPECTING SKULLS TO COME RESCUE ME?
SWP
SWP
NO, I'M NOT!
HAVE I BECOME A WEAK-LING?
THAT CAN'T BE!
SLAP
I'M STRONG!

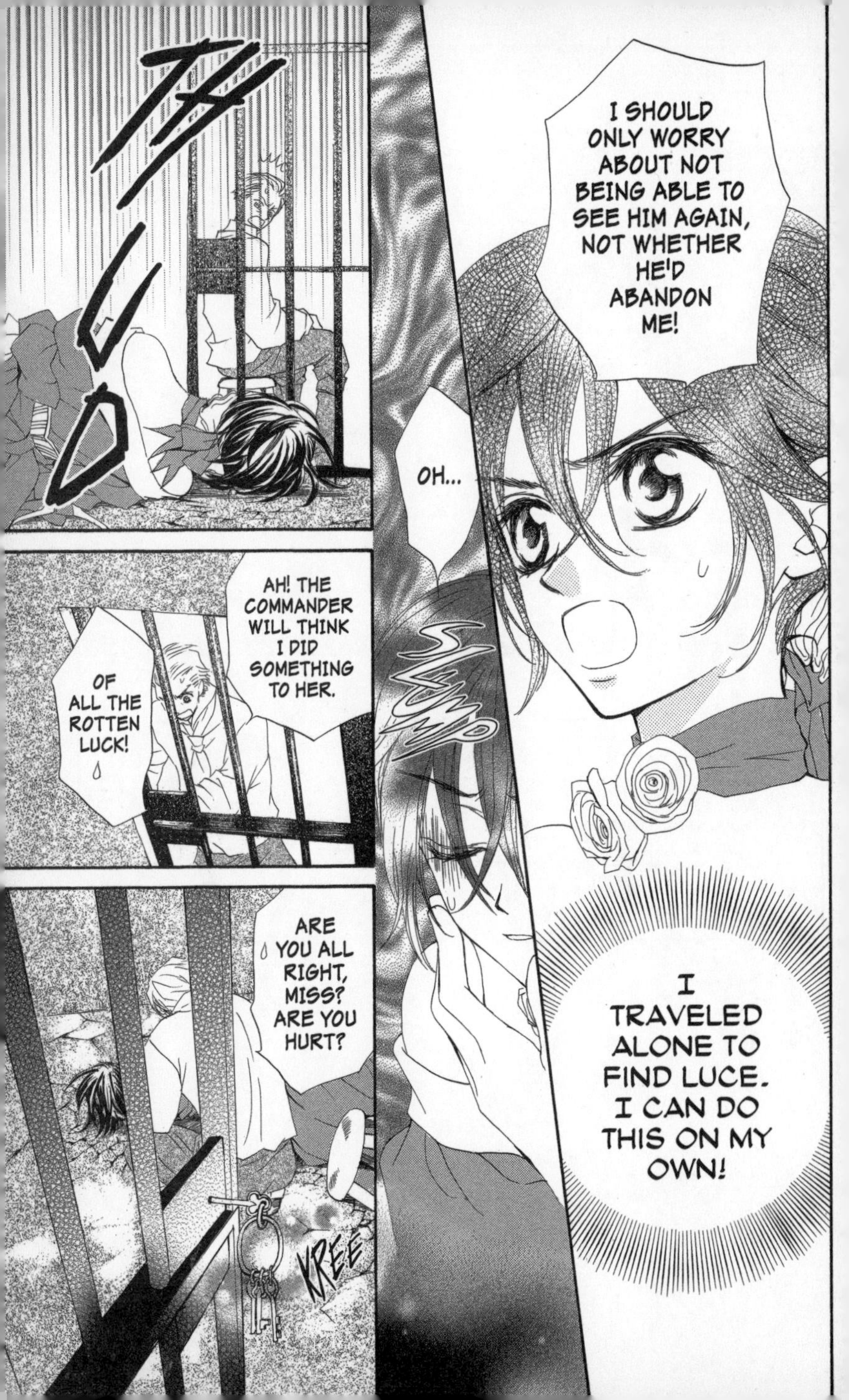
I SHOULD ONLY WORRY ABOUT NOT BEING ABLE TO SEE HIM AGAIN, NOT WHETHER HE'D ABANDON ME!
OH...
I TRAVELED ALONE TO FIND LUCE. I CAN DO THIS ON MY OWN!
THUD
AH! THE COMMANDER WILL THINK I DID SOMETHING TO HER.
OF ALL THE ROTTEN LUCK!
ARE YOU ALL RIGHT, MISS? ARE YOU HURT?
KREE

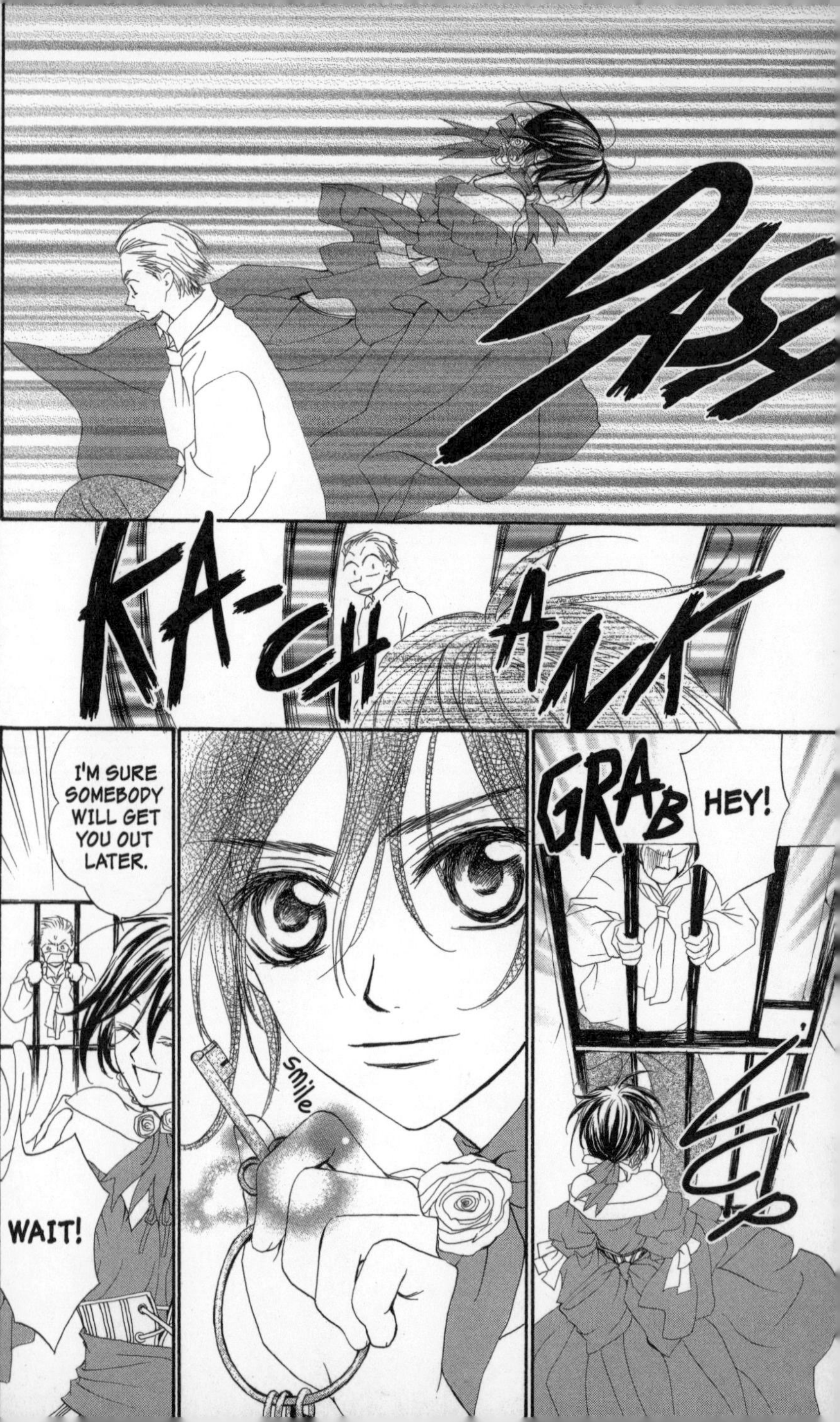
DASH
KA-CHANK
GRAB
HEY!
smile
I'M SURE SOMEBODY WILL GET YOU OUT LATER.
WAIT!

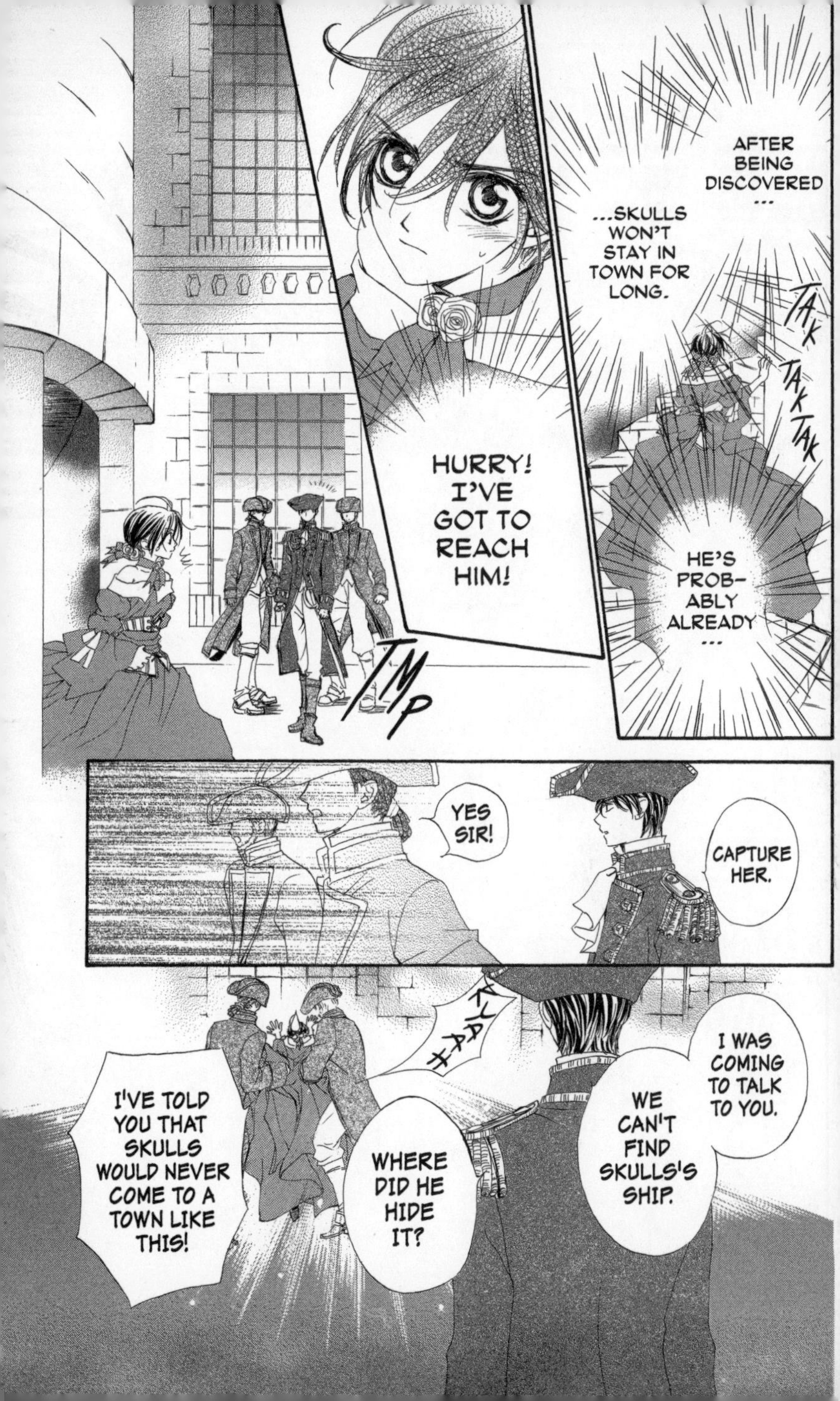
AFTER BEING DISCOVERED...
...SKULLS WON'T STAY IN TOWN FOR LONG.
TAK TAK TAK
HE'S PROB-ABLY ALREADY...
HURRY! I'VE GOT TO REACH HIM!
TMP
CAPTURE HER.
YES SIR!
I WAS COMING TO TALK TO YOU.
WE CAN'T FIND SKULLS'S SHIP.
KYAAH
WHERE DID HE HIDE IT?
I'VE TOLD YOU THAT SKULLS WOULD NEVER COME TO A TOWN LIKE THIS!

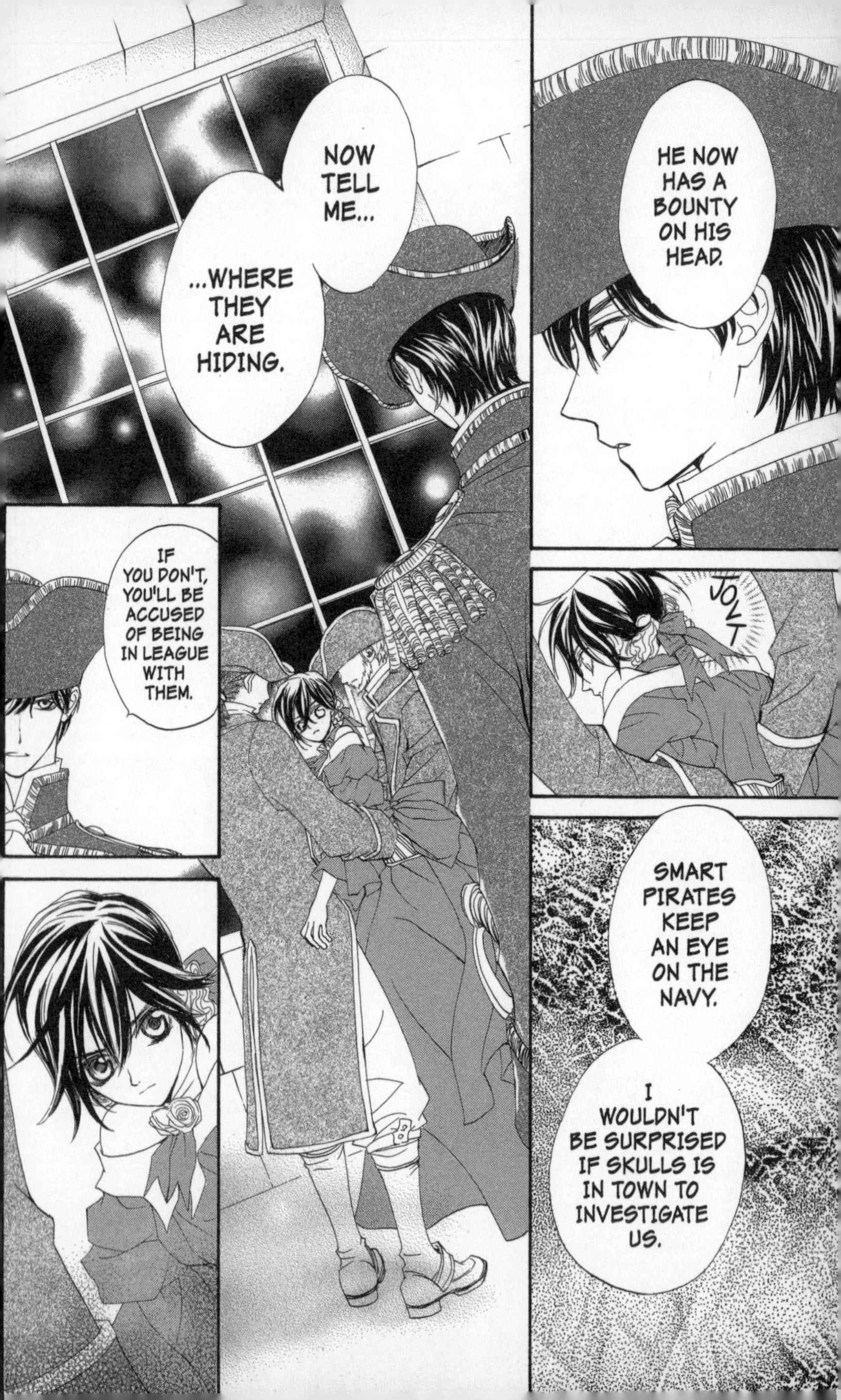
HE NOW HAS A BOUNTY ON HIS HEAD.
NOW TELL ME...
...WHERE THEY ARE HIDING.
IF YOU DON'T, YOU'LL BE ACCUSED OF BEING IN LEAGUE WITH THEM.
JOLT
SMART PIRATES KEEP AN EYE ON THE NAVY.
I WOULDN'T BE SURPRISED IF SKULLS IS IN TOWN TO INVESTIGATE US.

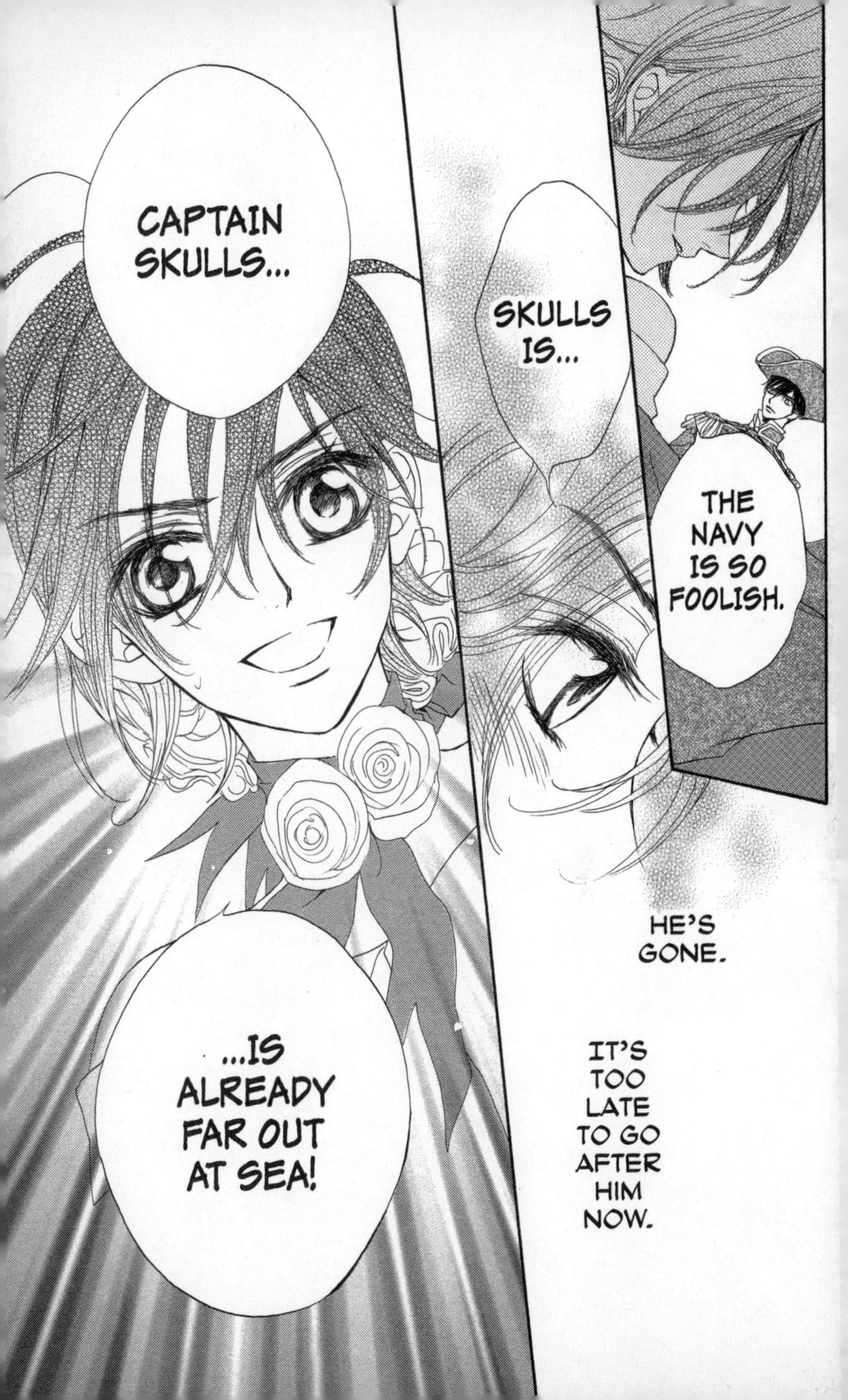
THE NAVY IS SO FOOLISH.
SKULLS IS...
HE'S GONE.
IT'S TOO LATE TO GO AFTER HIM NOW.
CAPTAIN SKULLS...
...IS ALREADY FAR OUT AT SEA!

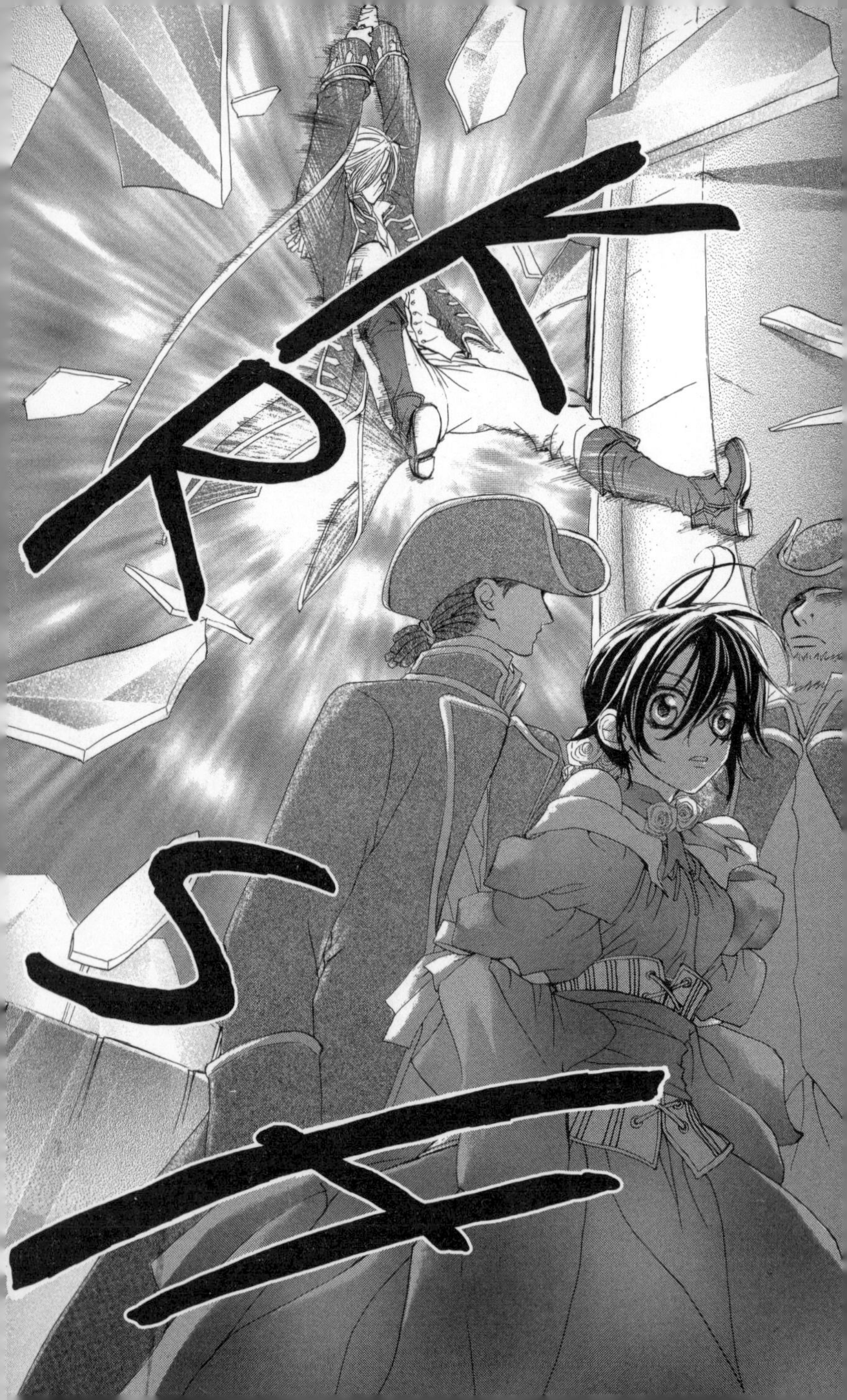
KRSH

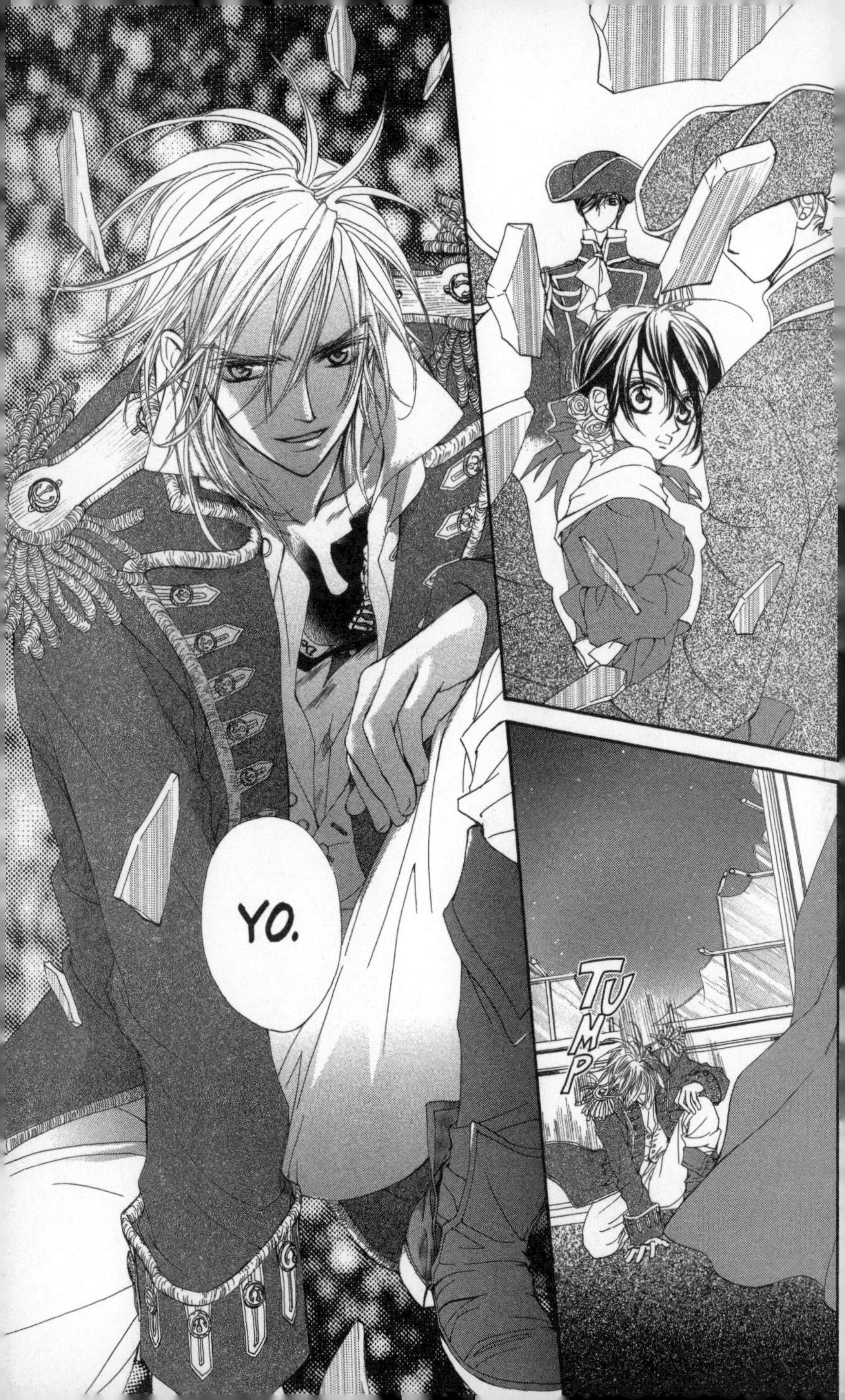
YO.
TUMP

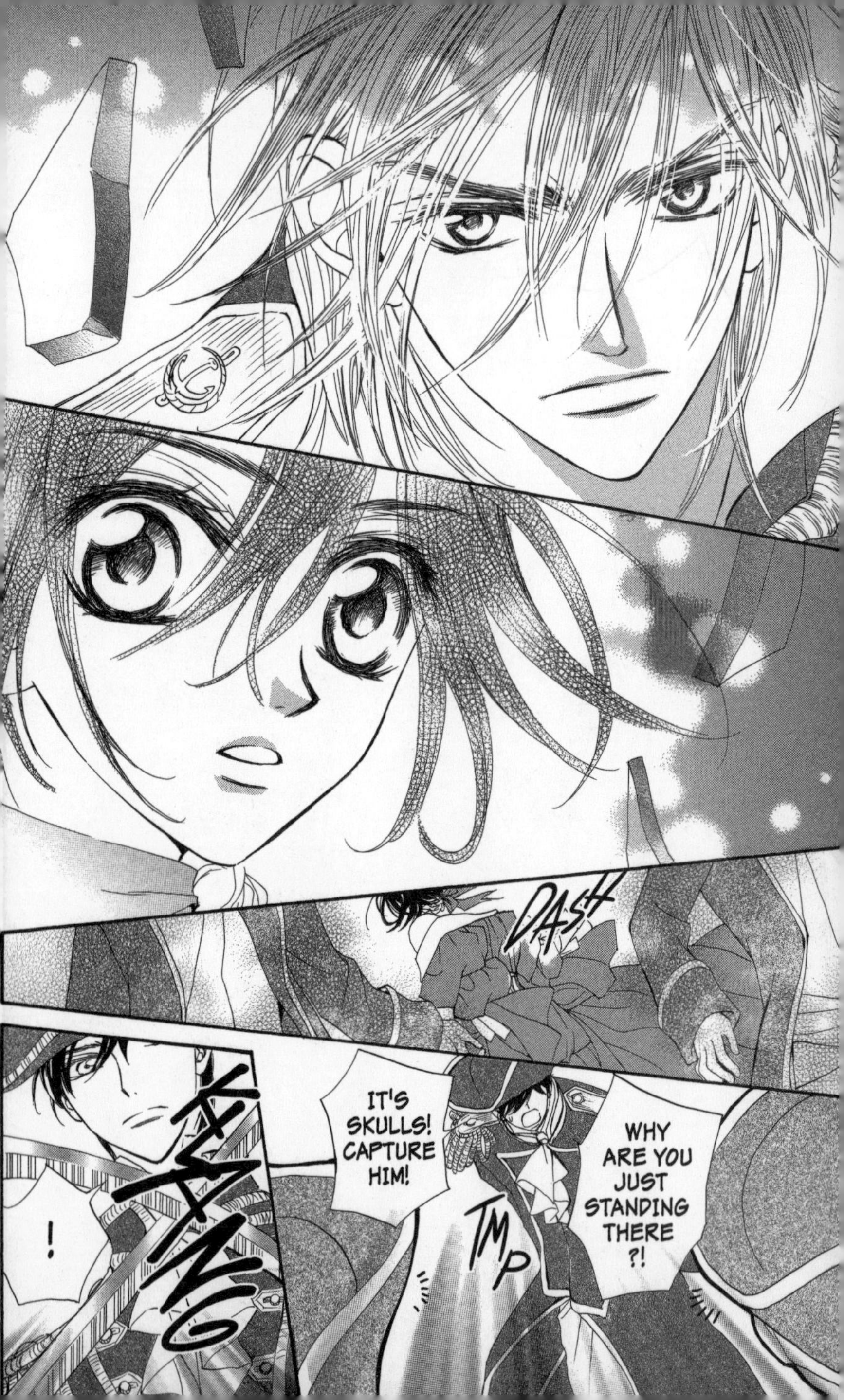
DASH
WHY ARE YOU JUST STANDING THERE ?!
TMP
IT'S SKULLS! CAPTURE HIM!
!

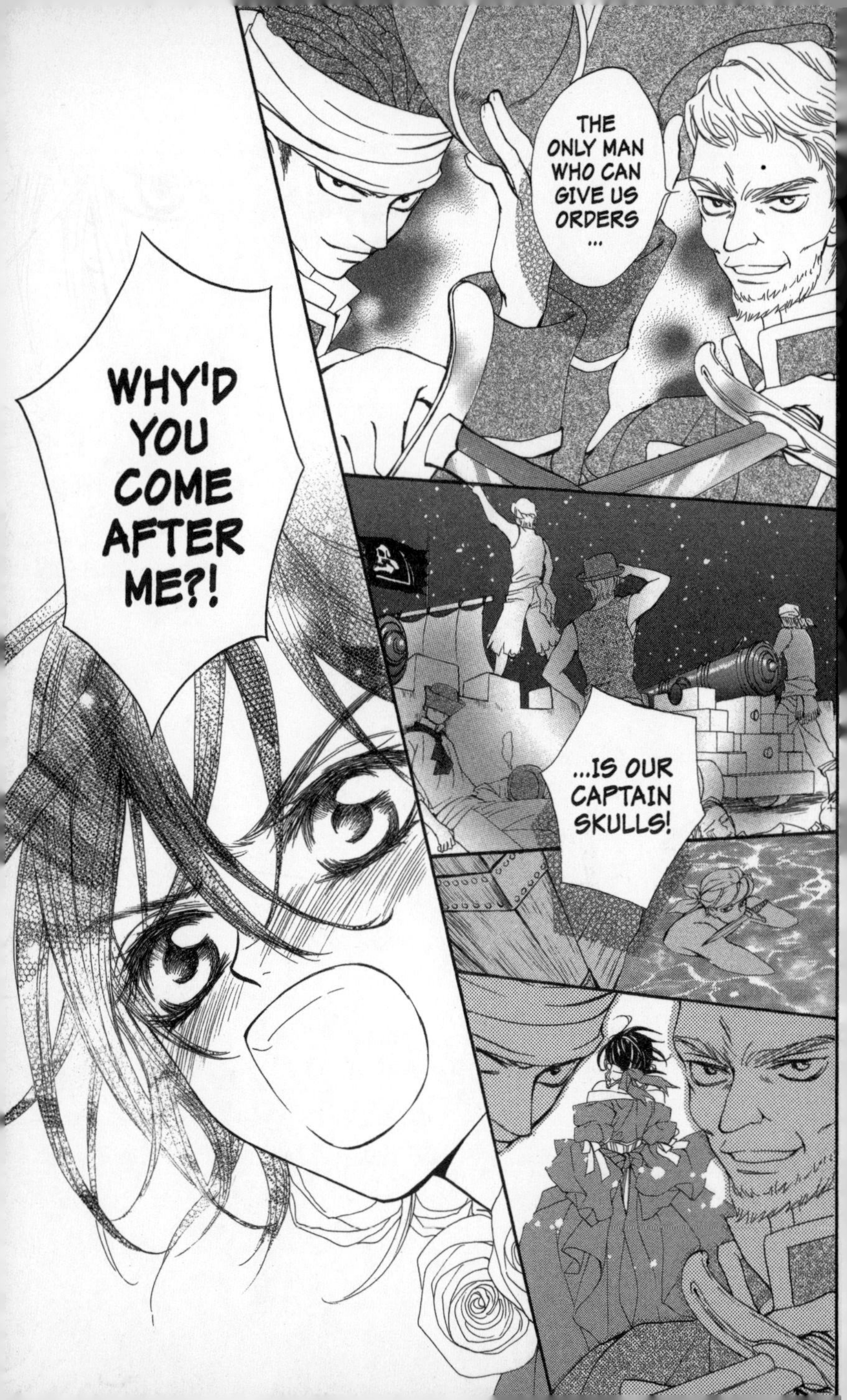
THE ONLY MAN WHO CAN GIVE US ORDERS ...
...IS OUR CAPTAIN SKULLS!
WHY'D YOU COME AFTER ME?!

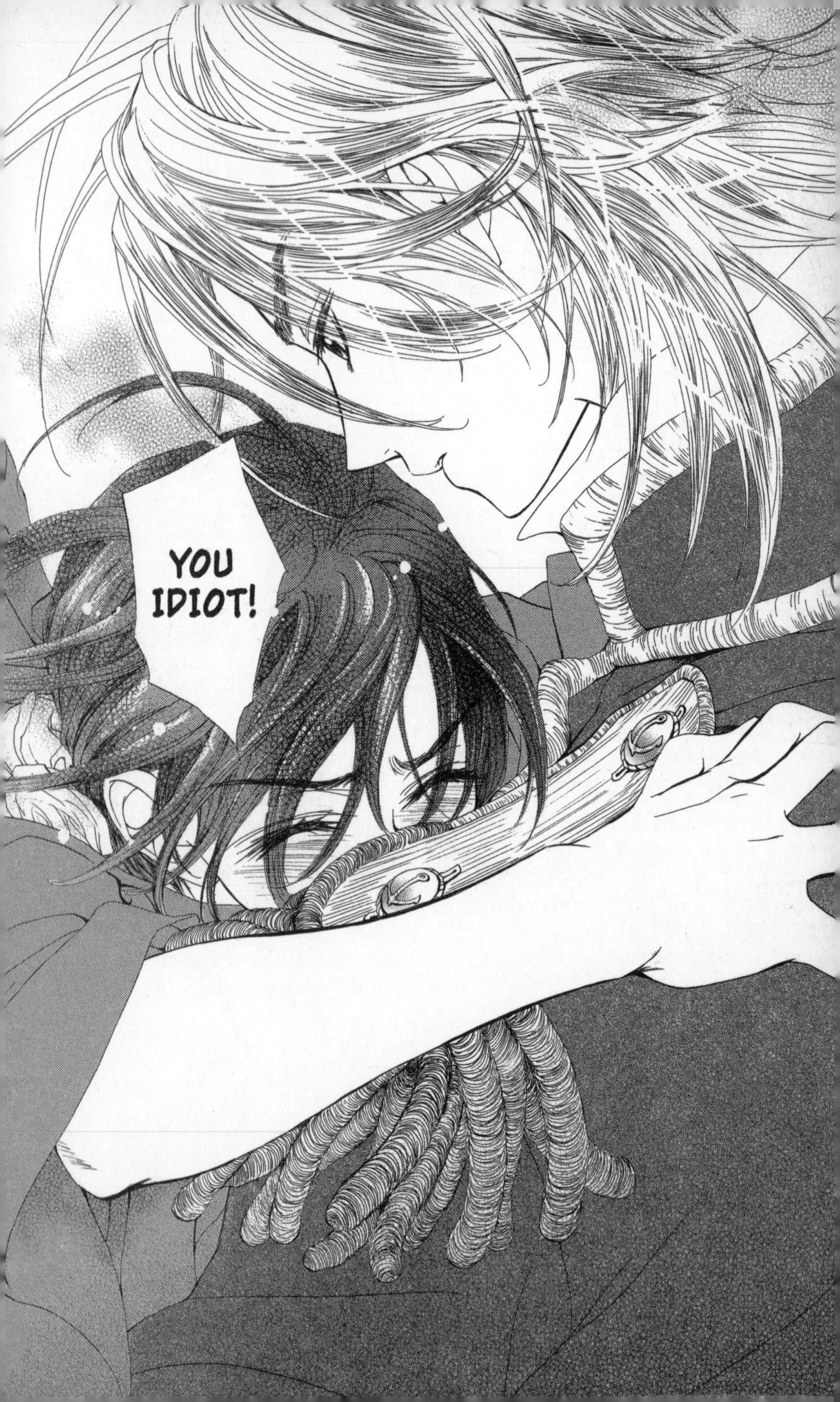
YOU IDIOT!

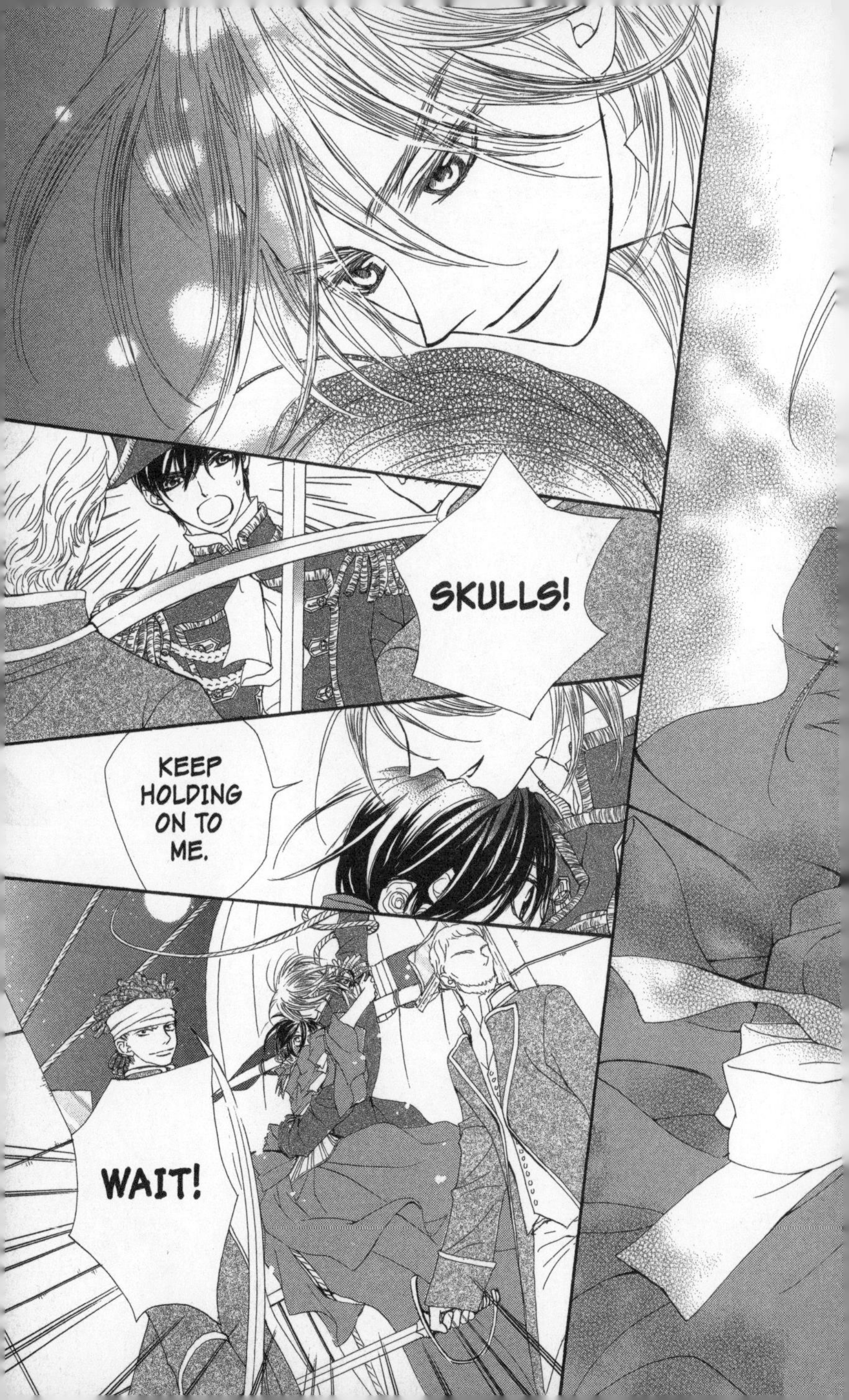
SKULLS!
KEEP HOLDING ON TO ME.
WAIT!

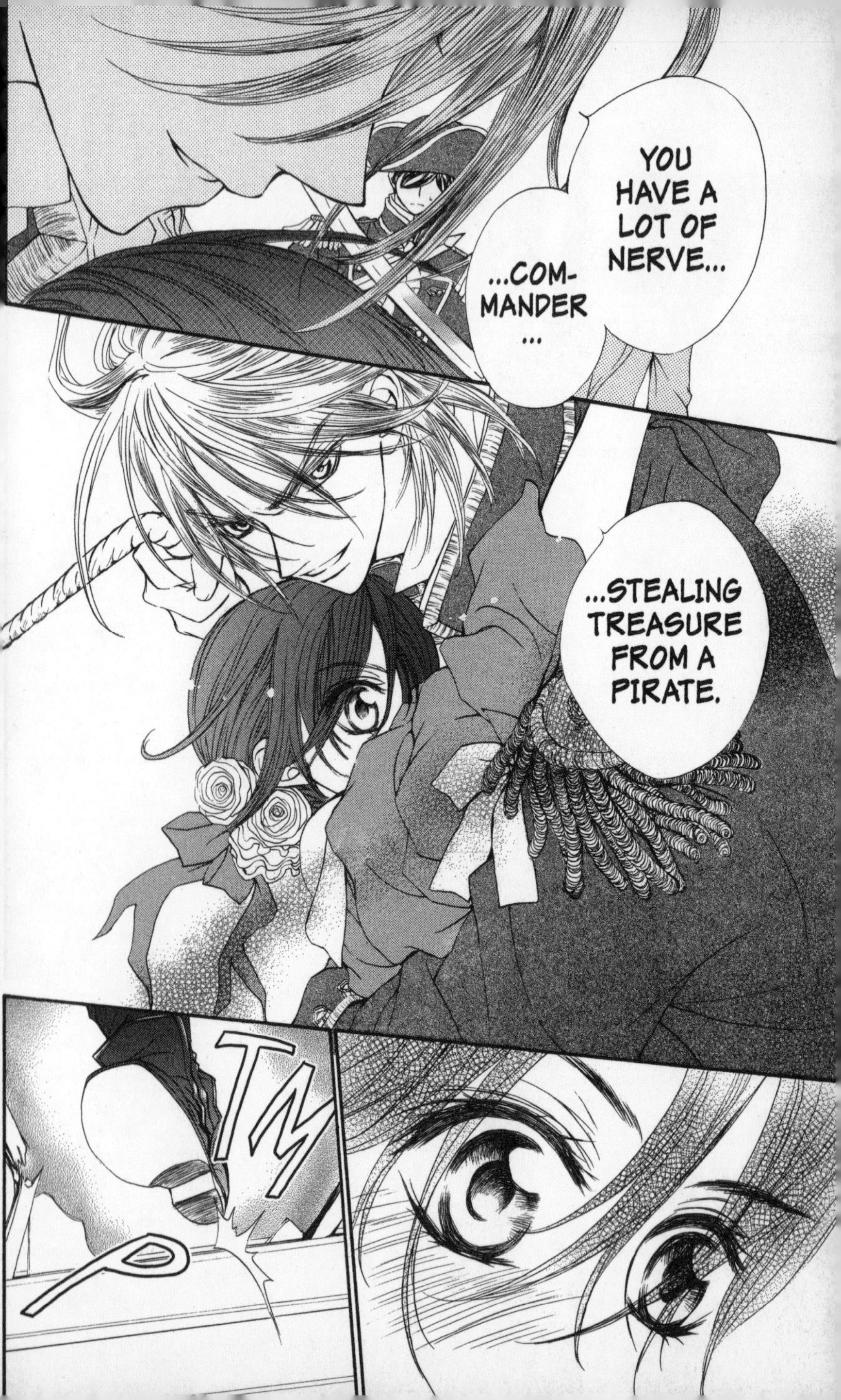
YOU HAVE A LOT OF NERVE...
...COM-MANDER...
...STEALING TREASURE FROM A PIRATE.
TMP

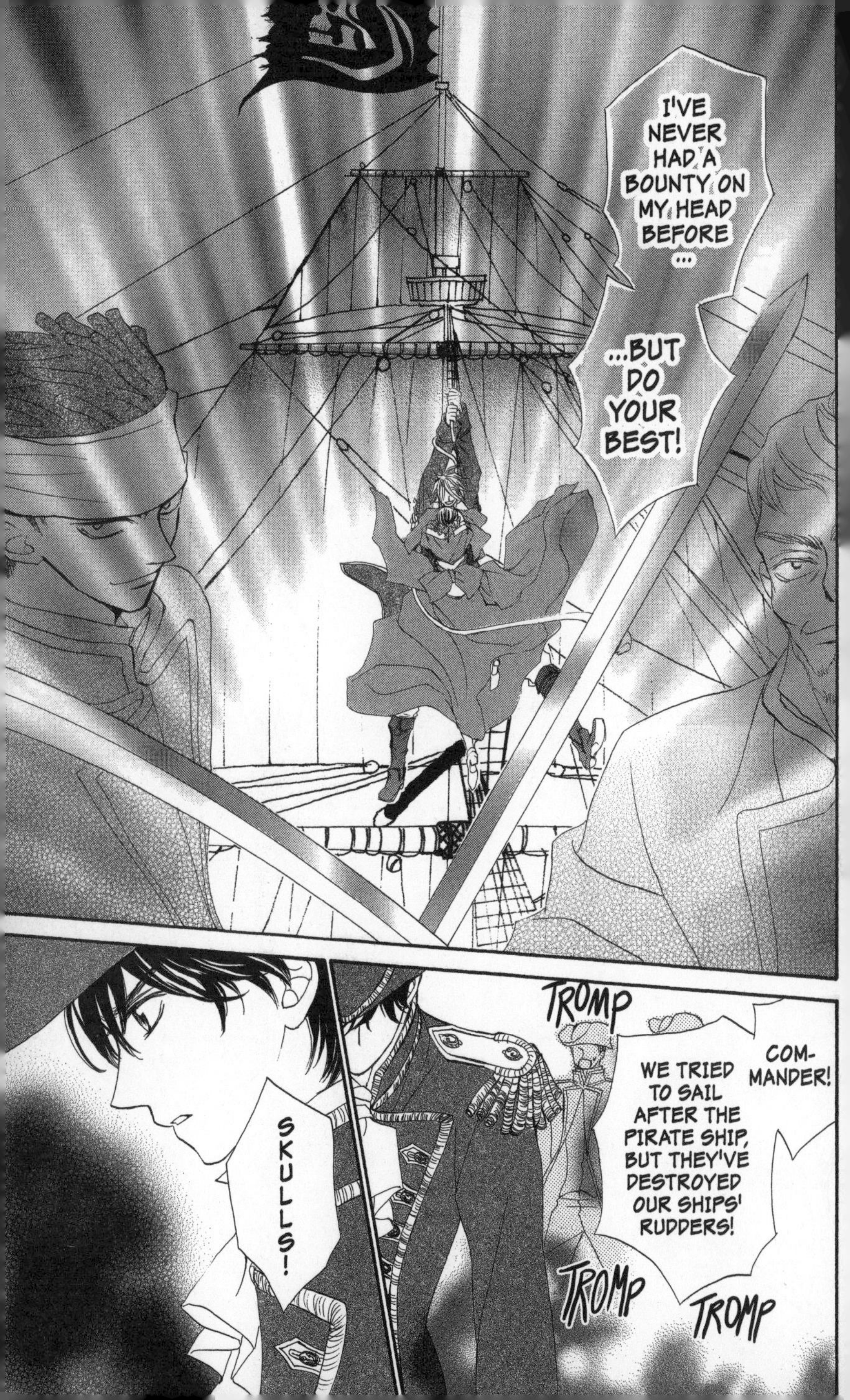
I'VE NEVER HAD A BOUNTY ON MY HEAD BEFORE ...
...BUT DO YOUR BEST!
TROMP
COM-MANDER!
WE TRIED TO SAIL AFTER THE PIRATE SHIP, BUT THEY'VE DESTROYED OUR SHIPS' RUDDERS!
TROMP
TROMP
SKULLS!

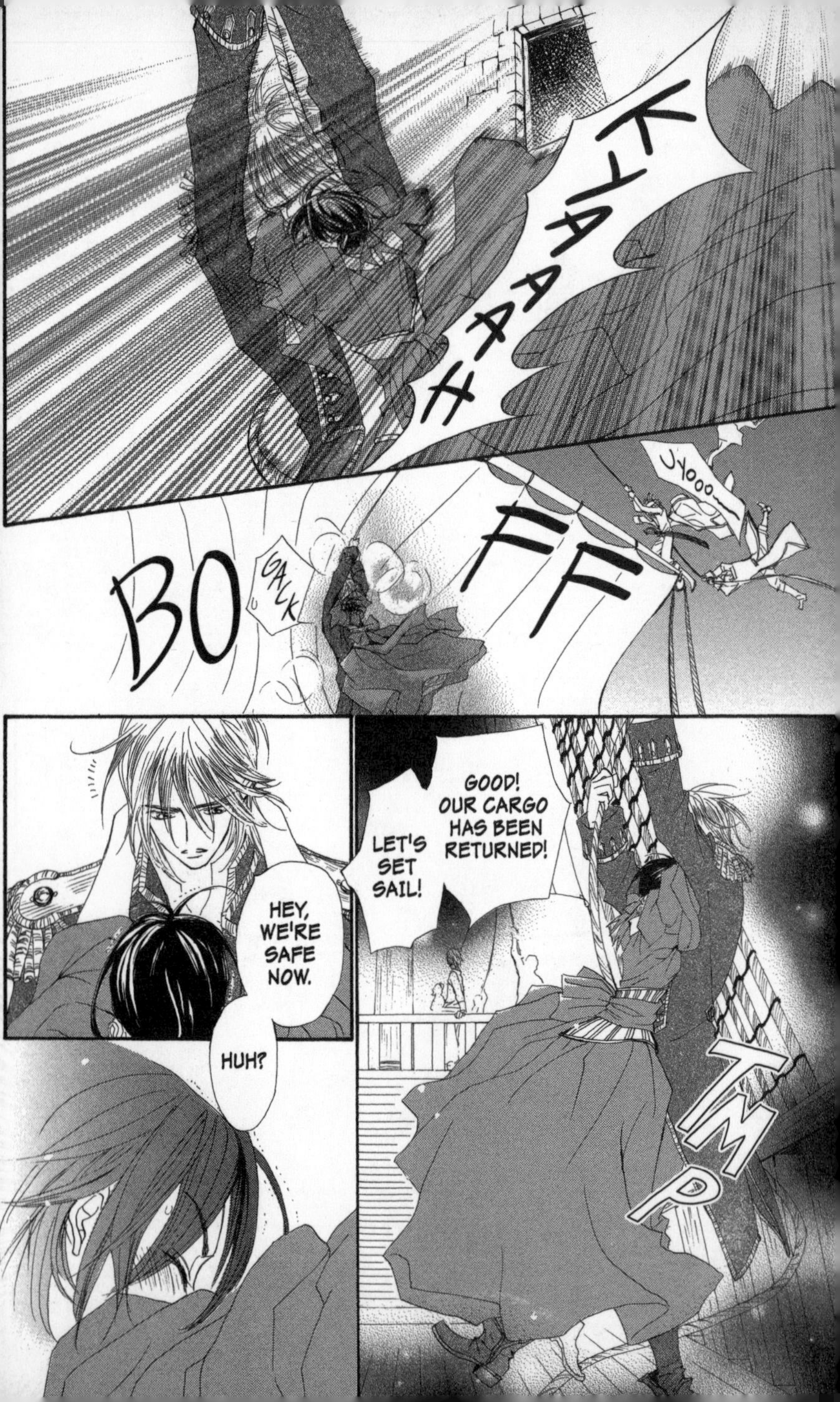
KYAAAH
JYOOO~
BOFF
GACK
GOOD! OUR CARGO HAS BEEN RETURNED!
LET'S SET SAIL!
TMP
HEY, WE'RE SAFE NOW.
HUH?

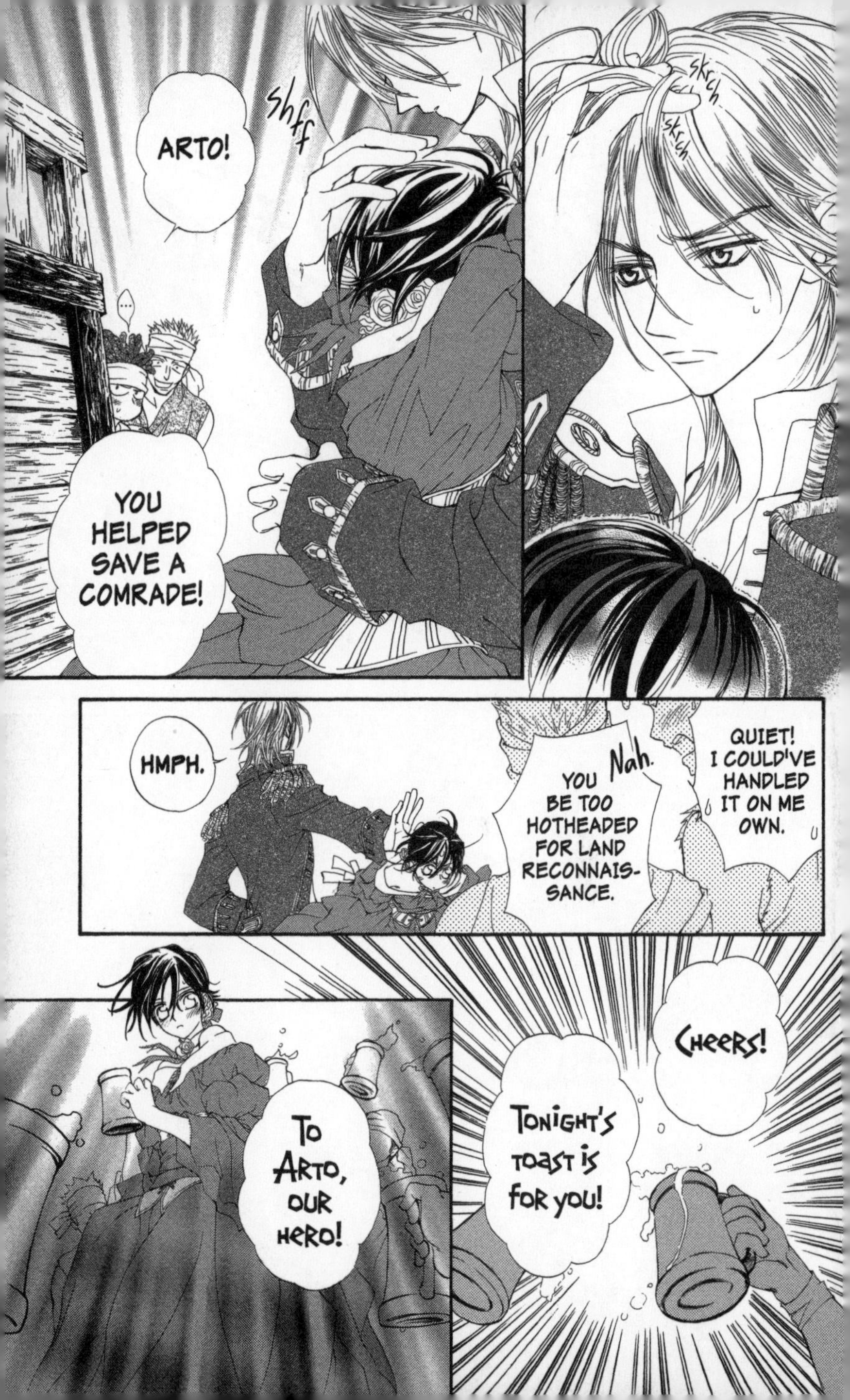
skrch
skrch
shff
ARTO!
...
YOU HELPED SAVE A COMRADE!
QUIET! I COULD'VE HANDLED IT ON ME OWN.
Nah.
YOU BE TOO HOTHEADED FOR LAND RECONNAIS-SANCE.
HMPH.
Cheers!
Tonight's toast is for you!
To Arto, our hero!

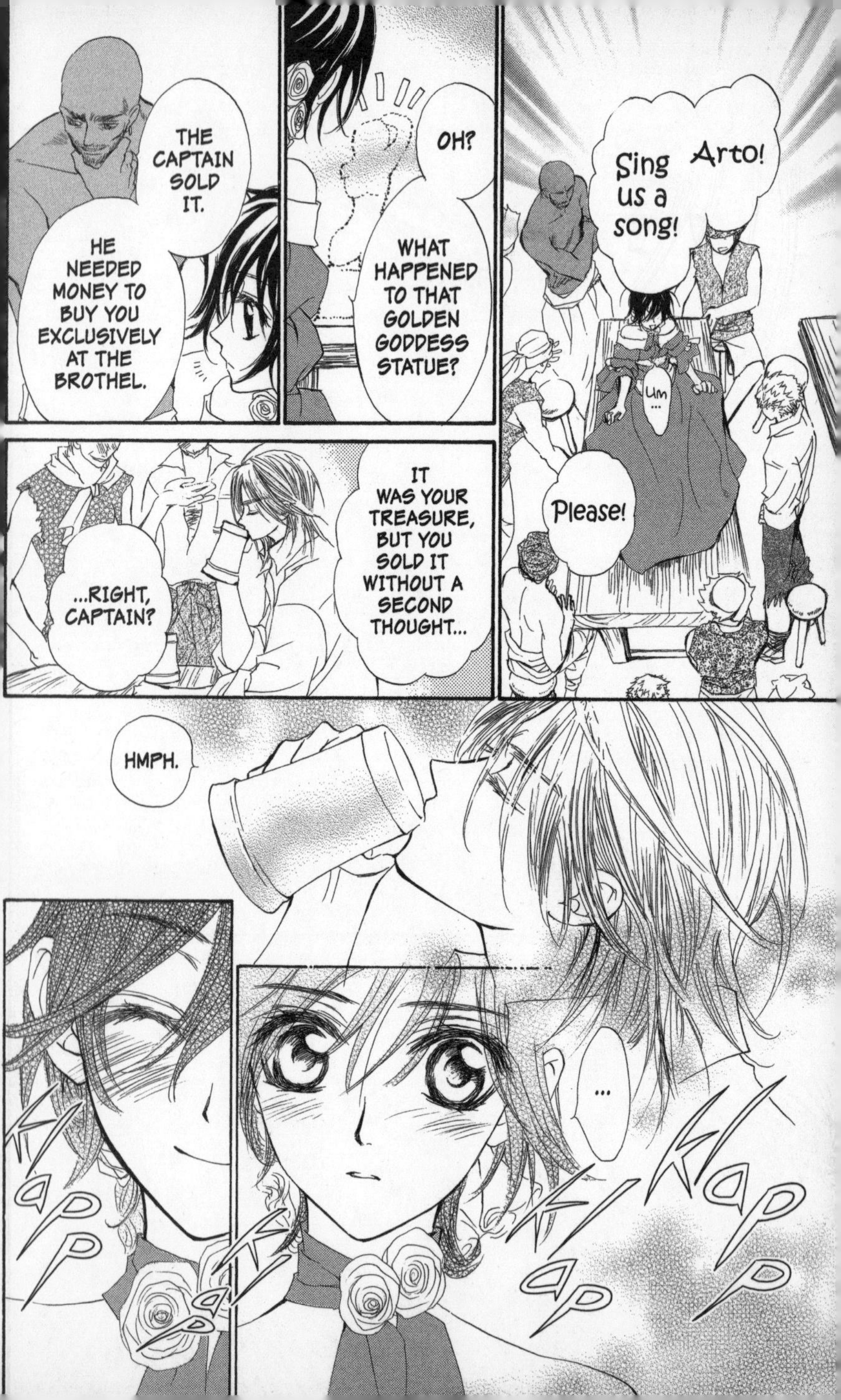
Arto!
Sing us a song!
Um...
Please!
OH?
WHAT HAPPENED TO THAT GOLDEN GODDESS STATUE?
THE CAPTAIN SOLD IT.
HE NEEDED MONEY TO BUY YOU EXCLUSIVELY AT THE BROTHEL.
IT WAS YOUR TREASURE, BUT YOU SOLD IT WITHOUT A SECOND THOUGHT...
...RIGHT, CAPTAIN?
HMPH.
...
Klap klap
klap klap
klap klap
pap pap

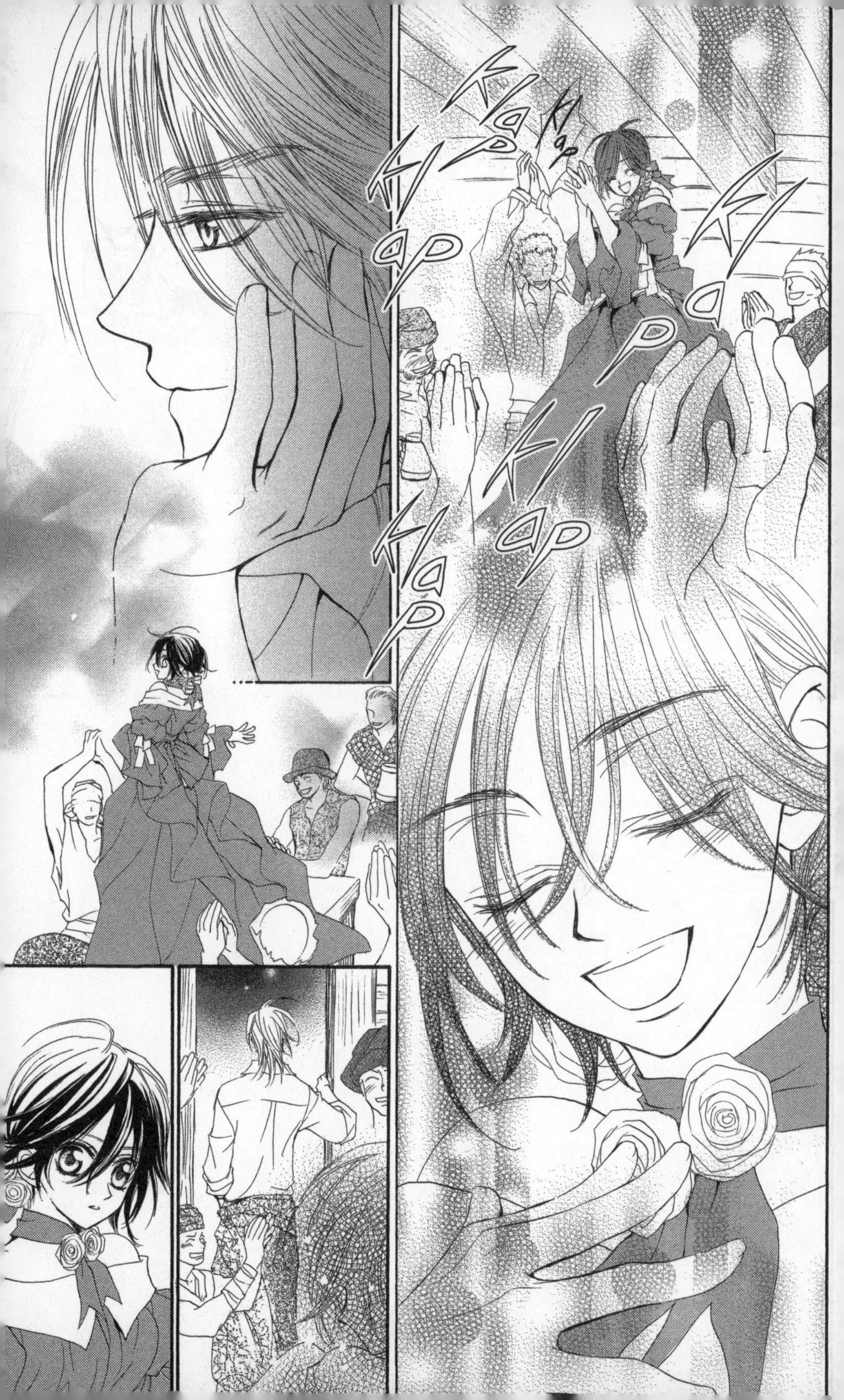

Klap
Klap
Klap
Klap
Klap
Klap
...

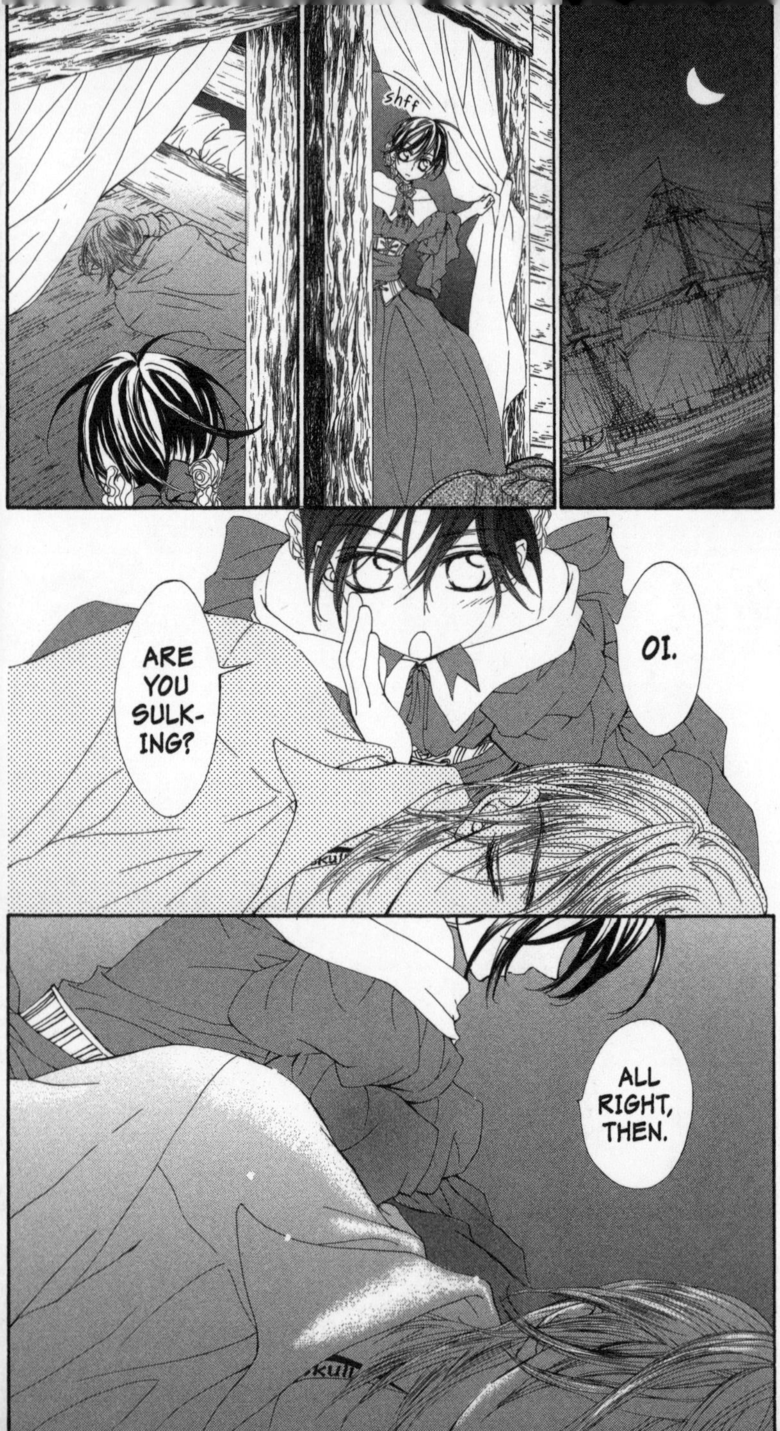
shff
OI.
ARE YOU SULK-ING?
ALL RIGHT, THEN.

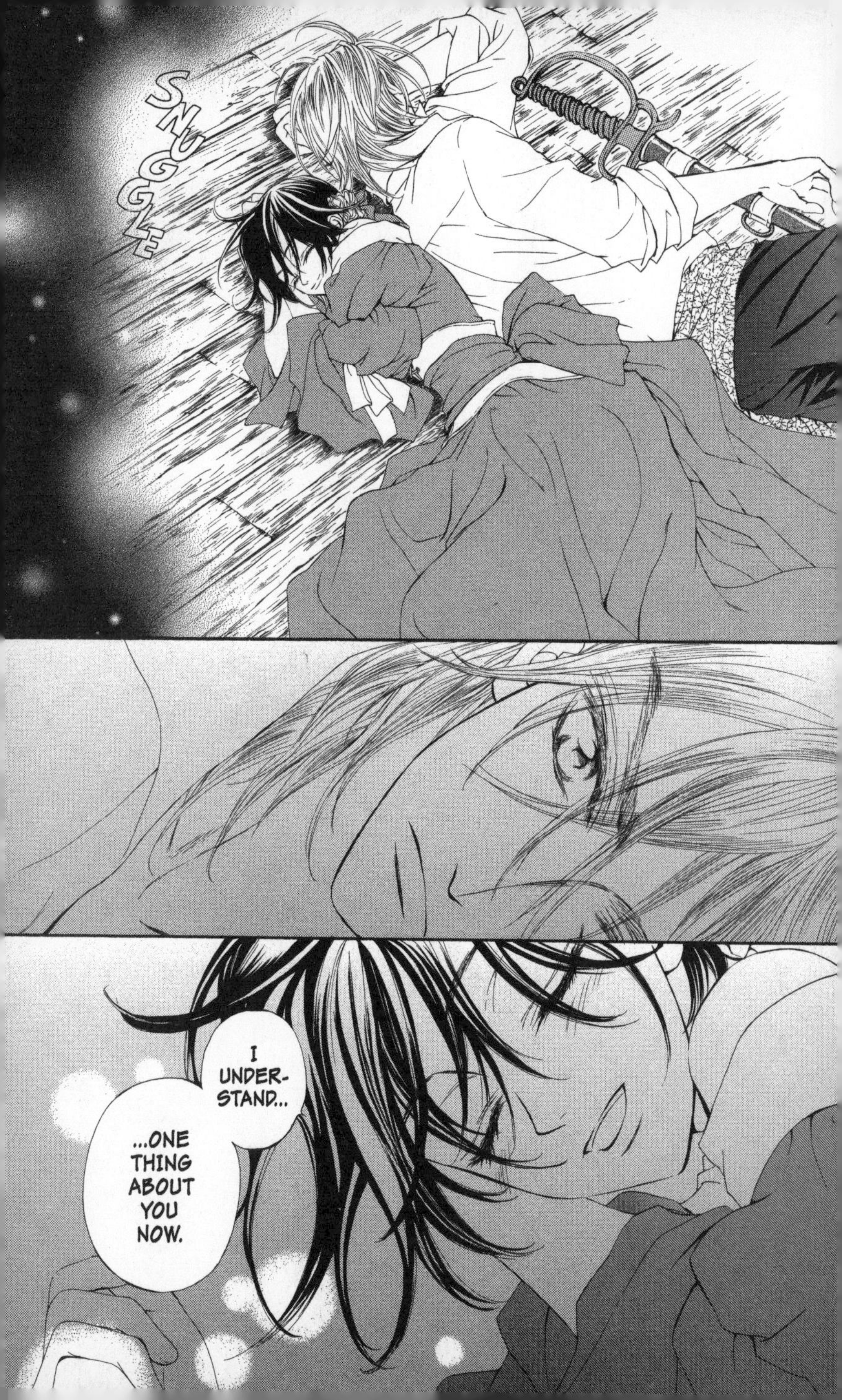
SNUGGLE
I UNDER-STAND...
...ONE THING ABOUT YOU NOW.

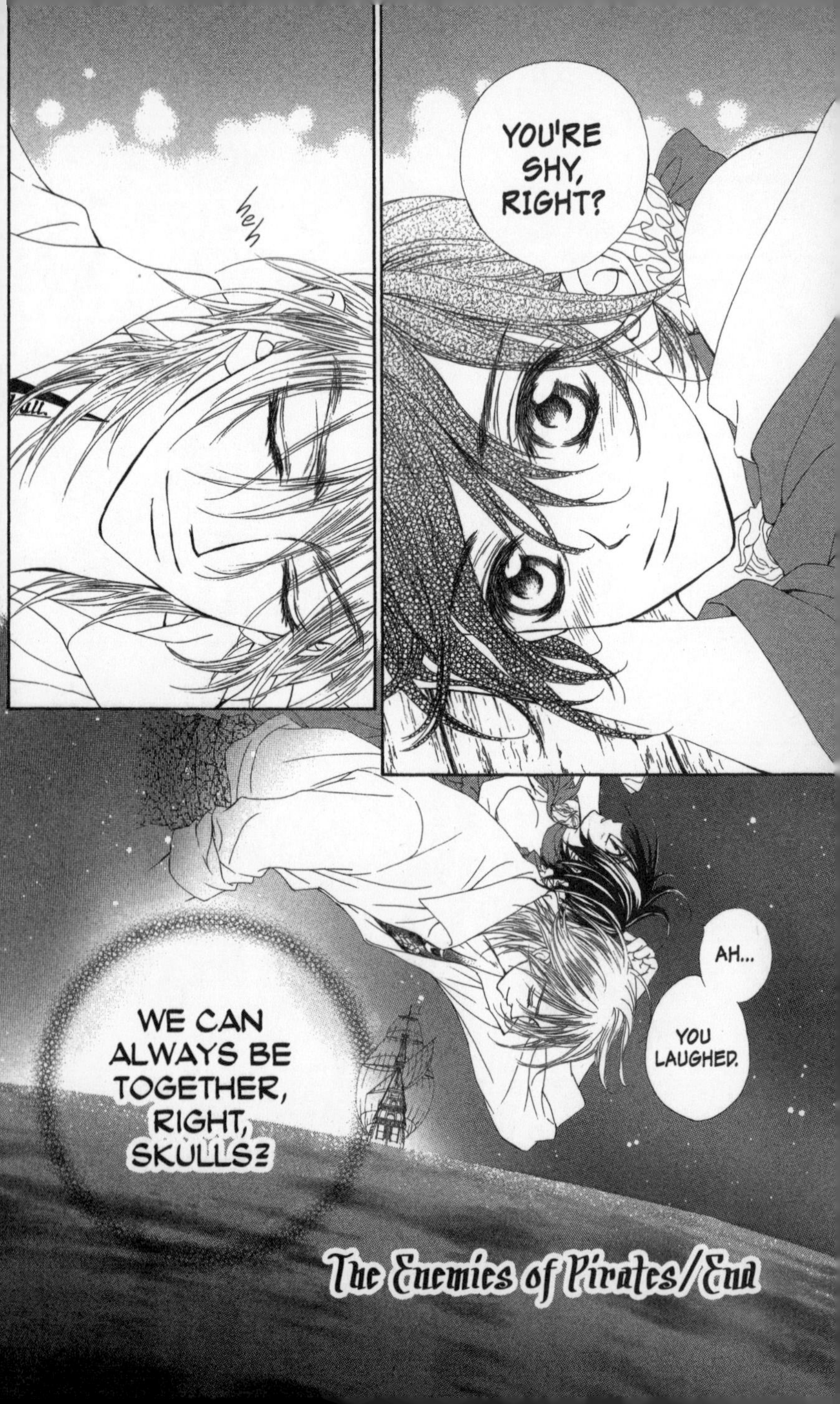
YOU'RE SHY, RIGHT?
heh
AH...
YOU LAUGHED.
WE CAN ALWAYS BE TOGETHER, RIGHT, SKULLS?
The Enemies of Pirates/End

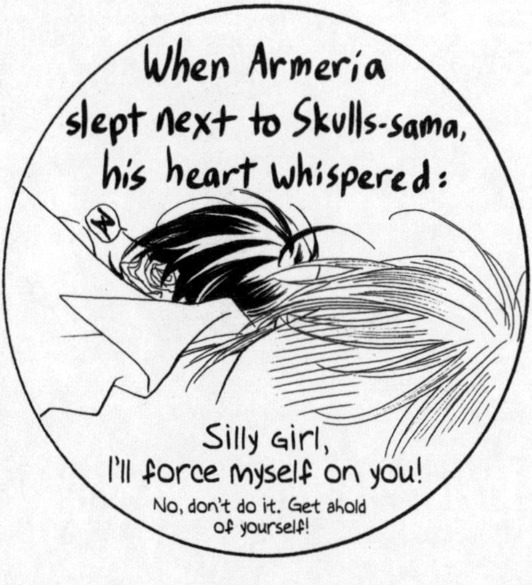
When Armeria slept next to Skulls-sama, his heart whispered:
Silly Girl, I'll force myself on you!
No, don't do it. Get ahold of yourself!

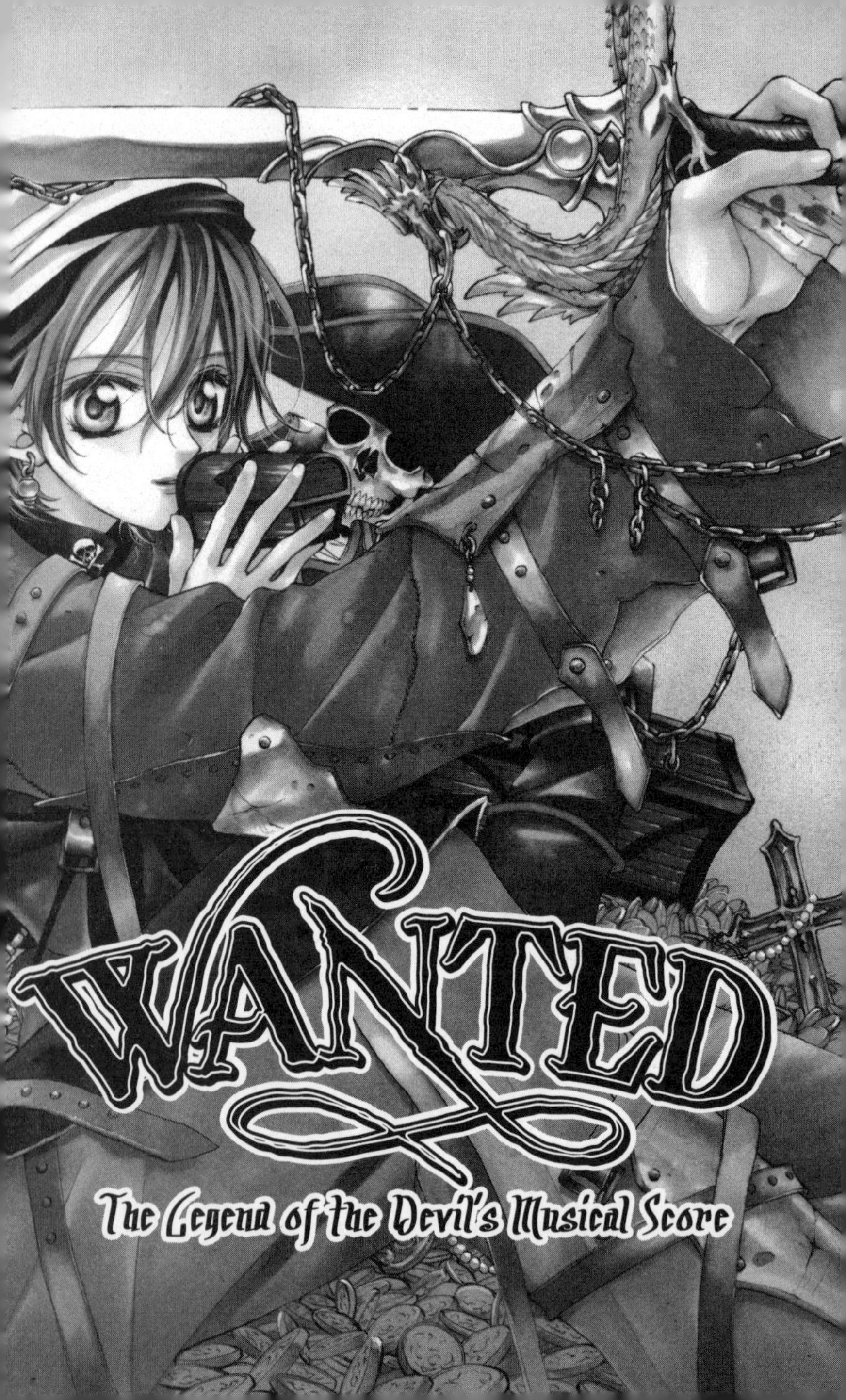
WANTED
The Legend of the Devil's Musical Score

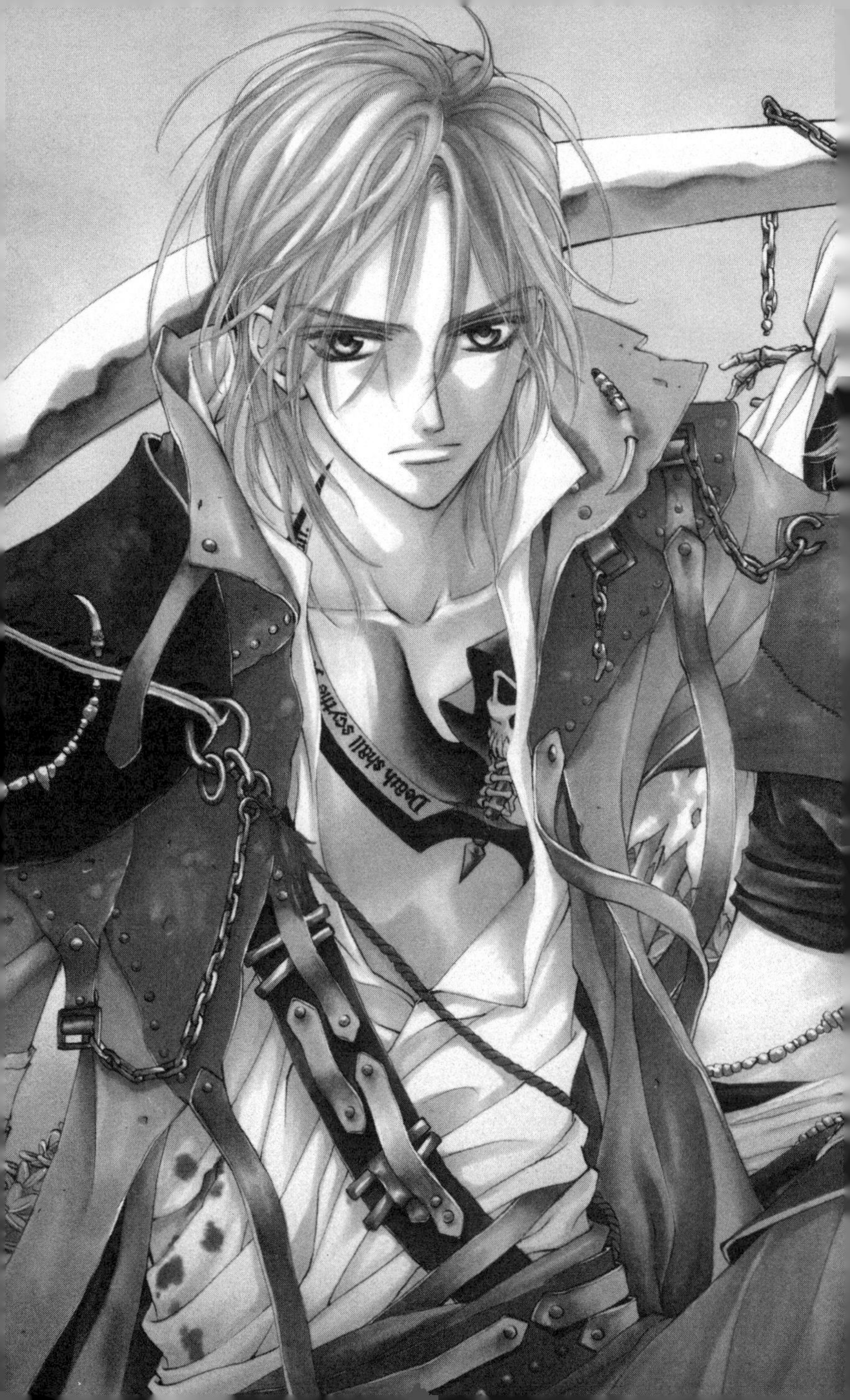
Death shall scythe

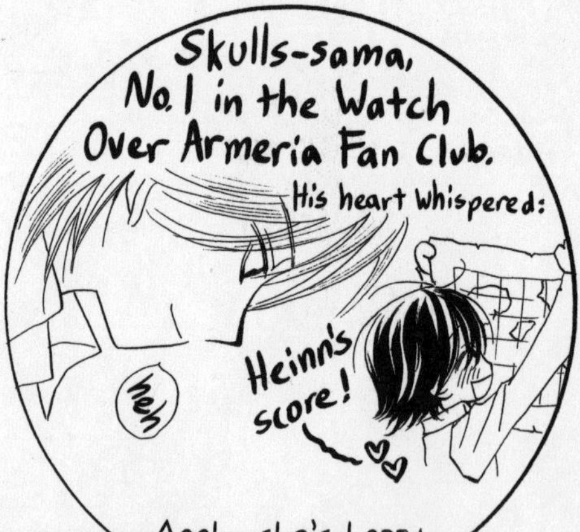
Skulls-sama, No. 1 in the Watch Over Armeria Fan Club.
His heart whispered:
Heinn's score!
heh
Aaah...she's happy.

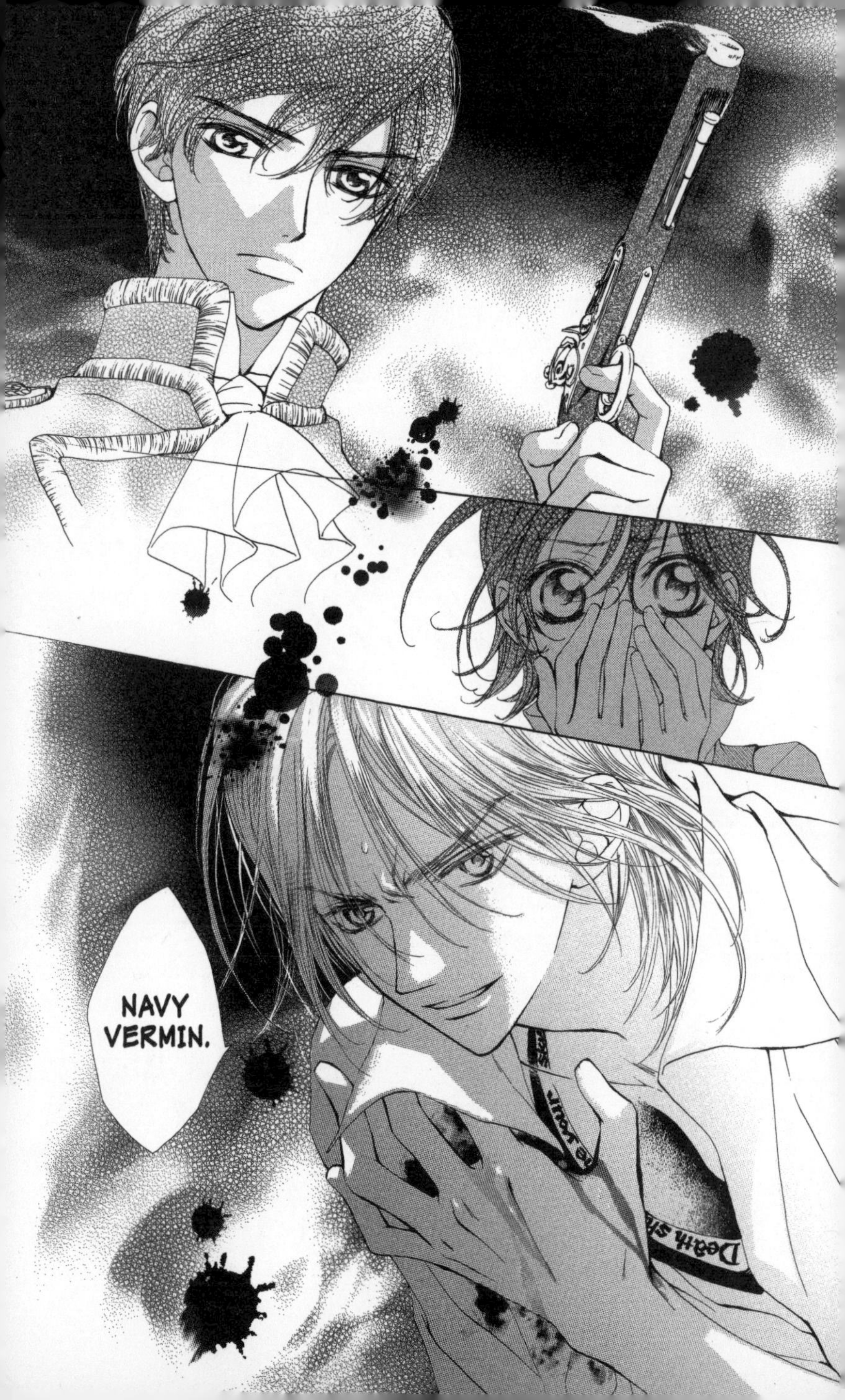
NAVY VERMIN.

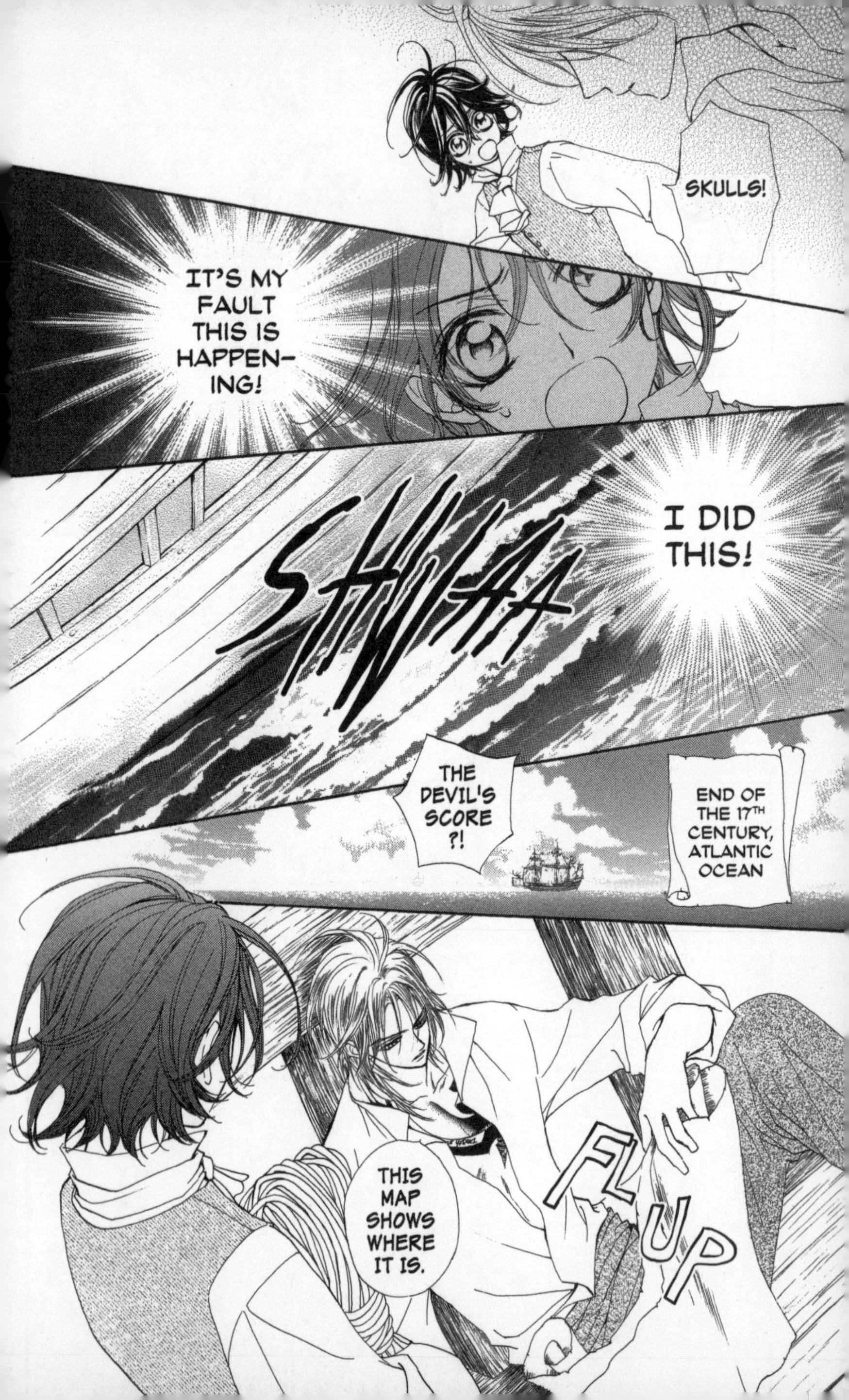
SKULLS!
IT'S MY FAULT THIS IS HAPPENING!
I DID THIS!
SHWAA
END OF THE 17TH CENTURY, ATLANTIC OCEAN
THE DEVIL'S SCORE?!
FLUP
THIS MAP SHOWS WHERE IT IS.

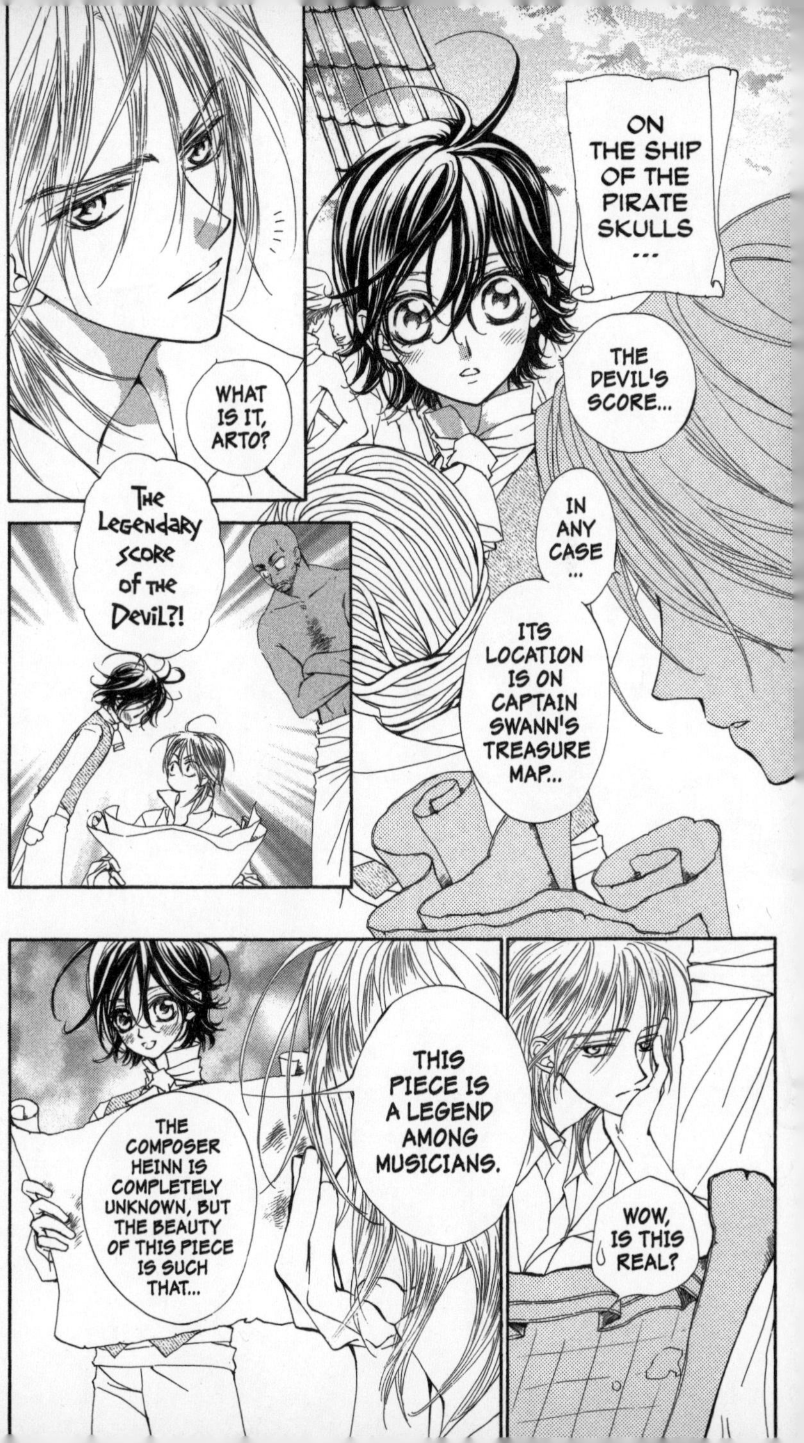
ON THE SHIP OF THE PIRATE SKULLS...
THE DEVIL'S SCORE...
IN ANY CASE...
ITS LOCATION IS ON CAPTAIN SWANN'S TREASURE MAP...
WHAT IS IT, ARTO?
The Legendary score of the Devil?!
WOW, IS THIS REAL?
THIS PIECE IS A LEGEND AMONG MUSICIANS.
THE COMPOSER HEINN IS COMPLETELY UNKNOWN, BUT THE BEAUTY OF THIS PIECE IS SUCH THAT...

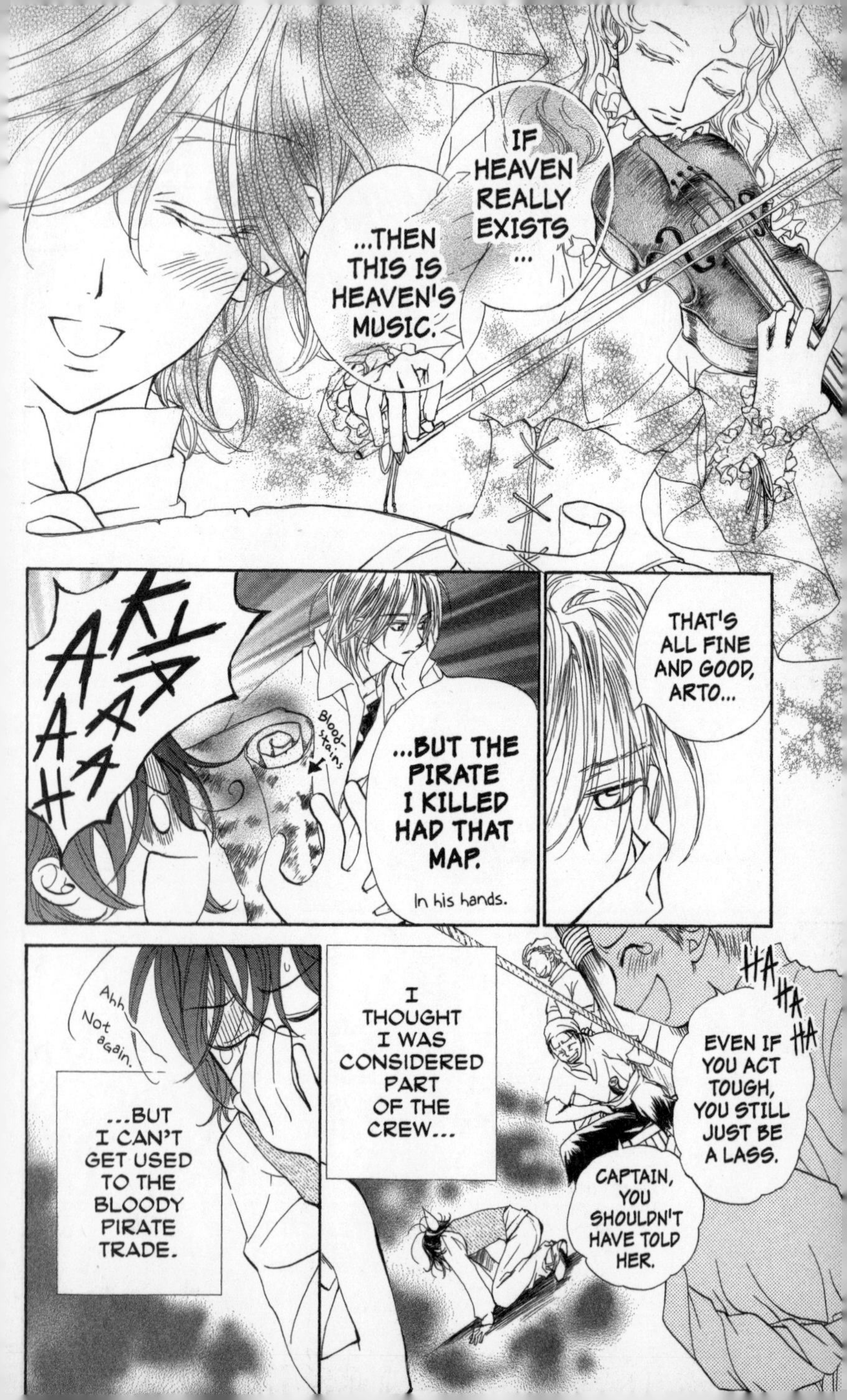
IF HEAVEN REALLY EXISTS...
...THEN THIS IS HEAVEN'S MUSIC.
THAT'S ALL FINE AND GOOD, ARTO...
...BUT THE PIRATE I KILLED HAD THAT MAP.
In his hands.
Blood-stains
KYAAAAAH
HA HA HA
EVEN IF YOU ACT TOUGH, YOU STILL JUST BE A LASS.
CAPTAIN, YOU SHOULDN'T HAVE TOLD HER.
I THOUGHT I WAS CONSIDERED PART OF THE CREW...
Ahh Not again.
...BUT I CAN'T GET USED TO THE BLOODY PIRATE TRADE.

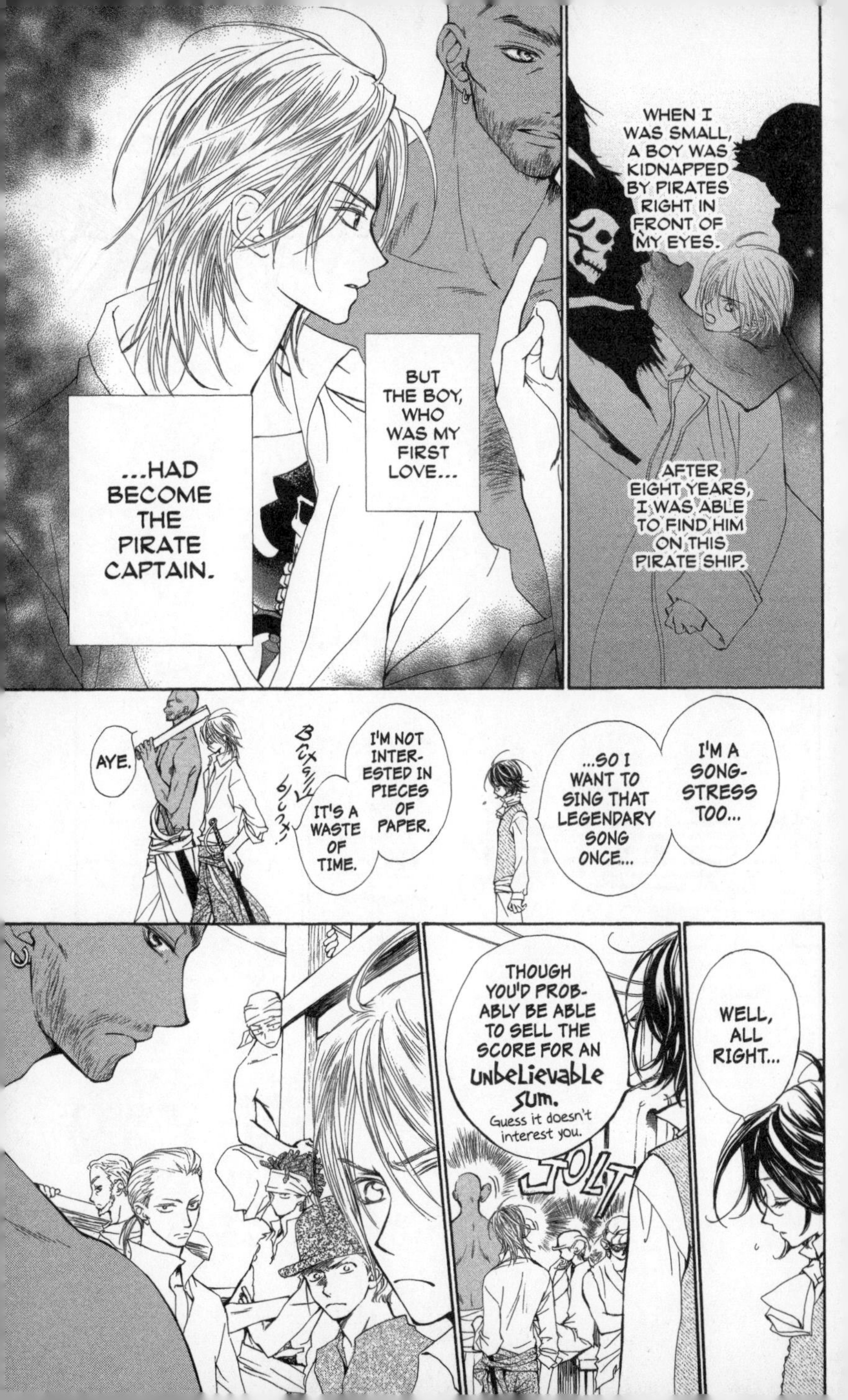
WHEN I WAS SMALL, A BOY WAS KIDNAPPED BY PIRATES RIGHT IN FRONT OF MY EYES.
AFTER EIGHT YEARS, I WAS ABLE TO FIND HIM ON THIS PIRATE SHIP.
BUT THE BOY, WHO WAS MY FIRST LOVE...
...HAD BECOME THE PIRATE CAPTAIN.
I'M A SONG-STRESS TOO...
...SO I WANT TO SING THAT LEGENDARY SONG ONCE...
I'M NOT INTER-ESTED IN PIECES OF PAPER.
IT'S A WASTE OF TIME.
AYE.
WELL, ALL RIGHT...
THOUGH YOU'D PROB-ABLY BE ABLE TO SELL THE SCORE FOR AN UNBELIEVABLE SUM.
Guess it doesn't interest you.
JOLT

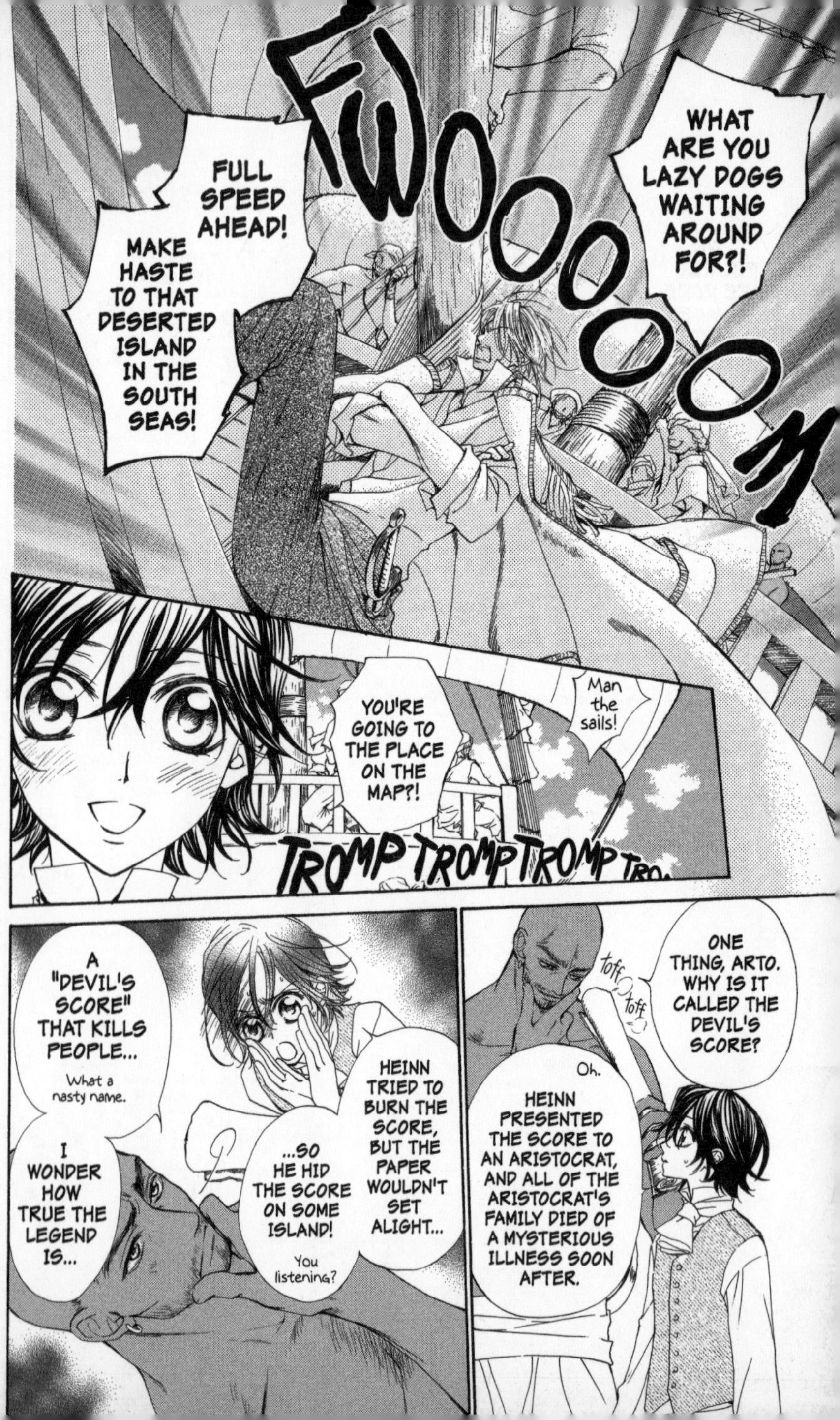
WHAT ARE YOU LAZY DOGS WAITING AROUND FOR?!
FWOOOOOOOM
FULL SPEED AHEAD!
MAKE HASTE TO THAT DESERTED ISLAND IN THE SOUTH SEAS!
Man the sails!
YOU'RE GOING TO THE PLACE ON THE MAP?!
TROMP TROMP TROMP TRO...
ONE THING, ARTO. WHY IS IT CALLED THE DEVIL'S SCORE?
toff toff
Oh.
HEINN PRESENTED THE SCORE TO AN ARISTOCRAT, AND ALL OF THE ARISTOCRAT'S FAMILY DIED OF A MYSTERIOUS ILLNESS SOON AFTER.
HEINN TRIED TO BURN THE SCORE, BUT THE PAPER WOULDN'T SET ALIGHT...
...SO HE HID THE SCORE ON SOME ISLAND!
You listening?
A "DEVIL'S SCORE" THAT KILLS PEOPLE...
What a nasty name.
I WONDER HOW TRUE THE LEGEND IS...

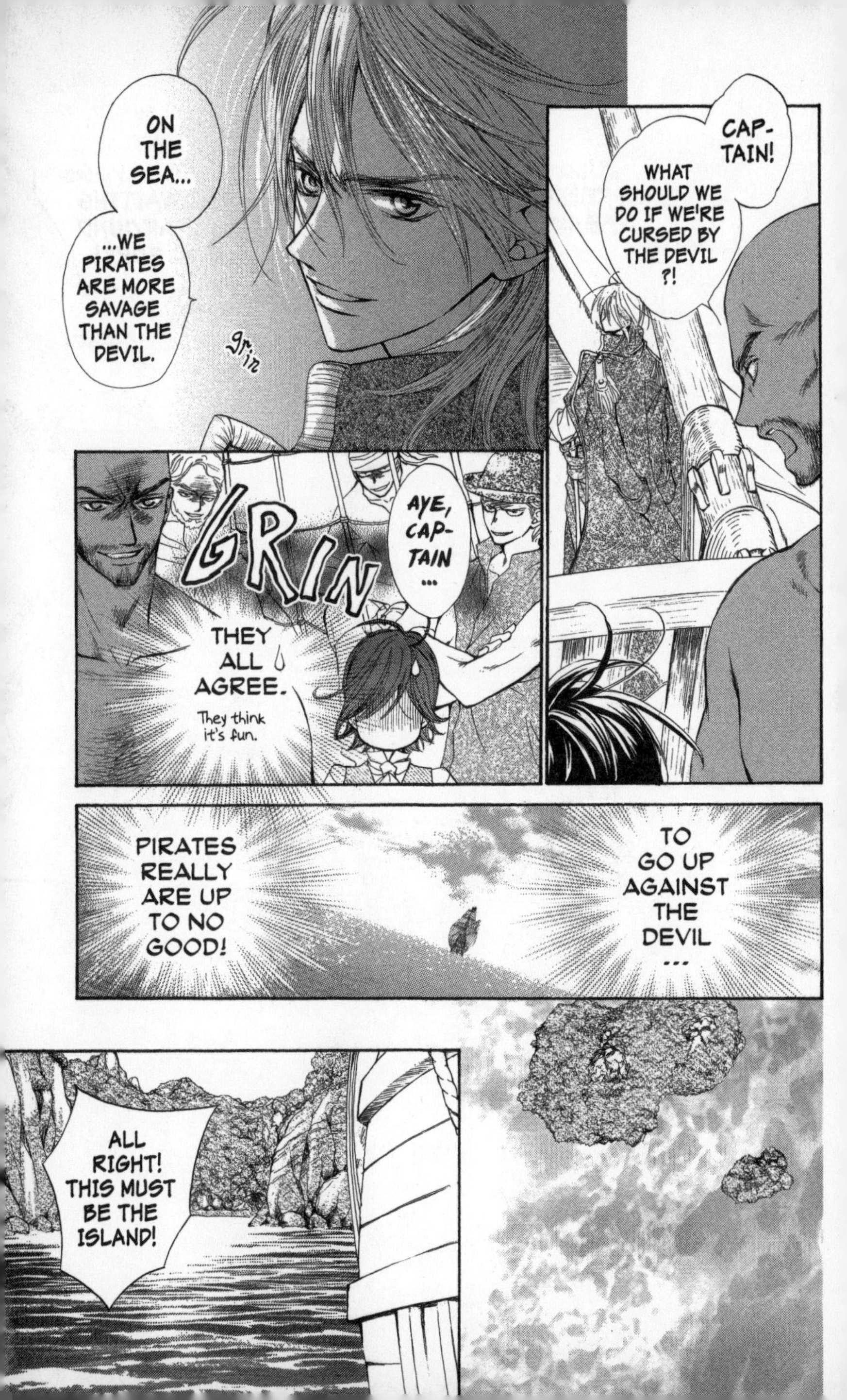
CAP-TAIN!
WHAT SHOULD WE DO IF WE'RE CURSED BY THE DEVIL?!
ON THE SEA...
...WE PIRATES ARE MORE SAVAGE THAN THE DEVIL.
grin
GRIN
AYE, CAP-TAIN...
THEY ALL AGREE.
They think it's fun.
TO GO UP AGAINST THE DEVIL...
PIRATES REALLY ARE UP TO NO GOOD!
ALL RIGHT! THIS MUST BE THE ISLAND!

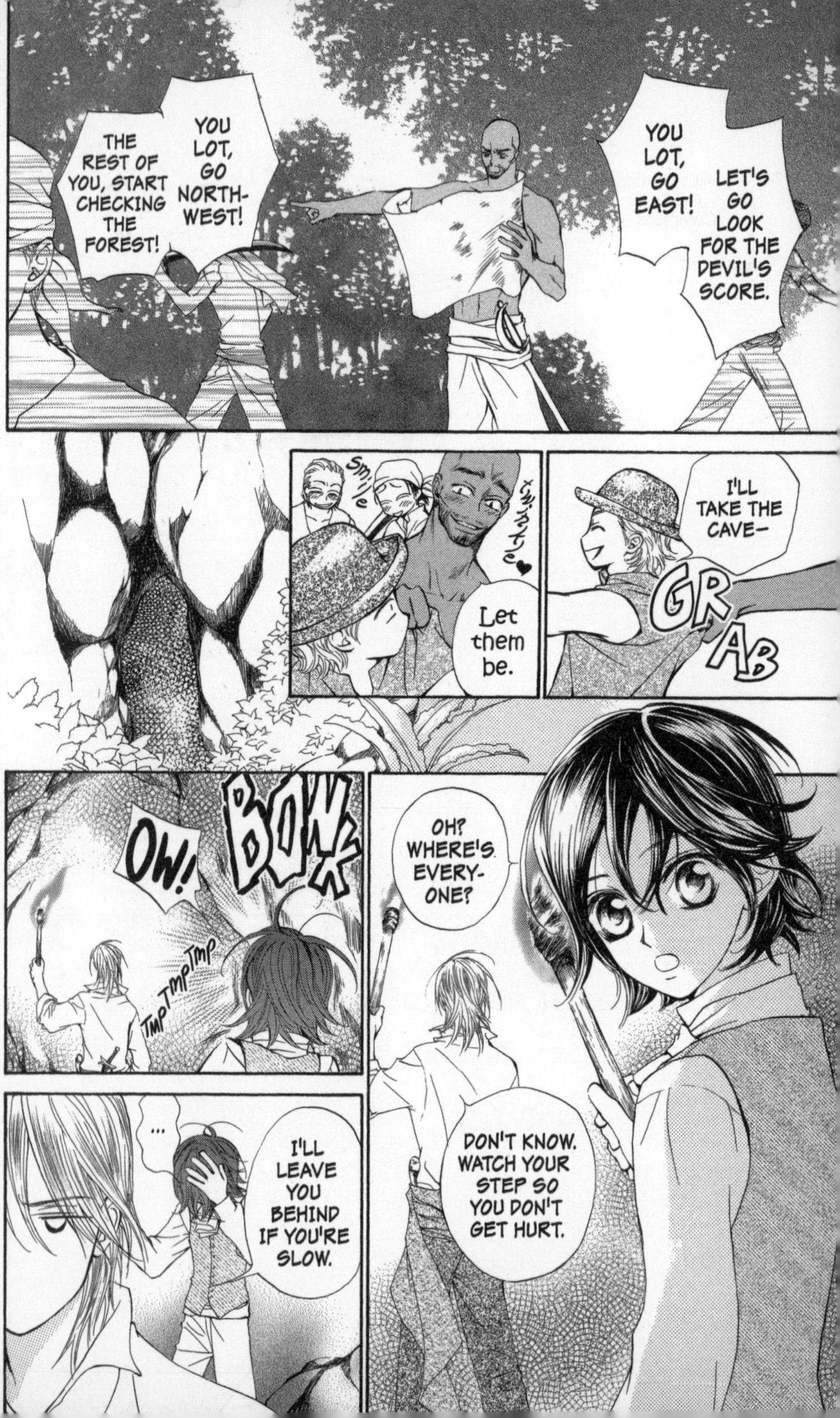
LET'S GO LOOK FOR THE DEVIL'S SCORE.
YOU LOT, GO EAST!
YOU LOT, GO NORTH-WEST!
THE REST OF YOU, START CHECKING THE FOREST!
I'LL TAKE THE CAVE—
GRAB
twinkle♥
Smile
Let them be.
OH? WHERE'S EVERYONE?
DON'T KNOW. WATCH YOUR STEP SO YOU DON'T GET HURT.
BONK
OW!
TMP TMP TMP
...
I'LL LEAVE YOU BEHIND IF YOU'RE SLOW.

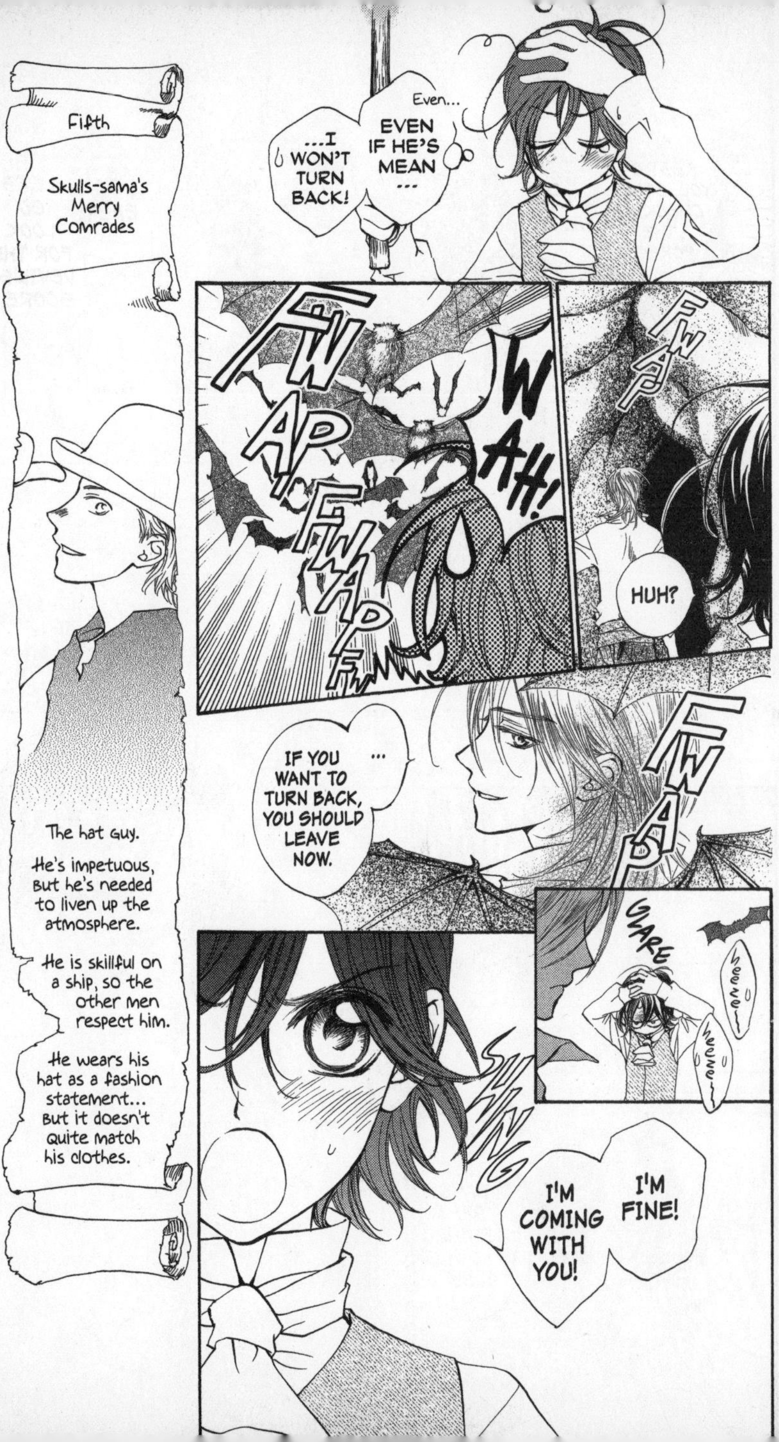
Even...
EVEN IF HE'S MEAN ...
...I WON'T TURN BACK!
FWAP
HUH?
WAH!
FWAP
FWAP
...
IF YOU WANT TO TURN BACK, YOU SHOULD LEAVE NOW.
FWAP
GLARE
heeze~
heeze~
SHING
I'M FINE!
I'M COMING WITH YOU!
Fifth
Skulls-sama's Merry Comrades
The hat guy.
He's impetuous, but he's needed to liven up the atmosphere.
He is skillful on a ship, so the other men respect him.
He wears his hat as a fashion statement... But it doesn't quite match his clothes.

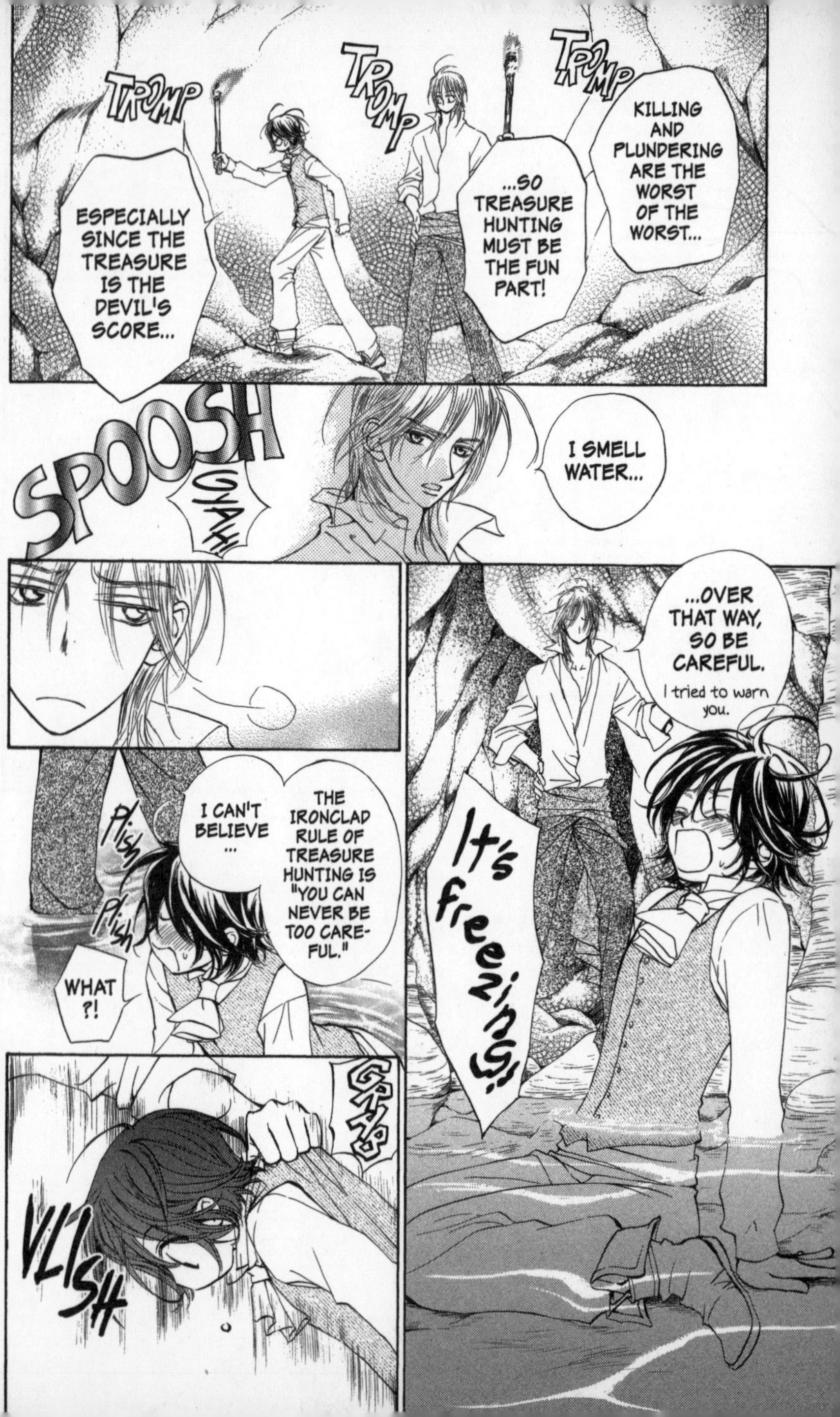
TROMP
KILLING AND PLUNDERING ARE THE WORST OF THE WORST...
TROMP
...SO TREASURE HUNTING MUST BE THE FUN PART!
TROMP
ESPECIALLY SINCE THE TREASURE IS THE DEVIL'S SCORE...
I SMELL WATER...
SPOOSH
GYAH!!
...OVER THAT WAY, SO BE CAREFUL.
I tried to warn you.
It's freezing!!
THE IRONCLAD RULE OF TREASURE HUNTING IS "YOU CAN NEVER BE TOO CAREFUL."
I CAN'T BELIEVE ...
Plish
Plish
WHAT?!
GRAB
VLISH

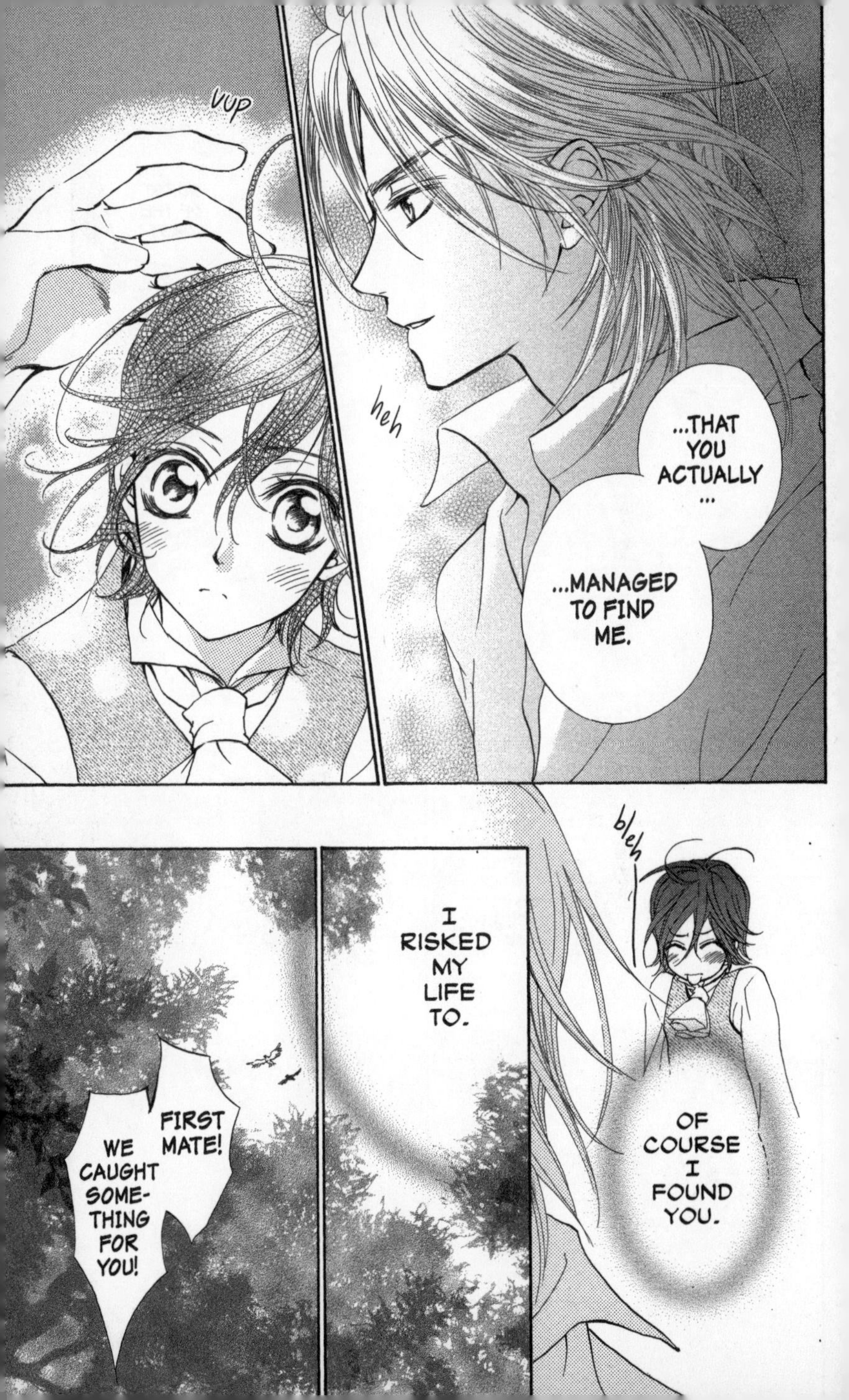
...THAT YOU ACTUALLY ...
heh
...MANAGED TO FIND ME.
vup
bleh
OF COURSE I FOUND YOU.
I RISKED MY LIFE TO.
FIRST MATE!
WE CAUGHT SOMETHING FOR YOU!

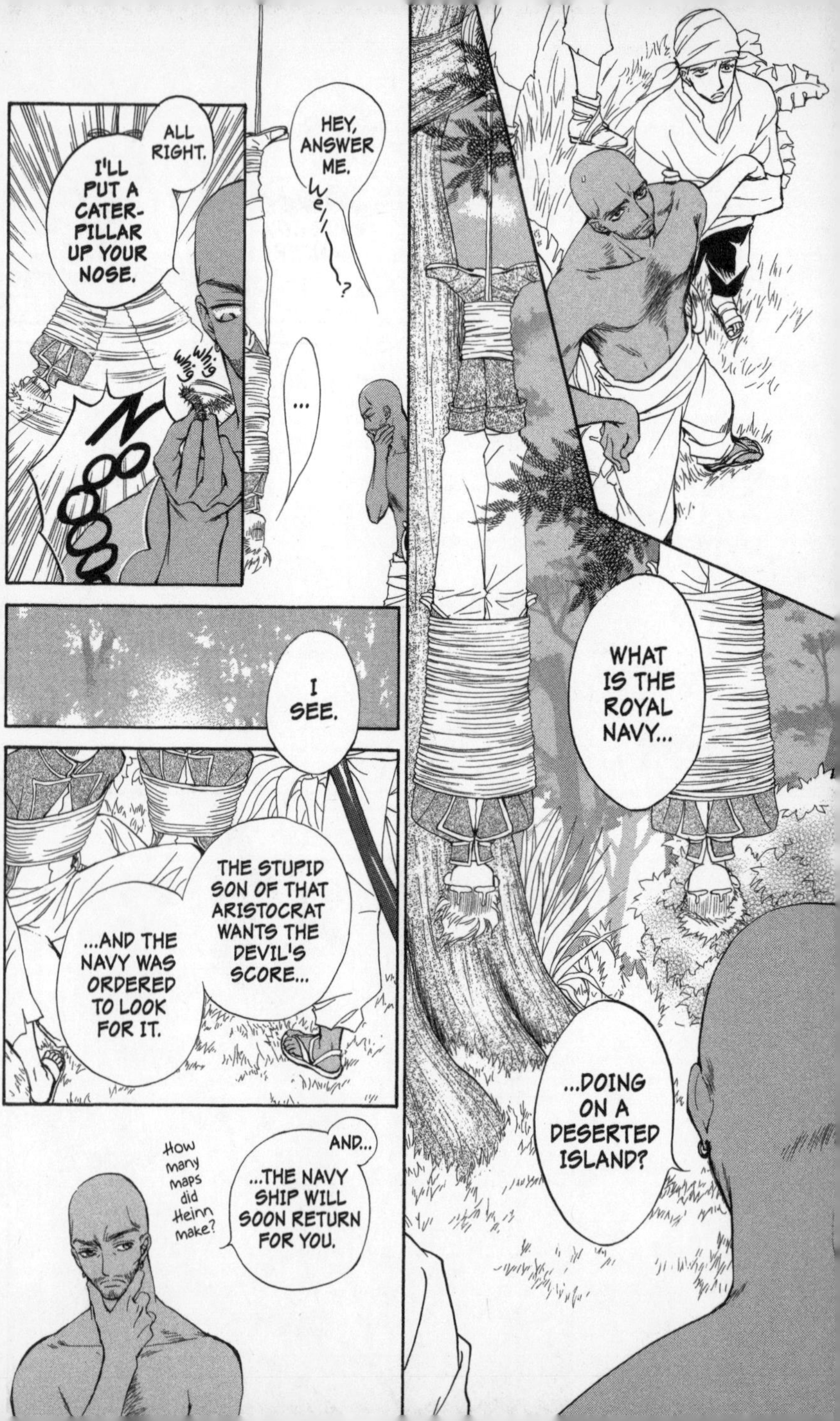
WHAT IS THE ROYAL NAVY...
...DOING ON A DESERTED ISLAND?
HEY, ANSWER ME.
Well...?
...
ALL RIGHT.
I'LL PUT A CATER-PILLAR UP YOUR NOSE.
whig whig
NOOOOO
I SEE.
THE STUPID SON OF THAT ARISTOCRAT WANTS THE DEVIL'S SCORE...
...AND THE NAVY WAS ORDERED TO LOOK FOR IT.
AND...
...THE NAVY SHIP WILL SOON RETURN FOR YOU.
How many maps did Heinn make?

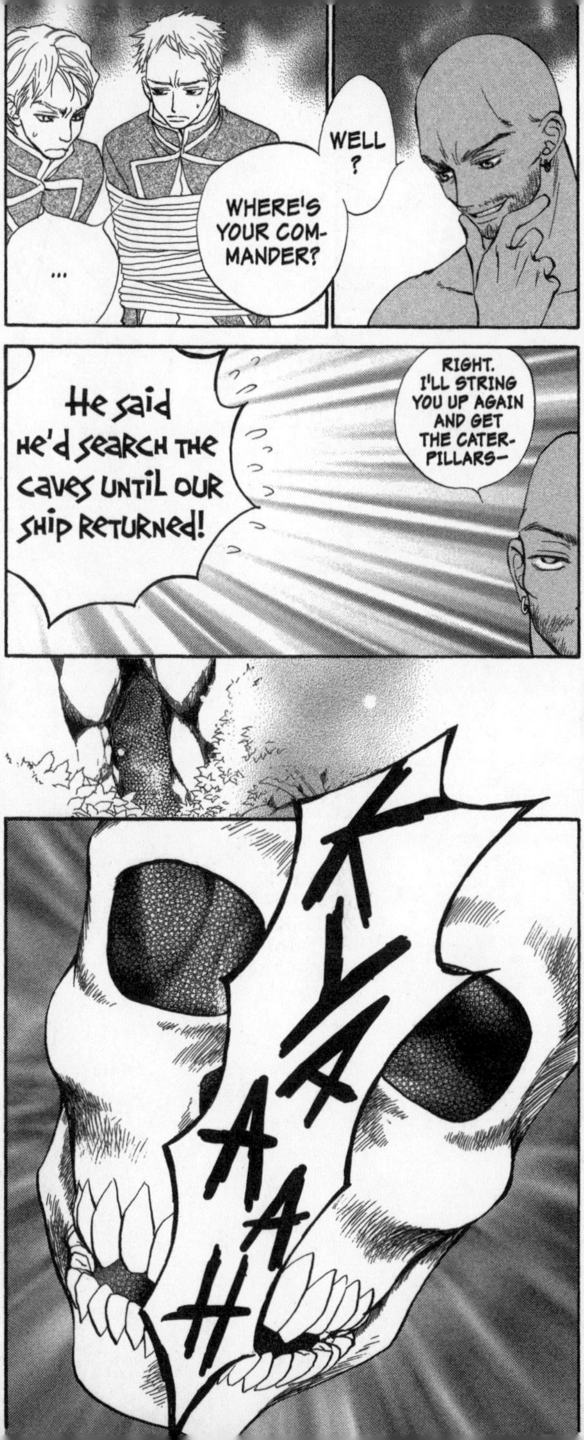
WELL ?
WHERE'S YOUR COMMANDER?
...
RIGHT. I'LL STRING YOU UP AGAIN AND GET THE CATERPILLARS—
He said he'd search the caves until our ship returned!
KYAAAAH

Sixth

Skulls-sama's Merry Comrades

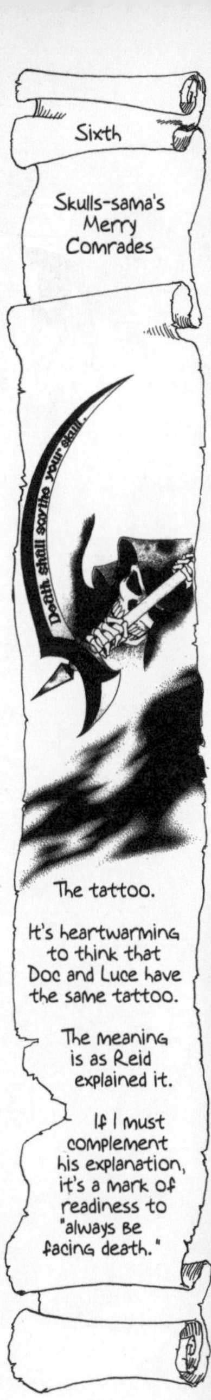
Death shall scythe your skull.

The tattoo.

It's heartwarming to think that Doc and Luce have the same tattoo.

The meaning is as Reid explained it.

If I must complement his explanation, it's a mark of readiness to "always be facing death."

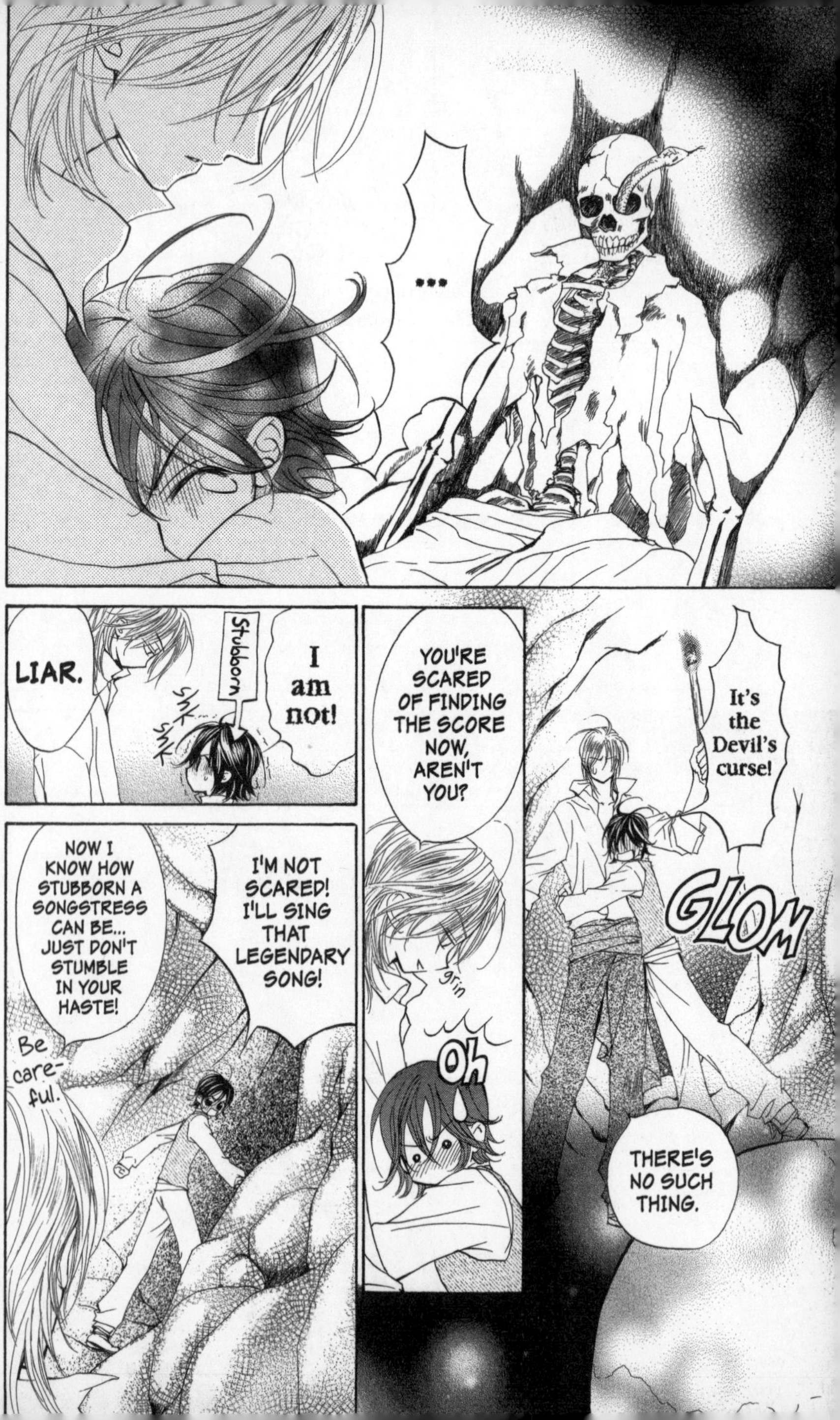
...
It's the Devil's curse!
GLOM
THERE'S NO SUCH THING.
YOU'RE SCARED OF FINDING THE SCORE NOW, AREN'T YOU?
grin
Oh
I am not!
Stubborn
shk shk
LIAR.
I'M NOT SCARED! I'LL SING THAT LEGENDARY SONG!
NOW I KNOW HOW STUBBORN A SONGSTRESS CAN BE... JUST DON'T STUMBLE IN YOUR HASTE!
Be care-ful.

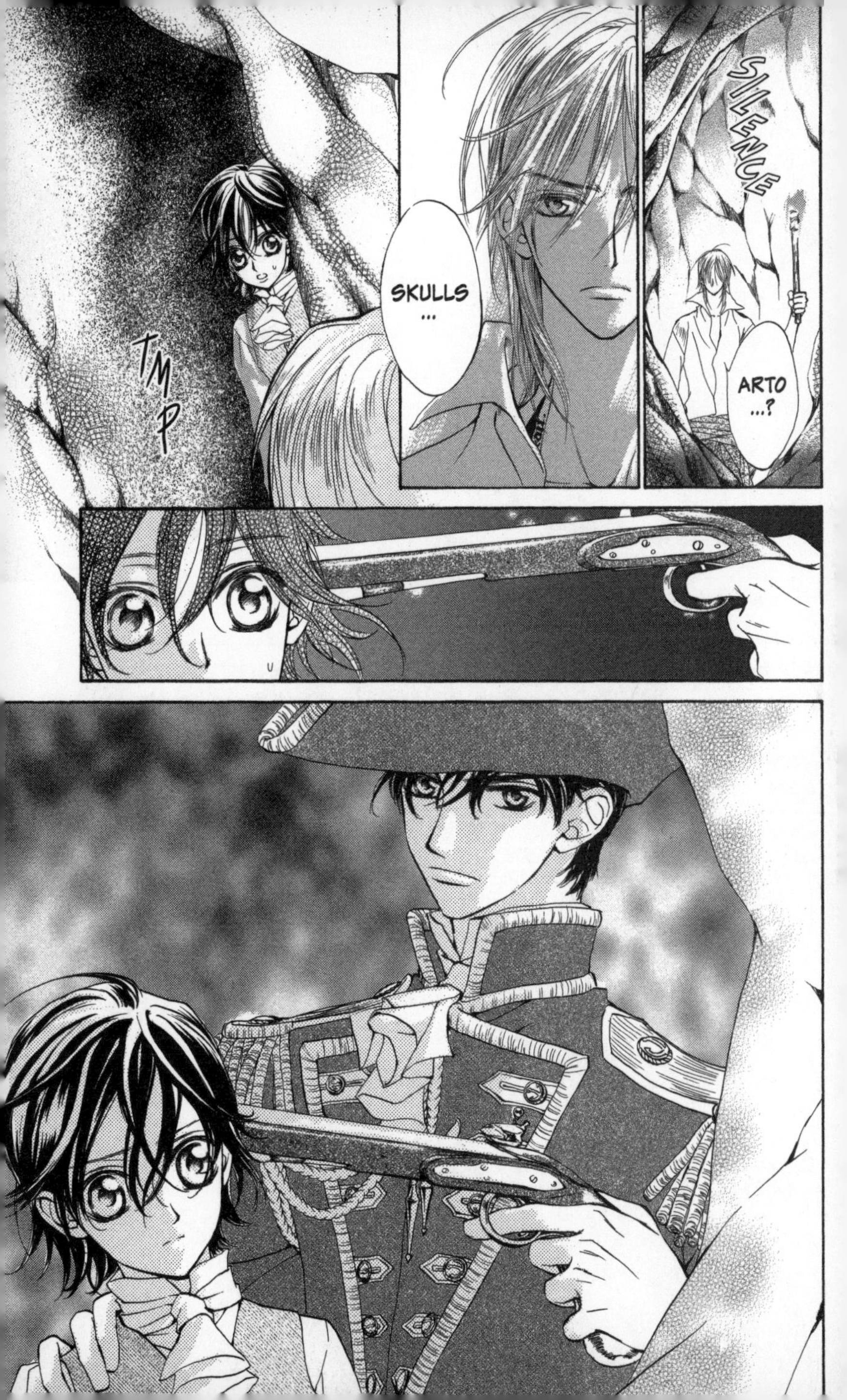
SILENCE
ARTO ...?
SKULLS ...
TMP

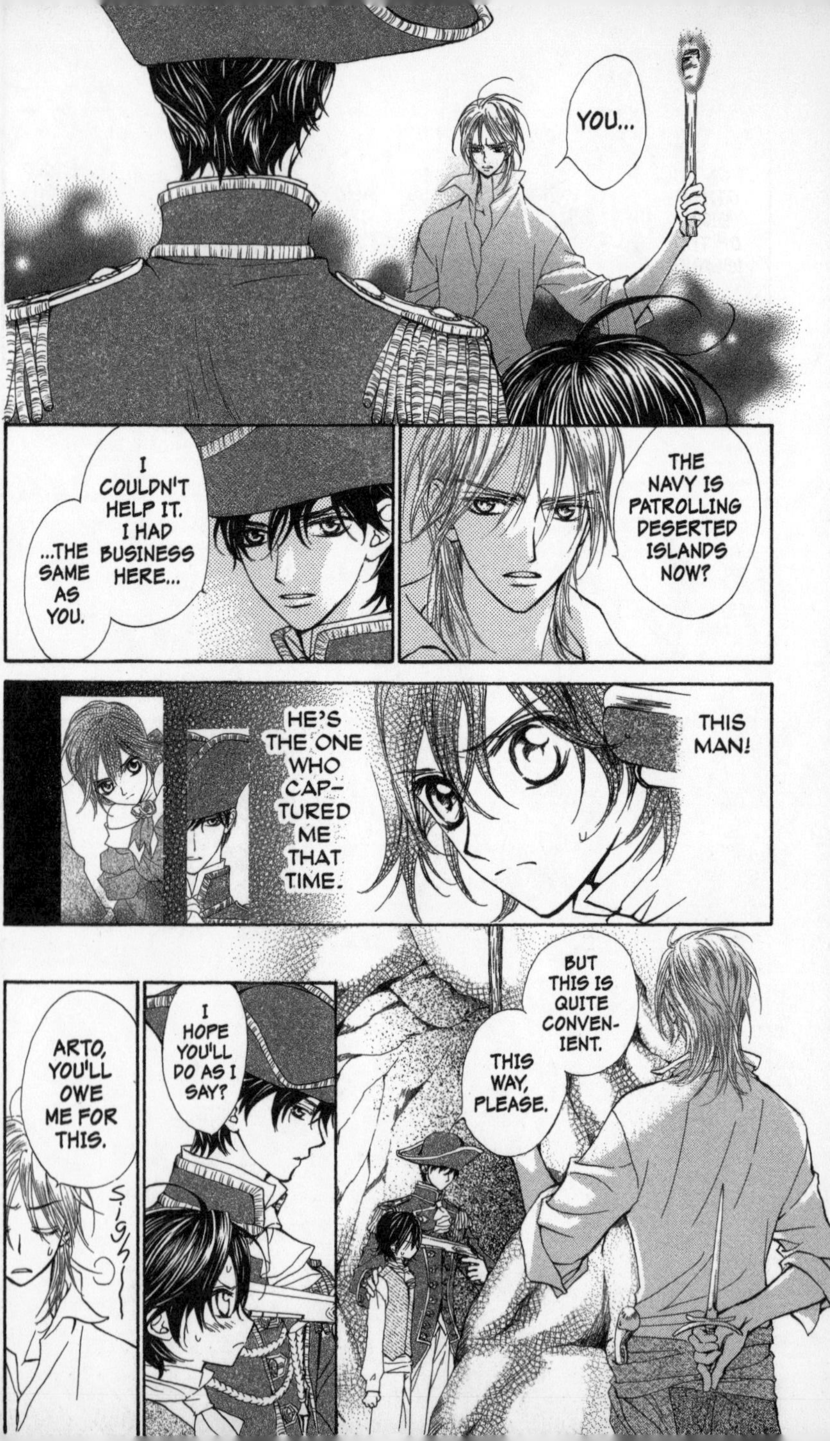
YOU...
THE NAVY IS PATROLLING DESERTED ISLANDS NOW?
I COULDN'T HELP IT. I HAD BUSINESS HERE...
...THE SAME AS YOU.
THIS MAN!
HE'S THE ONE WHO CAP-TURED ME THAT TIME.
BUT THIS IS QUITE CONVEN-IENT.
THIS WAY, PLEASE.
I HOPE YOU'LL DO AS I SAY?
ARTO, YOU'LL OWE ME FOR THIS.
SIGH

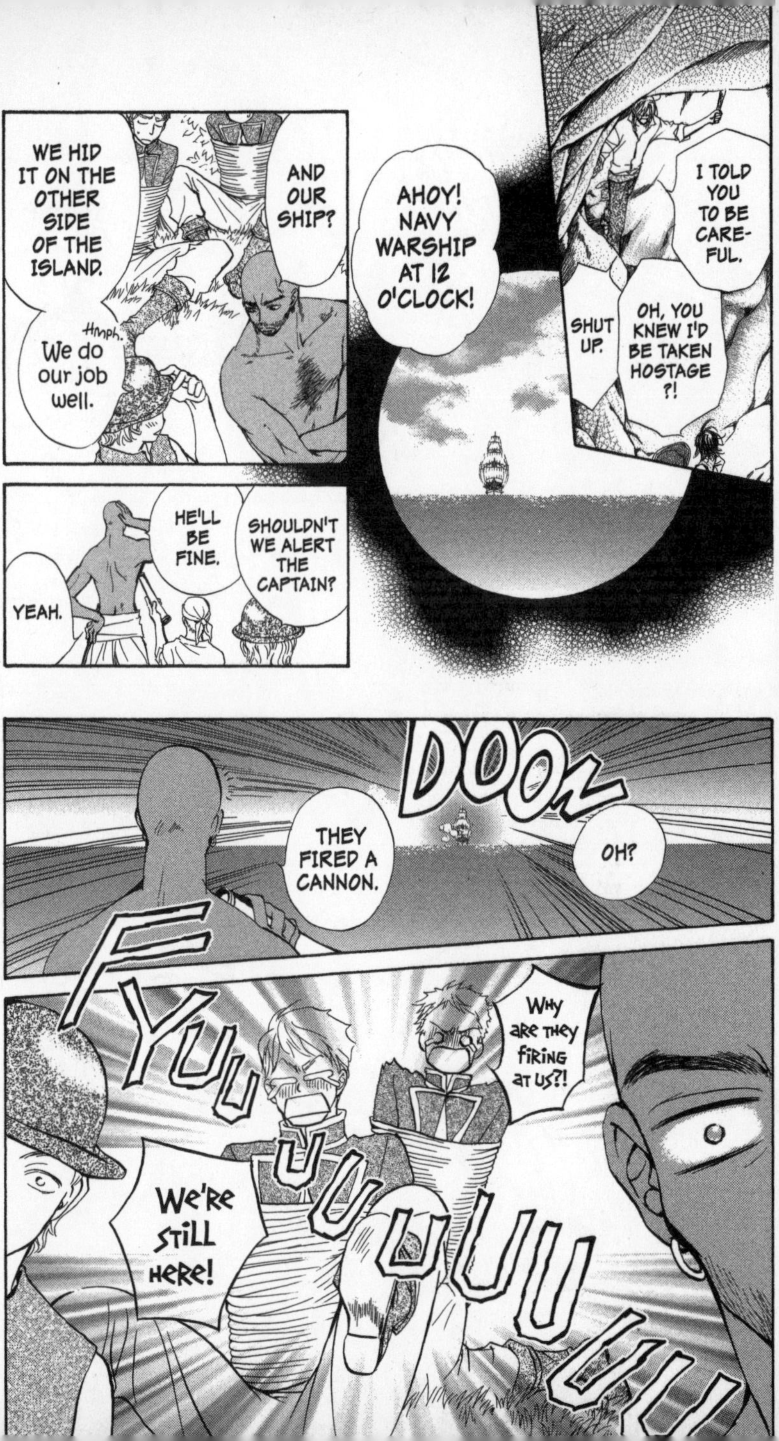
I TOLD YOU TO BE CARE-FUL.
OH, YOU KNEW I'D BE TAKEN HOSTAGE?!
SHUT UP.
AHOY! NAVY WARSHIP AT 12 O'CLOCK!
AND OUR SHIP?
WE HID IT ON THE OTHER SIDE OF THE ISLAND.
Hmph.
We do our job well.
SHOULDN'T WE ALERT THE CAPTAIN?
HE'LL BE FINE.
YEAH.
DOON
OH?
THEY FIRED A CANNON.
FYUUUUUUUUU
Why are they firing at us?!
We're still here!

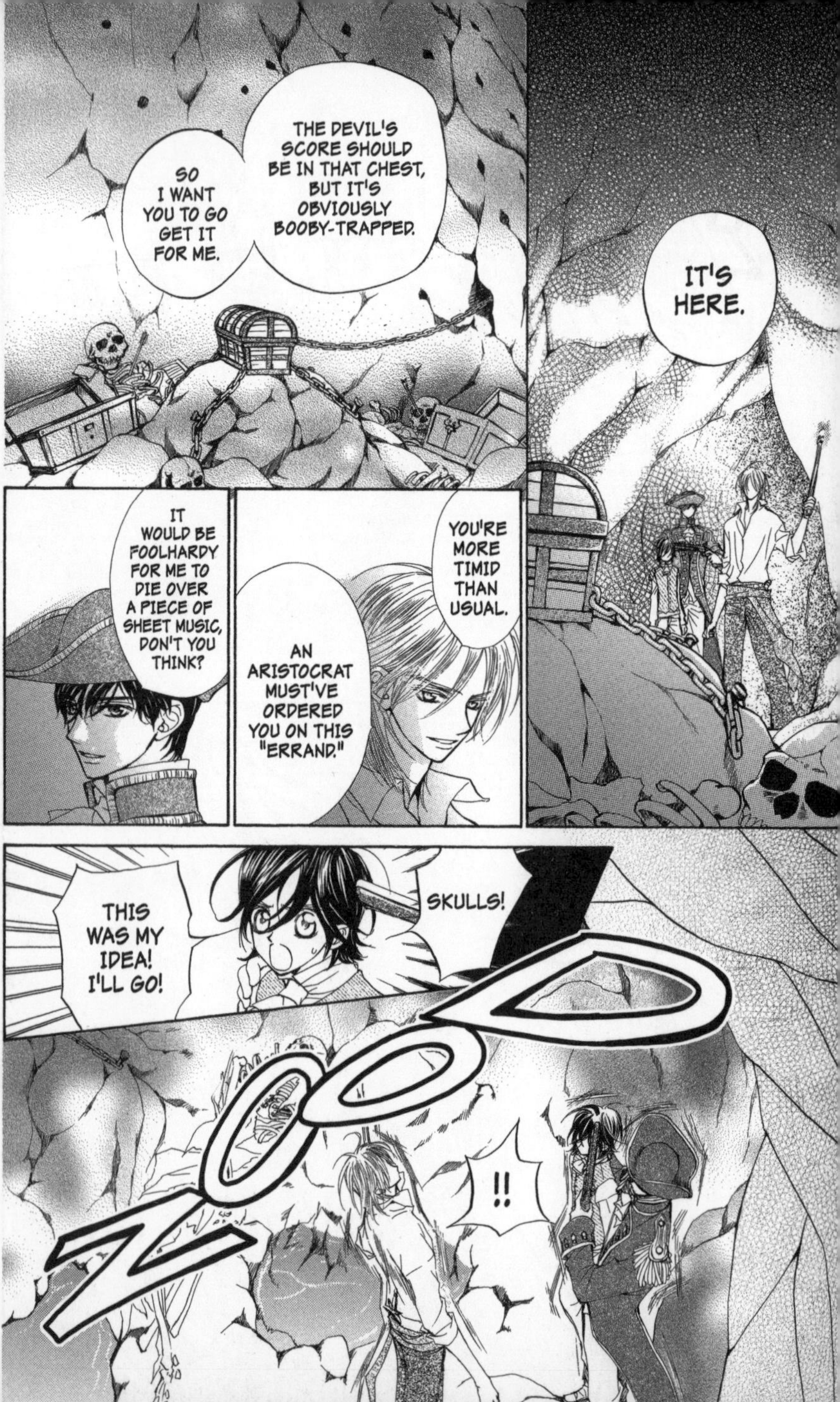
IT'S HERE.
THE DEVIL'S SCORE SHOULD BE IN THAT CHEST, BUT IT'S OBVIOUSLY BOOBY-TRAPPED.
SO I WANT YOU TO GO GET IT FOR ME.
YOU'RE MORE TIMID THAN USUAL.
AN ARISTOCRAT MUST'VE ORDERED YOU ON THIS "ERRAND."
IT WOULD BE FOOLHARDY FOR ME TO DIE OVER A PIECE OF SHEET MUSIC, DON'T YOU THINK?
SKULLS!
THIS WAS MY IDEA! I'LL GO!
!!

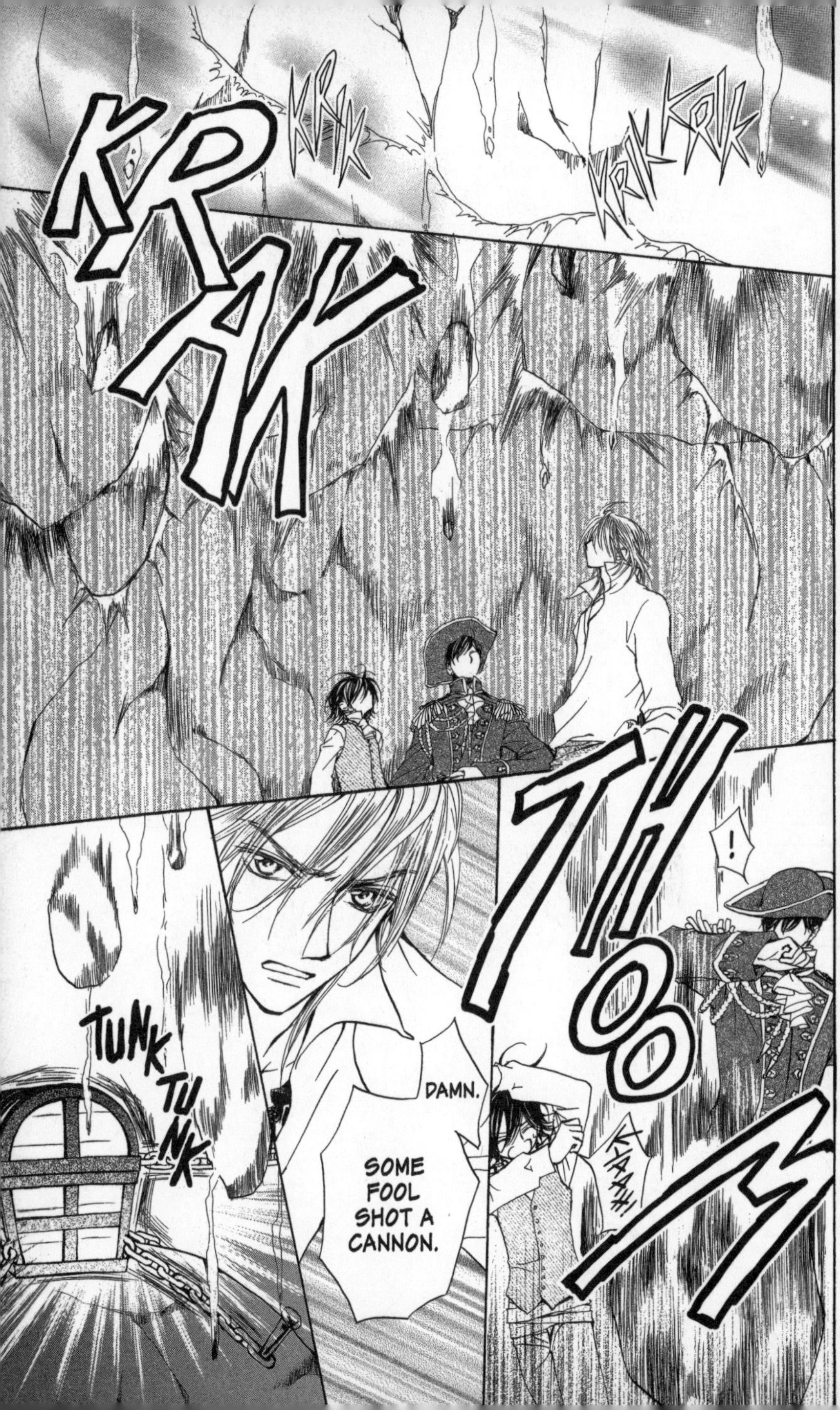
KRAK
KRAK
KRAK KRAK
!
THOOM
KYAAH!
DAMN.
SOME FOOL SHOT A CANNON.
TUNK TUNK

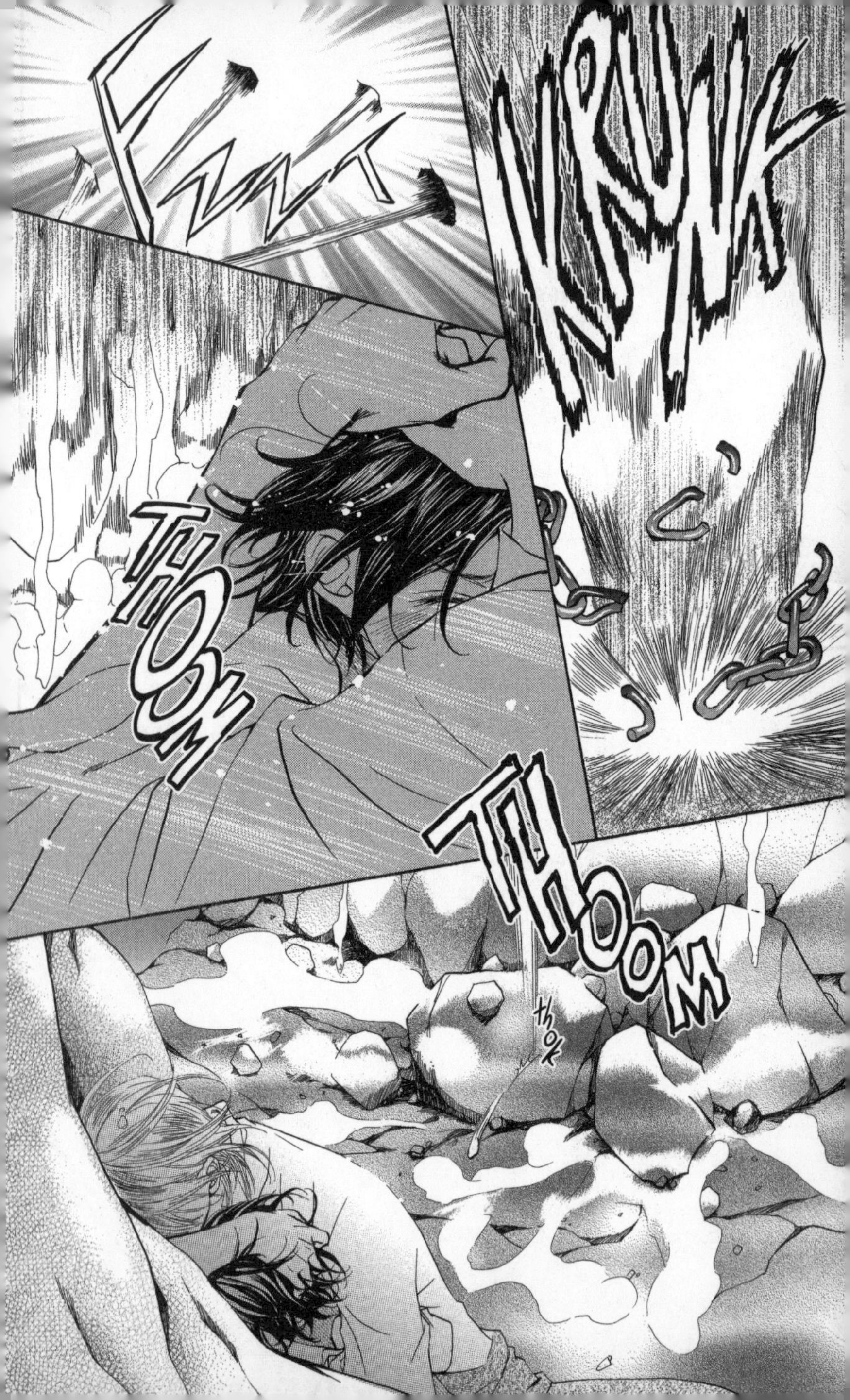
KRUNK
FZZT
THOOM
THOOM
thok

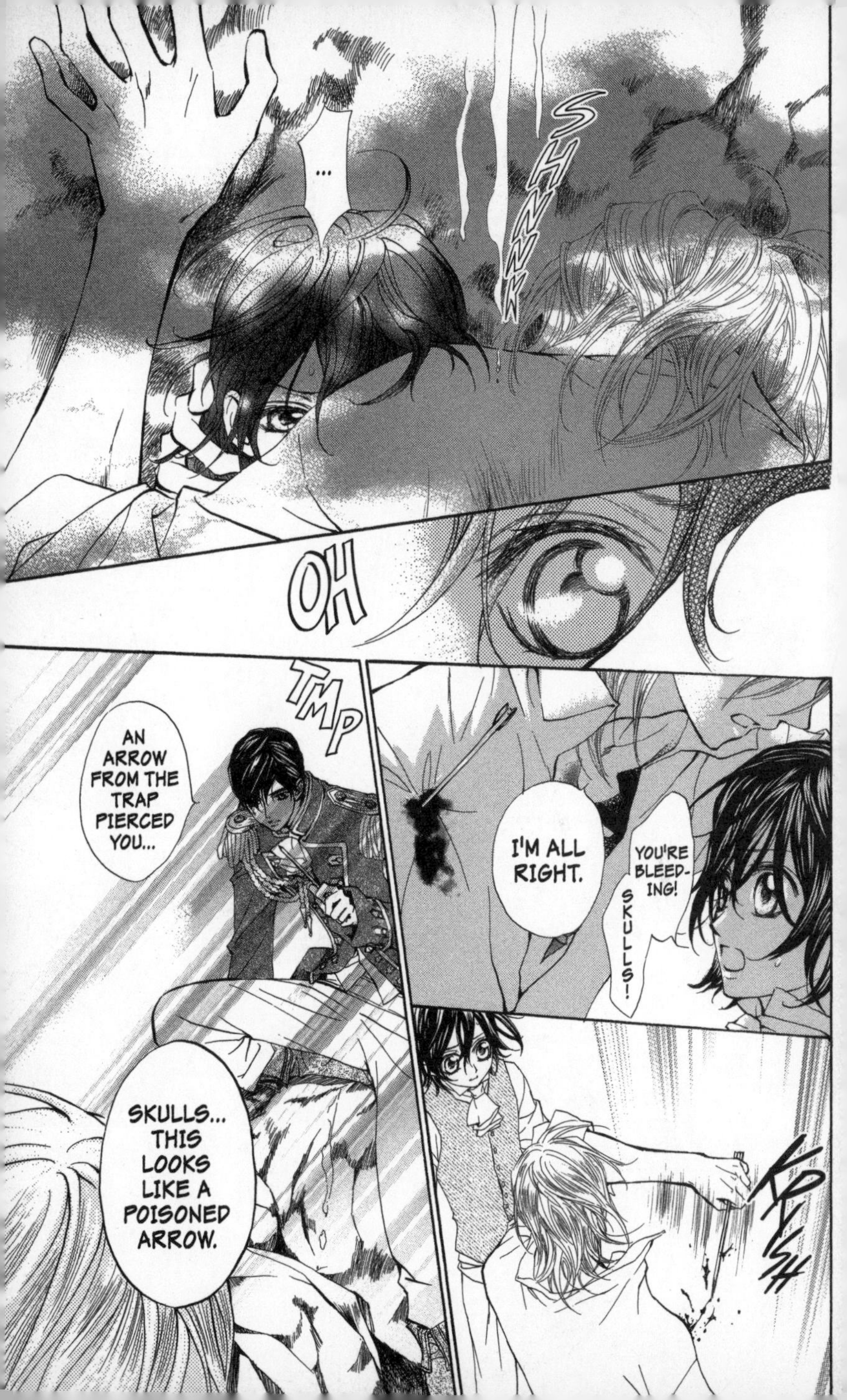
SHNWK
...
OH
YOU'RE BLEEDING!
SKULLS!
I'M ALL RIGHT.
KRISH
TMP
AN ARROW FROM THE TRAP PIERCED YOU...
SKULLS... THIS LOOKS LIKE A POISONED ARROW.

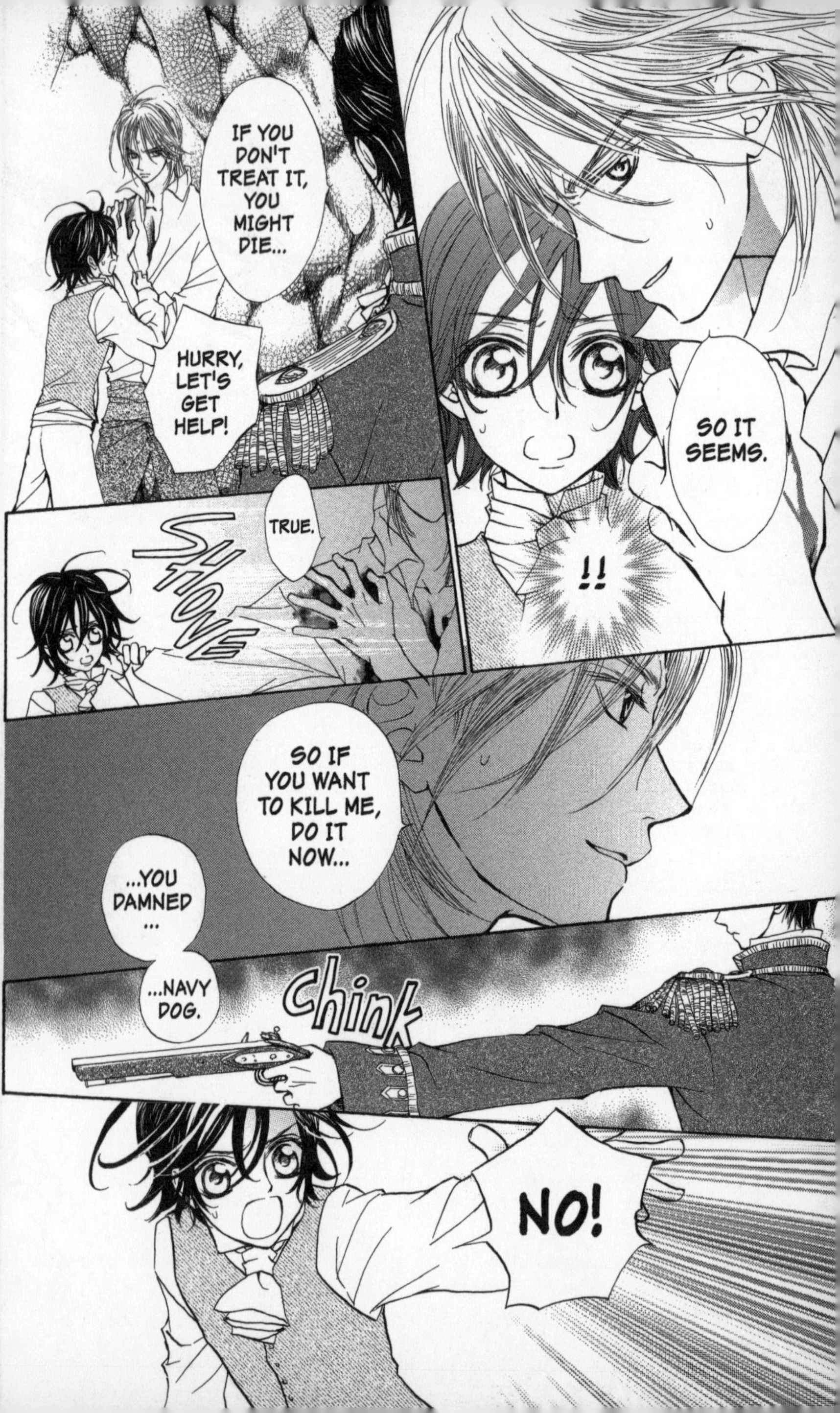
SO IT SEEMS.
!!
IF YOU DON'T TREAT IT, YOU MIGHT DIE...
HURRY, LET'S GET HELP!
TRUE.
SHOVE
SO IF YOU WANT TO KILL ME, DO IT NOW...
...YOU DAMNED ...
...NAVY DOG.
Chink
NO!

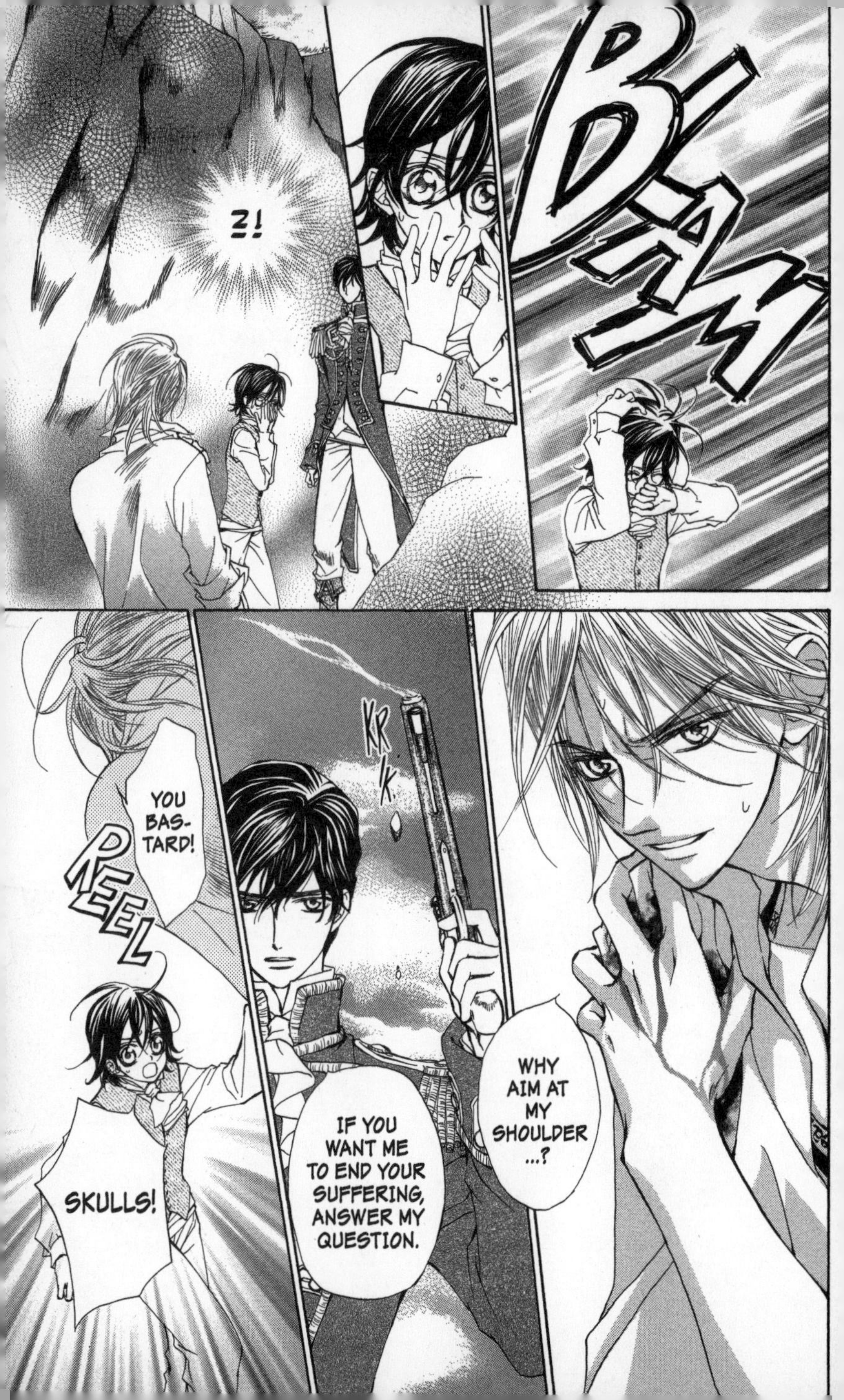
BLAM
Z!
WHY AIM AT MY SHOULDER ...?
KRIK
IF YOU WANT ME TO END YOUR SUFFERING, ANSWER MY QUESTION.
YOU BAS-TARD!
REEL
SKULLS!

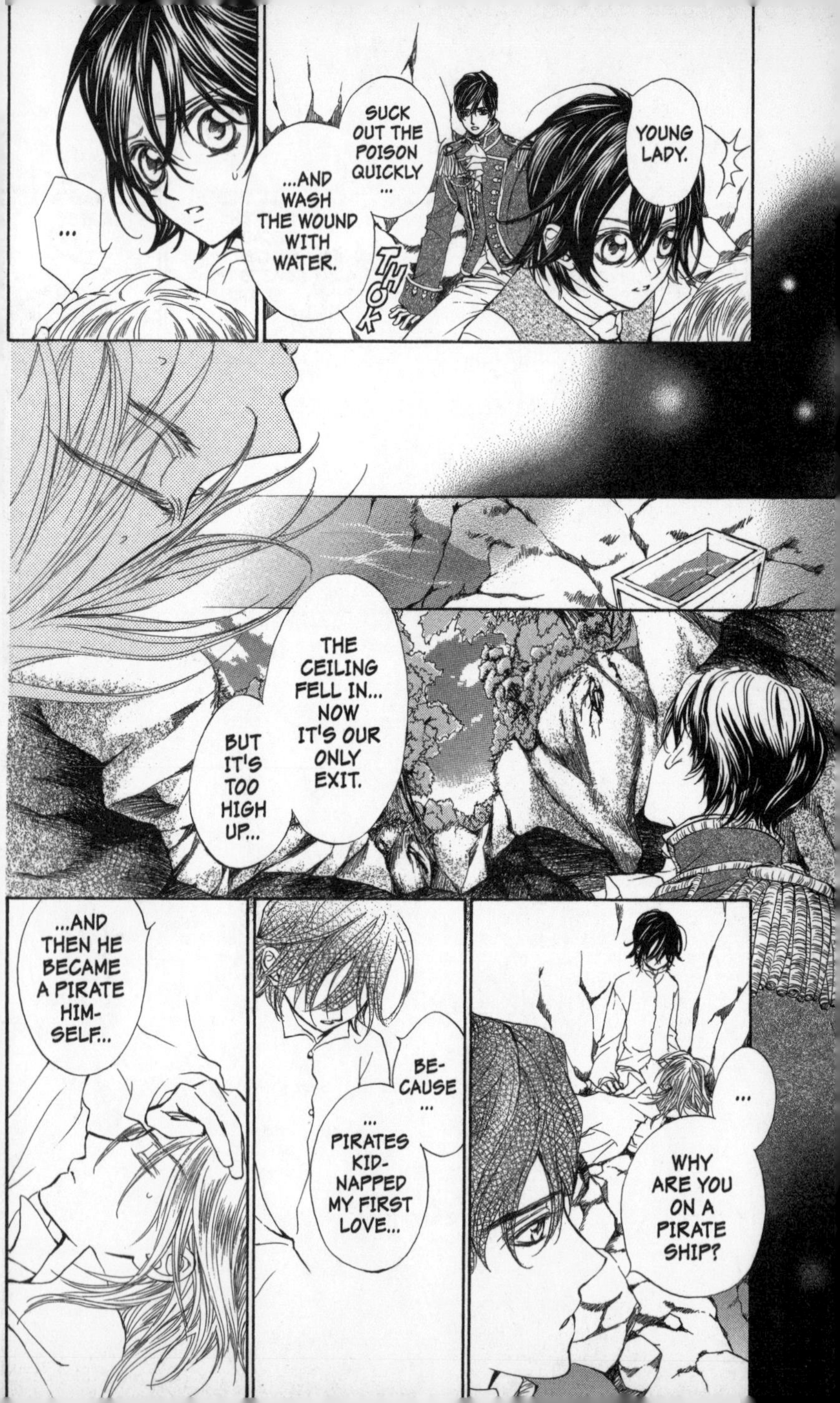
YOUNG LADY.
SUCK OUT THE POISON QUICKLY ...
...AND WASH THE WOUND WITH WATER.
THOK
...
THE CEILING FELL IN... NOW IT'S OUR ONLY EXIT.
BUT IT'S TOO HIGH UP...
...
WHY ARE YOU ON A PIRATE SHIP?
BE-CAUSE ...
... PIRATES KID-NAPPED MY FIRST LOVE...
...AND THEN HE BECAME A PIRATE HIM-SELF...

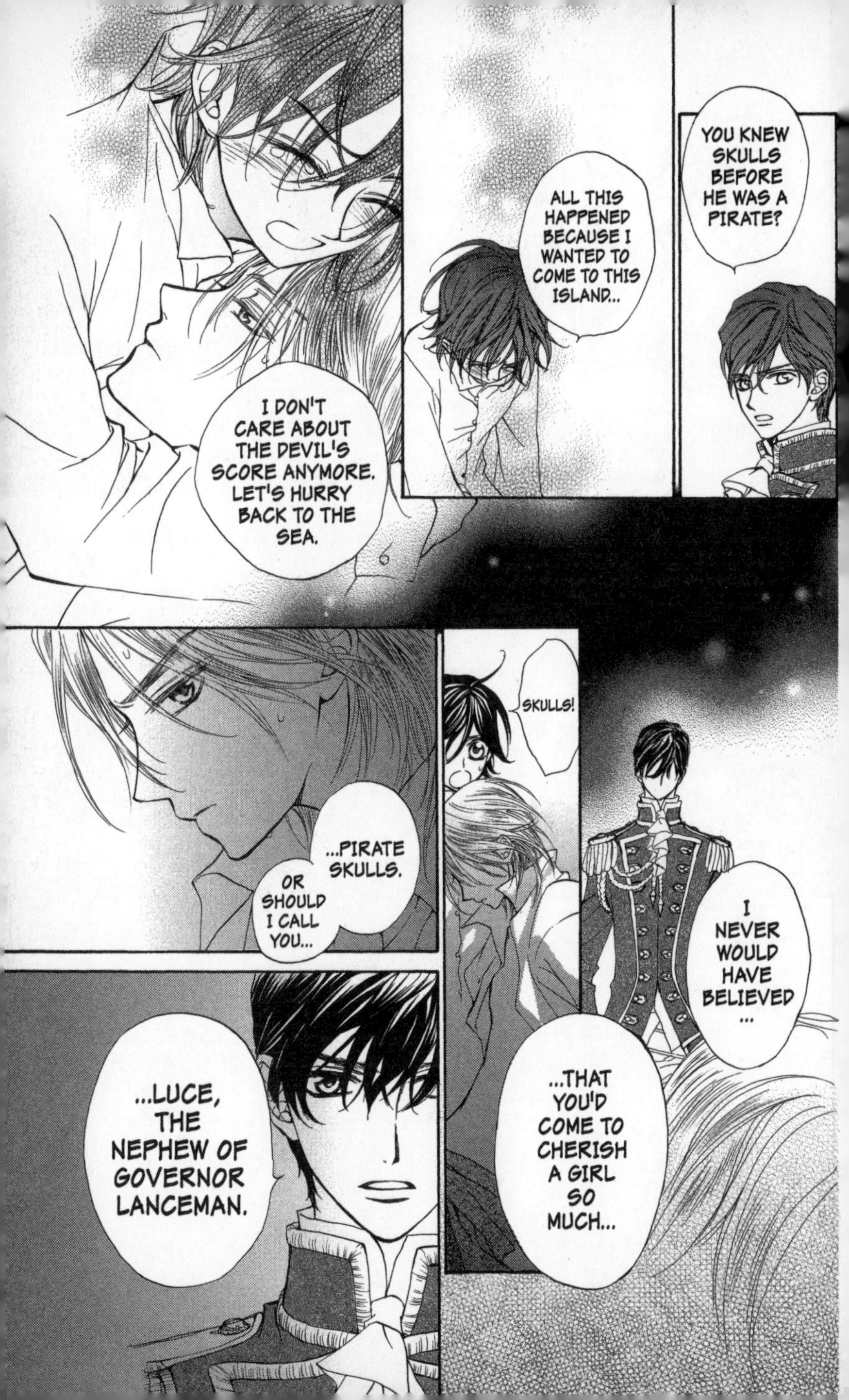
YOU KNEW SKULLS BEFORE HE WAS A PIRATE?
ALL THIS HAPPENED BECAUSE I WANTED TO COME TO THIS ISLAND...
I DON'T CARE ABOUT THE DEVIL'S SCORE ANYMORE. LET'S HURRY BACK TO THE SEA.
SKULLS!
I NEVER WOULD HAVE BELIEVED...
...THAT YOU'D COME TO CHERISH A GIRL SO MUCH...
...PIRATE SKULLS.
OR SHOULD I CALL YOU...
...LUCE, THE NEPHEW OF GOVERNOR LANCEMAN.

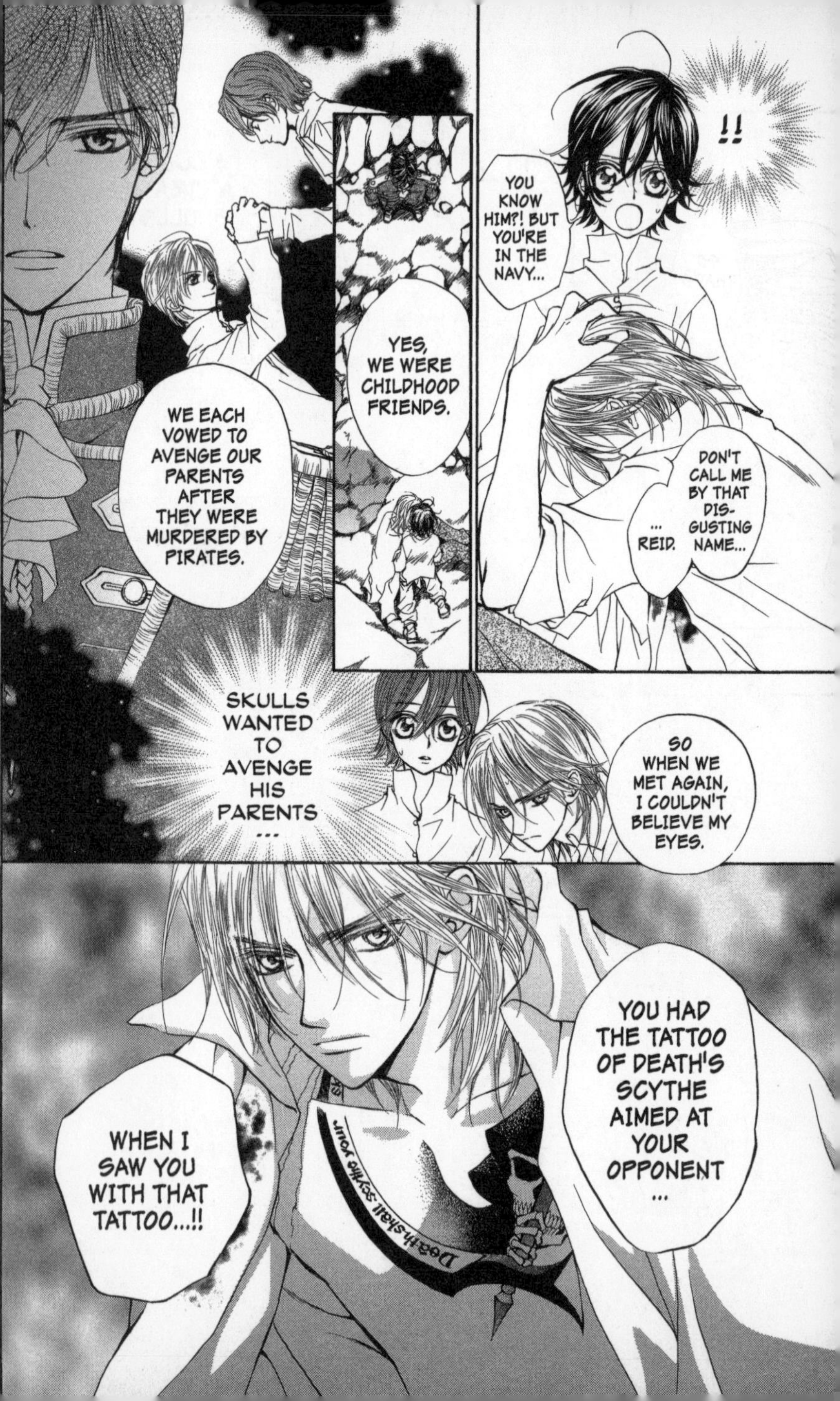
!!
YOU KNOW HIM?! BUT YOU'RE IN THE NAVY...
DON'T CALL ME BY THAT DIS-GUSTING NAME...
... REID.
YES, WE WERE CHILDHOOD FRIENDS.
WE EACH VOWED TO AVENGE OUR PARENTS AFTER THEY WERE MURDERED BY PIRATES.
SO WHEN WE MET AGAIN, I COULDN'T BELIEVE MY EYES.
SKULLS WANTED TO AVENGE HIS PARENTS ...
YOU HAD THE TATTOO OF DEATH'S SCYTHE AIMED AT YOUR OPPONENT ...
WHEN I SAW YOU WITH THAT TATTOO...!!

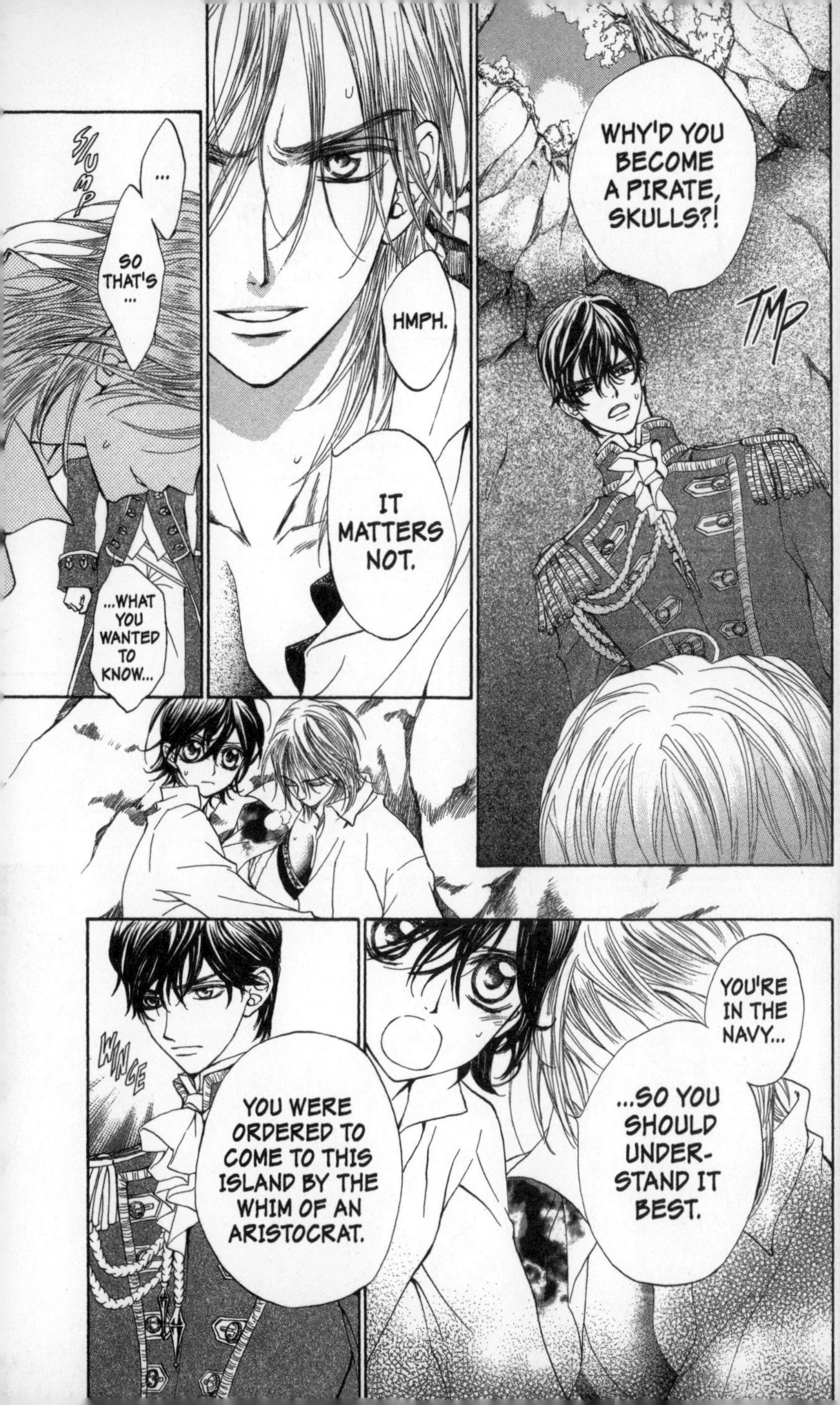
WHY'D YOU BECOME A PIRATE, SKULLS?!
TMP
HMPH.
IT MATTERS NOT.
SLUMP
...
SO THAT'S ...
...WHAT YOU WANTED TO KNOW...
YOU'RE IN THE NAVY...
...SO YOU SHOULD UNDER-STAND IT BEST.
WINCE
YOU WERE ORDERED TO COME TO THIS ISLAND BY THE WHIM OF AN ARISTOCRAT.

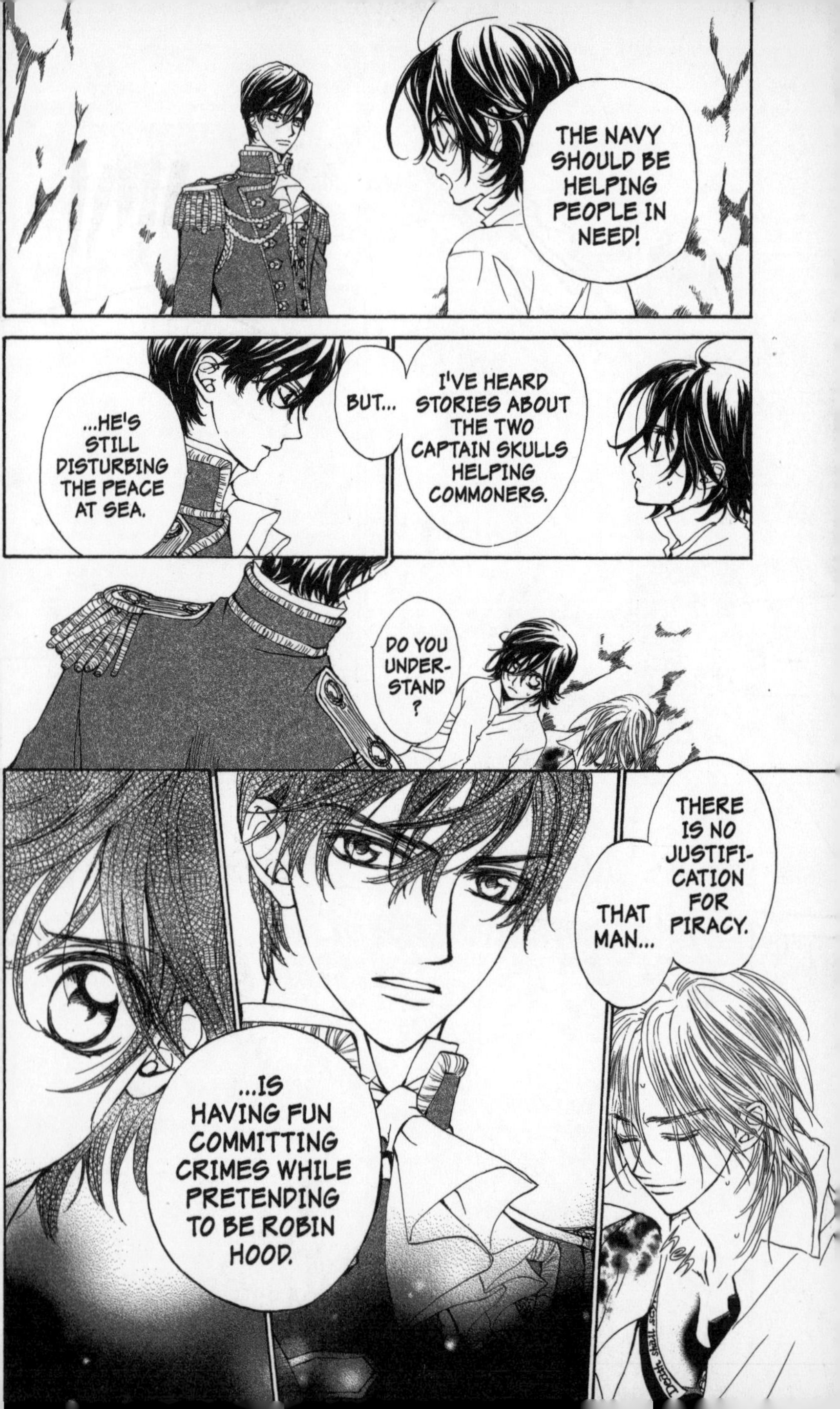
THE NAVY SHOULD BE HELPING PEOPLE IN NEED!
I'VE HEARD STORIES ABOUT THE TWO CAPTAIN SKULLS HELPING COMMONERS.
BUT...
...HE'S STILL DISTURBING THE PEACE AT SEA.
DO YOU UNDER-STAND?
THERE IS NO JUSTIFI-CATION FOR PIRACY.
THAT MAN...
...IS HAVING FUN COMMITTING CRIMES WHILE PRETENDING TO BE ROBIN HOOD.
heh

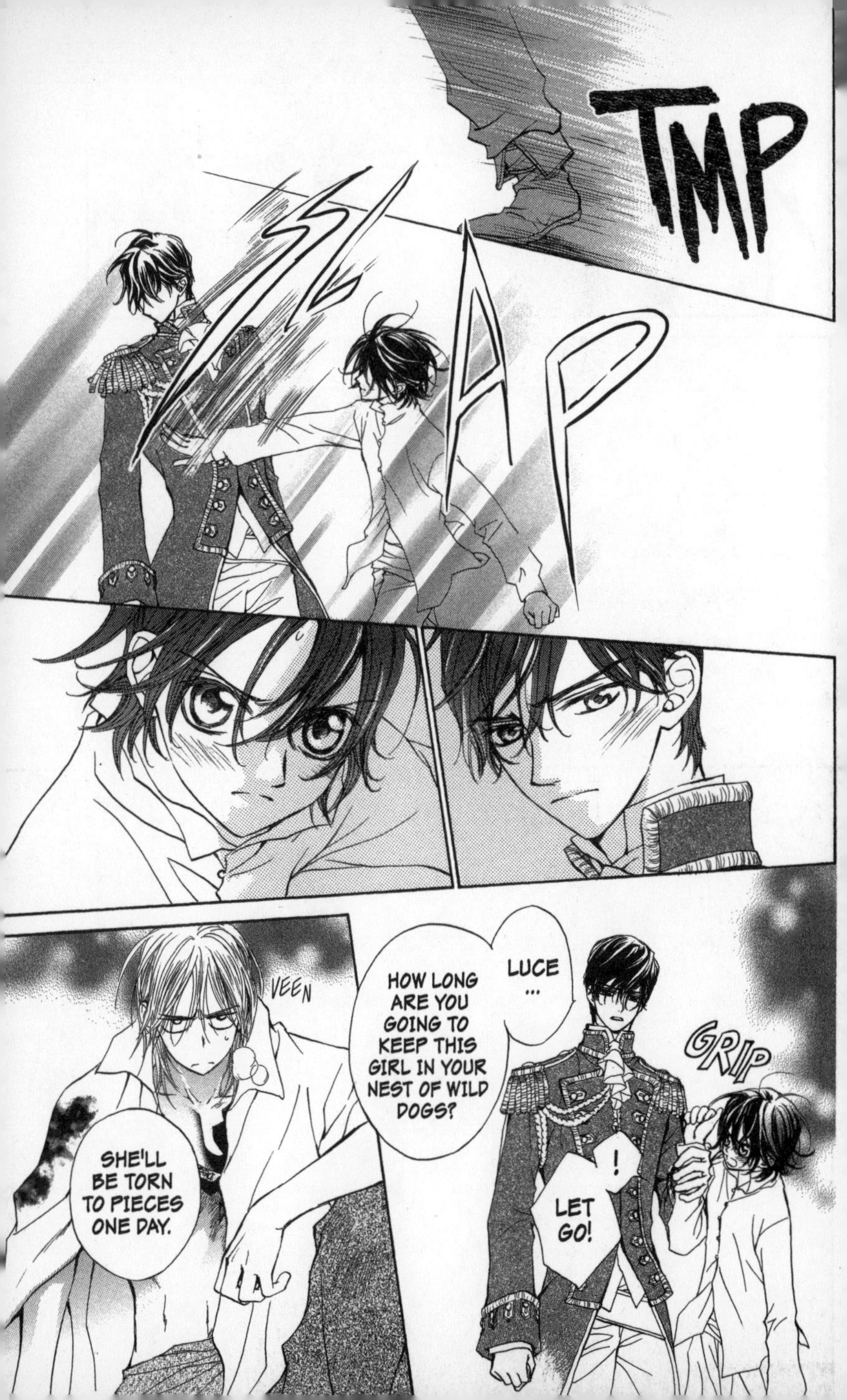
TMP
SLAP
LUCE ...
GRIP
!
LET GO!
VEEN
HOW LONG ARE YOU GOING TO KEEP THIS GIRL IN YOUR NEST OF WILD DOGS?
SHE'LL BE TORN TO PIECES ONE DAY.

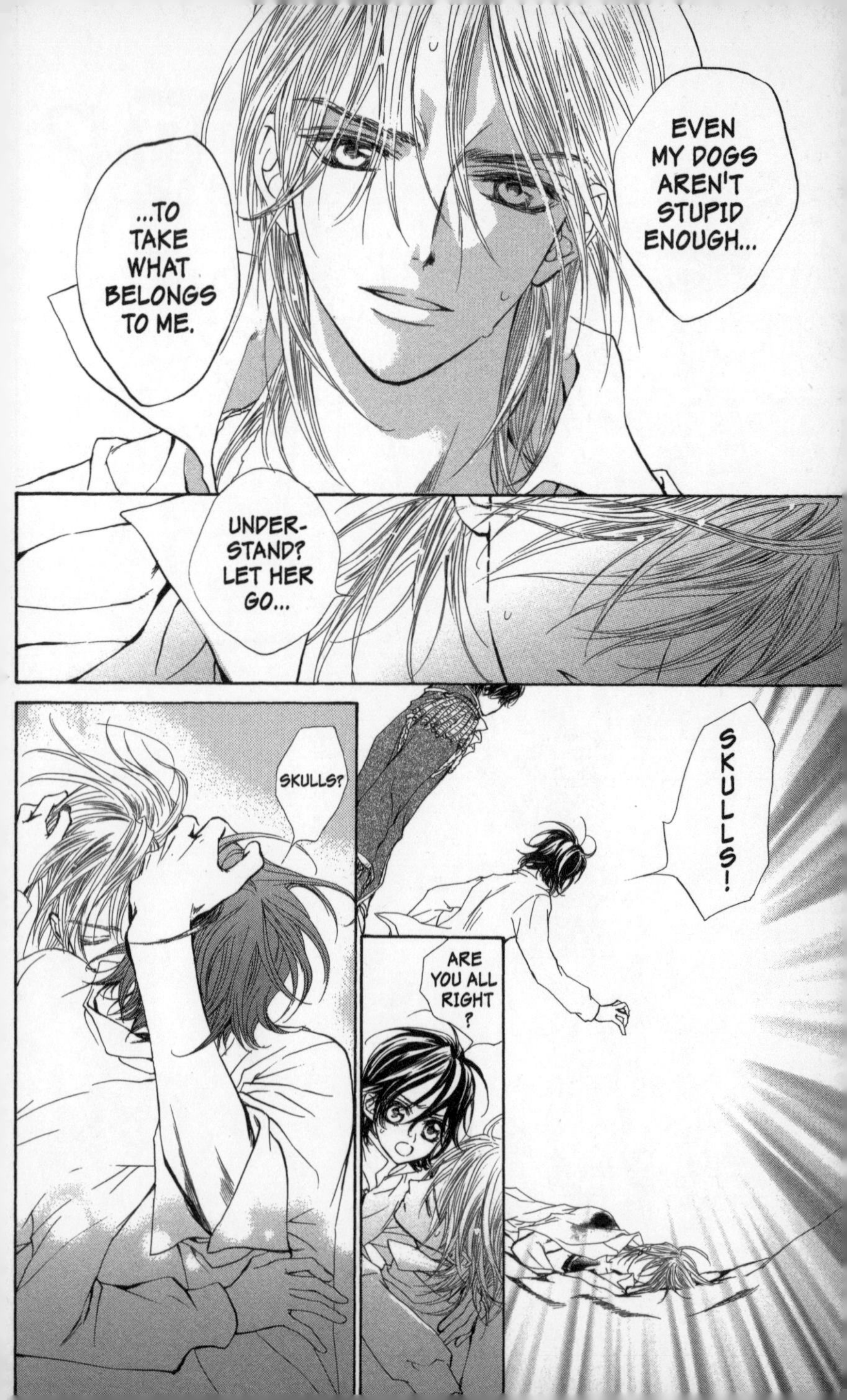
EVEN MY DOGS AREN'T STUPID ENOUGH...
...TO TAKE WHAT BELONGS TO ME.
UNDER-STAND? LET HER GO...
SKULLS!
SKULLS?
ARE YOU ALL RIGHT?

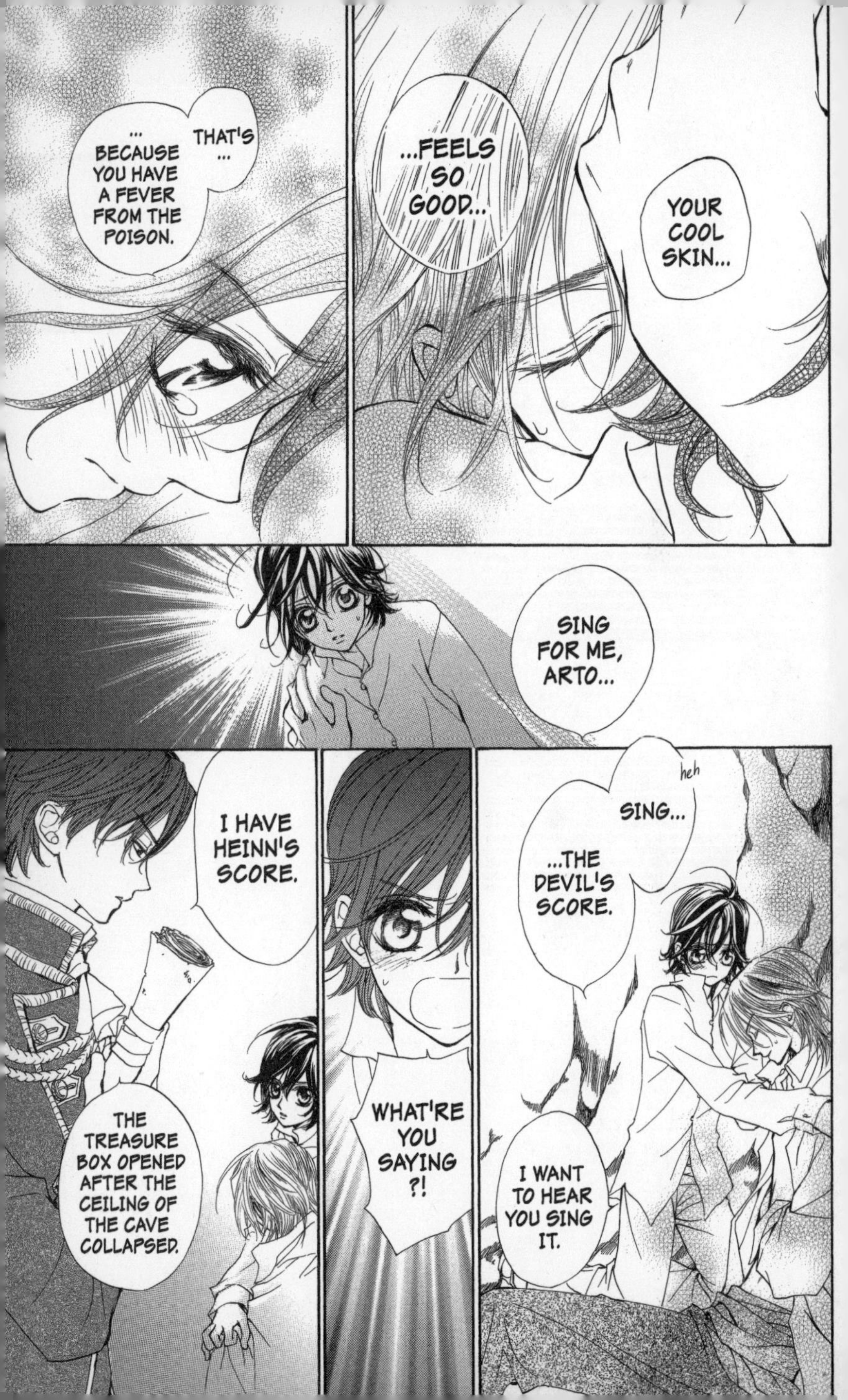
YOUR COOL SKIN...
...FEELS SO GOOD...
THAT'S...
...BECAUSE YOU HAVE A FEVER FROM THE POISON.
SING FOR ME, ARTO...
heh
SING...
...THE DEVIL'S SCORE.
I WANT TO HEAR YOU SING IT.
WHAT'RE YOU SAYING ?!
I HAVE HEINN'S SCORE.
THE TREASURE BOX OPENED AFTER THE CEILING OF THE CAVE COLLAPSED.

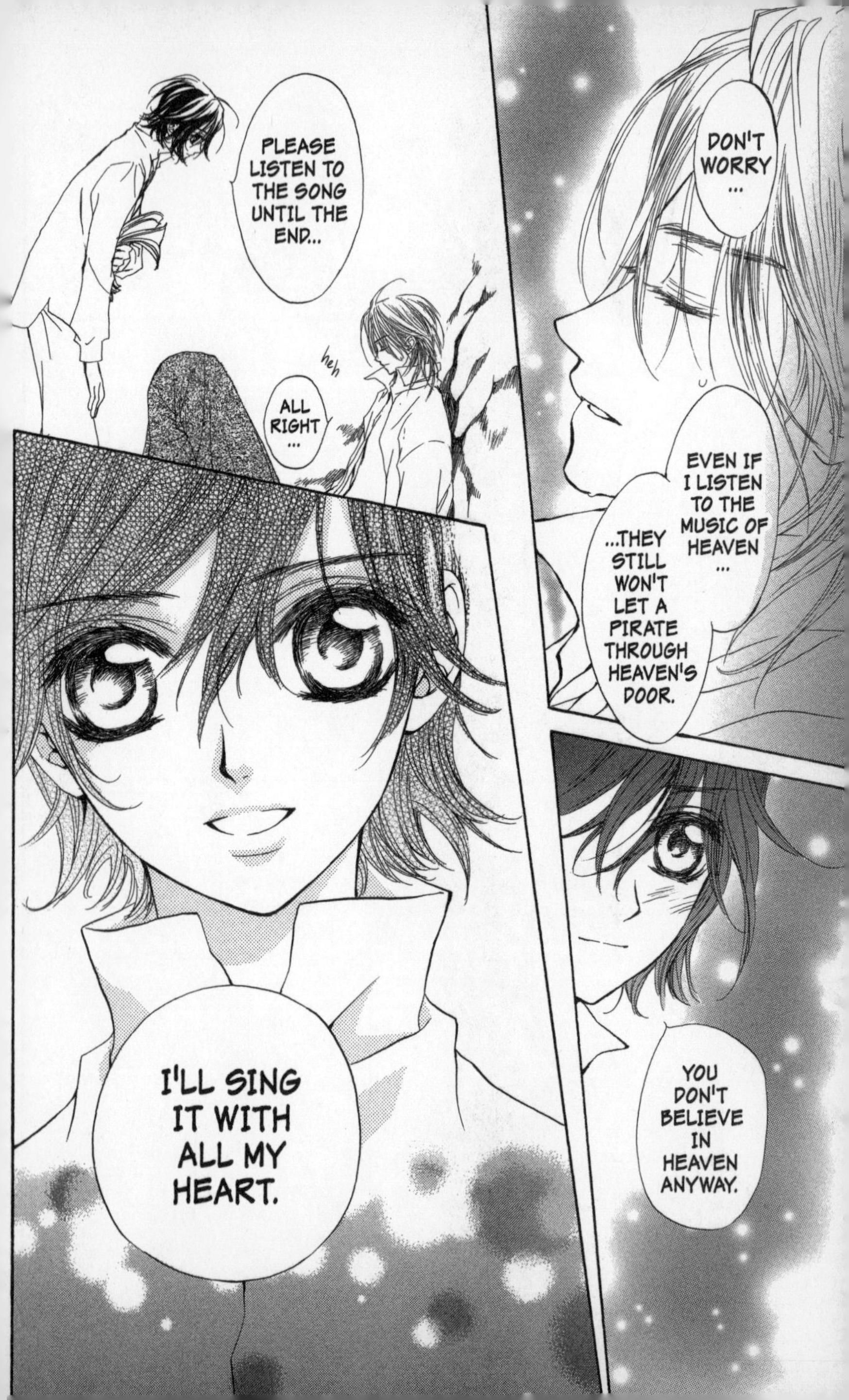
DON'T WORRY ...
EVEN IF I LISTEN TO THE MUSIC OF HEAVEN ...
...THEY STILL WON'T LET A PIRATE THROUGH HEAVEN'S DOOR.
PLEASE LISTEN TO THE SONG UNTIL THE END...
heh
ALL RIGHT ...
YOU DON'T BELIEVE IN HEAVEN ANYWAY.
I'LL SING IT WITH ALL MY HEART.

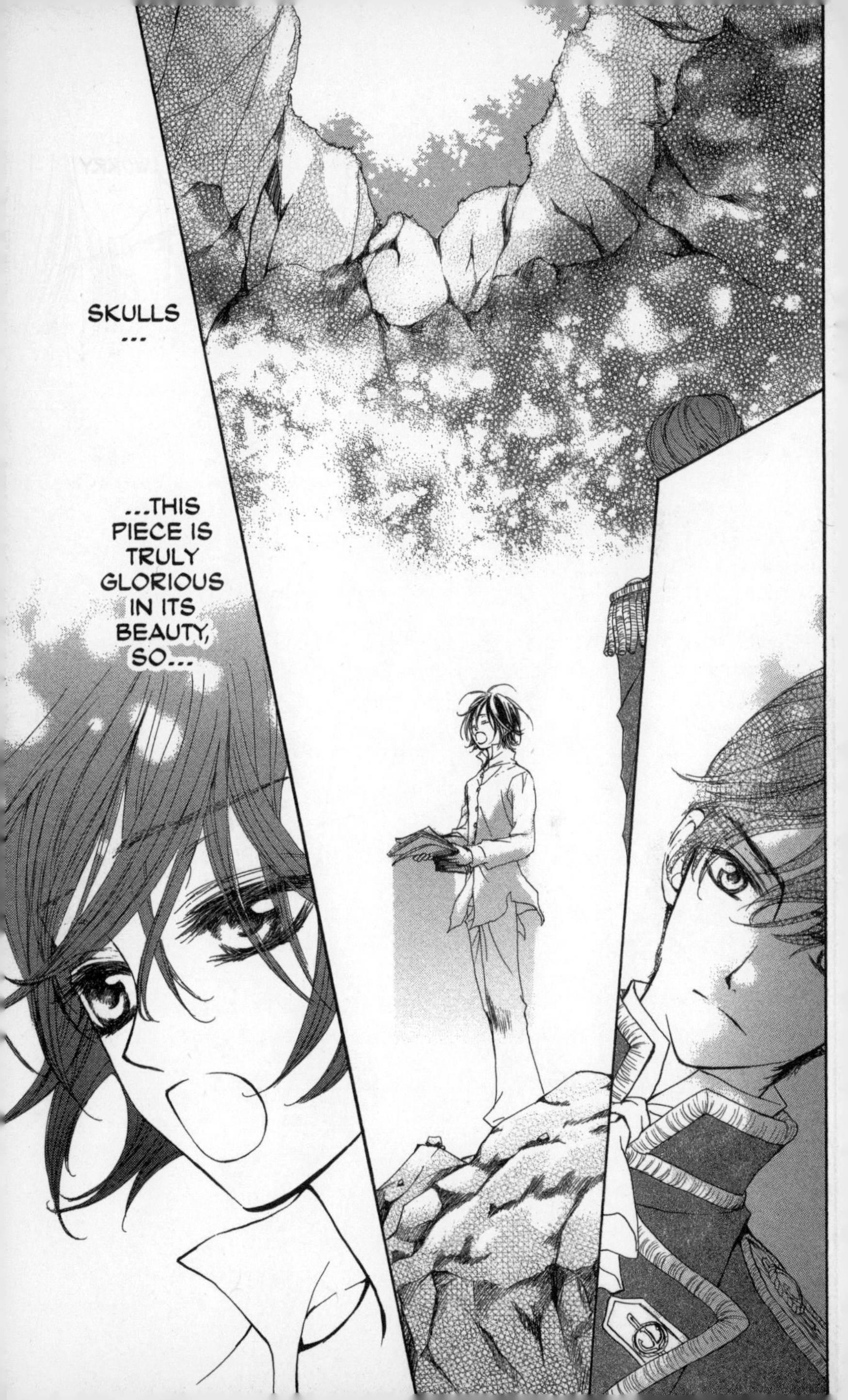
SKULLS ...
...THIS PIECE IS TRULY GLORIOUS IN ITS BEAUTY, SO...

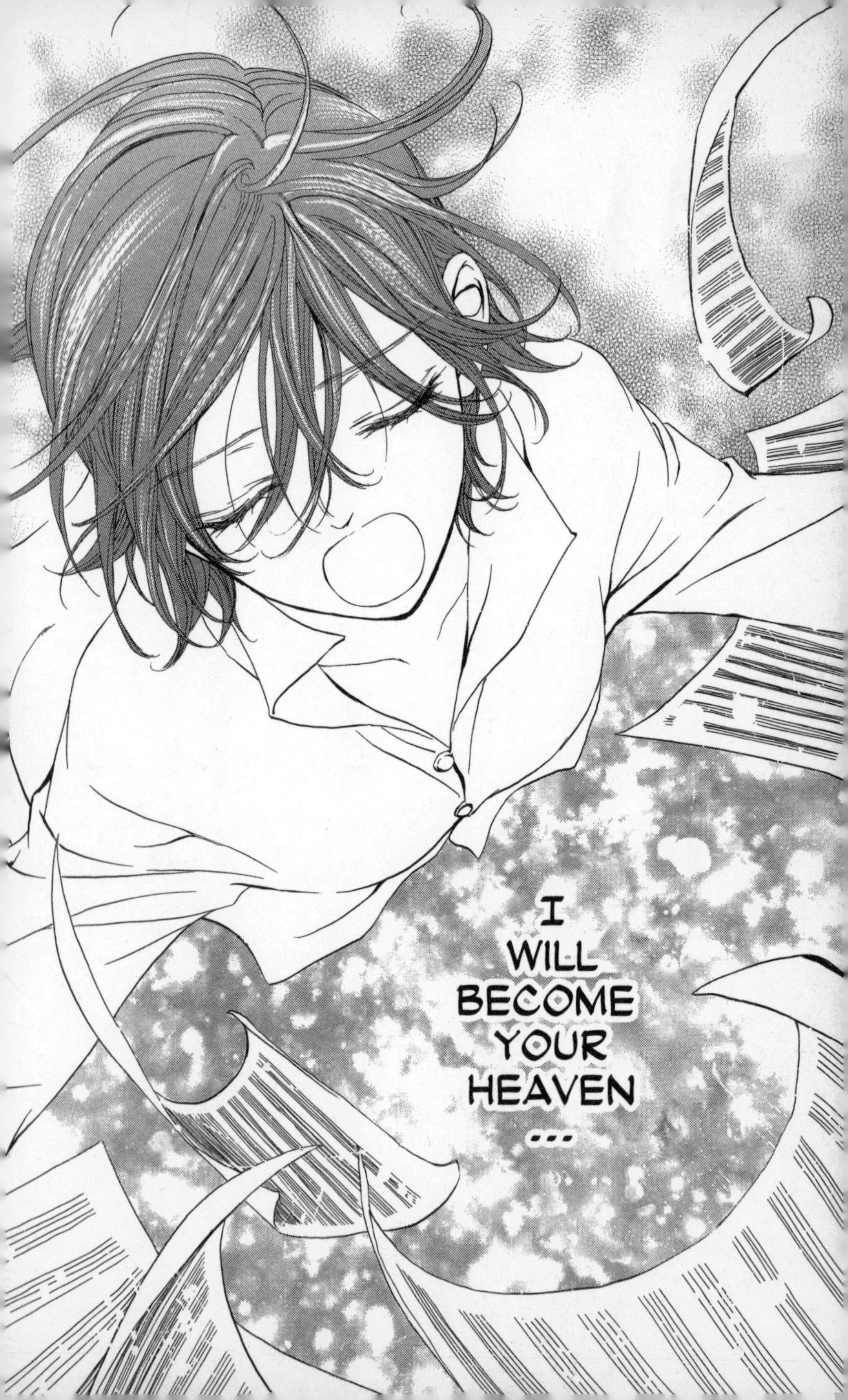
I WILL BECOME YOUR HEAVEN ...

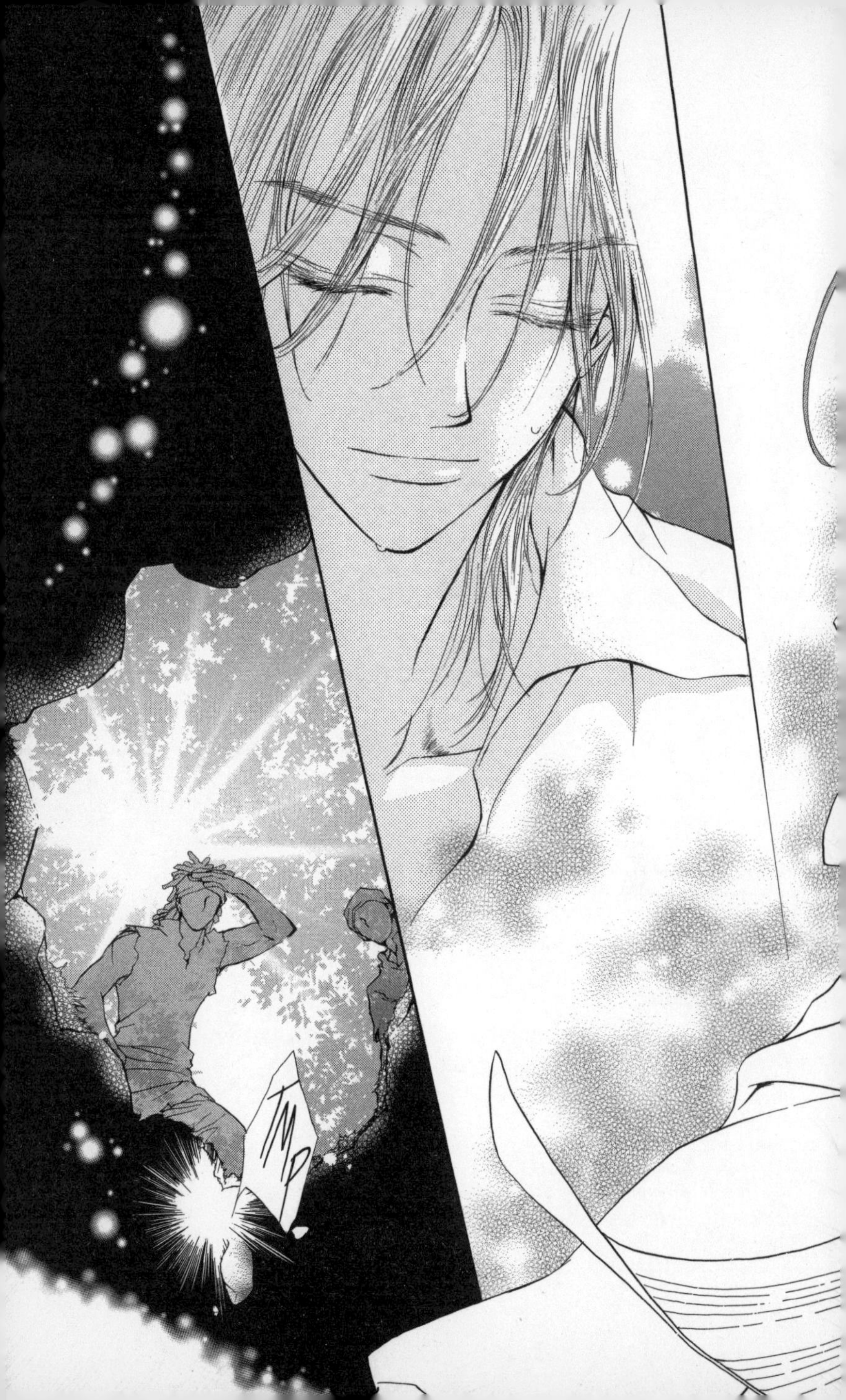
TMP

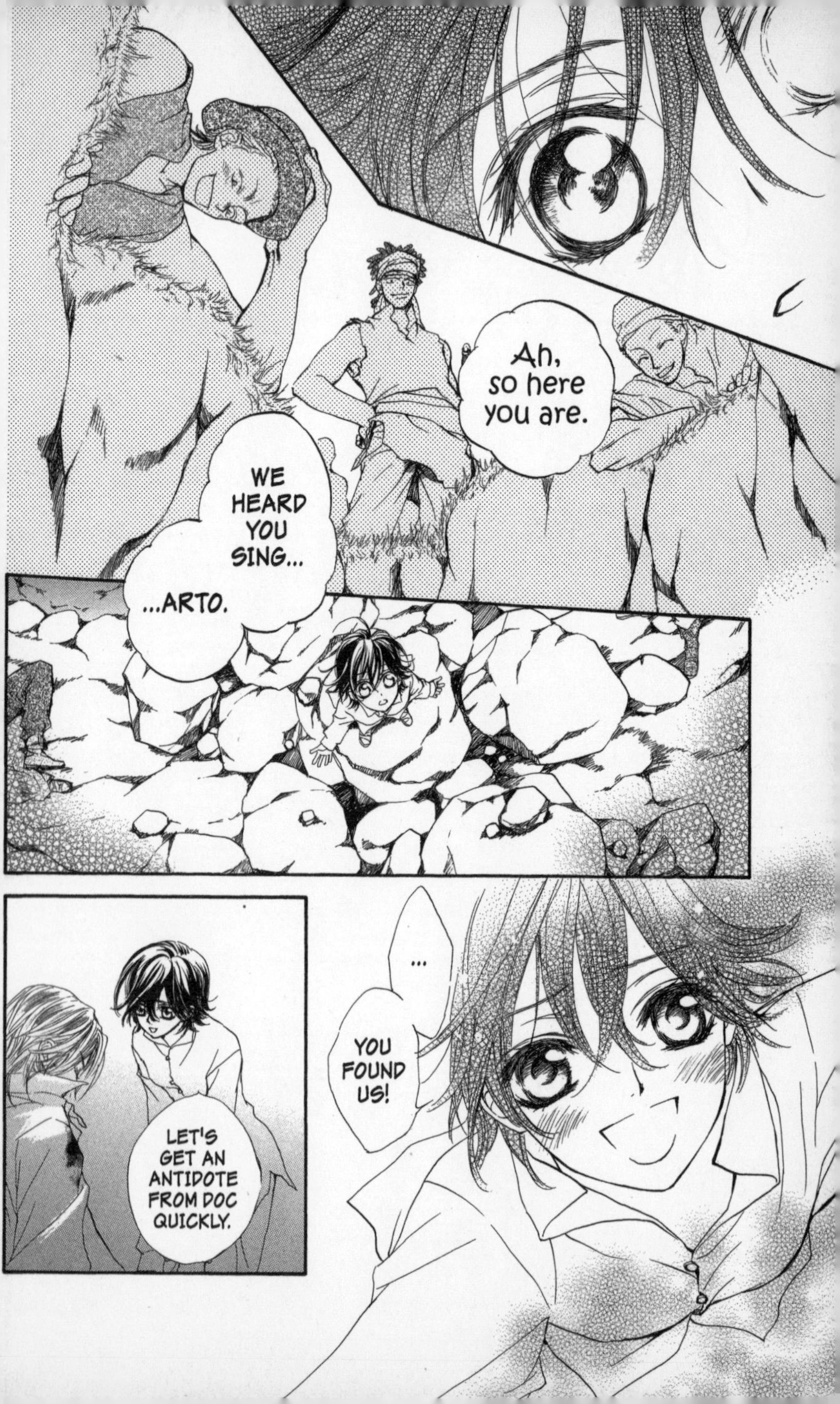
Ah, so here you are.
WE HEARD YOU SING...
...ARTO.
...
YOU FOUND US!
LET'S GET AN ANTIDOTE FROM DOC QUICKLY.

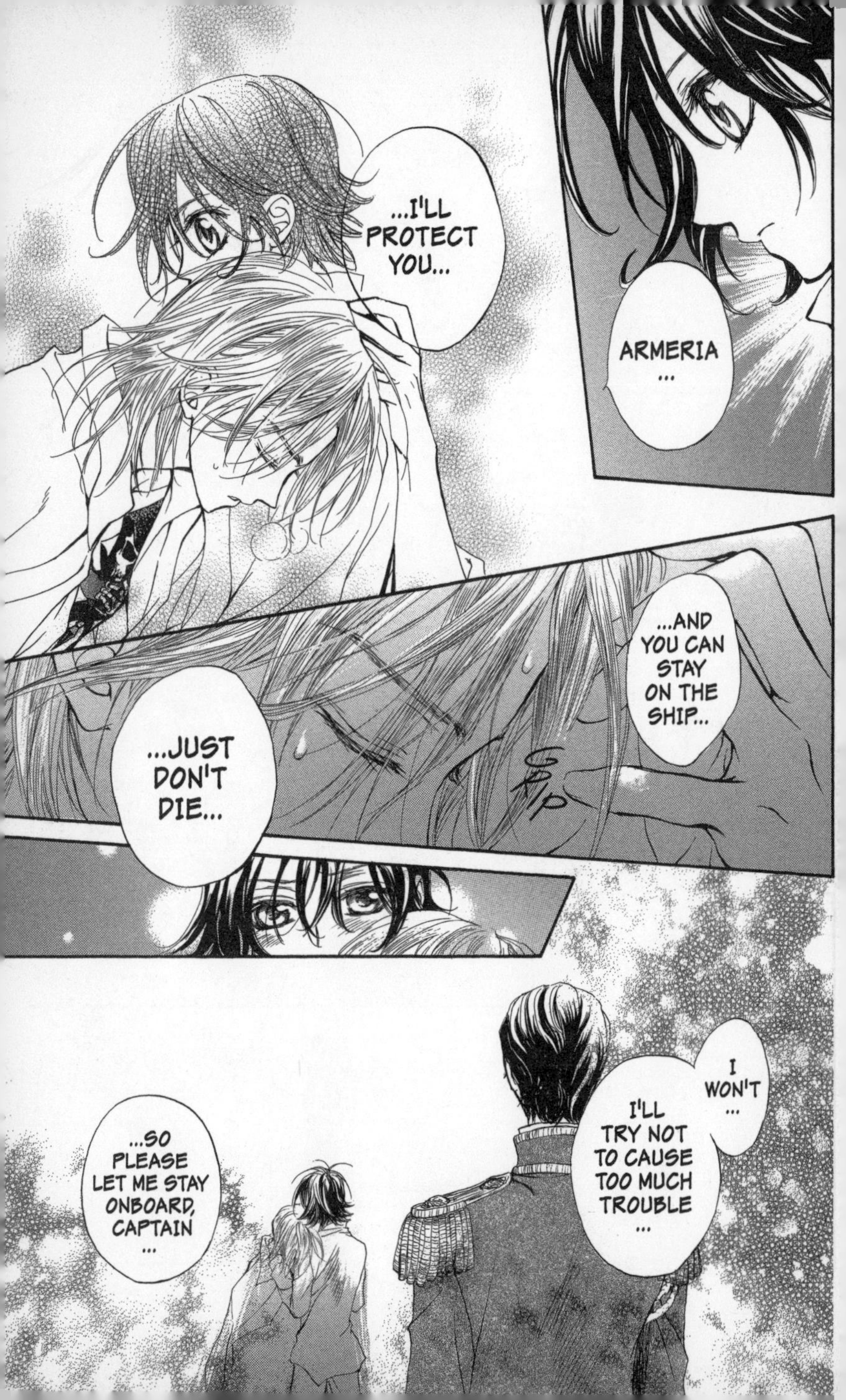
ARMERIA ...
...I'LL PROTECT YOU...
...AND YOU CAN STAY ON THE SHIP...
...JUST DON'T DIE...
I WON'T ...
I'LL TRY NOT TO CAUSE TOO MUCH TROUBLE ...
...SO PLEASE LET ME STAY ONBOARD, CAPTAIN ...

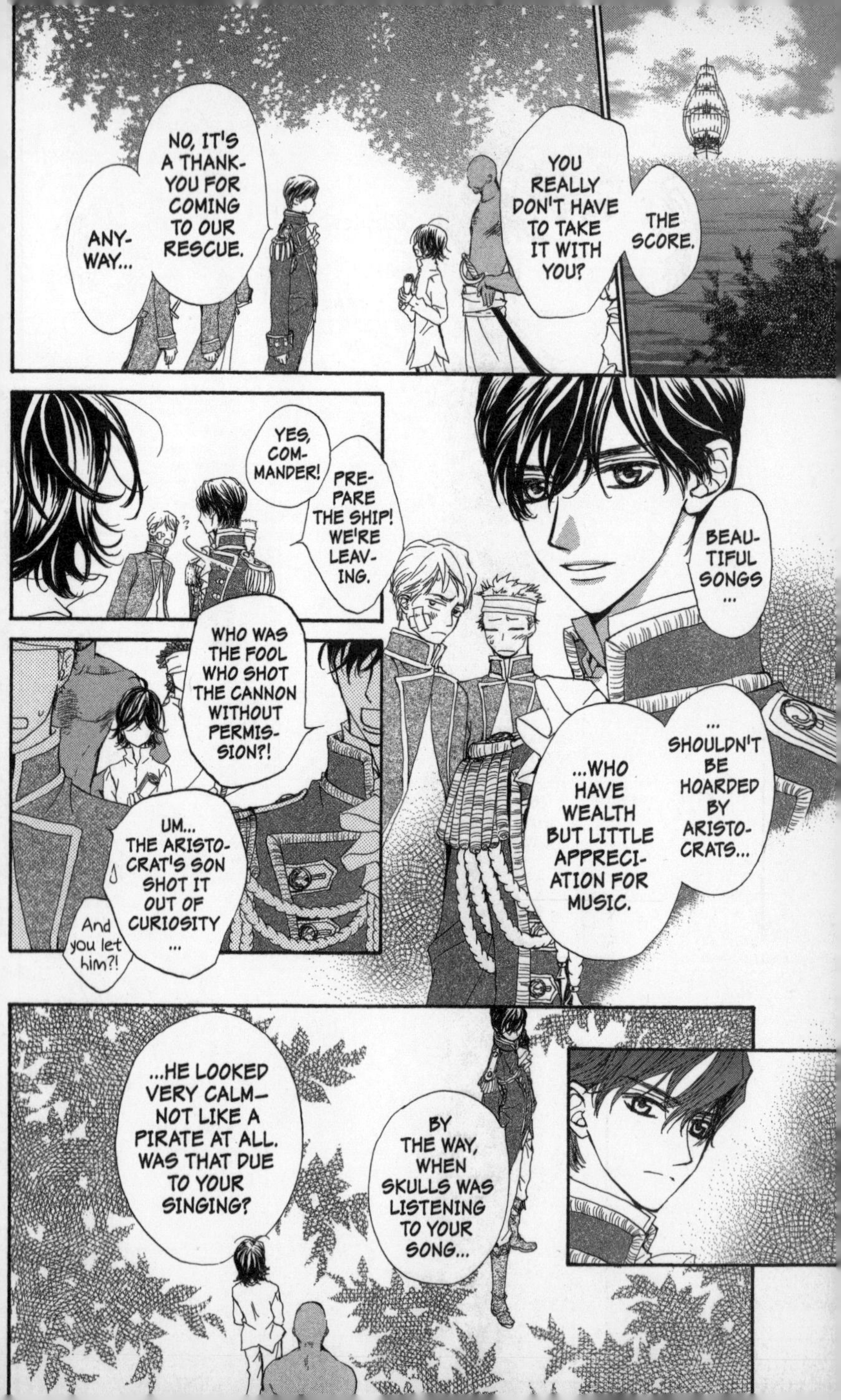
THE SCORE.
YOU REALLY DON'T HAVE TO TAKE IT WITH YOU?
NO, IT'S A THANK-YOU FOR COMING TO OUR RESCUE.
ANYWAY...
BEAUTIFUL SONGS...
...SHOULDN'T BE HOARDED BY ARISTOCRATS...
...WHO HAVE WEALTH BUT LITTLE APPRECIATION FOR MUSIC.
PREPARE THE SHIP! WE'RE LEAVING.
YES, COMMANDER!
WHO WAS THE FOOL WHO SHOT THE CANNON WITHOUT PERMISSION?!
UM... THE ARISTOCRAT'S SON SHOT IT OUT OF CURIOSITY...
And you let him?!
BY THE WAY, WHEN SKULLS WAS LISTENING TO YOUR SONG...
...HE LOOKED VERY CALM—NOT LIKE A PIRATE AT ALL. WAS THAT DUE TO YOUR SINGING?

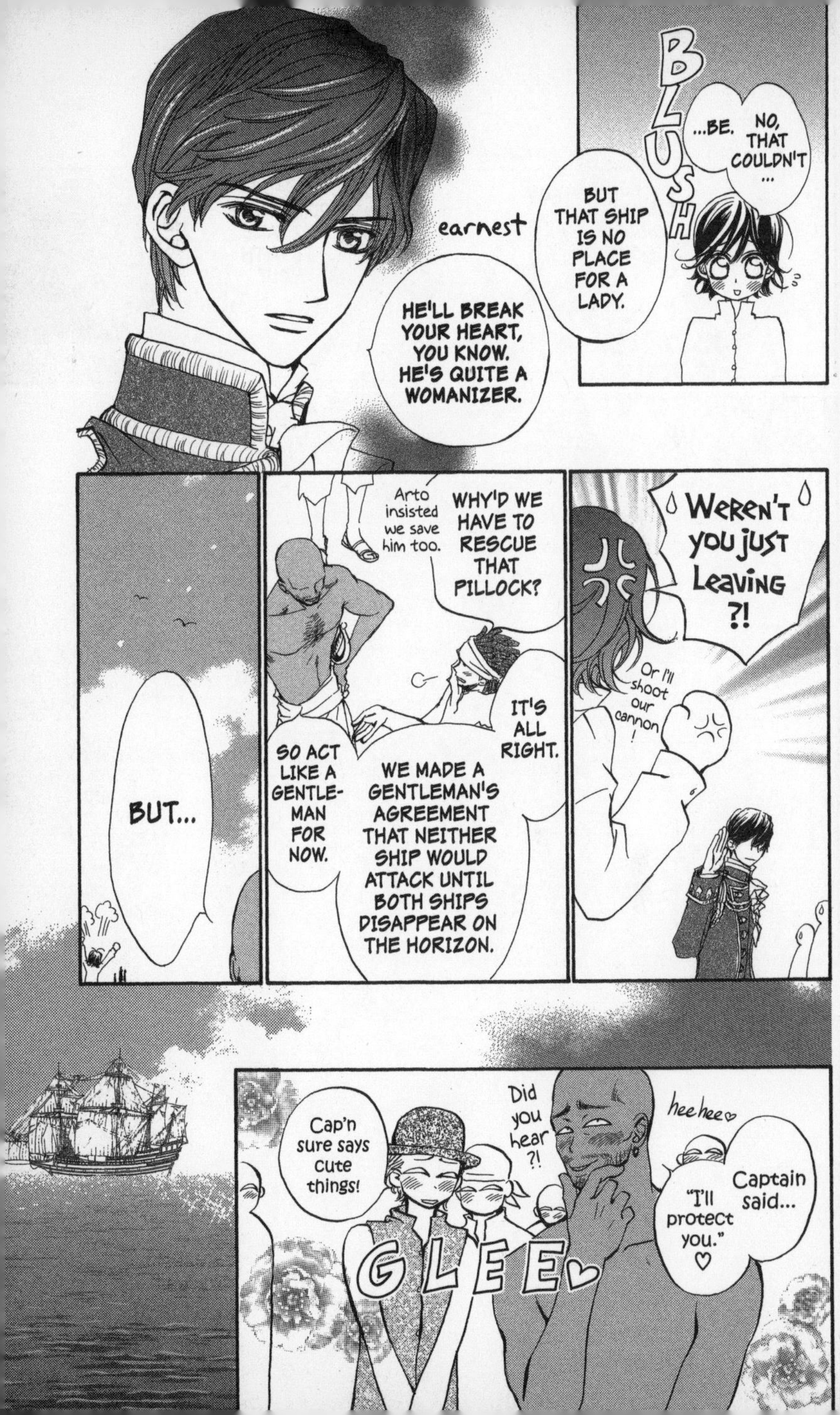
NO, THAT COULDN'T ...
...BE.
BLUSH
BUT THAT SHIP IS NO PLACE FOR A LADY.
earnest
HE'LL BREAK YOUR HEART, YOU KNOW. HE'S QUITE A WOMANIZER.
Weren't you just Leaving ?!
Or I'll shoot our cannon!
WHY'D WE HAVE TO RESCUE THAT PILLOCK?
Arto insisted we save him too.
IT'S ALL RIGHT.
WE MADE A GENTLEMAN'S AGREEMENT THAT NEITHER SHIP WOULD ATTACK UNTIL BOTH SHIPS DISAPPEAR ON THE HORIZON.
SO ACT LIKE A GENTLEMAN FOR NOW.
BUT...
Captain said... "I'll protect you." ♡
hee hee♡
Did you hear?!
Cap'n sure says cute things!
GLEE♡

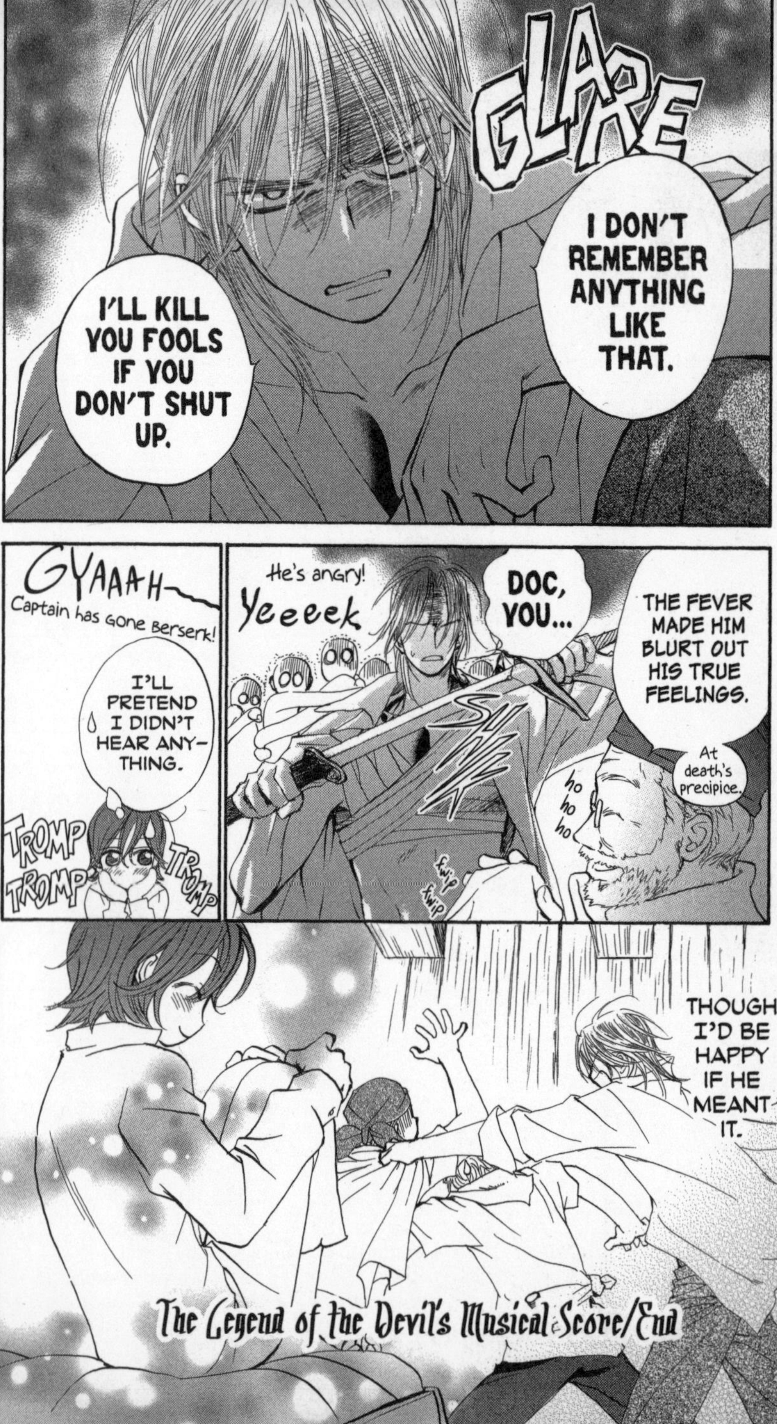
GLARE
I DON'T REMEMBER ANYTHING LIKE THAT.
I'LL KILL YOU FOOLS IF YOU DON'T SHUT UP.
THE FEVER MADE HIM BLURT OUT HIS TRUE FEELINGS.
DOC, YOU...
At death's precipice.
ho ho ho
He's angry!
Yeeeek
fwip fwip
GYAAAH
Captain has gone berserk!
I'LL PRETEND I DIDN'T HEAR ANYTHING.
TROMP TROMP TROMP
THOUGH I'D BE HAPPY IF HE MEANT IT.
The Legend of the Devil's Musical Score/End

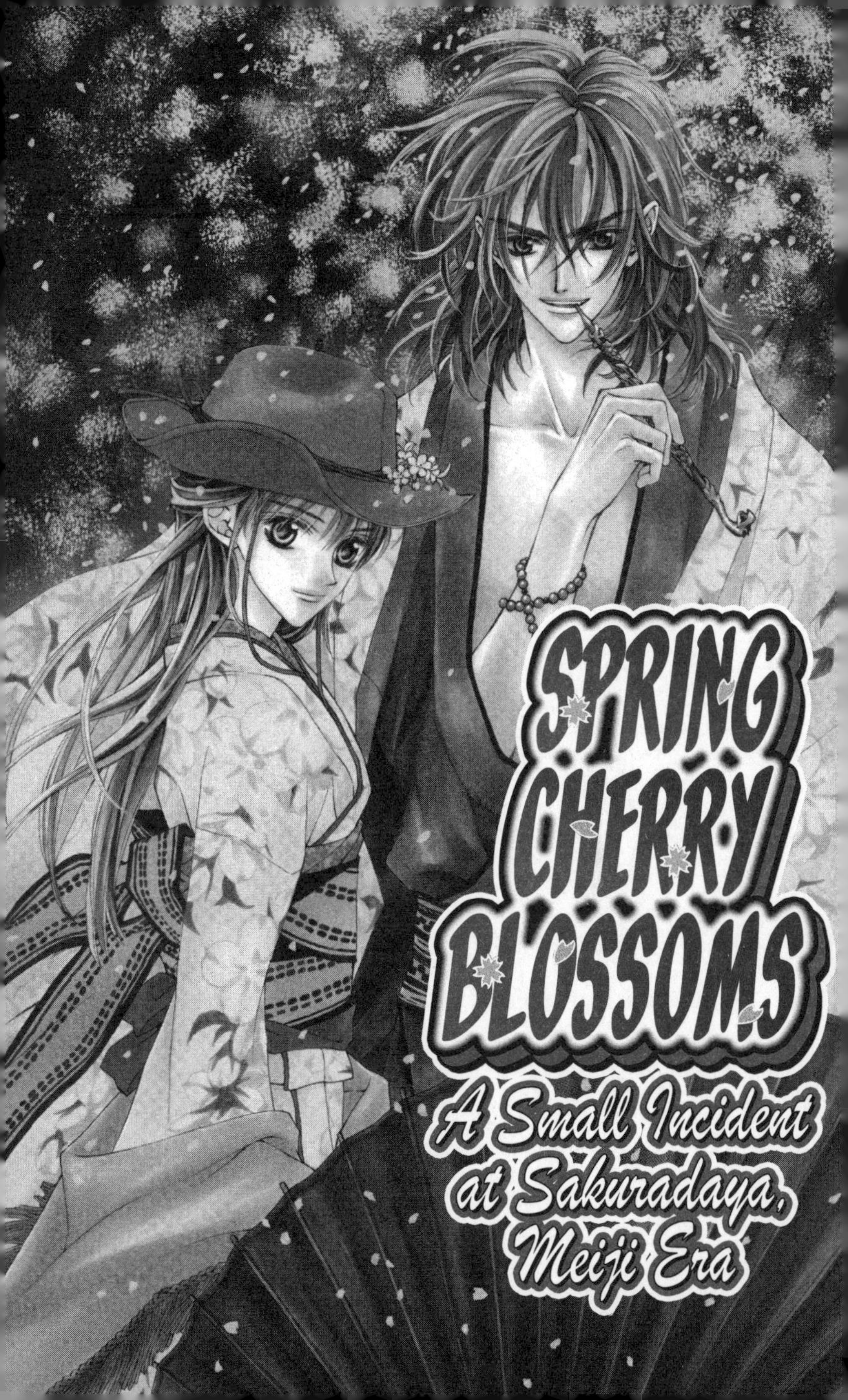
SPRING CHERRY BLOSSOMS
A Small Incident at Sakuradaya, Meiji Era

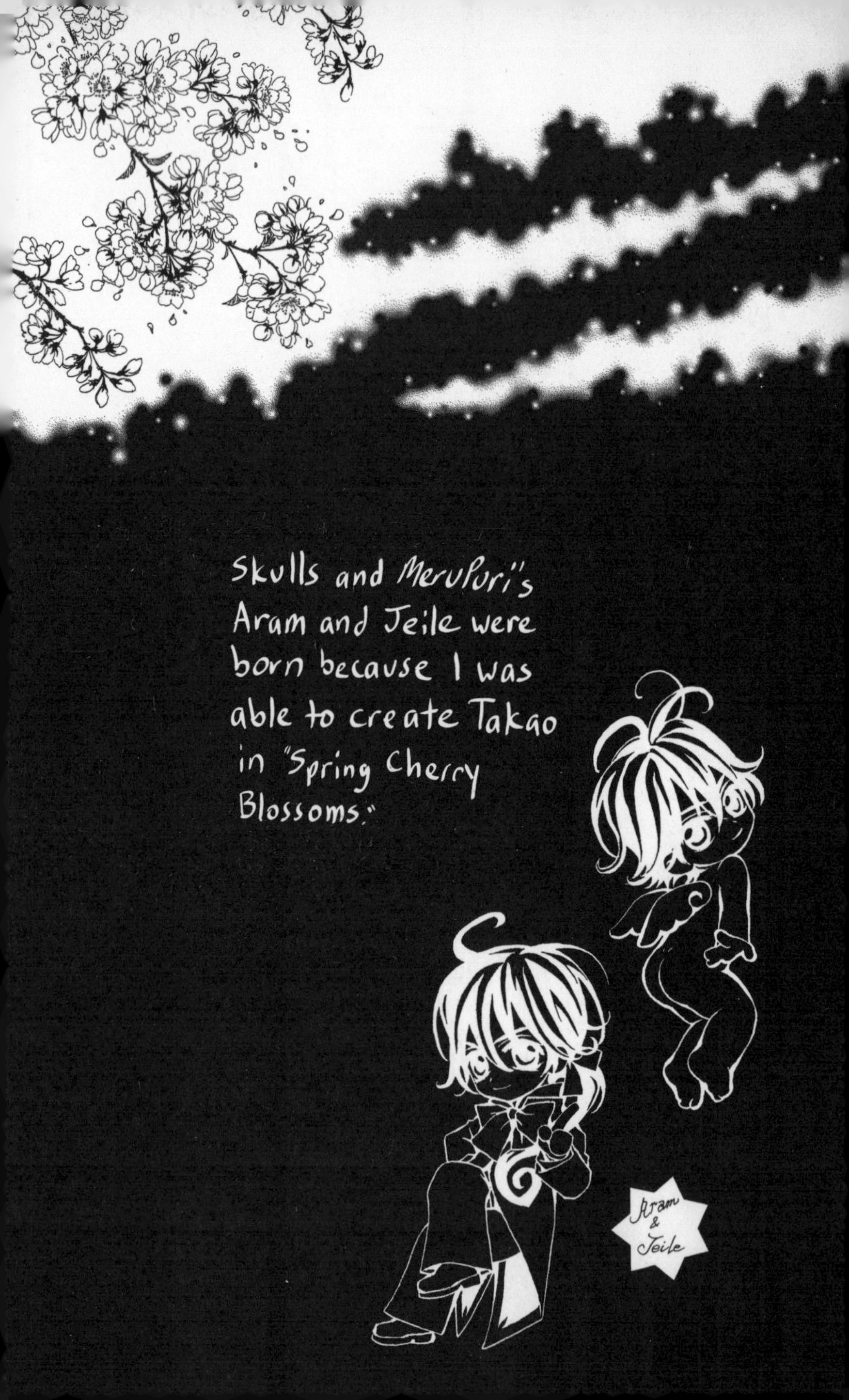
Skulls and MeruPuri's Aram and Jeile were born because I was able to create Takao in "Spring Cherry Blossoms."
Aram & Jeile

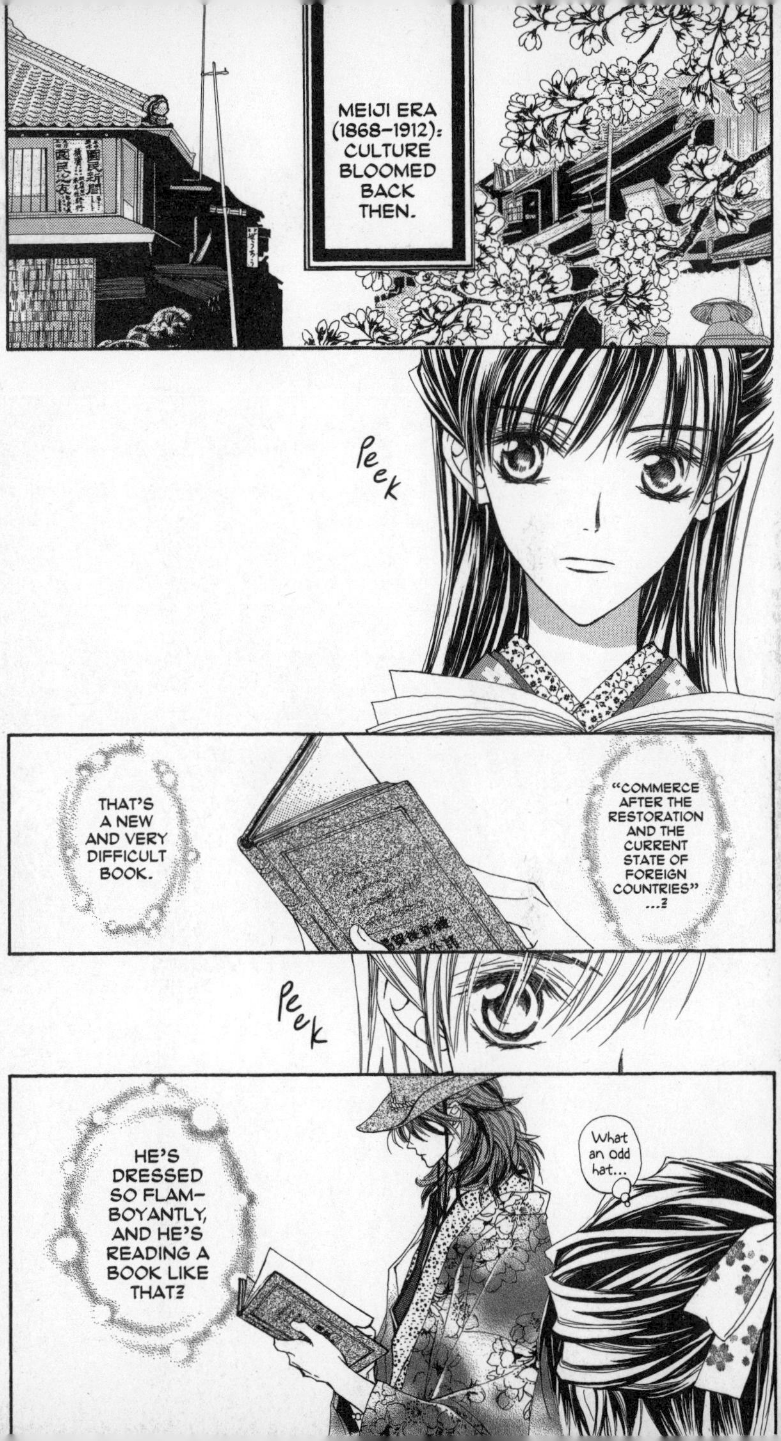
MEIJI ERA (1868–1912): CULTURE BLOOMED BACK THEN.
Peek
"COMMERCE AFTER THE RESTORATION AND THE CURRENT STATE OF FOREIGN COUNTRIES" ...?
THAT'S A NEW AND VERY DIFFICULT BOOK.
Peek
What an odd hat...
HE'S DRESSED SO FLAM-BOYANTLY, AND HE'S READING A BOOK LIKE THAT?

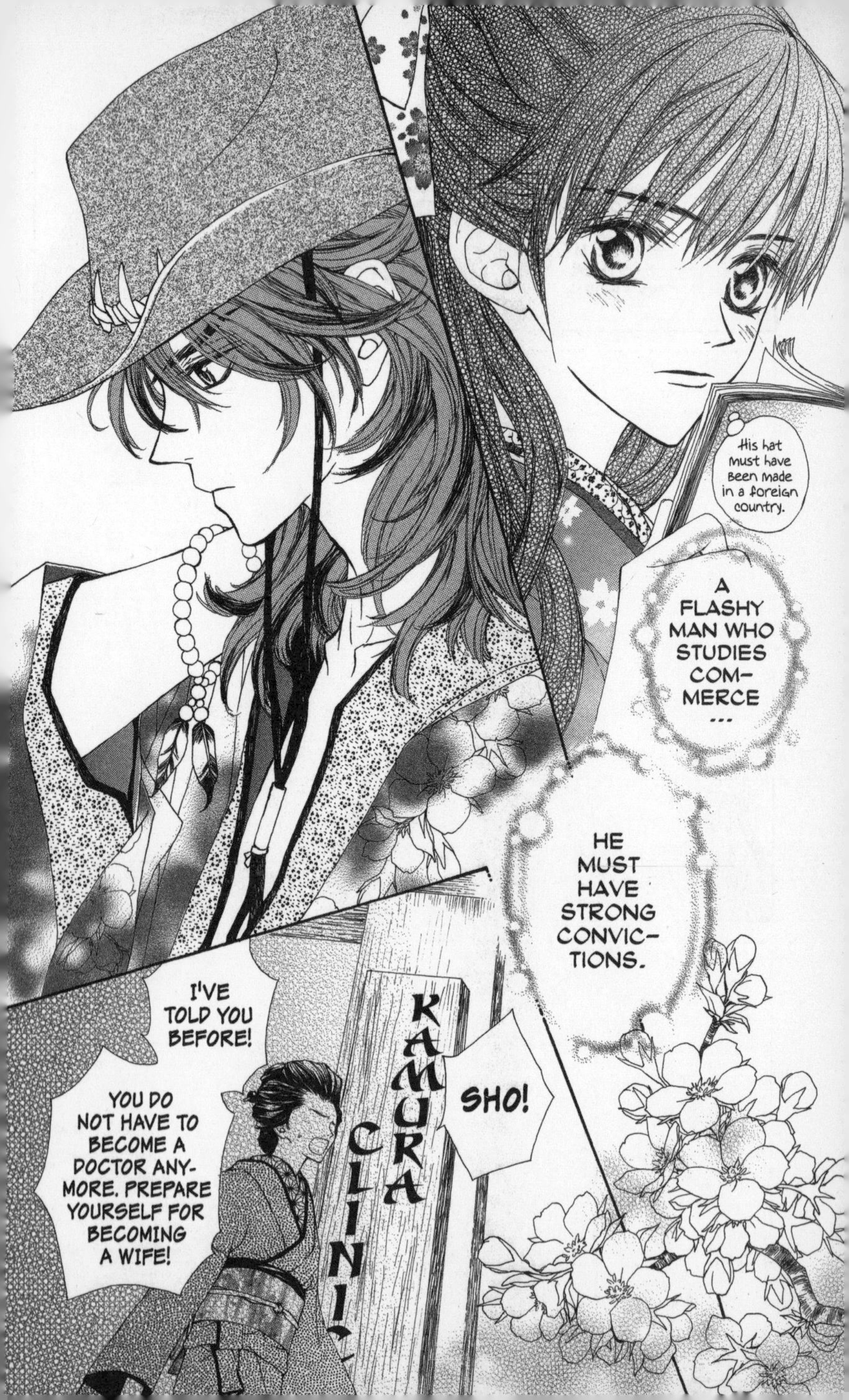
His hat must have been made in a foreign country.
A FLASHY MAN WHO STUDIES COM-MERCE...
HE MUST HAVE STRONG CONVIC-TIONS.
KAMURA
CLINI
SHO!
I'VE TOLD YOU BEFORE!
YOU DO NOT HAVE TO BECOME A DOCTOR ANY-MORE. PREPARE YOURSELF FOR BECOMING A WIFE!

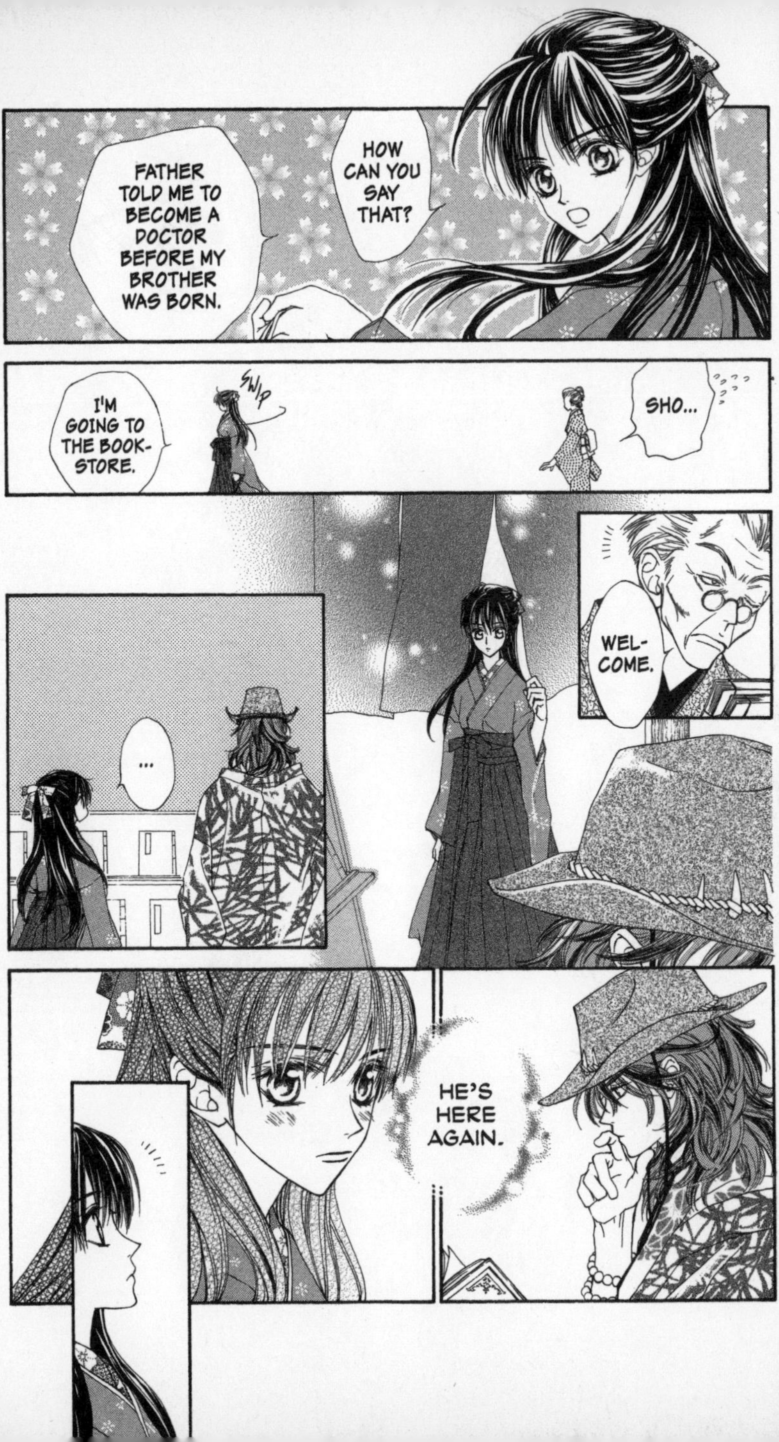
HOW CAN YOU SAY THAT?
FATHER TOLD ME TO BECOME A DOCTOR BEFORE MY BROTHER WAS BORN.
SHO...
SWIP
I'M GOING TO THE BOOK-STORE.
WEL-COME.
...
HE'S HERE AGAIN.

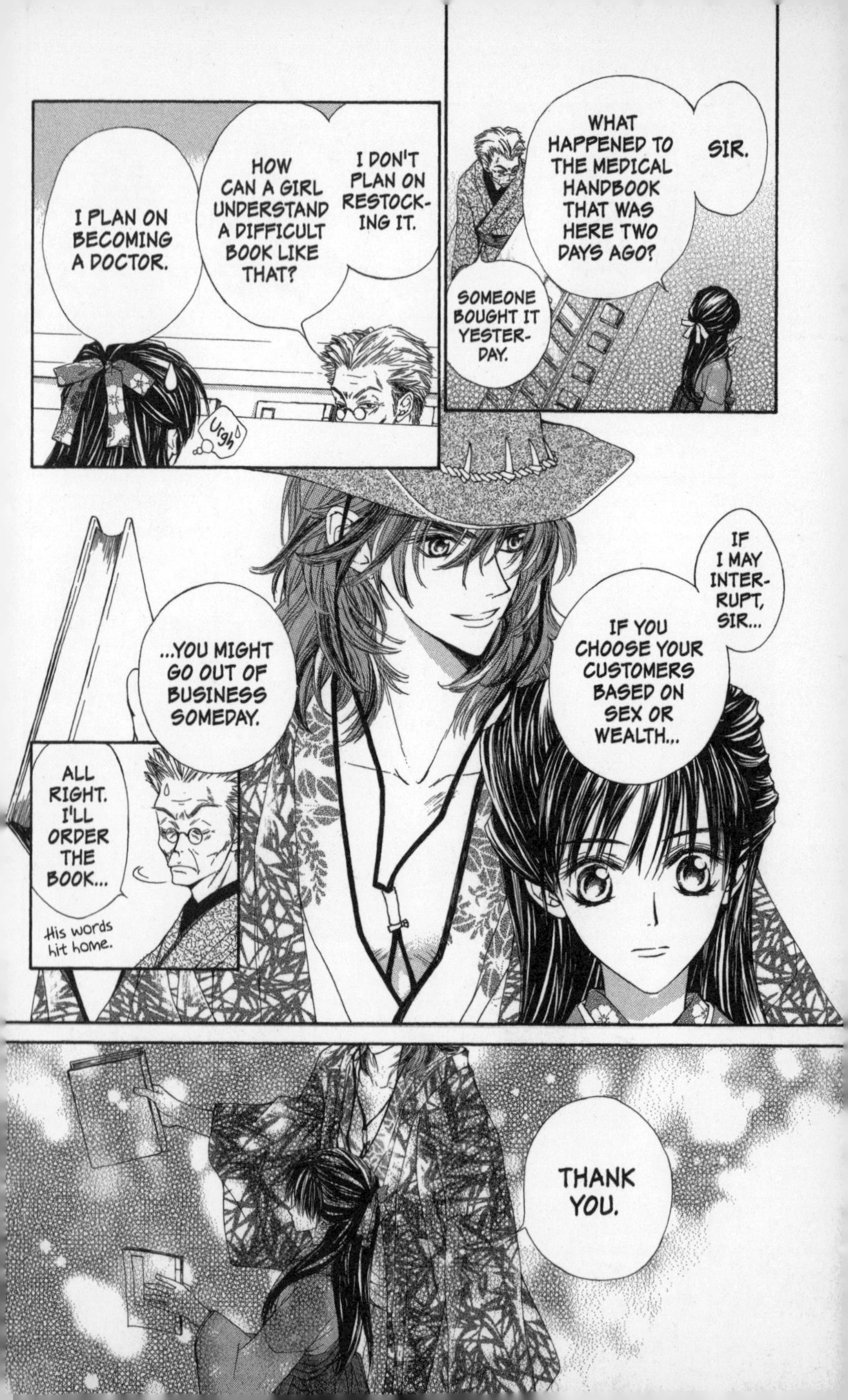
SIR.
WHAT HAPPENED TO THE MEDICAL HANDBOOK THAT WAS HERE TWO DAYS AGO?
SOMEONE BOUGHT IT YESTERDAY.
I DON'T PLAN ON RESTOCKING IT.
HOW CAN A GIRL UNDERSTAND A DIFFICULT BOOK LIKE THAT?
Urgh
I PLAN ON BECOMING A DOCTOR.
IF I MAY INTERRUPT, SIR...
IF YOU CHOOSE YOUR CUSTOMERS BASED ON SEX OR WEALTH...
...YOU MIGHT GO OUT OF BUSINESS SOMEDAY.
ALL RIGHT. I'LL ORDER THE BOOK...
His words hit home.
THANK YOU.

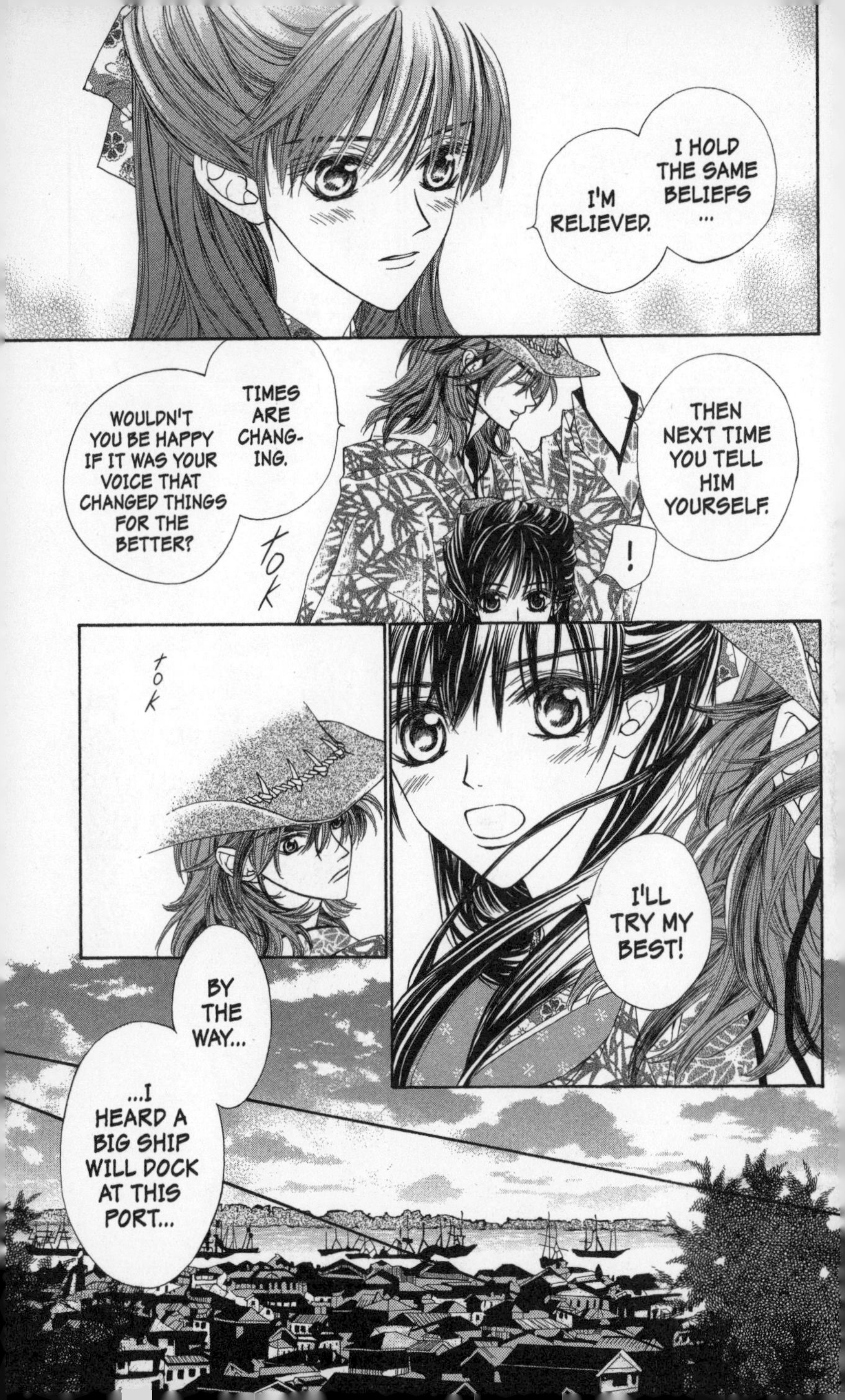
I HOLD THE SAME BELIEFS...
I'M RELIEVED.
THEN NEXT TIME YOU TELL HIM YOURSELF.
!
TIMES ARE CHANG-ING.
WOULDN'T YOU BE HAPPY IF IT WAS YOUR VOICE THAT CHANGED THINGS FOR THE BETTER?
TOK
I'LL TRY MY BEST!
TOK
BY THE WAY...
...I HEARD A BIG SHIP WILL DOCK AT THIS PORT...

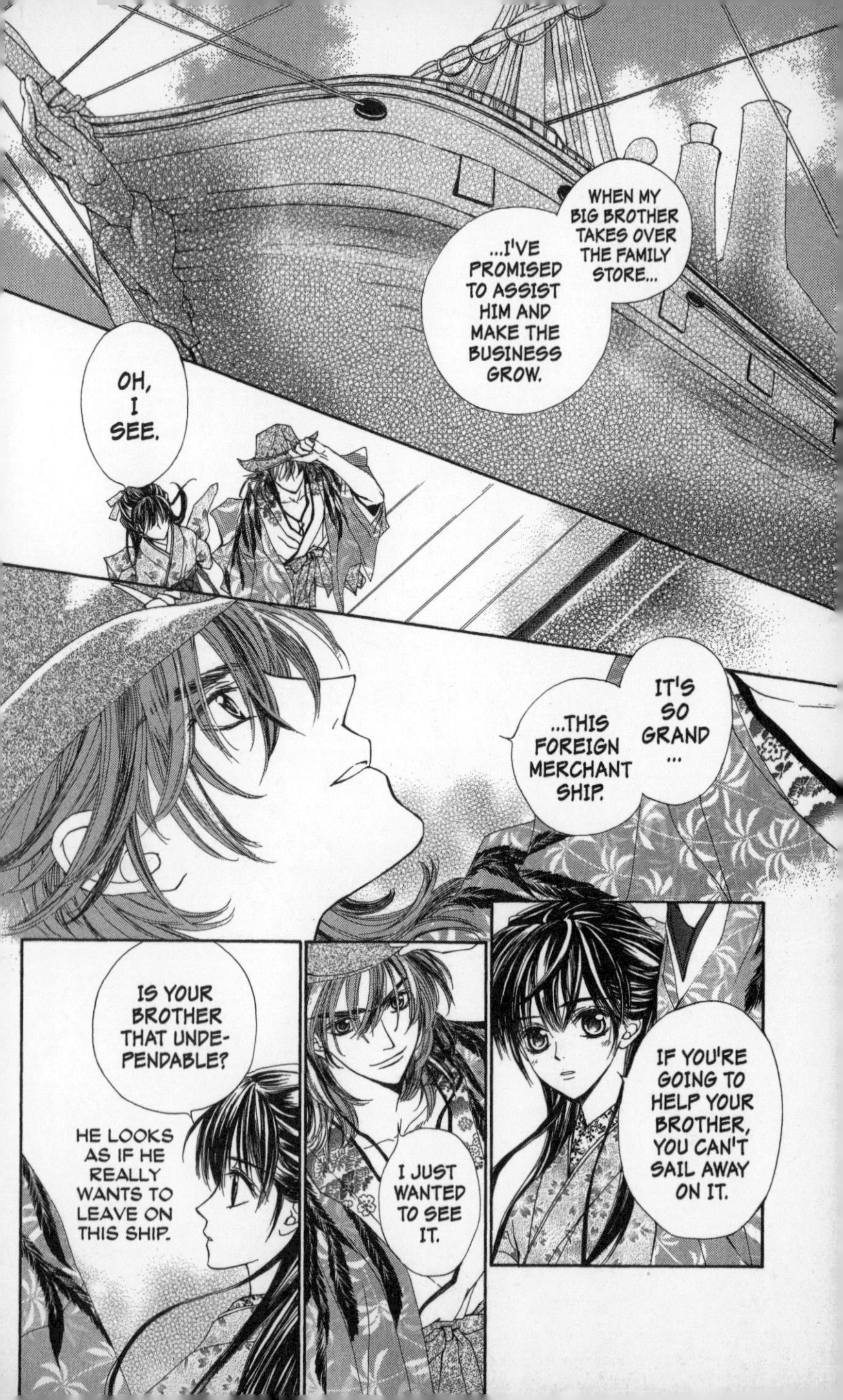
WHEN MY BIG BROTHER TAKES OVER THE FAMILY STORE...
...I'VE PROMISED TO ASSIST HIM AND MAKE THE BUSINESS GROW.
OH, I SEE.
IT'S SO GRAND ...
...THIS FOREIGN MERCHANT SHIP.
IF YOU'RE GOING TO HELP YOUR BROTHER, YOU CAN'T SAIL AWAY ON IT.
I JUST WANTED TO SEE IT.
IS YOUR BROTHER THAT UNDE-PENDABLE?
HE LOOKS AS IF HE REALLY WANTS TO LEAVE ON THIS SHIP.

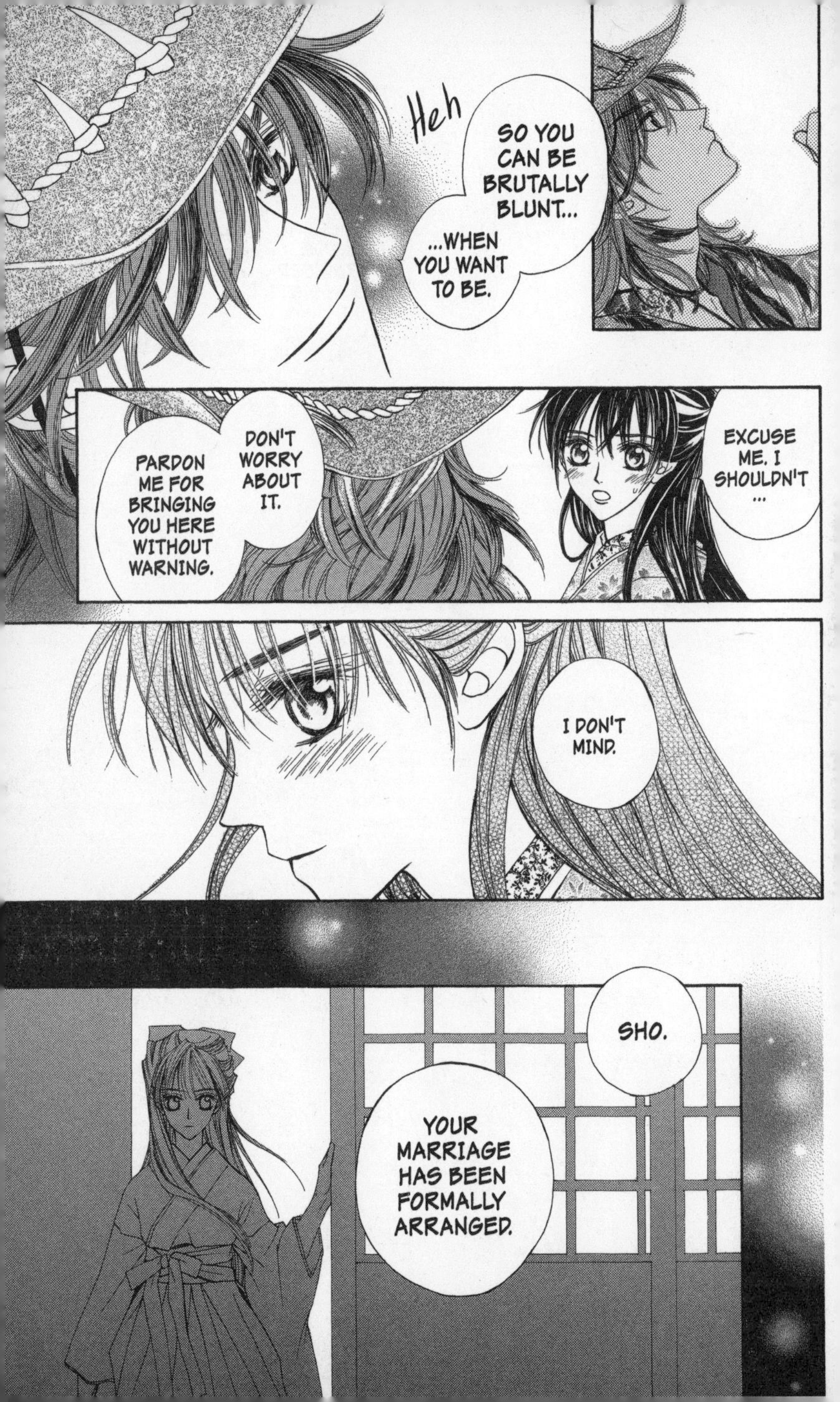
Heh
SO YOU CAN BE BRUTALLY BLUNT...
...WHEN YOU WANT TO BE.
EXCUSE ME. I SHOULDN'T ...
DON'T WORRY ABOUT IT.
PARDON ME FOR BRINGING YOU HERE WITHOUT WARNING.
I DON'T MIND.
SHO.
YOUR MARRIAGE HAS BEEN FORMALLY ARRANGED.

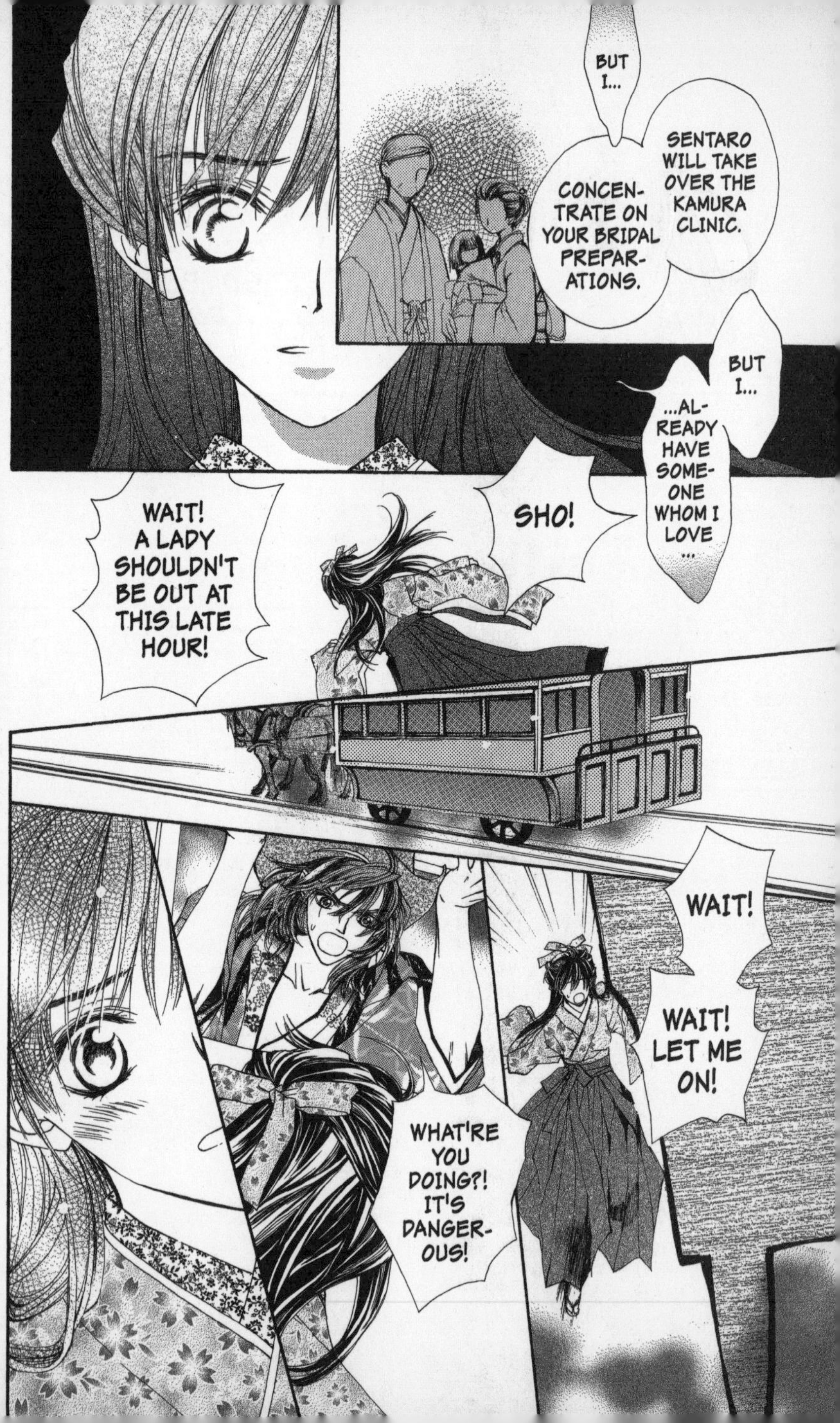
BUT I...
SENTARO WILL TAKE OVER THE KAMURA CLINIC.
CONCENTRATE ON YOUR BRIDAL PREPARATIONS.
BUT I...
...ALREADY HAVE SOMEONE WHOM I LOVE...
SHO!
WAIT! A LADY SHOULDN'T BE OUT AT THIS LATE HOUR!
WAIT!
WAIT! LET ME ON!
WHAT'RE YOU DOING?! IT'S DANGEROUS!

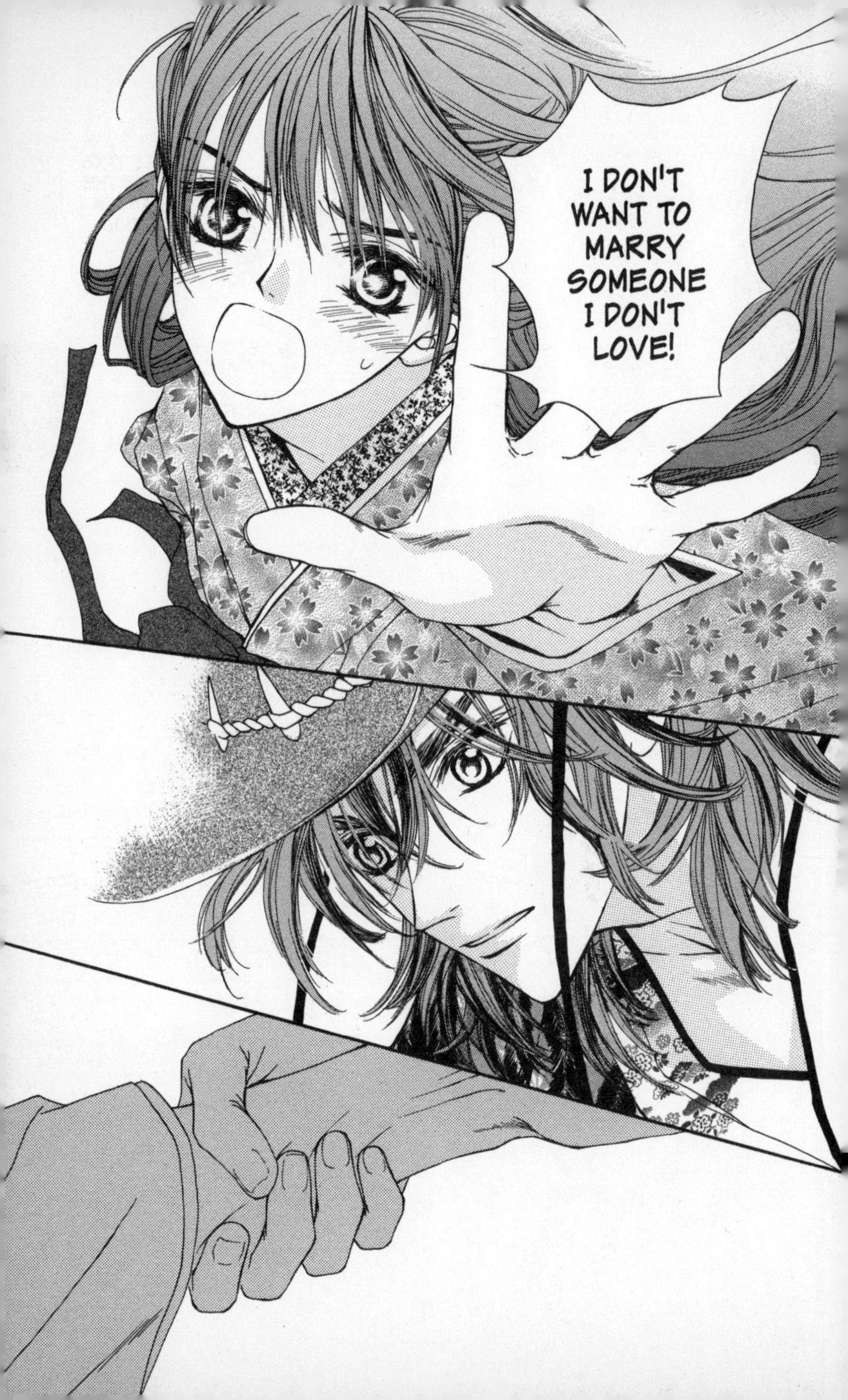
I DON'T WANT TO MARRY SOMEONE I DON'T LOVE!

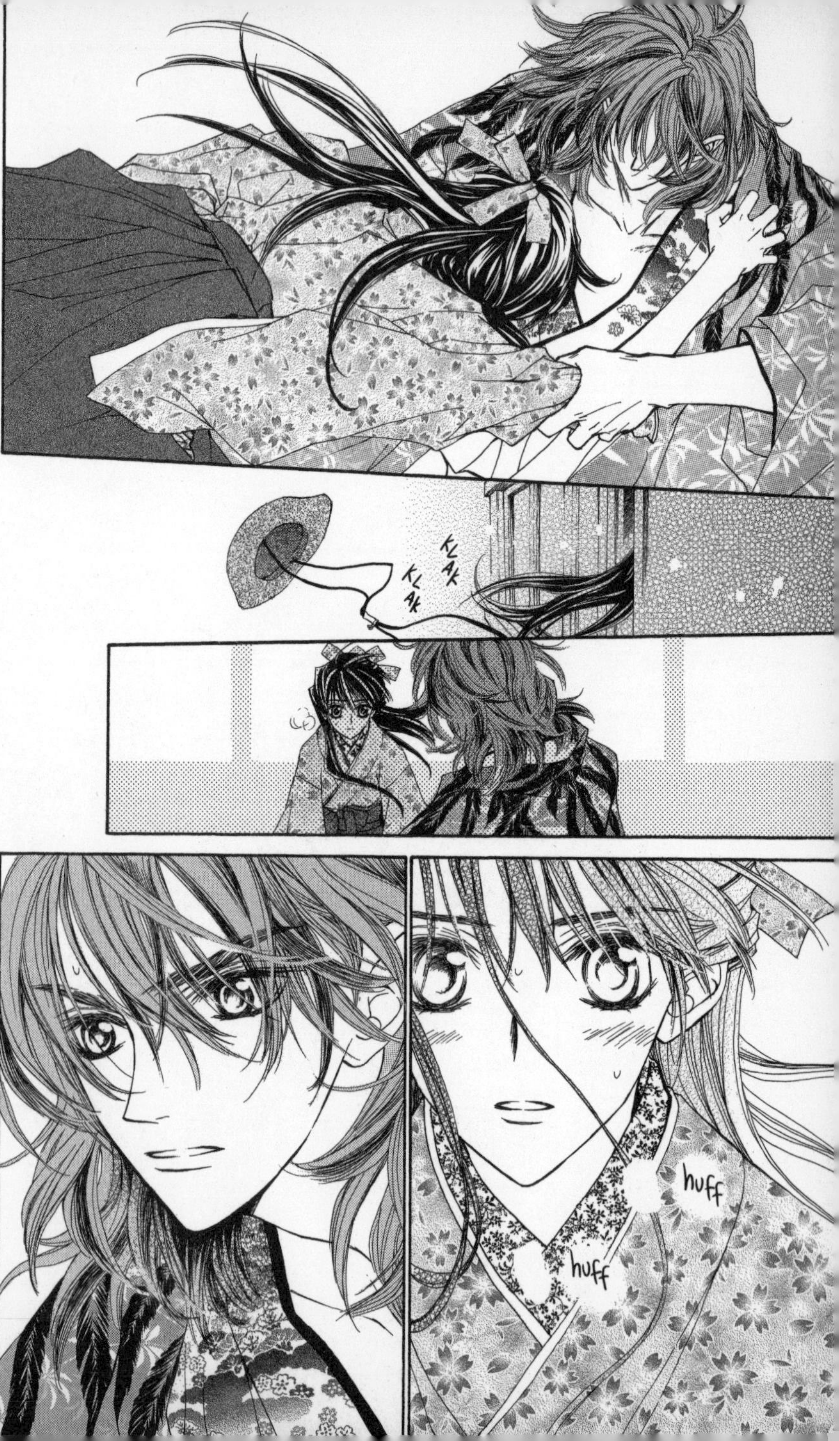
KLAK
KLAK
huff
huff

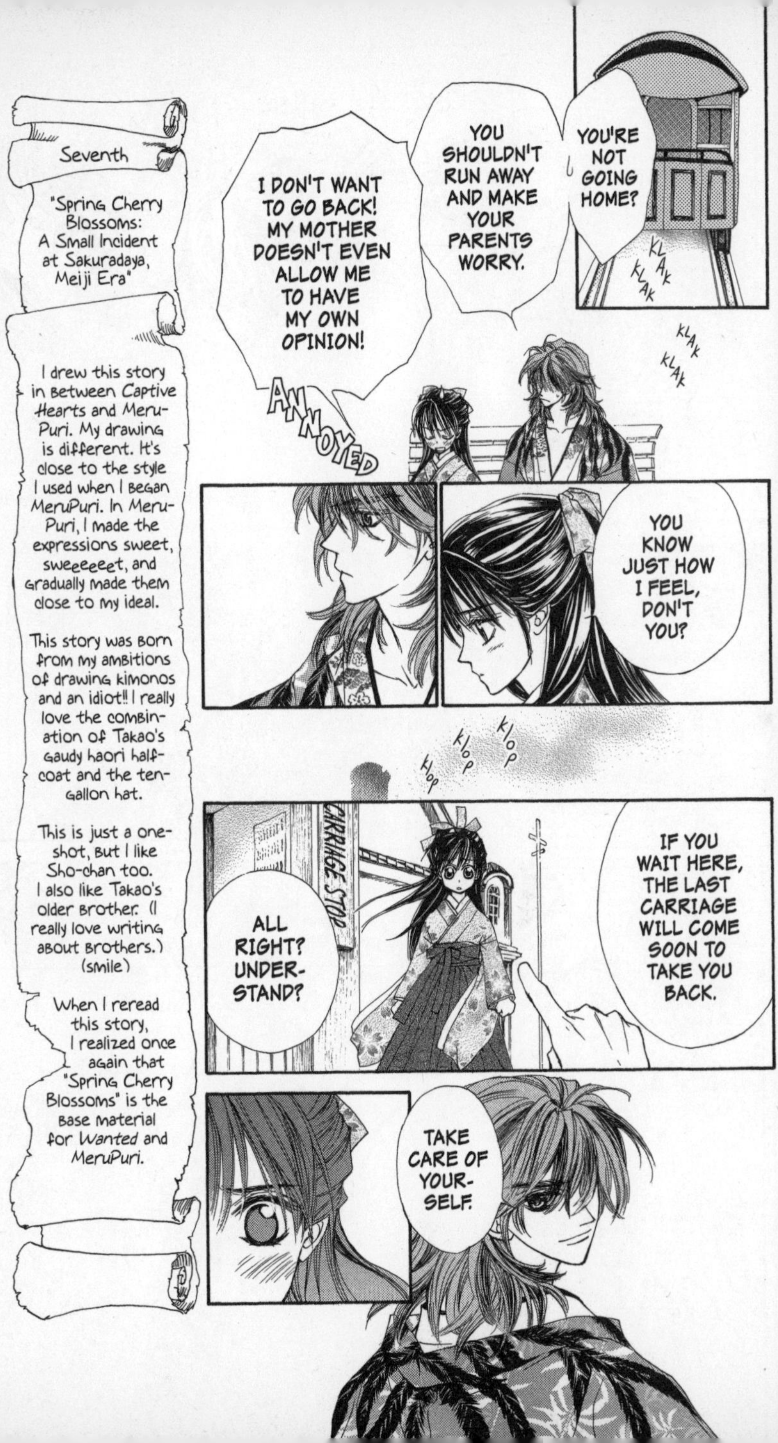
YOU'RE NOT GOING HOME?
KLAK KLAK
YOU SHOULDN'T RUN AWAY AND MAKE YOUR PARENTS WORRY.
I DON'T WANT TO GO BACK! MY MOTHER DOESN'T EVEN ALLOW ME TO HAVE MY OWN OPINION!
ANNOYED
KLAK KLAK
YOU KNOW JUST HOW I FEEL, DON'T YOU?
klop klop klop
IF YOU WAIT HERE, THE LAST CARRIAGE WILL COME SOON TO TAKE YOU BACK.
CARRIAGE STOP
ALL RIGHT? UNDERSTAND?
TAKE CARE OF YOUR-SELF.

Seventh

"Spring Cherry Blossoms: A Small Incident at Sakuradaya, Meiji Era"

I drew this story in between Captive Hearts and Meru-Puri. My drawing is different. It's close to the style I used when I began MeruPuri. In Meru-Puri, I made the expressions sweet, sweeeeeet, and gradually made them close to my ideal.

This story was born from my ambitions of drawing kimonos and an idiot!! I really love the combination of Takao's gaudy haori half-coat and the ten-gallon hat.

This is just a one-shot, but I like Sho-chan too. I also like Takao's older brother. (I really love writing about brothers.) (smile)

When I reread this story, I realized once again that "Spring Cherry Blossoms" is the base material for *Wanted* and MeruPuri.

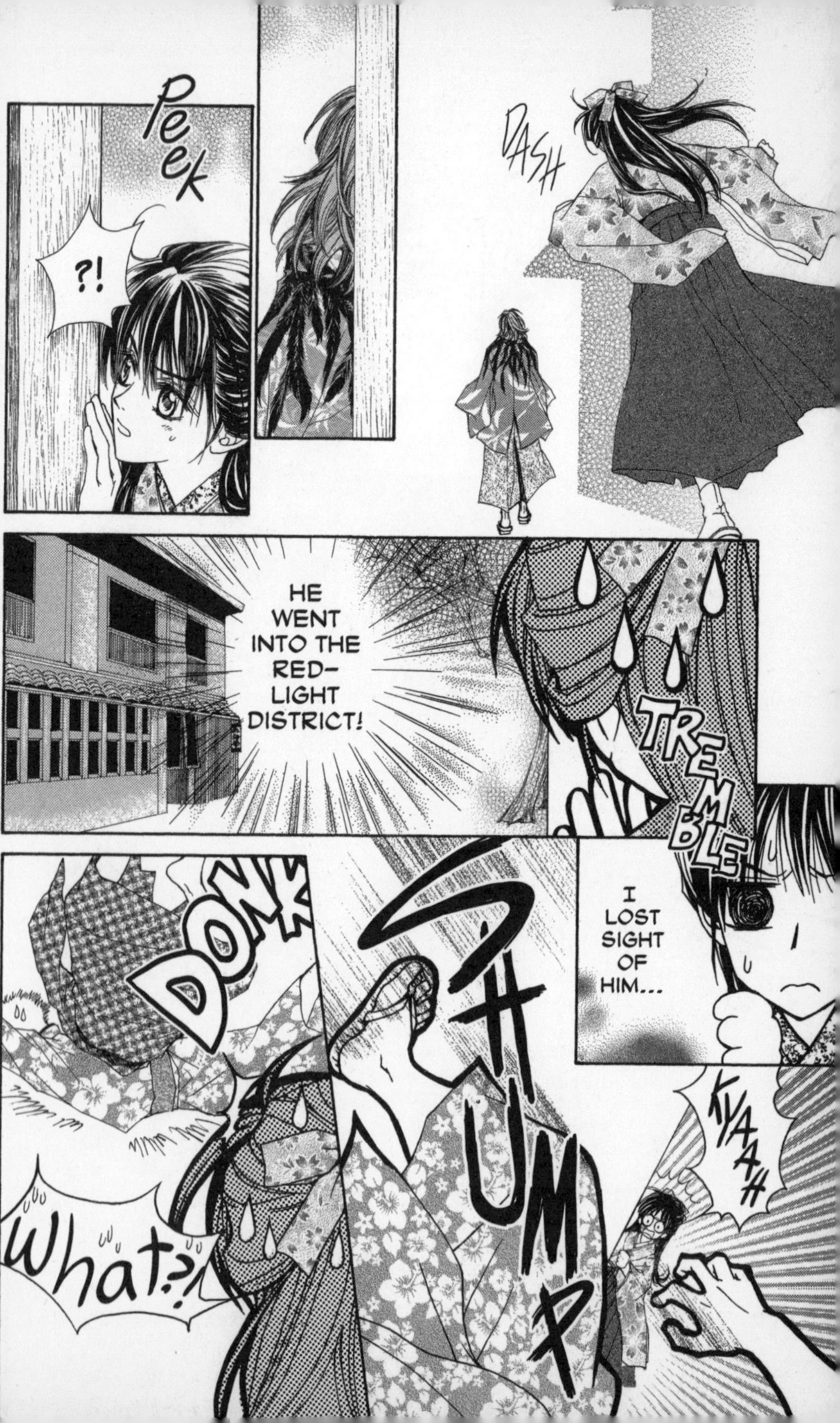
DASH
Peek
?!
TREMBLE
HE WENT INTO THE RED-LIGHT DISTRICT!
I LOST SIGHT OF HIM...
KYAAH
THUMP
DONK
What?!

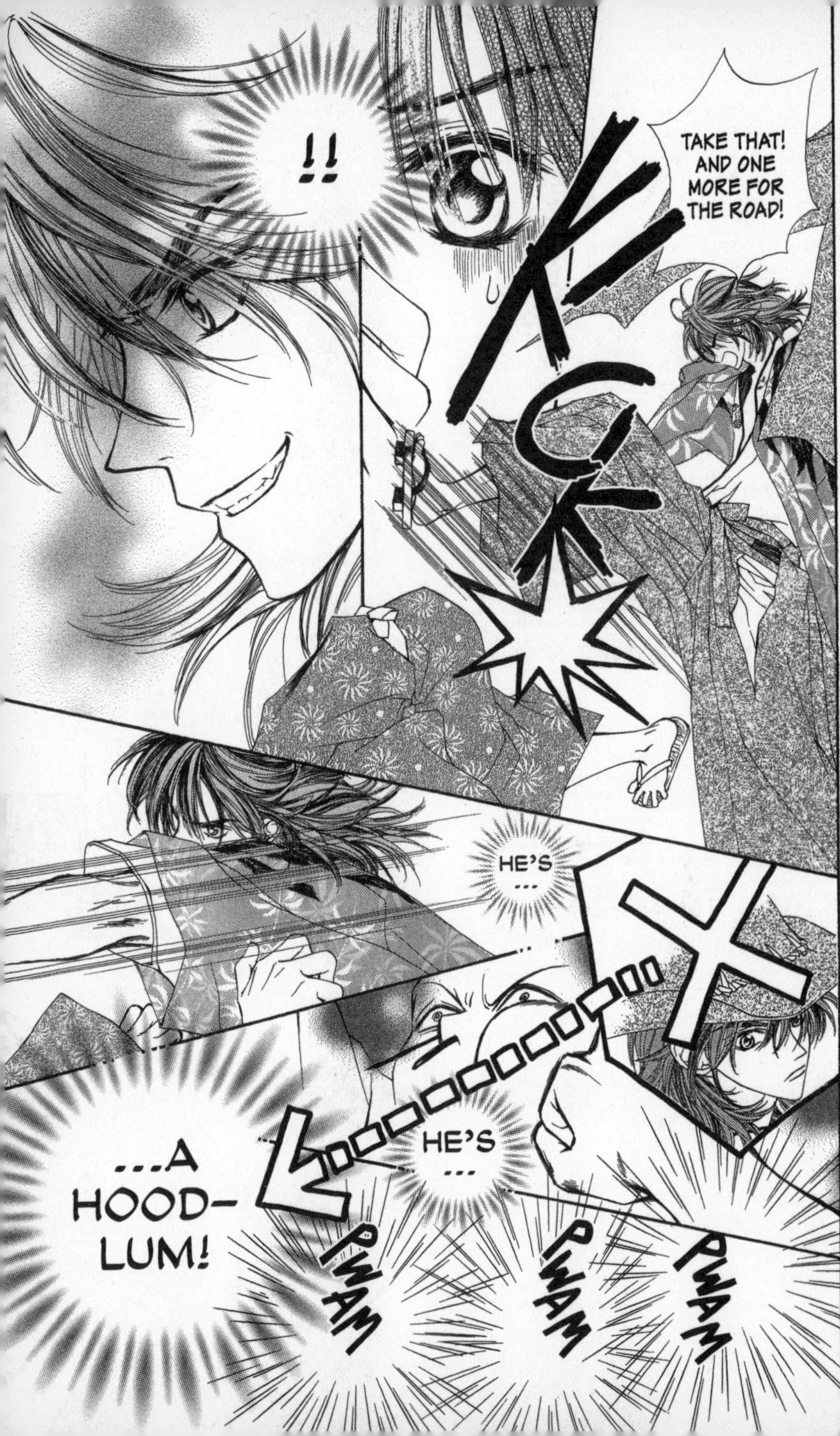
TAKE THAT! AND ONE MORE FOR THE ROAD!
KICK
!!
HE'S ...
HE'S ...
...A HOOD-LUM!
PWAM
PWAM
PWAM

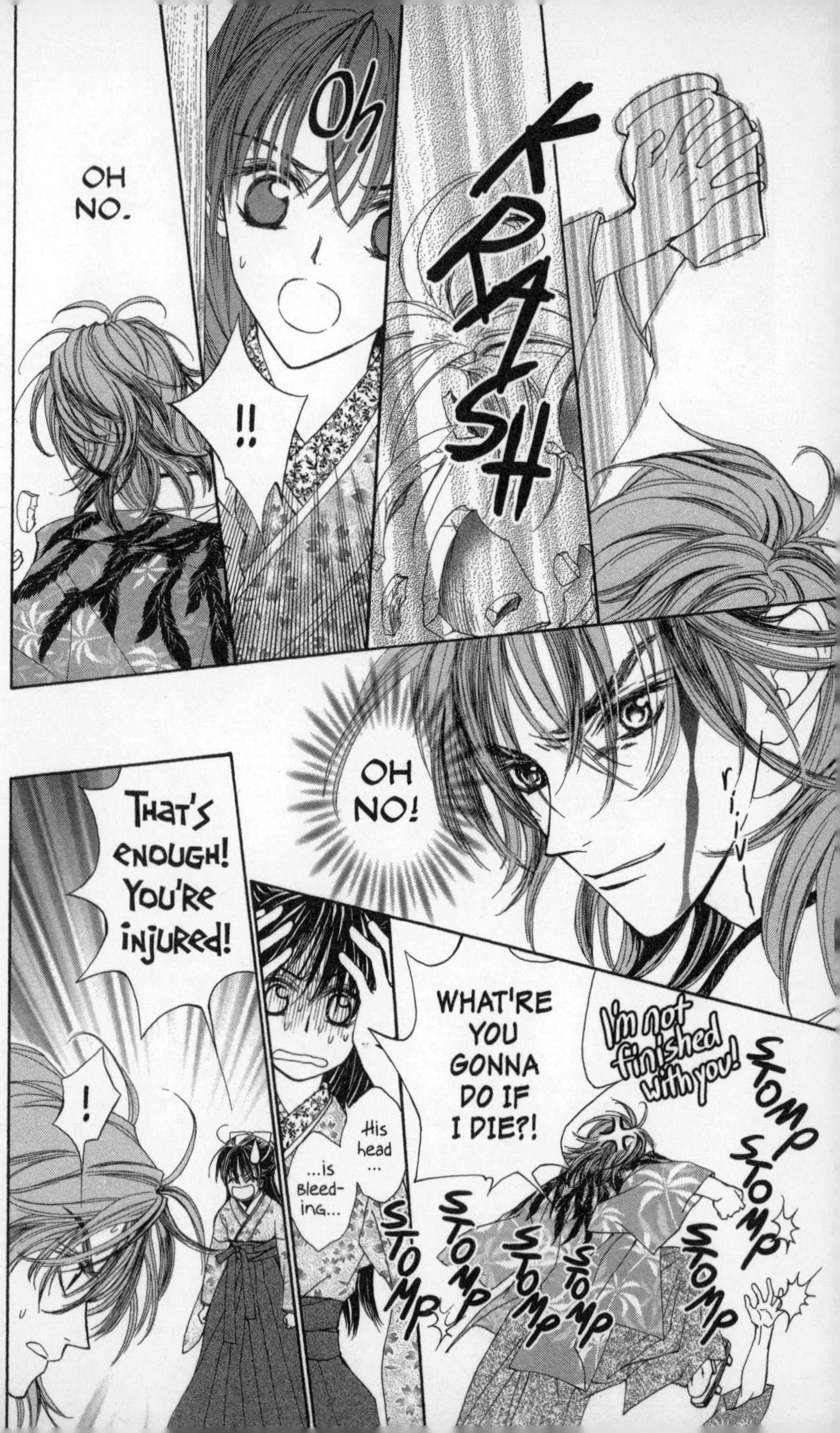
KRASH
Oh
!!
OH NO.
OH NO!
I'm not finished with you!
STOMP STOMP STOMP STOMP STOMP STOMP STOMP
WHAT'RE YOU GONNA DO IF I DIE?!
His head ...
...is bleeding...
That's enough! You're injured!
!

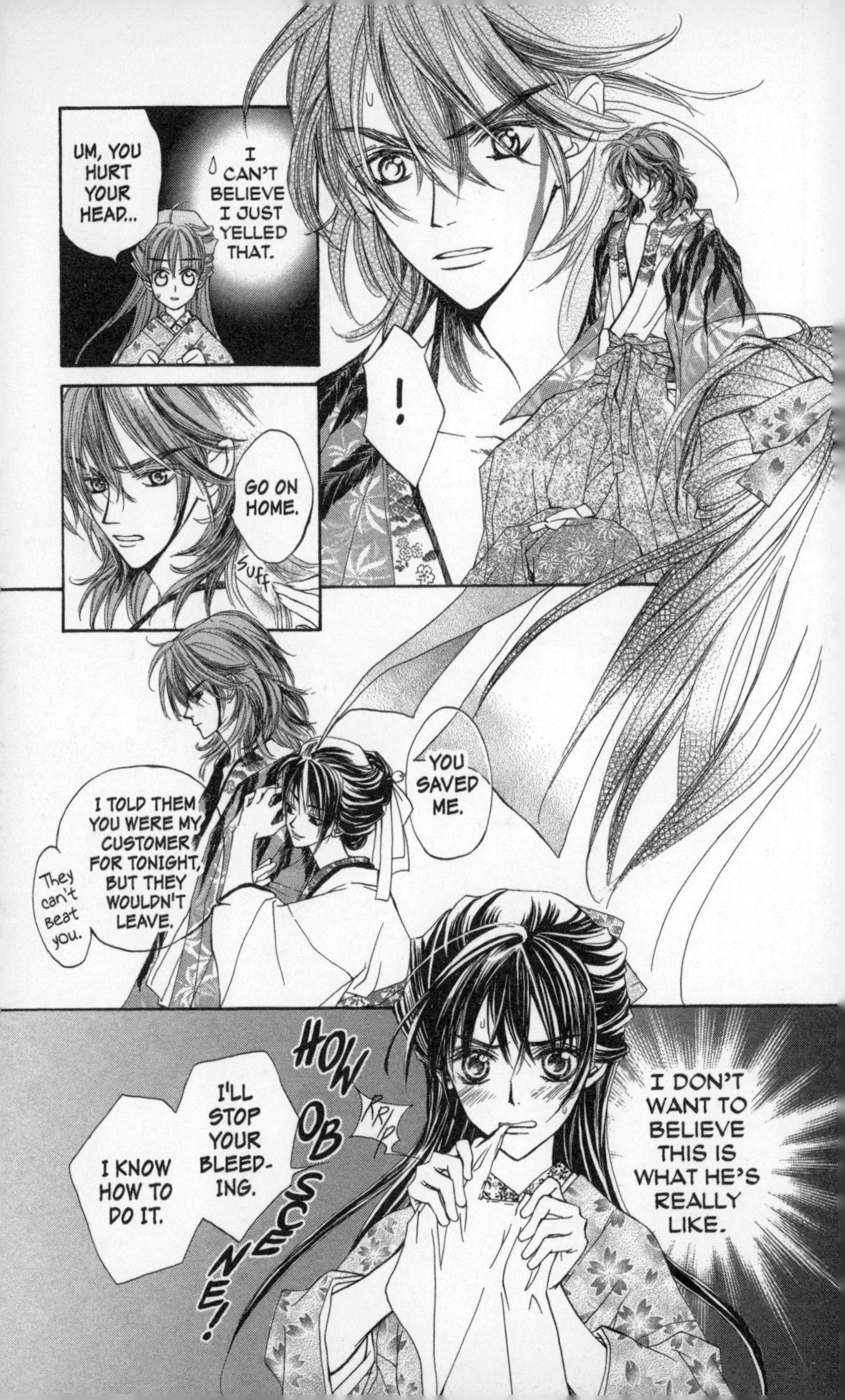

I CAN'T BELIEVE I JUST YELLED THAT.
UM, YOU HURT YOUR HEAD...
!
GO ON HOME.
SUFF
YOU SAVED ME.
I TOLD THEM YOU WERE MY CUSTOMER FOR TONIGHT, BUT THEY WOULDN'T LEAVE.
They can't beat you.
I DON'T WANT TO BELIEVE THIS IS WHAT HE'S REALLY LIKE.
HOW OBSCENE!
RRIP
I'LL STOP YOUR BLEEDING.
I KNOW HOW TO DO IT.

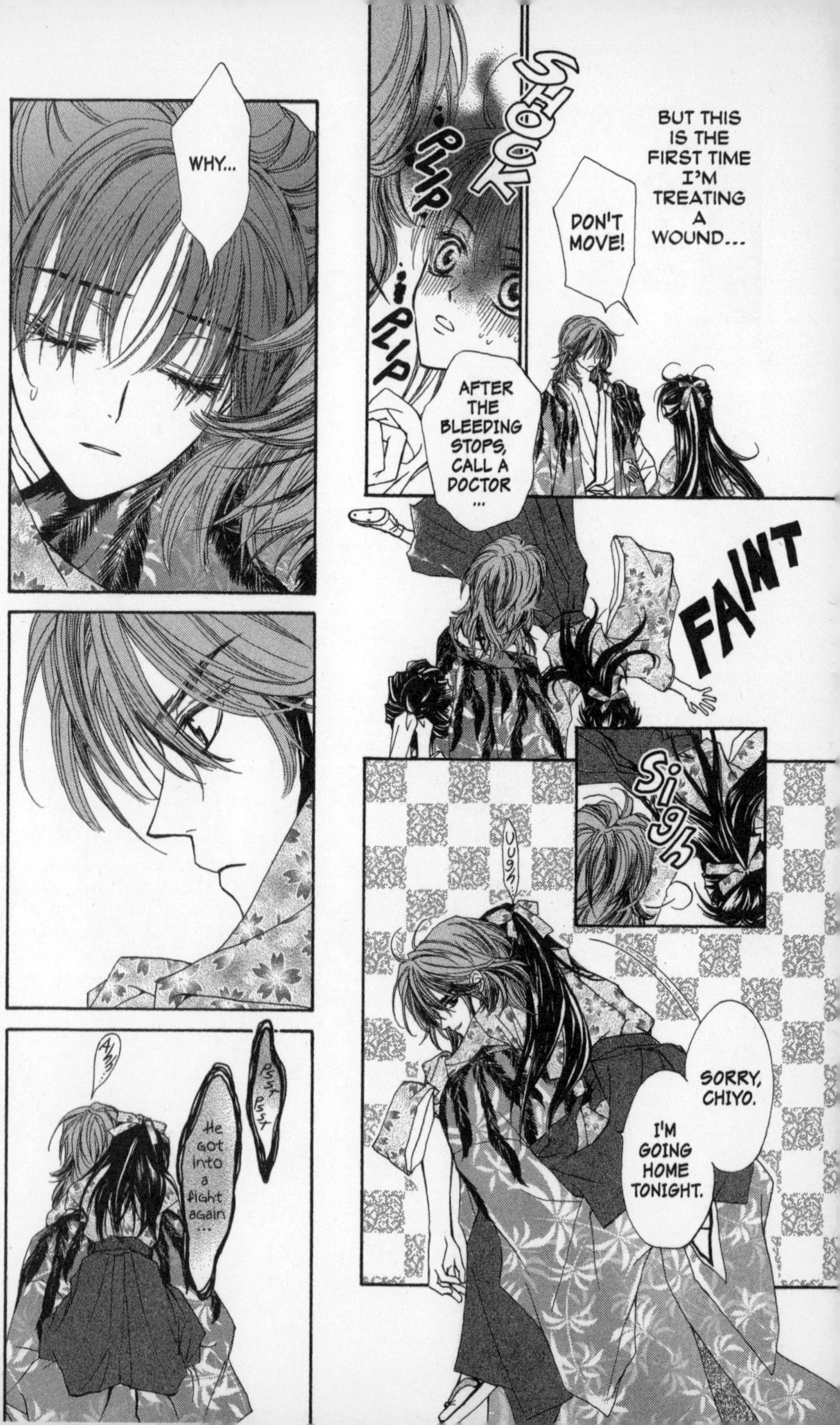
BUT THIS IS THE FIRST TIME I'M TREATING A WOUND...
DON'T MOVE!
SHOCK
PLIP PLIP
AFTER THE BLEEDING STOPS, CALL A DOCTOR ...
FAINT
Sigh
Uugh...
SORRY, CHIYO.
I'M GOING HOME TONIGHT.
WHY...
Psst psst
He got into a fight again...
Ah...

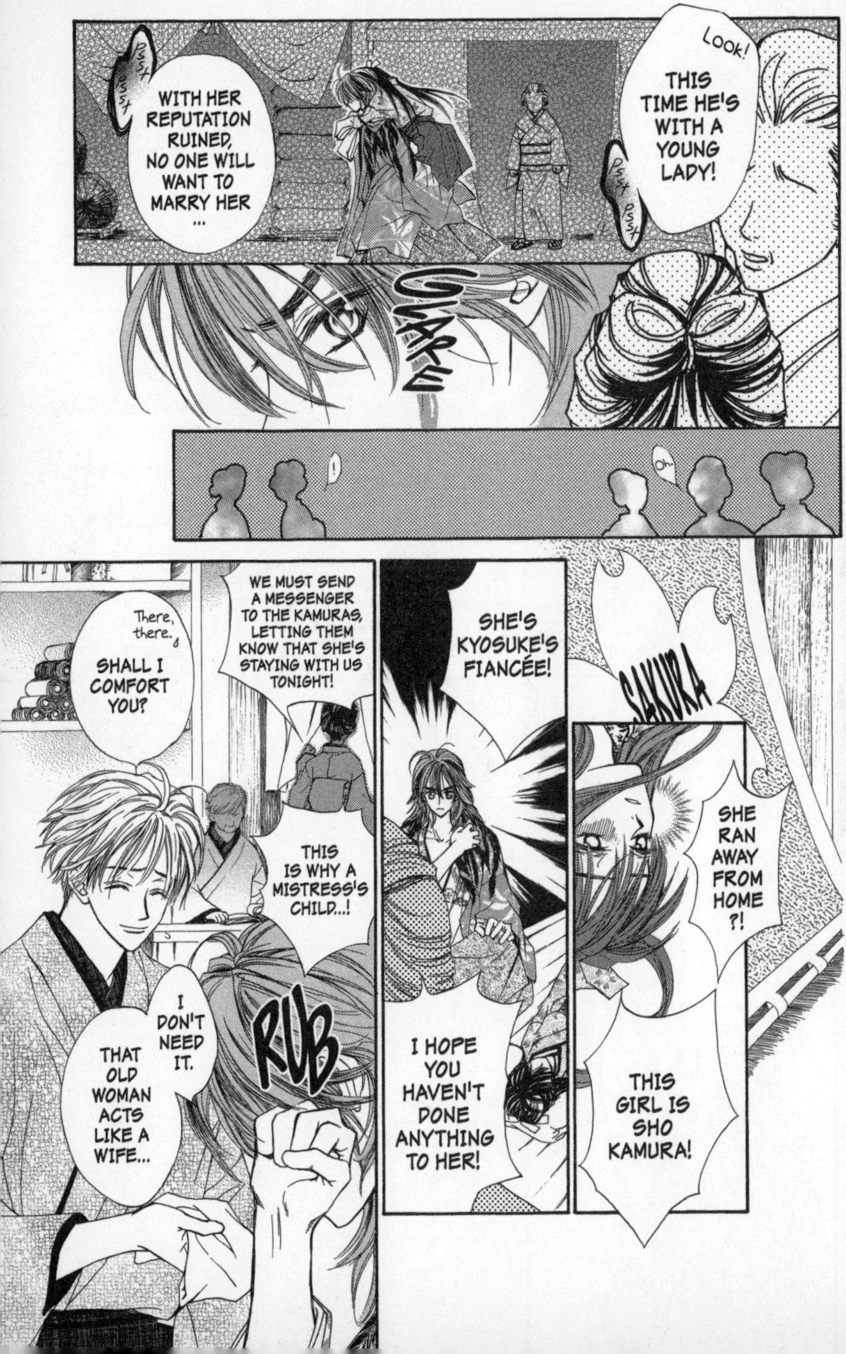
Look!
THIS TIME HE'S WITH A YOUNG LADY!
WITH HER REPUTATION RUINED, NO ONE WILL WANT TO MARRY HER ...
GLARE
Oh-
!
SAKURA
SHE RAN AWAY FROM HOME ?!
THIS GIRL IS SHO KAMURA!
SHE'S KYOSUKE'S FIANCÉE!
I HOPE YOU HAVEN'T DONE ANYTHING TO HER!
WE MUST SEND A MESSENGER TO THE KAMURAS, LETTING THEM KNOW THAT SHE'S STAYING WITH US TONIGHT!
There, there.
SHALL I COMFORT YOU?
THIS IS WHY A MISTRESS'S CHILD...!
RUB
I DON'T NEED IT.
THAT OLD WOMAN ACTS LIKE A WIFE...

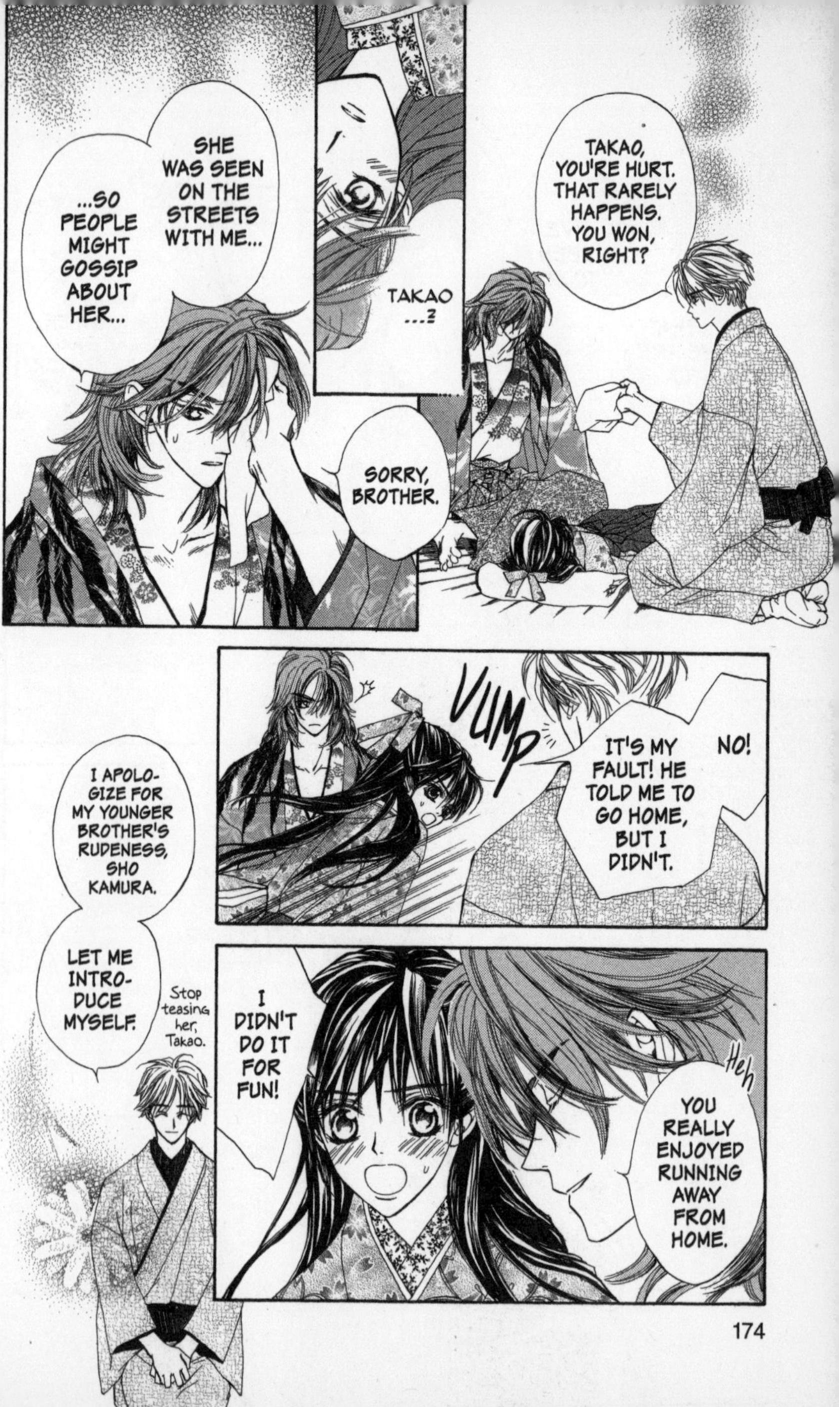
TAKAO, YOU'RE HURT. THAT RARELY HAPPENS. YOU WON, RIGHT?
TAKAO ...?
SORRY, BROTHER.
SHE WAS SEEN ON THE STREETS WITH ME...
...SO PEOPLE MIGHT GOSSIP ABOUT HER...
VUMP
NO!
IT'S MY FAULT! HE TOLD ME TO GO HOME, BUT I DIDN'T.
Heh
YOU REALLY ENJOYED RUNNING AWAY FROM HOME.
I DIDN'T DO IT FOR FUN!
Stop teasing her, Takao.
I APOLOGIZE FOR MY YOUNGER BROTHER'S RUDENESS, SHO KAMURA.
LET ME INTRODUCE MYSELF.

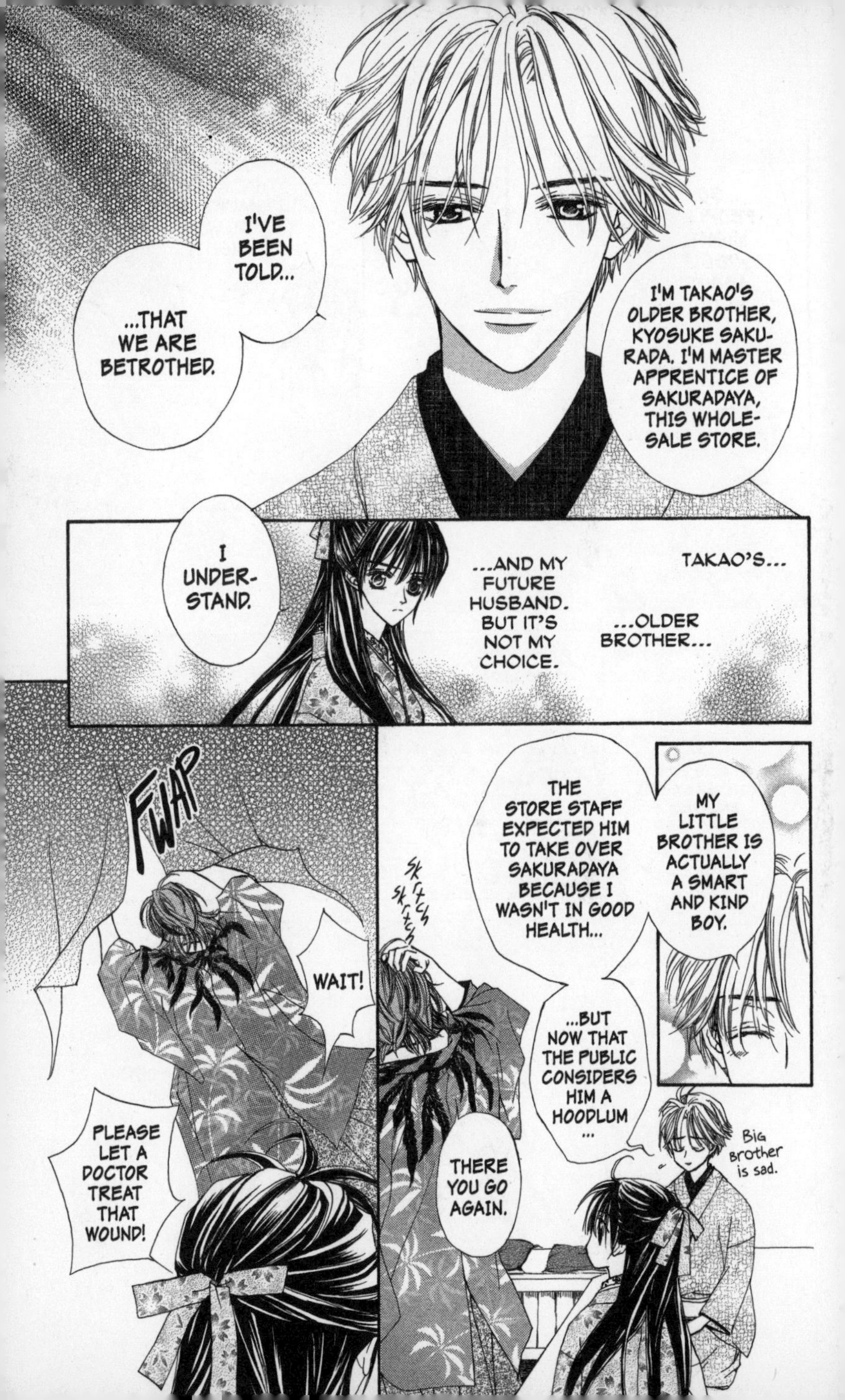
I'M TAKAO'S OLDER BROTHER, KYOSUKE SAKURADA. I'M MASTER APPRENTICE OF SAKURADAYA, THIS WHOLESALE STORE.
I'VE BEEN TOLD...
...THAT WE ARE BETROTHED.
TAKAO'S...
...OLDER BROTHER...
...AND MY FUTURE HUSBAND. BUT IT'S NOT MY CHOICE.
I UNDERSTAND.
MY LITTLE BROTHER IS ACTUALLY A SMART AND KIND BOY.
THE STORE STAFF EXPECTED HIM TO TAKE OVER SAKURADAYA BECAUSE I WASN'T IN GOOD HEALTH...
...BUT NOW THAT THE PUBLIC CONSIDERS HIM A HOODLUM ...
Big Brother is sad.
SKRTCH SKRTCH
THERE YOU GO AGAIN.
FWAP
WAIT!
PLEASE LET A DOCTOR TREAT THAT WOUND!

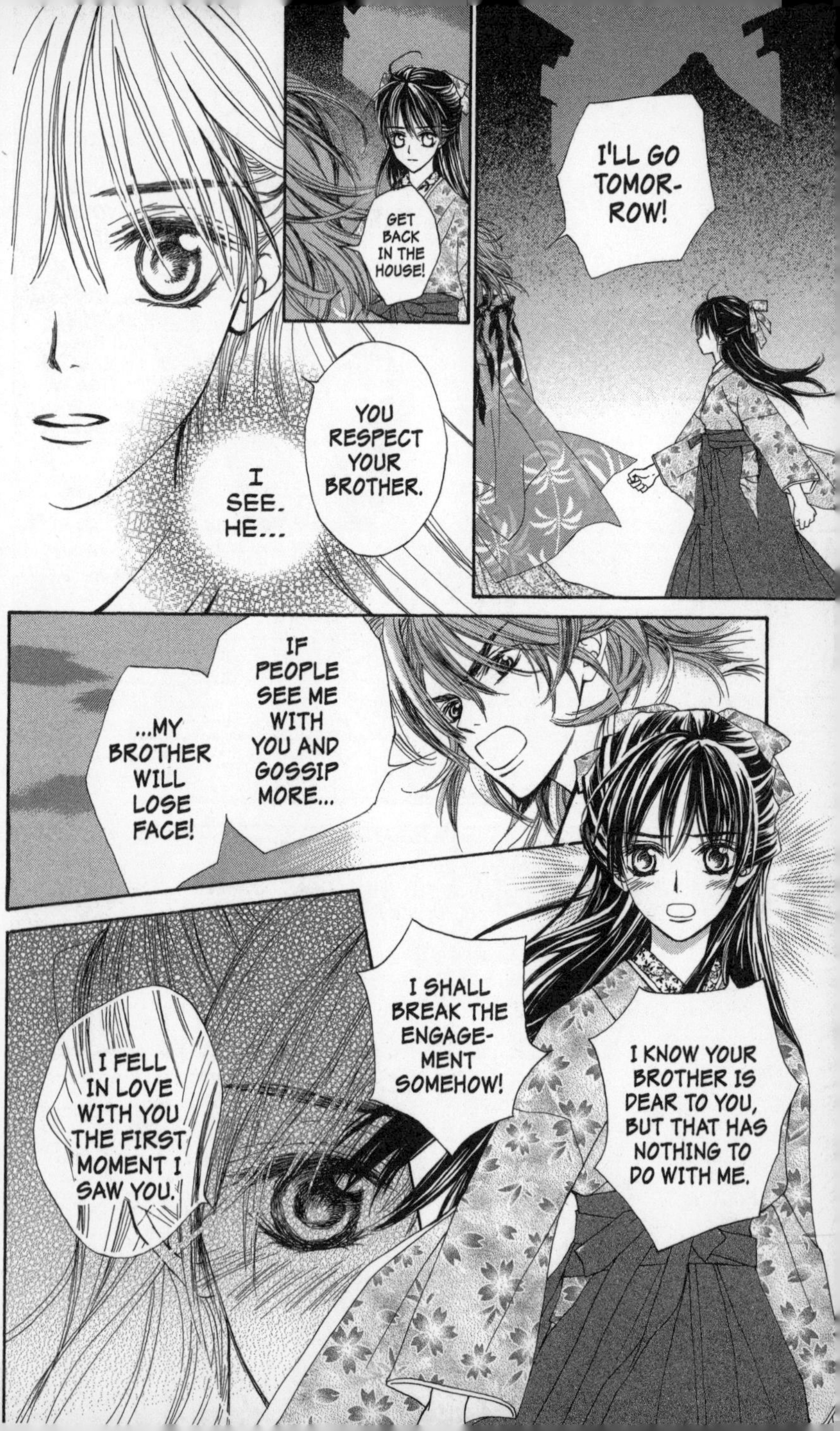
I'LL GO TOMOR-ROW!
GET BACK IN THE HOUSE!
YOU RESPECT YOUR BROTHER.
I SEE. HE...
IF PEOPLE SEE ME WITH YOU AND GOSSIP MORE...
...MY BROTHER WILL LOSE FACE!
I KNOW YOUR BROTHER IS DEAR TO YOU, BUT THAT HAS NOTHING TO DO WITH ME.
I SHALL BREAK THE ENGAGE-MENT SOMEHOW!
I FELL IN LOVE WITH YOU THE FIRST MOMENT I SAW YOU.

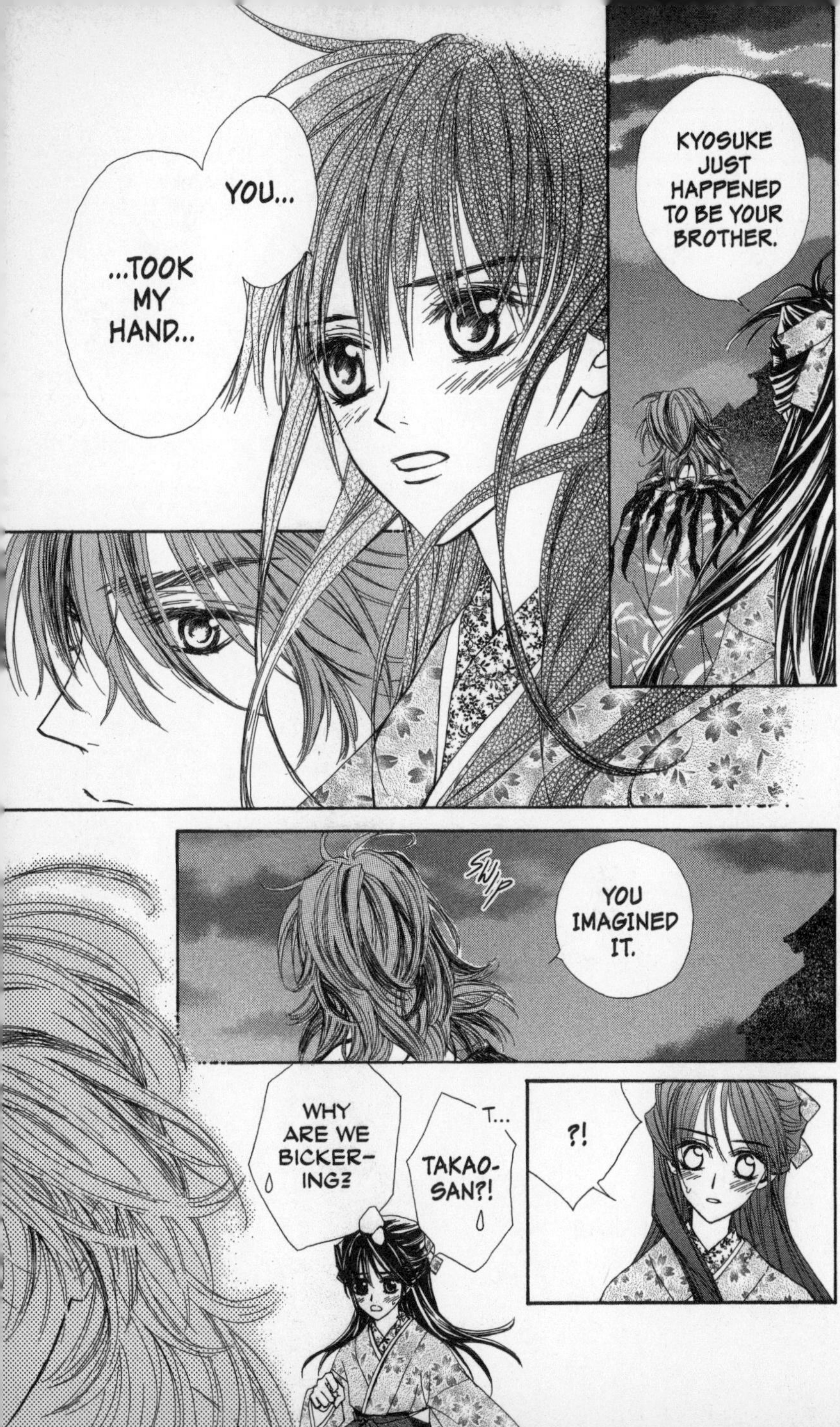
KYOSUKE JUST HAPPENED TO BE YOUR BROTHER.
YOU...
...TOOK MY HAND...
SWIP
YOU IMAGINED IT.
?!
T... TAKAO-SAN?!
WHY ARE WE BICKER-ING?

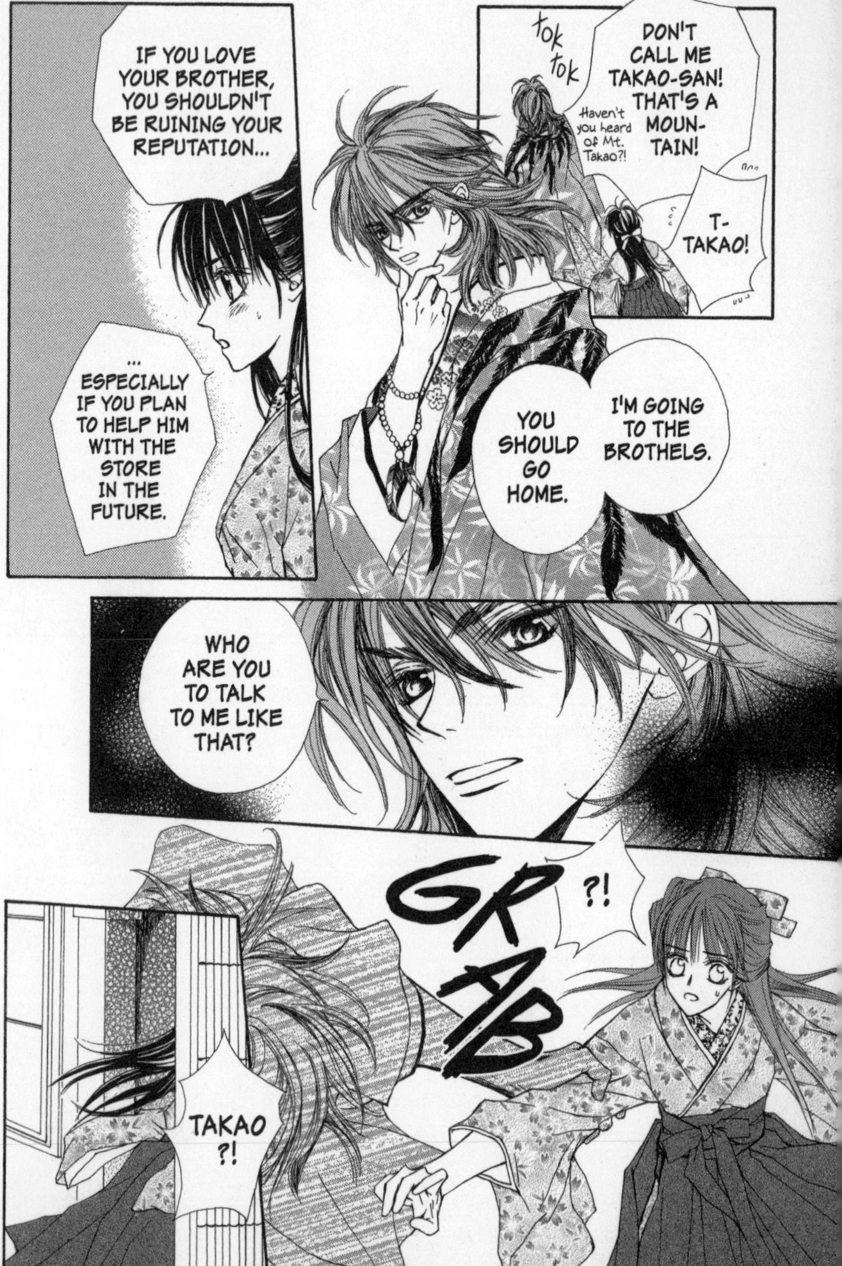

tok tok
DON'T CALL ME TAKAO-SAN! THAT'S A MOUN-TAIN!
Haven't you heard of Mt. Takao?!
T-TAKAO!
IF YOU LOVE YOUR BROTHER, YOU SHOULDN'T BE RUINING YOUR REPUTATION...
... ESPECIALLY IF YOU PLAN TO HELP HIM WITH THE STORE IN THE FUTURE.
I'M GOING TO THE BROTHELS.
YOU SHOULD GO HOME.
WHO ARE YOU TO TALK TO ME LIKE THAT?
GRAB
?!
TAKAO ?!

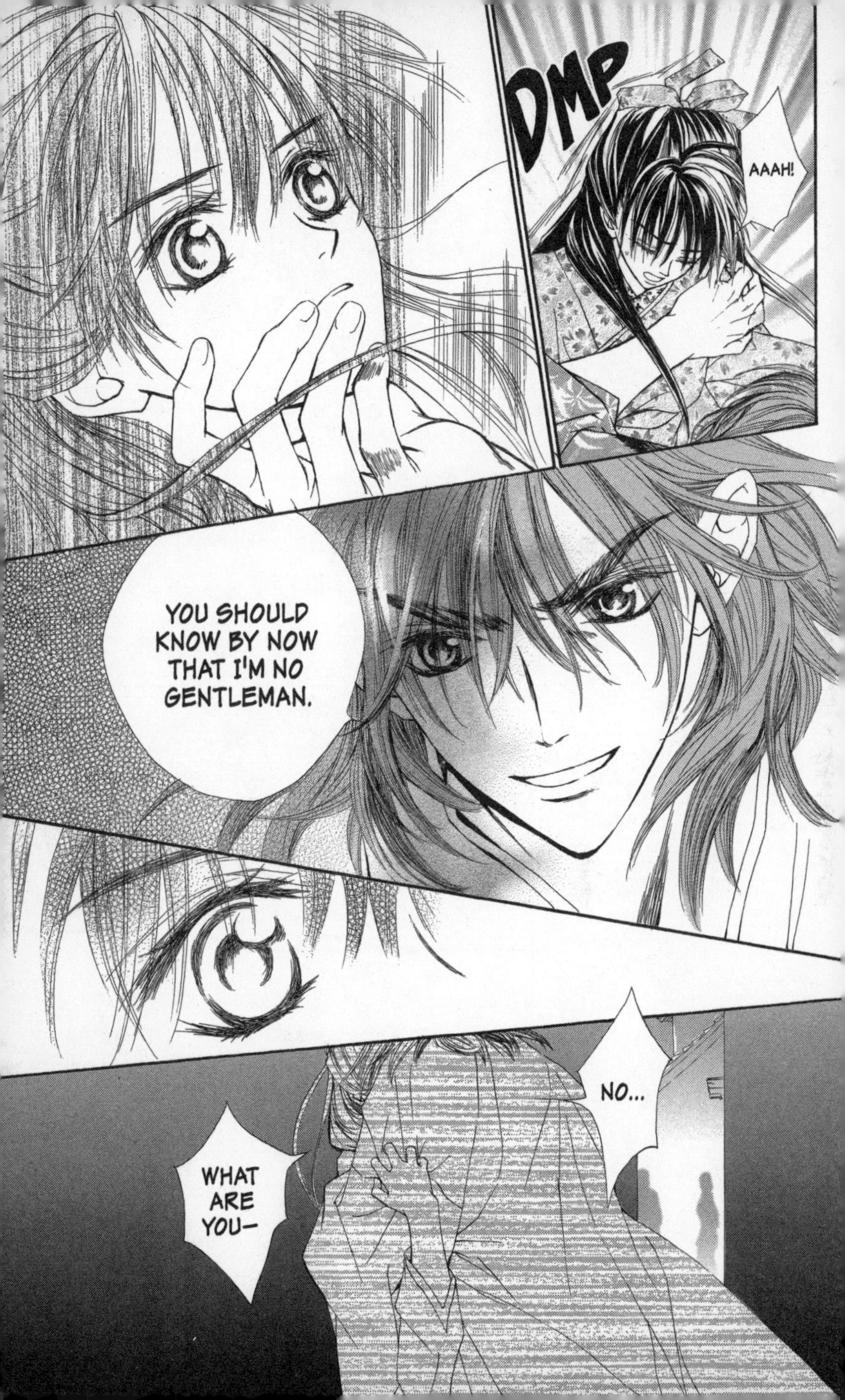
DMP
AAAH!
YOU SHOULD KNOW BY NOW THAT I'M NO GENTLEMAN.
NO...
WHAT ARE YOU–

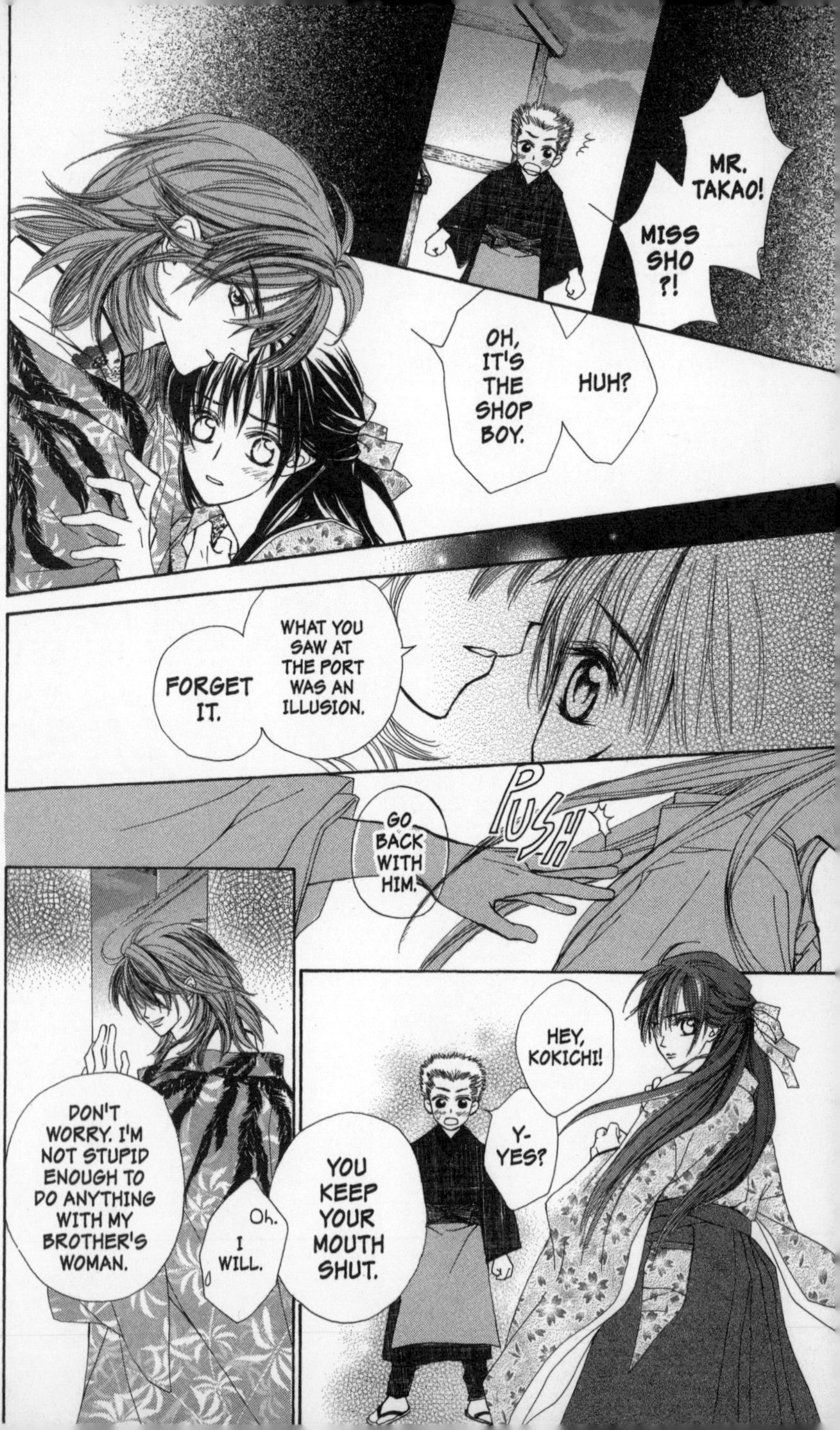
MR. TAKAO!
MISS SHO?!
HUH?
OH, IT'S THE SHOP BOY.
WHAT YOU SAW AT THE PORT WAS AN ILLUSION.
FORGET IT.
PUSH
GO BACK WITH HIM.
HEY, KOKICHI!
Y-YES?
YOU KEEP YOUR MOUTH SHUT.
Oh. I WILL.
DON'T WORRY. I'M NOT STUPID ENOUGH TO DO ANYTHING WITH MY BROTHER'S WOMAN.

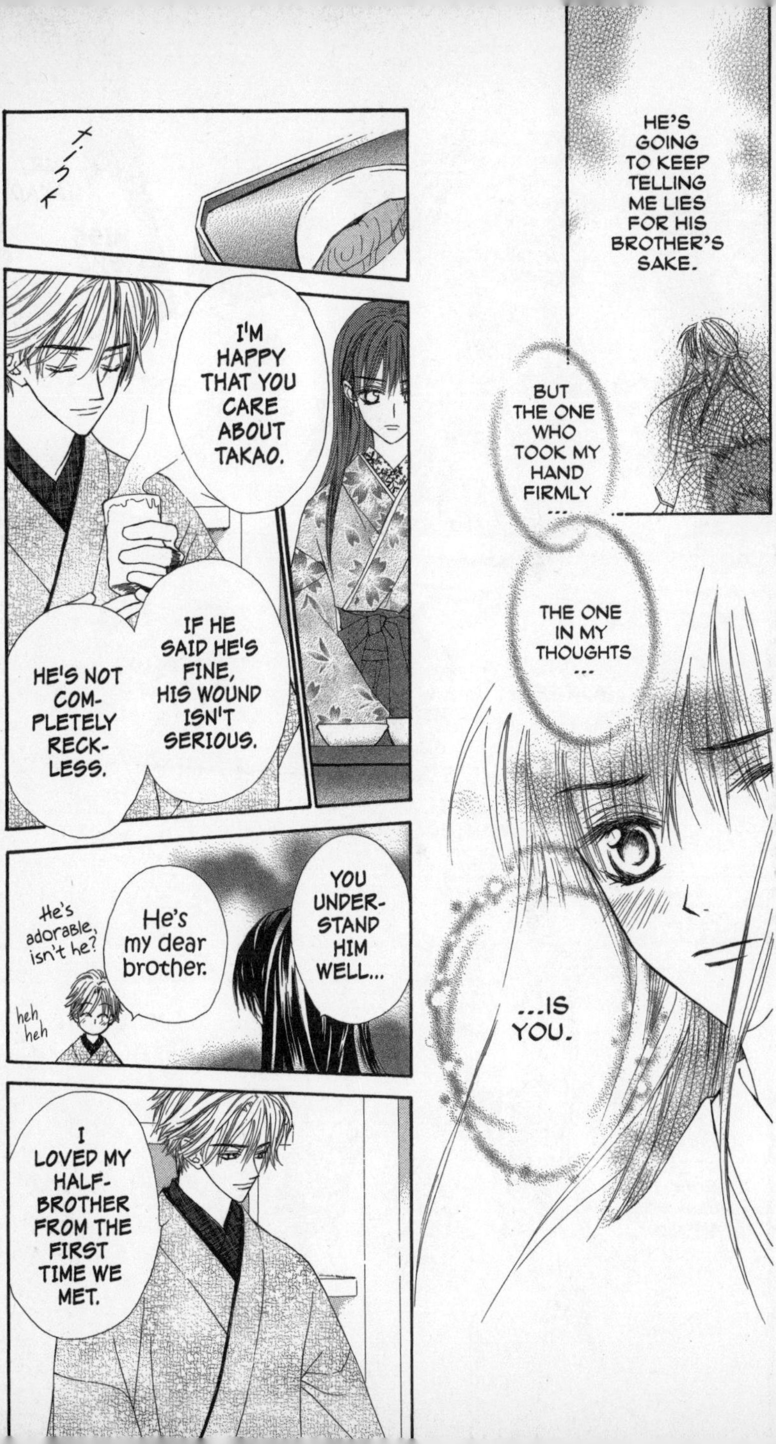
HE'S GOING TO KEEP TELLING ME LIES FOR HIS BROTHER'S SAKE.
BUT THE ONE WHO TOOK MY HAND FIRMLY...
THE ONE IN MY THOUGHTS...
...IS YOU.
I'M HAPPY THAT YOU CARE ABOUT TAKAO.
IF HE SAID HE'S FINE, HIS WOUND ISN'T SERIOUS.
HE'S NOT COMPLETELY RECKLESS.
YOU UNDERSTAND HIM WELL...
He's my dear brother.
He's adorable, isn't he?
heh heh
I LOVED MY HALF-BROTHER FROM THE FIRST TIME WE MET.

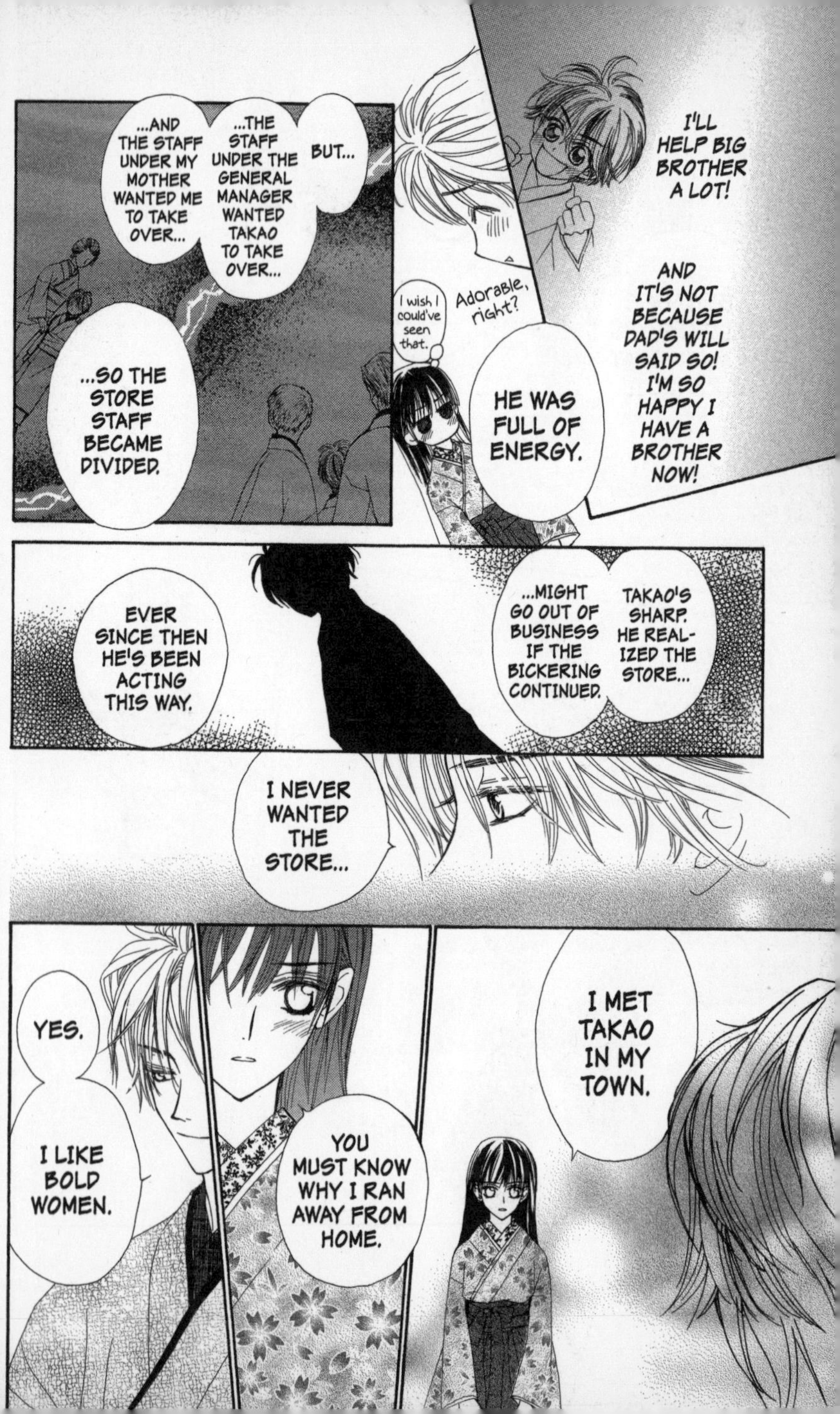
I'LL HELP BIG BROTHER A LOT!
AND IT'S NOT BECAUSE DAD'S WILL SAID SO! I'M SO HAPPY I HAVE A BROTHER NOW!
Adorable, right?
HE WAS FULL OF ENERGY.
I wish I could've seen that.
BUT...
...THE STAFF UNDER THE GENERAL MANAGER WANTED TAKAO TO TAKE OVER...
...AND THE STAFF UNDER MY MOTHER WANTED ME TO TAKE OVER...
...SO THE STORE STAFF BECAME DIVIDED.
TAKAO'S SHARP. HE REAL-IZED THE STORE...
...MIGHT GO OUT OF BUSINESS IF THE BICKERING CONTINUED.
EVER SINCE THEN HE'S BEEN ACTING THIS WAY.
I NEVER WANTED THE STORE...
I MET TAKAO IN MY TOWN.
YOU MUST KNOW WHY I RAN AWAY FROM HOME.
YES.
I LIKE BOLD WOMEN.

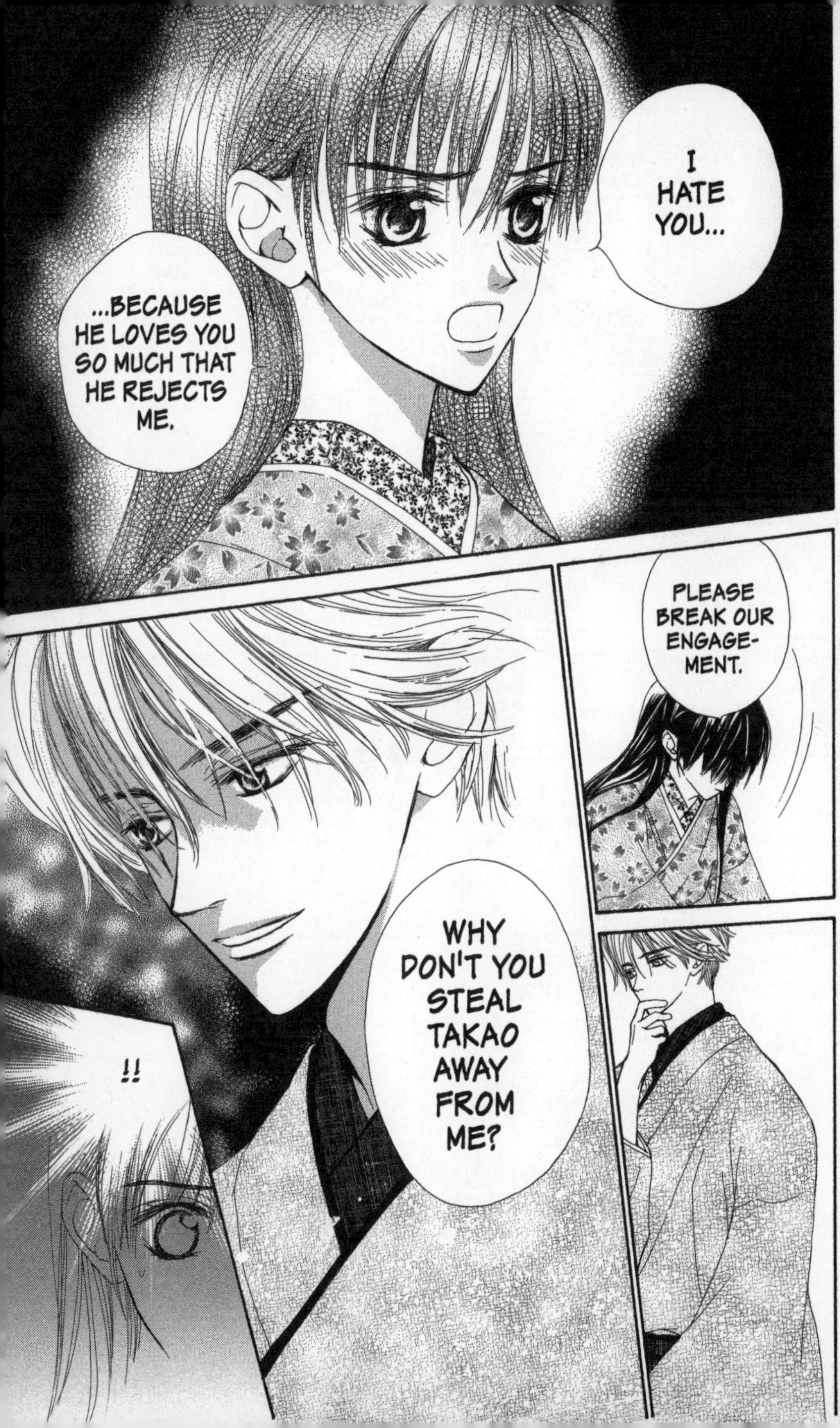
I HATE YOU...
...BECAUSE HE LOVES YOU SO MUCH THAT HE REJECTS ME.
PLEASE BREAK OUR ENGAGE-MENT.
WHY DON'T YOU STEAL TAKAO AWAY FROM ME?
!!

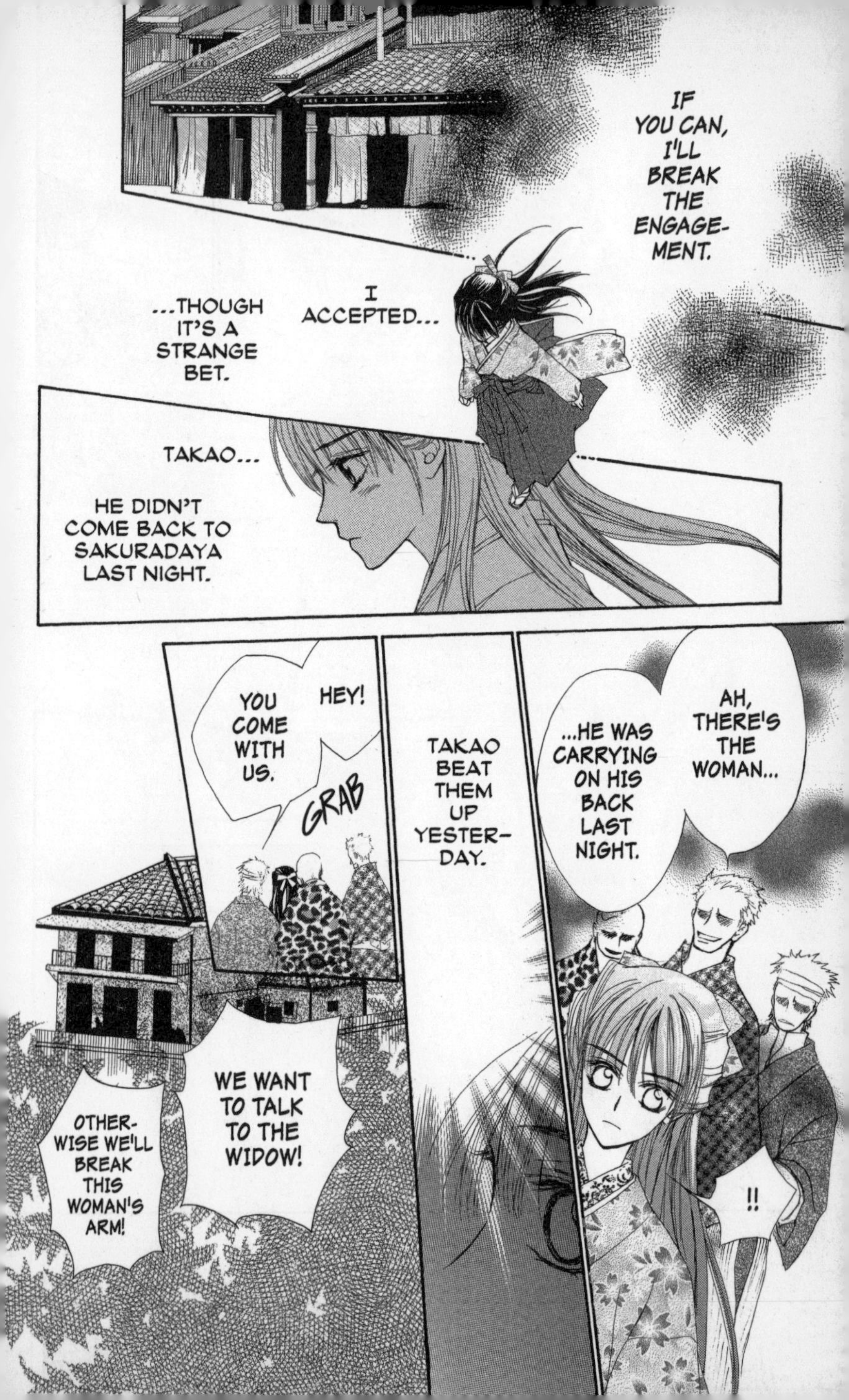
IF YOU CAN, I'LL BREAK THE ENGAGE-MENT.
I ACCEPTED...
...THOUGH IT'S A STRANGE BET.
TAKAO...
HE DIDN'T COME BACK TO SAKURADAYA LAST NIGHT.
AH, THERE'S THE WOMAN...
...HE WAS CARRYING ON HIS BACK LAST NIGHT.
!!
TAKAO BEAT THEM UP YESTER-DAY.
HEY!
YOU COME WITH US.
GRAB
WE WANT TO TALK TO THE WIDOW!
OTHER-WISE WE'LL BREAK THIS WOMAN'S ARM!

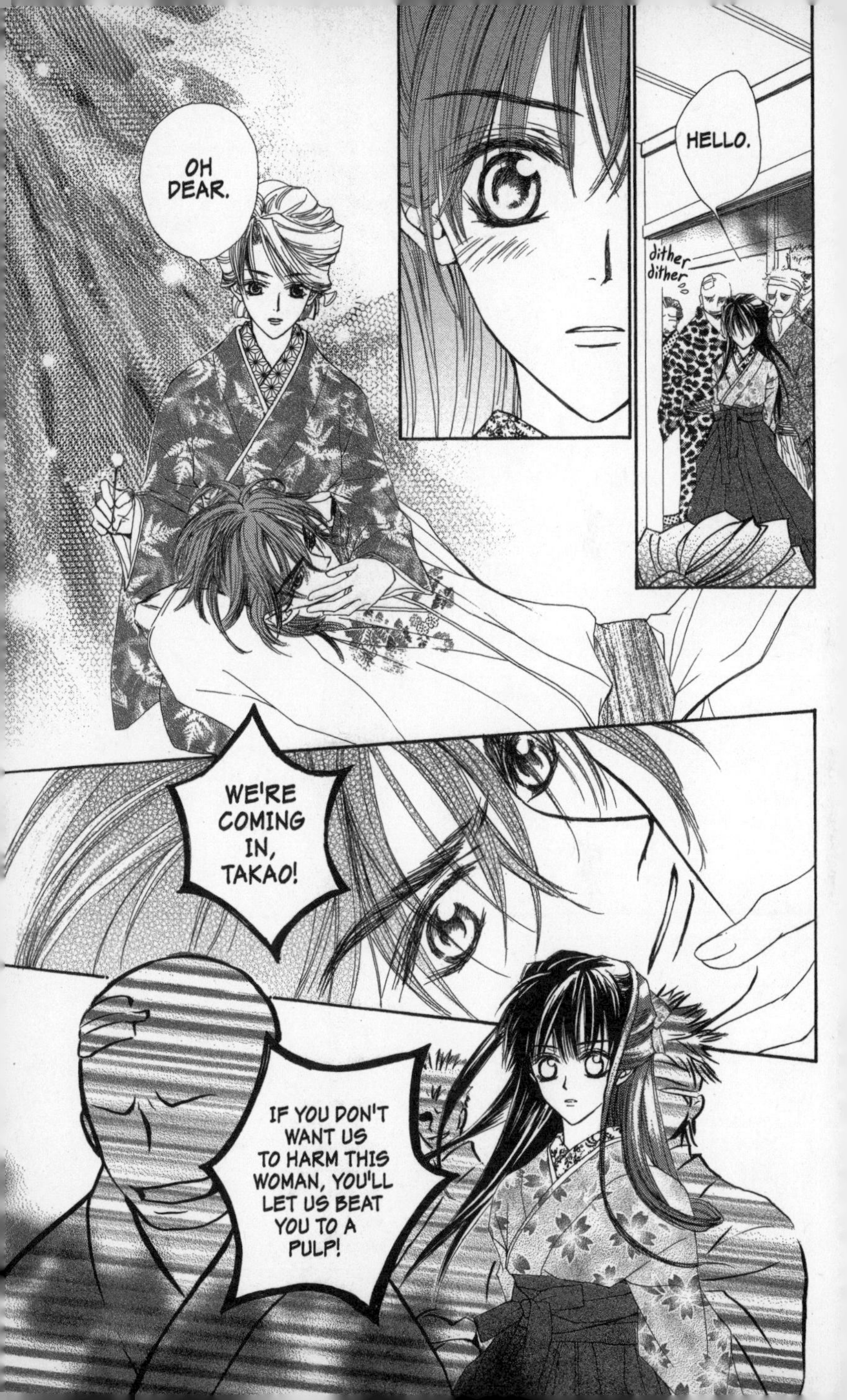
HELLO.
dither dither
OH DEAR.
WE'RE COMING IN, TAKAO!
IF YOU DON'T WANT US TO HARM THIS WOMAN, YOU'LL LET US BEAT YOU TO A PULP!

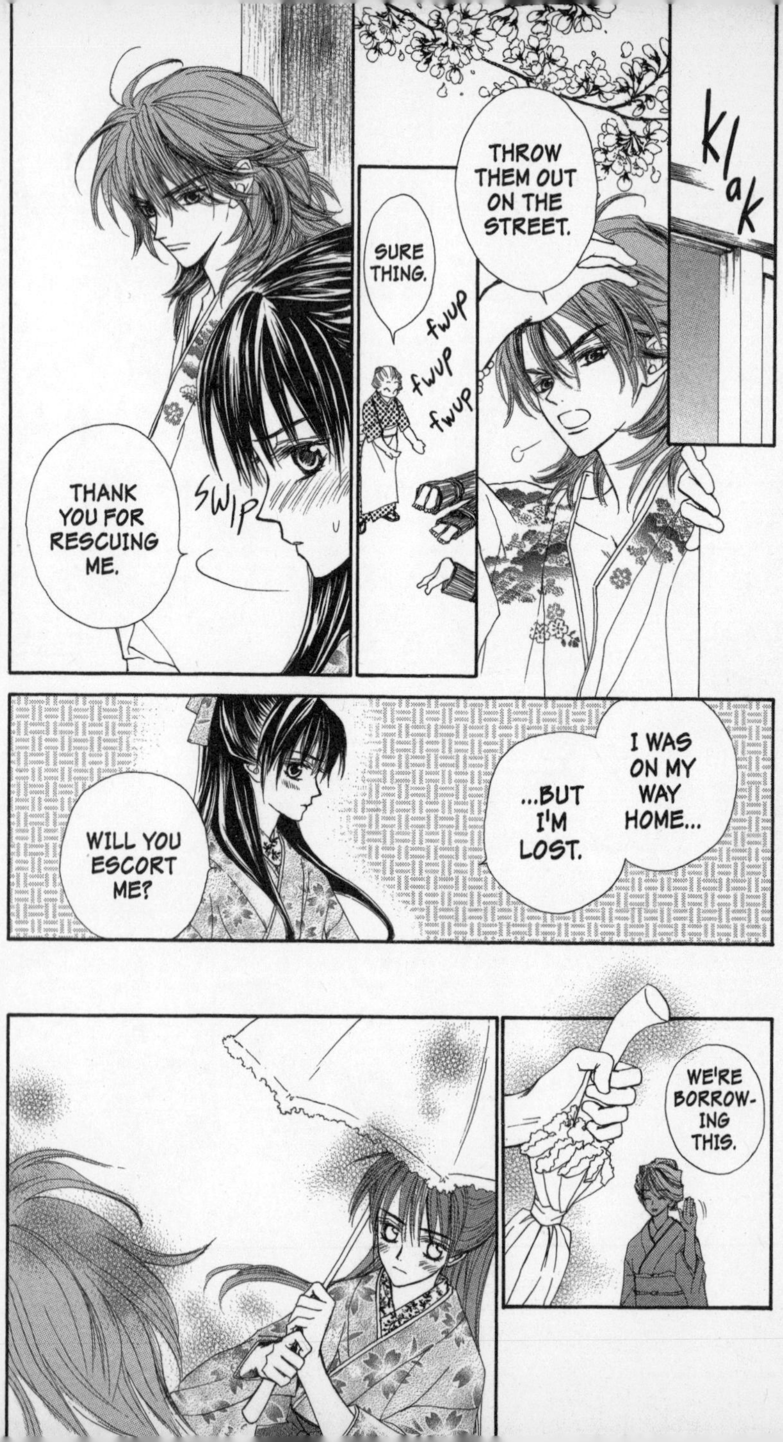
Klak
THROW THEM OUT ON THE STREET.
SURE THING.
fwup fwup fwup
SWIP
THANK YOU FOR RESCUING ME.
I WAS ON MY WAY HOME...
...BUT I'M LOST.
WILL YOU ESCORT ME?
WE'RE BORROW-ING THIS.

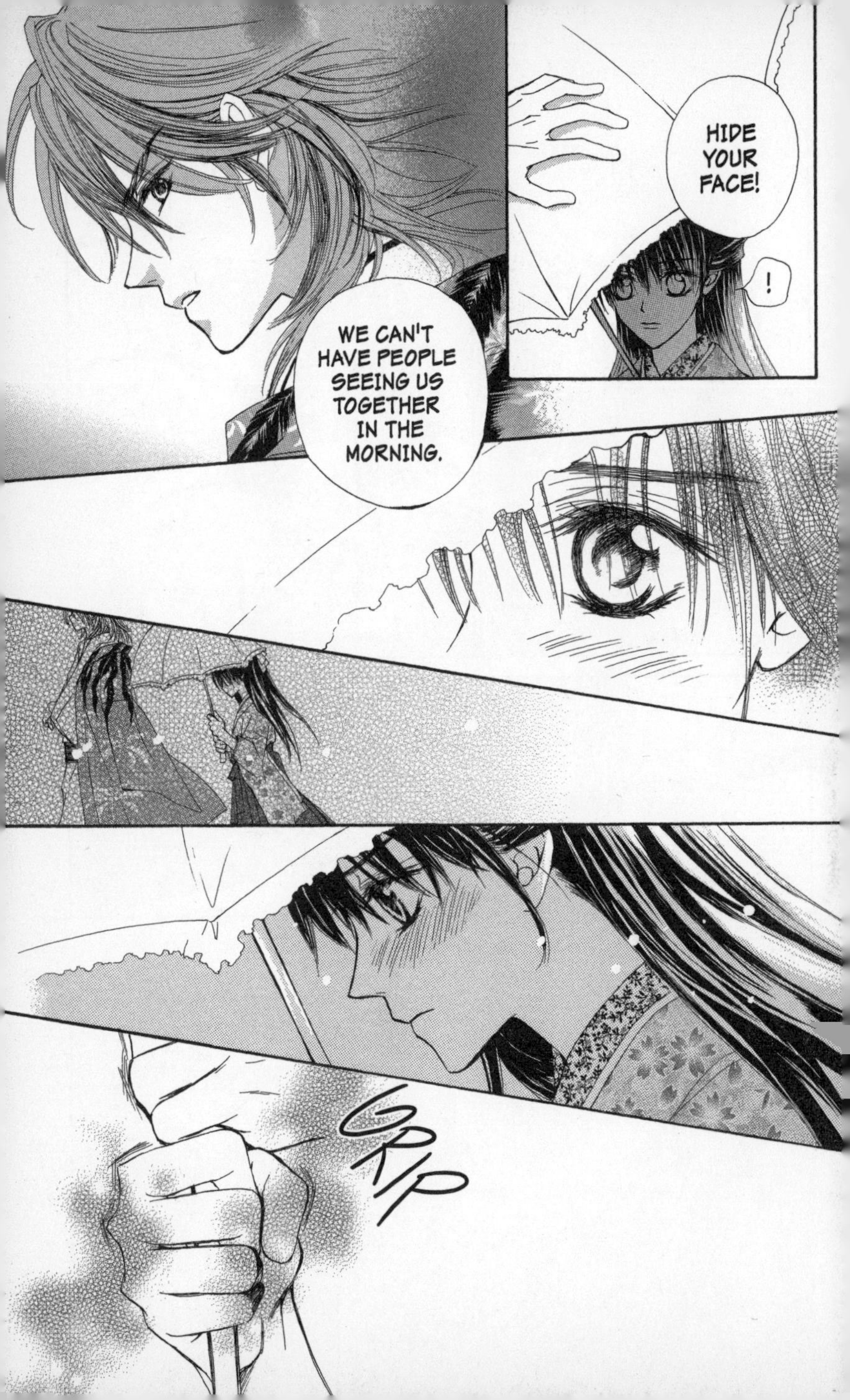
HIDE YOUR FACE!
!
WE CAN'T HAVE PEOPLE SEEING US TOGETHER IN THE MORNING.
GRIP

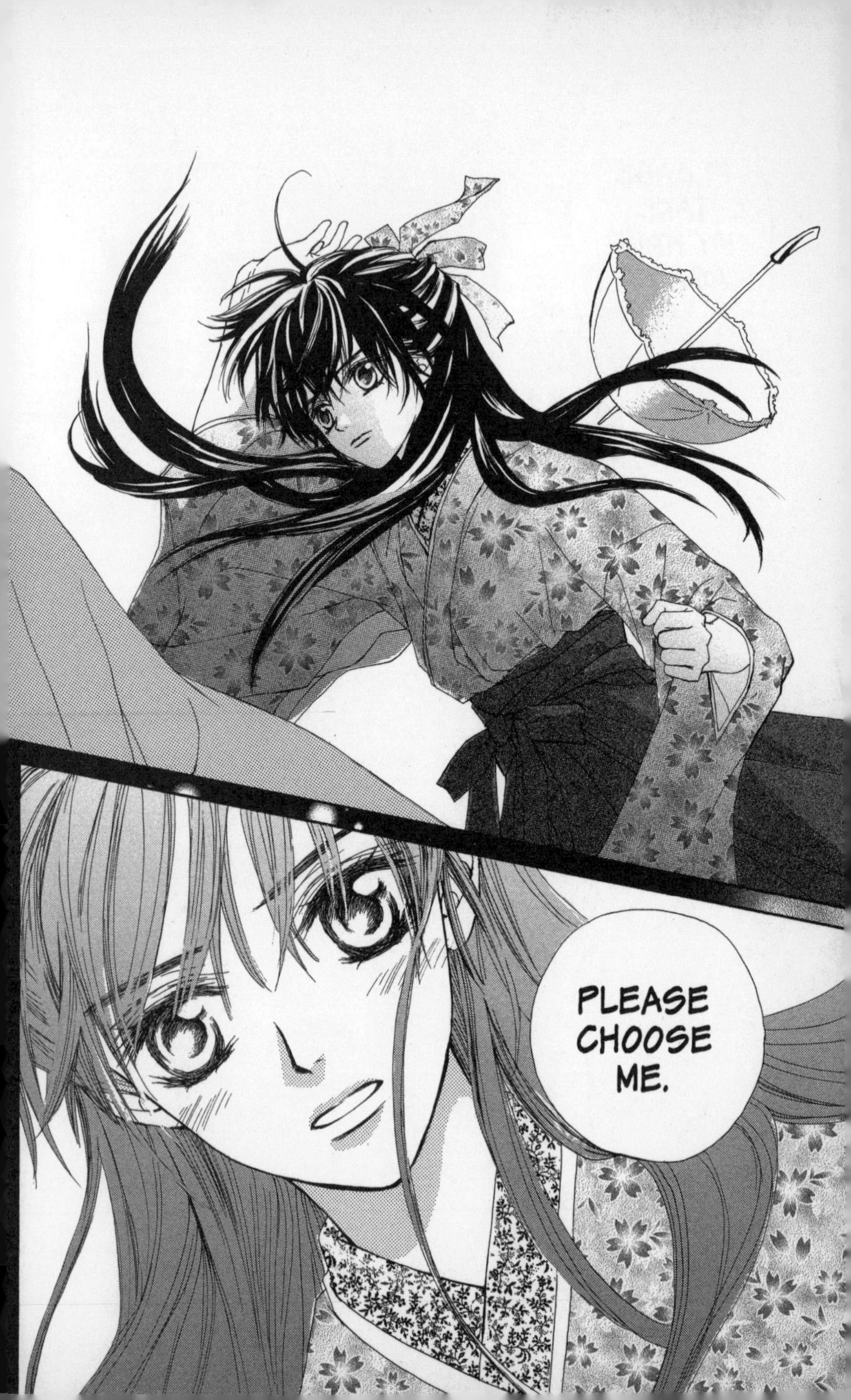
PLEASE CHOOSE ME.

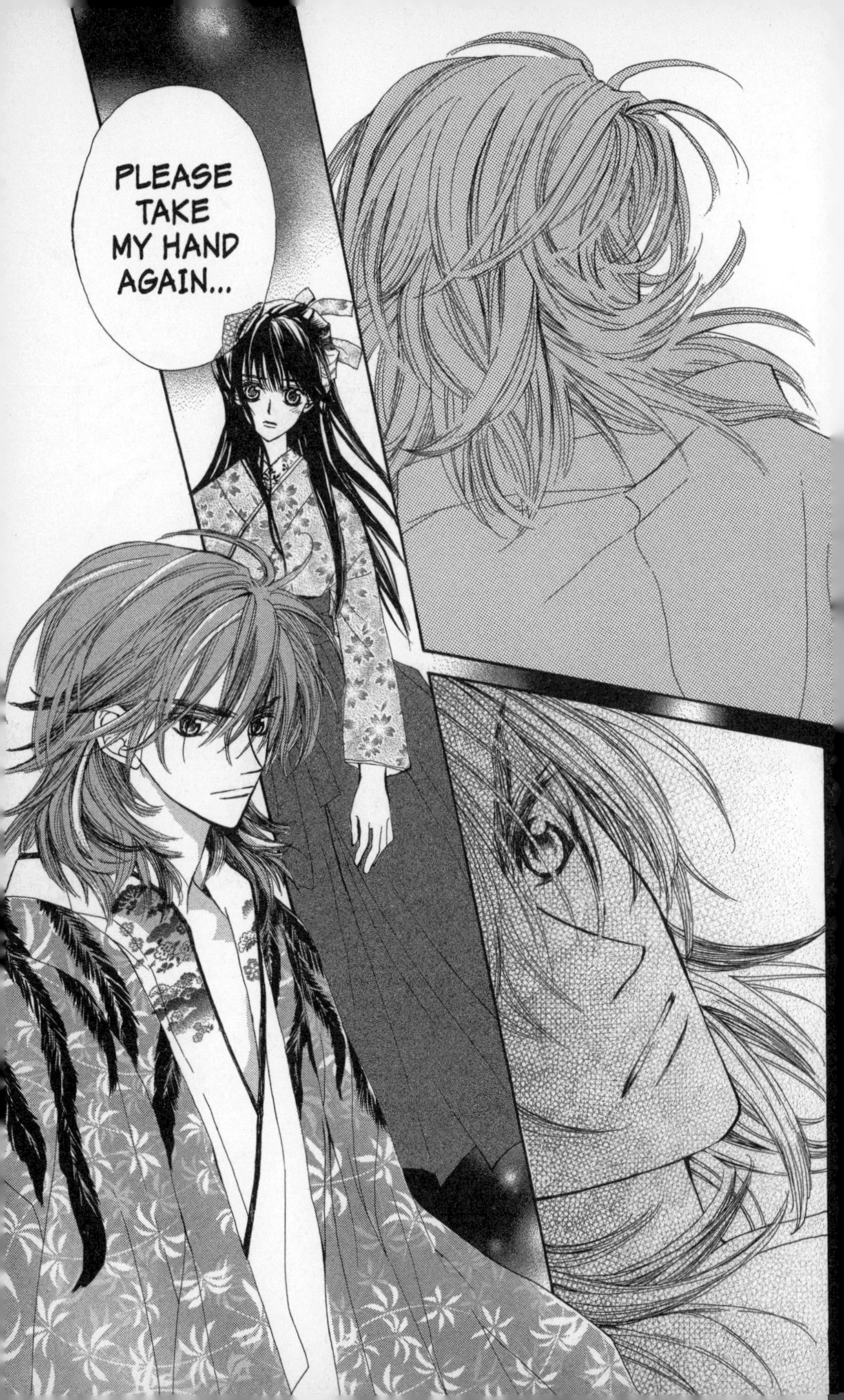
PLEASE TAKE MY HAND AGAIN...

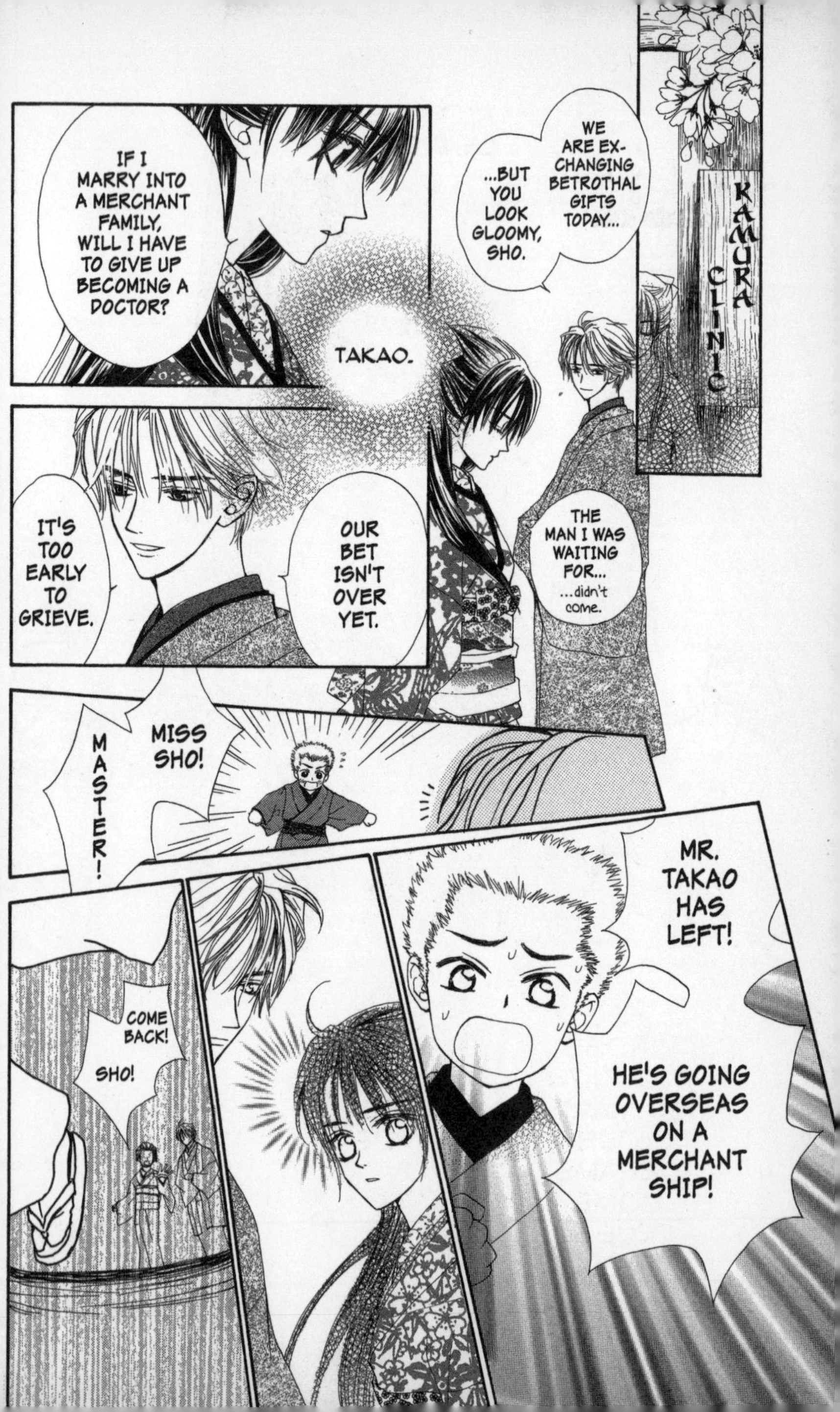
KAMURA CLINIC
WE ARE EX-CHANGING BETROTHAL GIFTS TODAY...
...BUT YOU LOOK GLOOMY, SHO.
THE MAN I WAS WAITING FOR...
...didn't come.
IF I MARRY INTO A MERCHANT FAMILY, WILL I HAVE TO GIVE UP BECOMING A DOCTOR?
TAKAO.
OUR BET ISN'T OVER YET.
IT'S TOO EARLY TO GRIEVE.
MISS SHO!
MASTER!
MR. TAKAO HAS LEFT!
HE'S GOING OVERSEAS ON A MERCHANT SHIP!
COME BACK!
SHO!

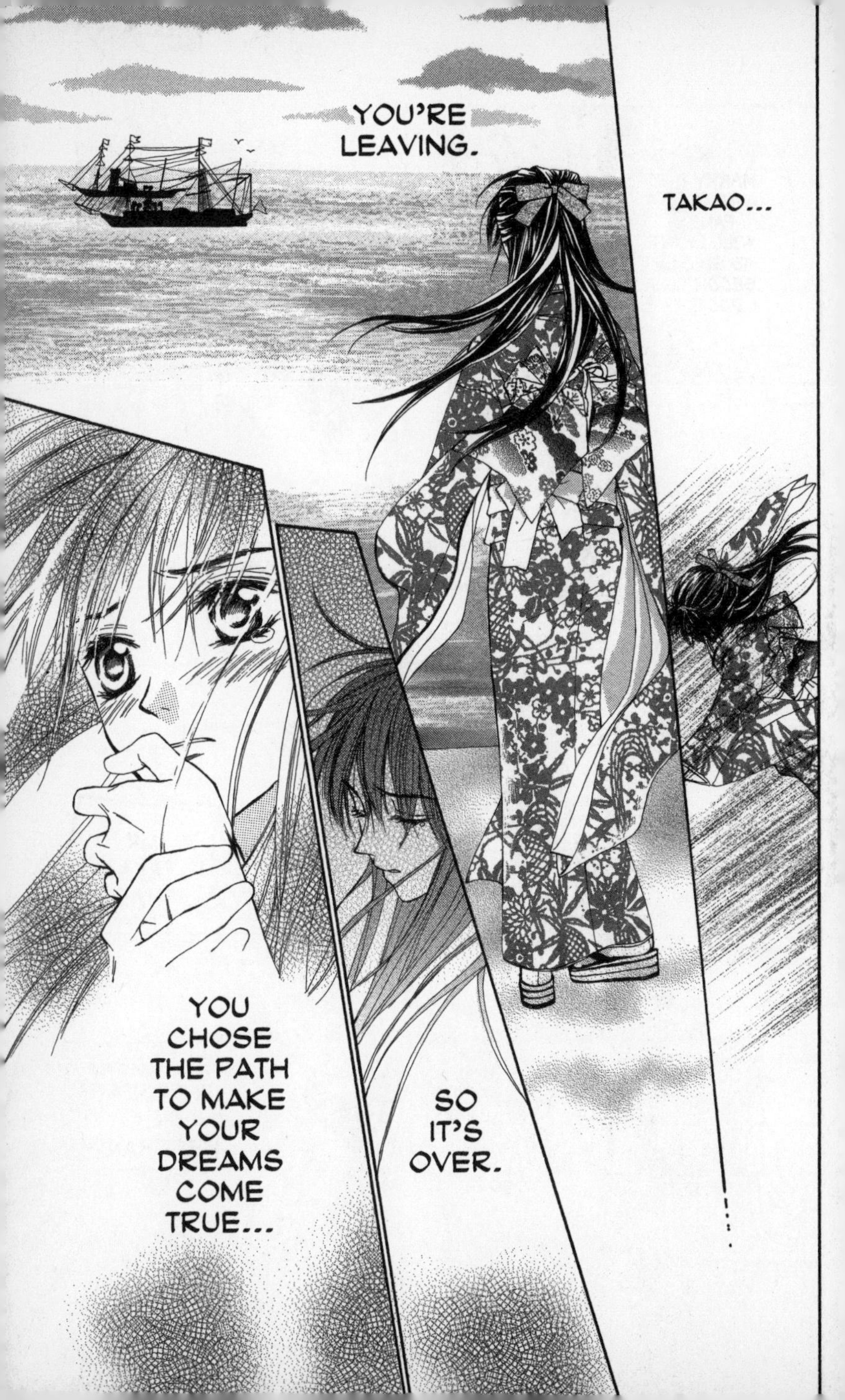
TAKAO...
YOU'RE LEAVING.
SO IT'S OVER.
YOU CHOSE THE PATH TO MAKE YOUR DREAMS COME TRUE...

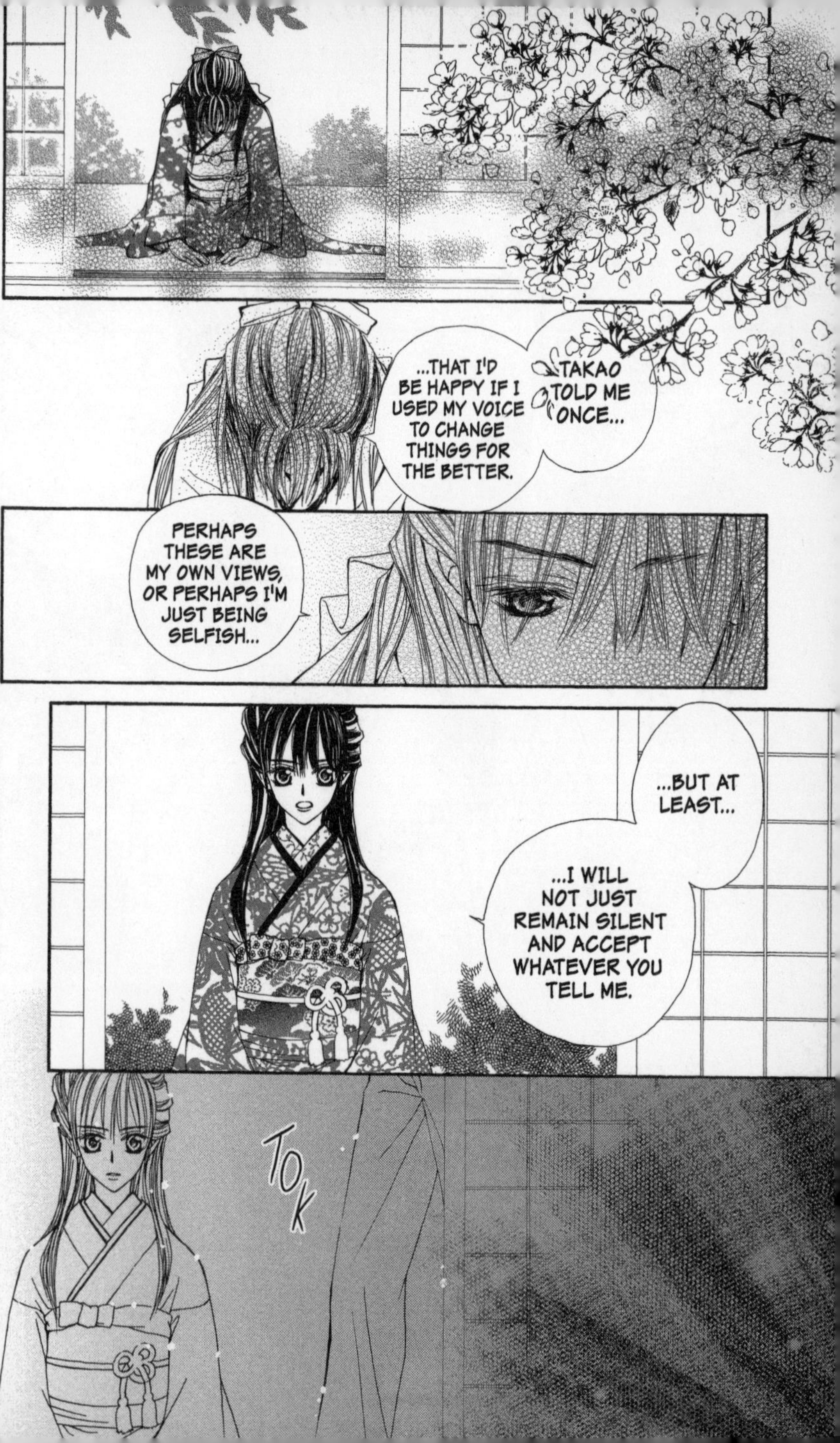
TAKAO TOLD ME ONCE...
...THAT I'D BE HAPPY IF I USED MY VOICE TO CHANGE THINGS FOR THE BETTER.
PERHAPS THESE ARE MY OWN VIEWS, OR PERHAPS I'M JUST BEING SELFISH...
...BUT AT LEAST...
...I WILL NOT JUST REMAIN SILENT AND ACCEPT WHATEVER YOU TELL ME.
TOK

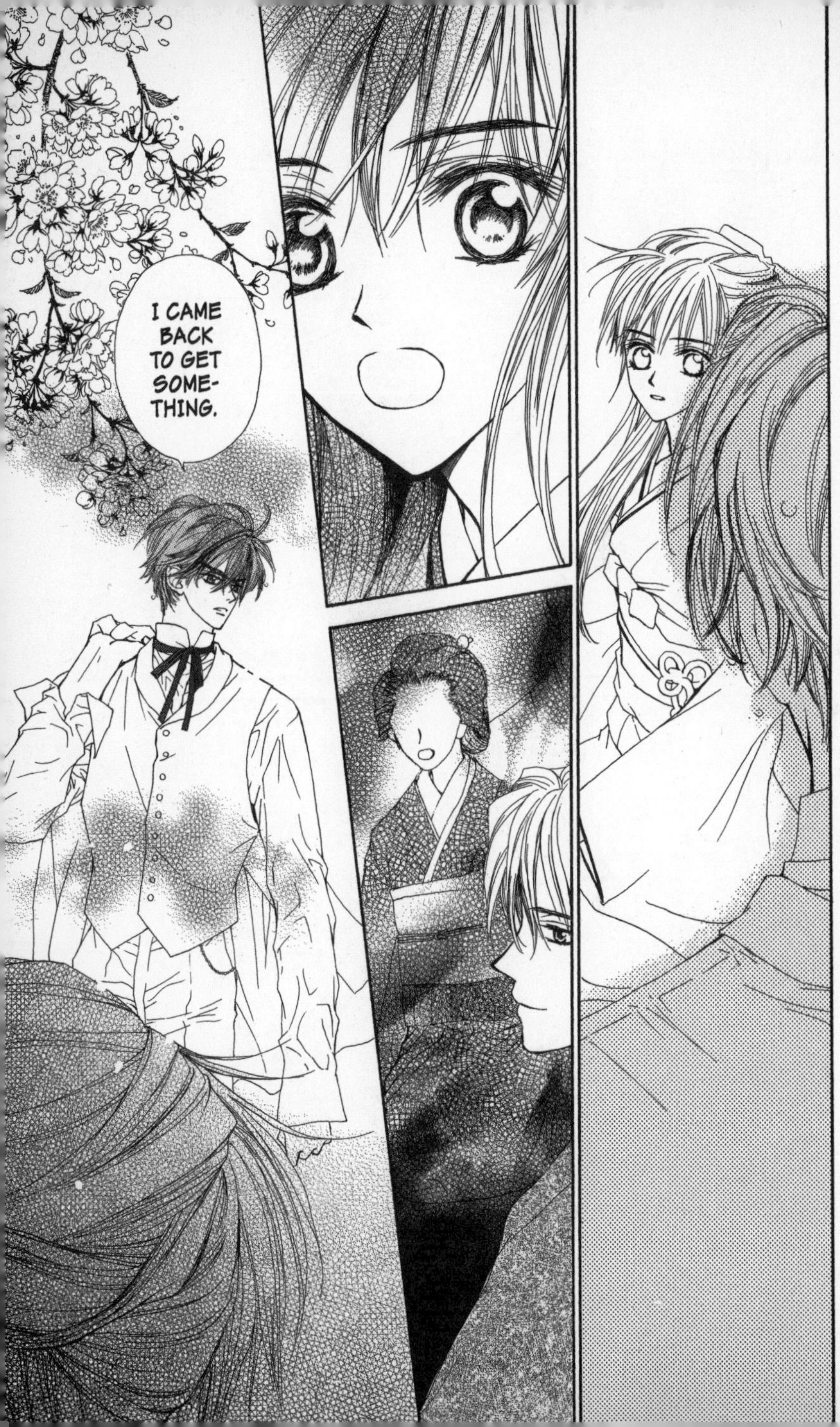
I CAME BACK TO GET SOME-THING.

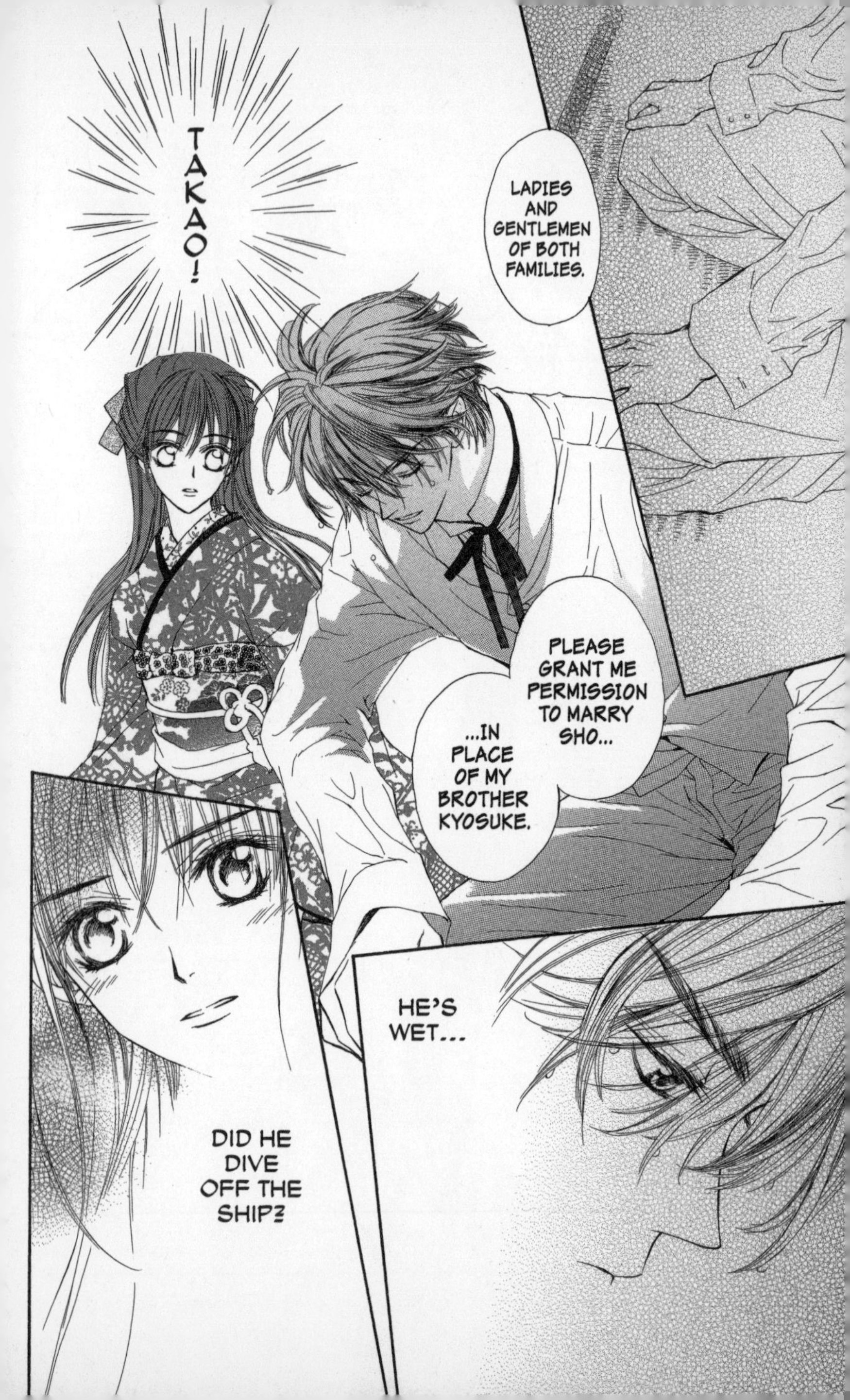
LADIES AND GENTLEMEN OF BOTH FAMILIES.
TAKAO!
PLEASE GRANT ME PERMISSION TO MARRY SHO...
...IN PLACE OF MY BROTHER KYOSUKE.
HE'S WET...
DID HE DIVE OFF THE SHIP?

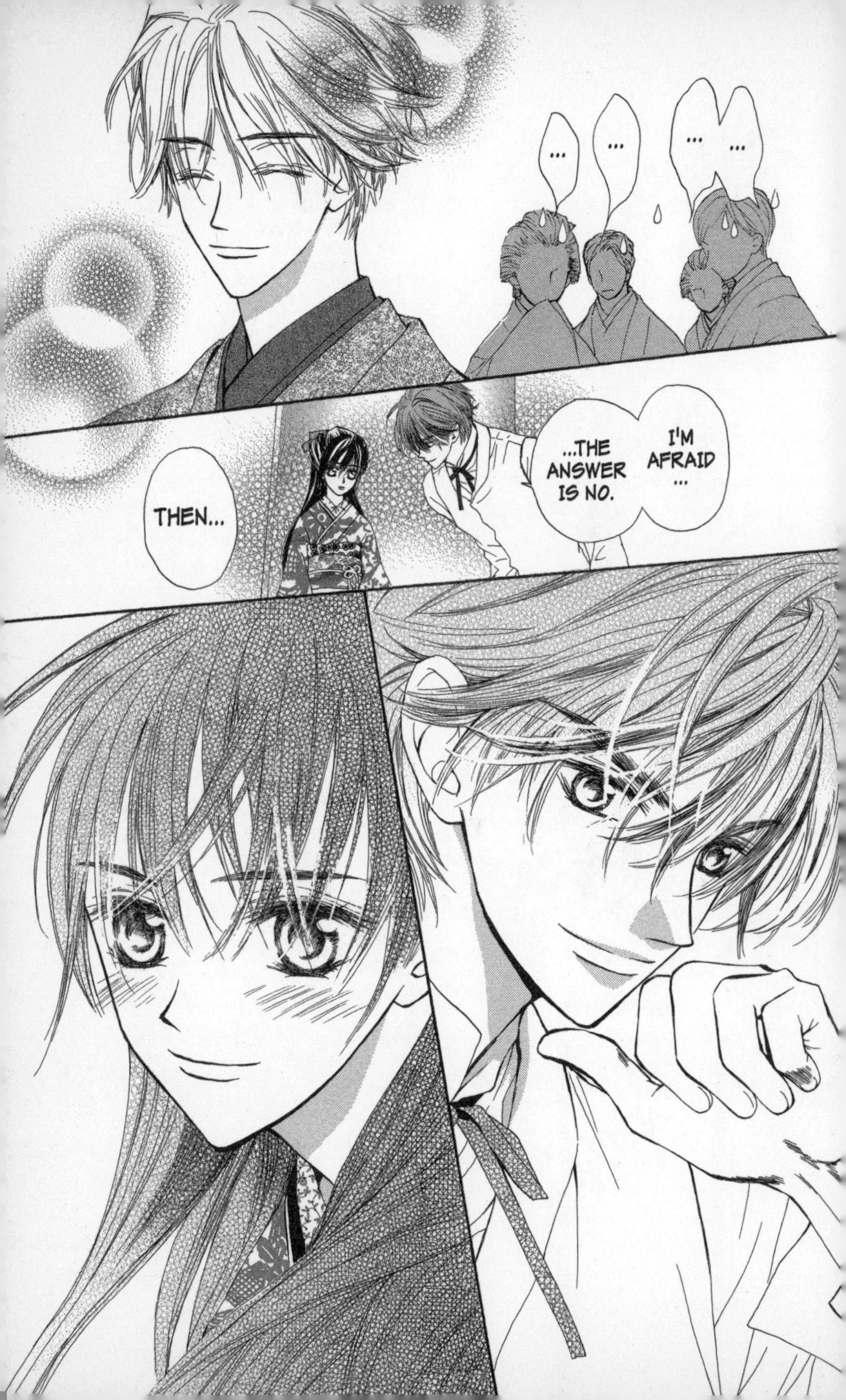

... ...
...
...
I'M AFRAID ...
...THE ANSWER IS NO.
THEN...

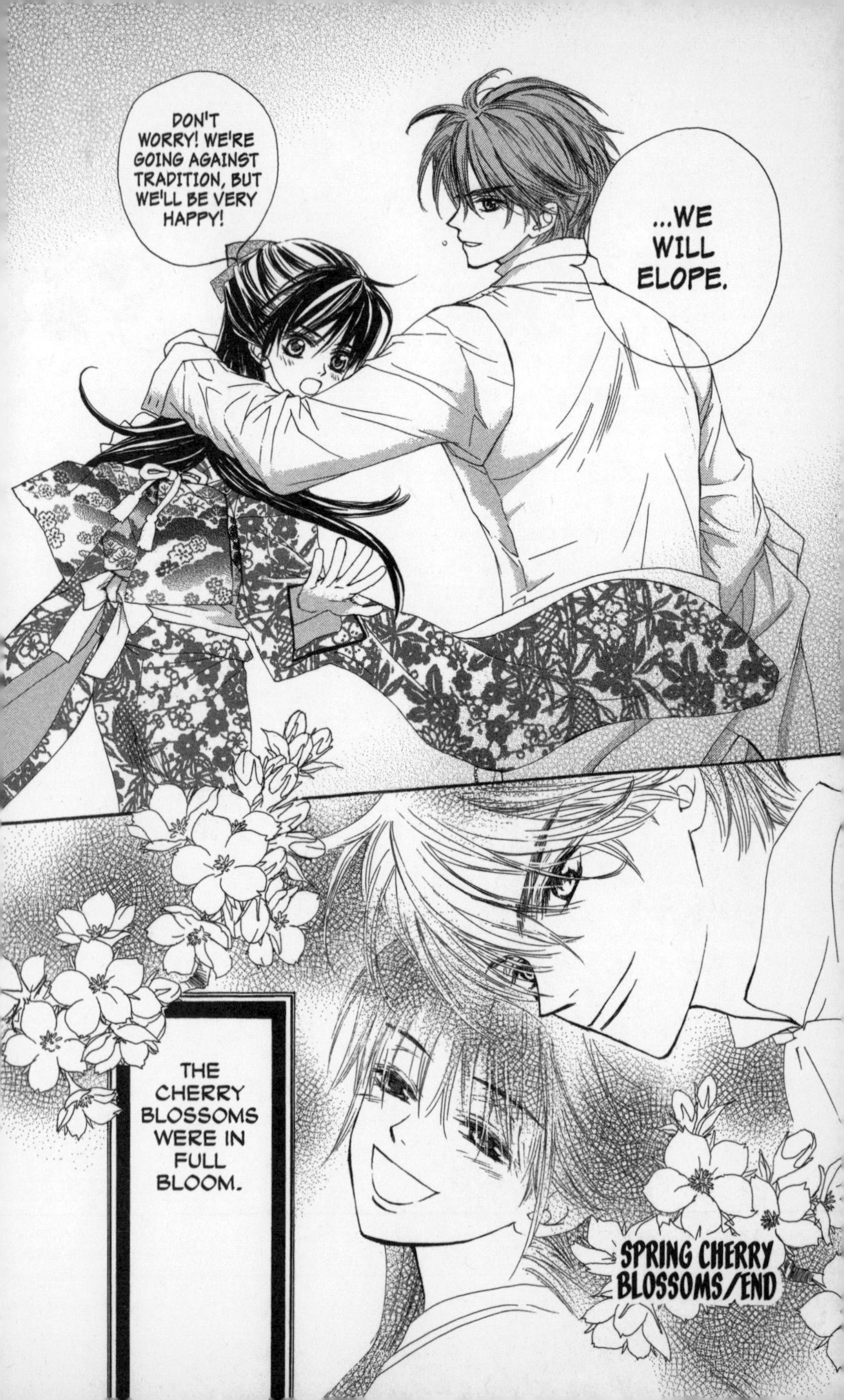
...WE WILL ELOPE.
DON'T WORRY! WE'RE GOING AGAINST TRADITION, BUT WE'LL BE VERY HAPPY!
THE CHERRY BLOSSOMS WERE IN FULL BLOOM.
SPRING CHERRY BLOSSOMS/END

SPRING
CHERRY
BLOSSOMS

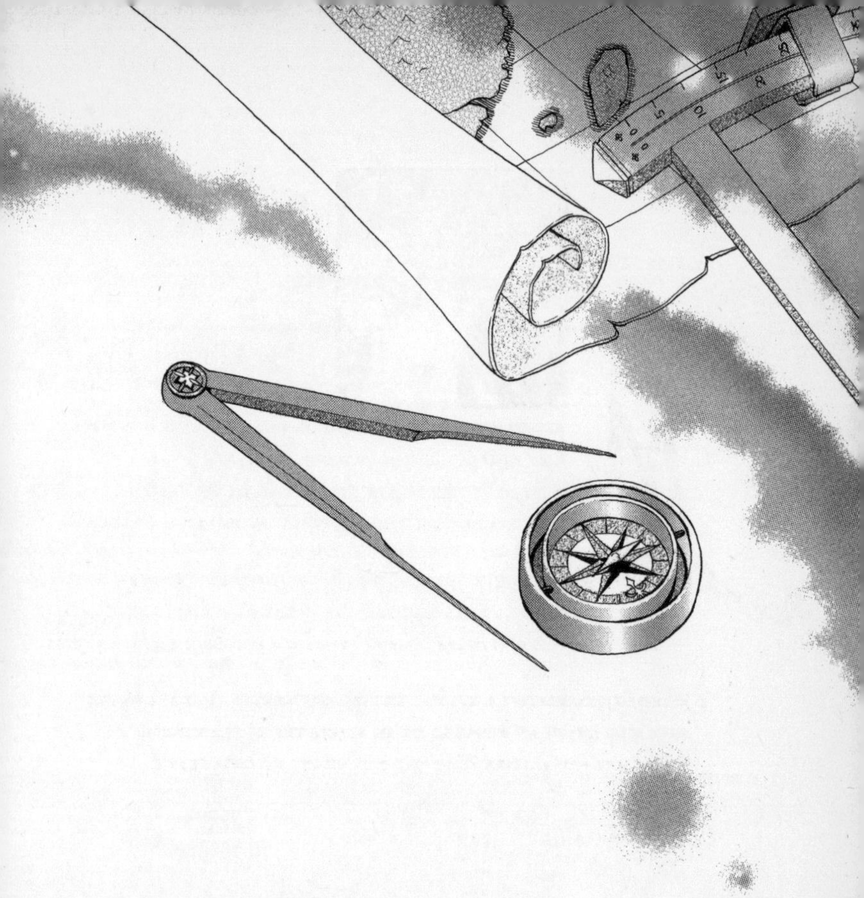

Afterword

For some reason, I still have lots of ideas for Wanted. For example, I'd like to draw a story where a female pirate appears...my thoughts are smoldering. I just started *Vampire Knight* in *LaLa*, so I must concentrate on that, though...

A sequel...whether I can do one is undecided, and I don't know how things will turn out (I won't be able to unless I can come up with interesting stories ♁), but I'd be happy if I can see all of you in Wanted again! And finally, thank you for reading this manga. Please read *Vampire Knight* too! ♡ Matsuri Hino

My heartfelt thanks to my editor, who's been taking good care of me; to I-san and to my mother, who helps me out every month; and to S.U.-sama and A.I.-sama, who I ended up asking for help in a rush.

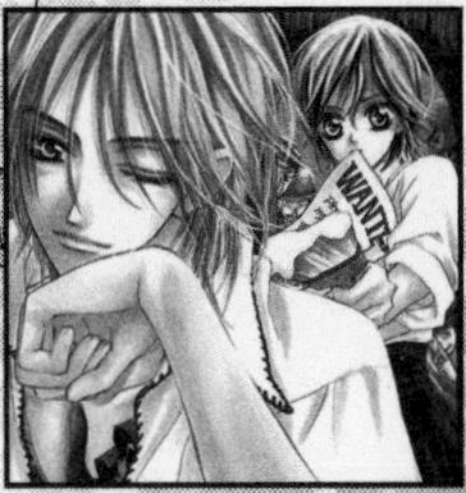
WANTED

Matsuri Hino burst onto the manga scene with her title *Kono Yume ga Sametara* (When This Dream Is Over), which was published in *LaLa DX* magazine. Hino was a manga artist a mere nine months after she decided to become one.

With the success of her popular series *Captive Hearts* and *MeruPuri*, Hino has established herself as a major player in the world of shojo manga. *Vampire Knight* is currently serialized in *LaLa* and *Shojo Beat* magazines.

Hino enjoys creative activities and has commented that she would have been either an architect or an apprentice to traditional Japanese craft masters if she had not become a manga artist.

WANTED

The Shojo Beat Manga Edition

STORY AND ART BY

Matsuri Hino

English Adaptation/NANCY THISTLETHWAITE
Translation/TOMO KIMURA
Touch-up Art & Lettering/SABRINA HEEP
Design/COURTNEY UTT
Logo Design/AARON CRUSE
Editor/NANCY THISTLETHWAITE

Editor in Chief, Books/ALVIN LU
Editor in Chief, Magazines/MARC WEIDENBAUM
VP, Publishing Licensing/RIKA INOUYE
VP, Sales & Product Marketing/GONZALO FERREYRA
VP, Creative/LINDA ESPINOSA
Publisher/HYOE NARITA

Printed in Canada

PUBLISHED BY VIZ MEDIA, LLC
P.O. BOX 77010
SAN FRANCISCO, CA 94107

SHOJO BEAT MANGA EDITION
10 9 8 7 6 5 4 3 2
FIRST PRINTING, SEPTEMBER 2008
SECOND PRINTING, OCTOBER 2008

RATED T+ FOR OLDER TEEN

PARENTAL ADVISORY
WANTED is rated T+ for Older Teen and is recommended for ages 16 and up. This volume contains brief nudity and suggestive themes.
ratings.viz.com

store.viz.com